Environmental Conflict

Environmental Conflict

Edited by

Paul F. Diehl
Department of Political Science,
University of Illinois

Nils Petter Gleditsch
Internationational Peace Research Institute,
Oslo (PRIO) and
Norwegian University of Science and
Technology, Trondheim

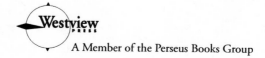

A Member of the Perseus Books Group

This book can be identified as a publication from the Oslo Project Office of the Global Environmental Change and Human Security Program (GECHS) of the International Human Dimensions Program on Global Environmental Change (IHDP).

Published in 2001 in the United States of America by Westview Press, 5500 Central Avenue, Boulder, Colorado 80301-2877, and in the United Kingdom by Westview Press, 12 Hid's Copse Road, Cumnor Hill, Oxford OX2 9JJ

Find us on the World Wide Web at www.westviewpress.com

Library of Congress Cataloging-in-Publication Data
Environmental conflict / edited by Paul F. Diehl and Nils Petter Gleditsch.
    p.   cm.
  Includes bibliographical references and index.
  ISBN 0-8133-9754-5 (pb)
    1. Environmental policy—International cooperation.   2. Environmental protection—International cooperation.   3. Global environmental change—International cooperation.   I. Diehl, Paul F. (Paul Francis).   II. Gleditsch, Nils Petter, 1942–   .

GE170.E57663   2000
363.7'0526—dc21
                                                                    00-063300

The paper used in this publication meets the requirements of the American National Standard for Permanence of Paper for Printed Library Materials Z39.48-1984.

10   9   8   7   6   5   4   3   2

Contents

v

Illustrations

Maps

Chapter One

Controversies and Questions

PAUL F. DIEHL
NILS PETTER GLEDITSCH

'Nations have often fought to assert or resist control over war materials, energy supplies, land, river basins, sea passages and other key environmental resources'. This passage from the World Commission on Environment and Development (Brundtland, 1987: 290) summarizes a common view of armed conflict. Thus, Renner et al. (1991: 109) claim that 'throughout human history, but particularly since the system of sovereign nation states, struggles over access to and control over natural resources . . . have been a root cause of tension and conflict' and that 'history provides numerous examples of how states and nations were destabilized by environmental collapse leading to famine, migration and rebellion'. Johan Galtung (1982: 99) has argued that 'wars are often over resources'. Lothar Brock (1991: 409) asserts that 'control over natural resources has always been important in enabling a country to wage war', citing as an example the Pacific War (1879–1884) between Chile and Peru over guano deposits. Arthur Westing (1986) has examined how resource competition has contributed to the onset of twelve armed confrontations in the twentieth century, ranging from the two world wars to the Anglo-Icelandic 'Cod Wars' of 1972–1973. A more ambitious claim is made by Paul Colinvaux (1980: 10), who asserts that 'history has been a long progression of changing ways of life and changing population', with 'wars, trade and empire' as the results. Paul Ehrlich and Anne Ehrlich (1970: 425) argue that 'population-related problems seem to be increasing the probability of triggering a thermonuclear Armageddon'.

The belief that environment factors are responsible for wars in the past is mirrored in the projections about the future sources of violent conflict. For example, Galtung (1982: 99) has argued that 'destruction of the environment may lead to more wars over resources', and suggests that 'environmental effects make a country more offensive because it is more vulnerable to attack and because it may wish to make up for the deficit by extending the ecocycles abroad, diluting and hiding the pollution, getting access to new resources'. Johannes Opschoor (1989: 137) asserts that 'ecological stress and the consequences thereof may exacerbate tension within and between countries', and Sverre Lodgaard (1992: 119) has argued that 'where there is environmental degradation, or acute scarcity of vital resources, war may follow'. Similarly, the then Norwegian defense minister Johan Jørgen Holst (1989: 123) argued that environmental stress seems likely to become an increasingly potent factor in major conflicts between nations: 'environmental degradation may be viewed as a *contribution* to armed conflict in the sense of exacerbating conflicts or adding new dimensions'. Anthony McMichael (1993: 321) believes that 'the end-stage of unequal power relations and economic exploitation in the world will be tension and struggle over life-sustaining resources. Fossil fuels, freshwater, farming and fish have already become the foci of armed struggles'. Also on an alarmist note, Kaplan (1994), in a widely publicized article, predicted coming world anarchy—sparked in large measure by environmental degradation. The secretary-general of the Habitat conference in 1996 was reported to have told the participants that 'the scarcity of water is replacing oil as a flashpoint for conflict between nations' (quoted in Lonergan, 1997: 375).

Although there have long been broad assertions that resource competitions were at the root of modern warfare, past and future, it was not until the recent emergence of environmental issues on the international political agenda that more specific claims about environmental disruption and violent conflict emerged.[1] Unlike the vague, sometimes overgeneralized statements of the past, some of the recent wave of environmental conflict debates contained detailed theoretical arguments. Nevertheless, despite the conventional wisdom that environmental factors may be critical in the outbreak of civil and interstate war, research on this interconnection has lagged behind the polemics. Below, we outline some limitations and gaps in the so-called environmental security field. It is from these problems that the impetus of this collection emerges.

Insights Without Evidence

The diminution of some traditional security issues at the end of the Cold War and the emergence of environmental concerns on the international agenda merged to create a topic of scholarly study called 'environmental security'(Mathews, 1989). The specific merits and defects of this field are discussed in the last part of this book. A general problem is to delineate exactly what constitutes environmental security. A wide range of environmental concerns were lumped under the rubric of environmental security, making the boundaries of the field very unclear. Environmental security studies have frequently come under attack from scholars who did not regard it as a legitimate area of study or who criticized the elasticity of the security concept as it was applied beyond the traditional military realm (e.g., Deudney, 1990; Levy, 1995). In effect, much of the controversy over environmental security has been fought on conceptual grounds, although one cannot dismiss the political motives of those who wished to elevate—or prevent the elevation—of environmental concerns to the same status as military ones.

We do not dismiss these debates as unimportant. Nevertheless, we believe that an exclusive focus on conceptual issues is likely to impede theoretical development in the long run. Understanding the causal linkages, if any, between environmental factors and conflict requires theorizing about those relationships and then subjecting them to empirical testing. Debating about what should or should not be included under the rubric of environmental security does not move the field forward in this way and ultimately cannot be answered anyway without empirical analysis. Unfortunately, environmental security studies have been notably limited in their theorizing about conflict and underdeveloped in their empirical applications. We also do not believe that a concentration on conceptual concerns will provide the policy guidance needed to deal with environmental degradation and scarcity. Most of the links between environmental factors and violent conflict imply cumulative processes, and therefore decisionmakers cannot wait until conceptual controversies are settled or violence is manifest. If environmental factors are important for the outbreak of conflict, then action must be taken soon. The questions remain, however, whether any action is required and what that action should be. Conceptual debates about whether to include environmental security in the realm of traditional security studies are moot if there are no empirical connections between the environment and violent conflict. These questions have to be resolved by theoretical and empirical analysis.

The purpose of this book is to address the two central shortcomings, the empirical and the theoretical. The kinds of claims represented at the outset of this chapter represent questions that are largely empirical. Unfortunately, until recently (and even now limited to a few major efforts), there has been a dearth of empirical analyses that test if, when, and under what conditions environmental factors affect the outbreak of violence. The first part of the book responds to that lacuna by offering a number of studies that provide empirical evidence directly, or review such evidence, on the environment-conflict nexus. Although we cannot claim that the empirical questions are put to rest by such contributions, they do provide some of the first evidence on the subject and point to the directions for future research.

Conflict Without Cooperation

Establishing if, when, and under what conditions environmental factors are associated with conflict would be a big step forward, but the environmental security field remains handicapped in its theoretical focus on only one side of the conflict-cooperation coin. That is, almost all the claims focus on the environment's conflict-generating capacity and ignore the cooperative elements that might be present. Environmental cooperation issues appear in two forms here. First, environmental degradation and scarcity may prompt groups or states to cooperate in order to solve those common problems rather than fight over the diminished resources; trade, treaties, and international organizations are mechanisms that might facilitate this. Most environmental security analyses do not even recognize these possibilities, much less account for them in their models or predictions. Second, even if environmental factors do promote the outbreak of conflict, this does not mean that such conflict cannot be mitigated or managed. Unfortunately, issues of conflict management as they apply to environmental security have been largely ignored. The second part of this book seeks to redress the imbalance. Four chapters consider a variety of mechanisms and factors that serve to mitigate environmental conflict and promote cooperation. Our goal here is not only to introduce the reader to this corner of the environmental security field, but also to stimulate further research.

The book is divided into three parts. The first deals with providing empirical evidence on the influence of environmental factors on conflict, both *intra*state and *inter*state. The second part considers the reduction of environmental conflict. The empirical focus of the volume continues here, but our authors also offer a number of prescriptions for how greater environmental cooperation and conflict management might be achieved. We conclude with a retrospective on the field of environmental security looking to where it has been in order to suggest where it should go. We provide a brief overview of these three parts below.

Environmental Factors as Sources of Conflict

The first part of the book contains chapters that explore the empirical connection (if any) between environmental conditions and violence. The Project on Environment, Population, and Security at the University of Toronto (commonly referred to as the Toronto Group) is one of the most prominent and controversial in this topic area. Led by Thomas Homer-Dixon, this project was at the forefront of developing models of how environmental factors induce conflict (Homer-Dixon, 1991, 1994). Much of their early work produced largely abstract conceptions of the environment-conflict relationship, with actual cases presented only as anecdotal evidence or as illustrative examples. The chapter by Val Percival and Homer-Dixon in Part 1 represents one of the first empirical tests of those theoretical models. The authors trace changes in South Africa during the later apartheid period and beyond; they argue that many of the violent conflicts in that country during those times have roots in the scarcity of renewable resources. The case study approach allows the reader to see the theoretical concepts and their impacts traced in great detail through real world events.

Wenche Hauge and Tanja Ellingsen carry a test of the Toronto Group framework one step further. They conduct one of the first large-N, multivariate studies of environmental degradation and civil conflict. This goes beyond establishing the plausibility of environment-conflict relationship in one or a few cases. Their chapter allows us to assess the broader empirical applicability of the theoretical framework. Hauge and Ellingsen are able not only to confirm some of the Toronto Group's hypotheses across a variety of countries, but also, perhaps more importantly, determine the *relative* importance (or substantive significance) of environmental factors, as opposed to other variables in civil conflict. Together, the first two chapters provide unique empirical evidence for the potential and limitations of studies that attempt to link the environment to civil conflict; they are also prototypes of the predominant methodological approaches to studying such questions.

There is a tendency for environmental security studies to concentrate on the outbreak of civil conflict. Yet many of the models and theoretical arguments in this field either derive from analyses of interstate conflict or appear equally applicable to that form of violence. Certainly, environmental problems can as easily occur across borders as they can within. Accordingly, the third chapter in this part, by Jaroslav Tir and Paul Diehl, shifts the focus from internal conflict to interstate conflict. They assess whether population pressures are associated with international conflict involvement, initiation, and escalation for all states in the international system for the period 1930–1989. This chapter provides one of the few empirical attempts to link population pressures and interstate conflict directly.

In most models of environmental conflict, population pressure is often the alleged driving force behind resource scarcity and environmental degradation. Tir and Diehl and Hauge and Ellingsen address some of the potential impacts of population pressure on international and domestic conflict. Jack Goldstone broadens the focus on demographic influences and provides an overview of the empirical findings on population and violent conflict. He also considers other factors as well, including the role of elites. This chapter stakes out a more skeptical position about the environment-conflict relationship than is reflected in the previous chapters.

The remaining two chapters in this part take one step back from the alleged environment-conflict relationship and consider the question of scarcity. All studies and models in environmental security implicitly assume that resource constraints or degradation have occurred or will occur at some point in time. This fundamental assumption has been challenged by Julian Simon (1981, 1996) and others. If resource scarcity does not occur empirically and if environmental degradation and overconsumption will not produce scarcity in the future, there is little reason to be concerned about environmental security. Lonergan considers the resource that most frequently figures into policy assessments and projections of conflict: water. Starting from the question: How scarce is water? he assesses the empirical evidence for the occurrence of 'water wars' in the past as well as suggesting what conditions might precipitate such conflicts in the future. Lomborg also explores whether the environment is really deteriorating, but cuts a wider swath, exploring a range of different resources, such as food supply, energy, and raw materials. He considers current supplies in the context of historical trends and argues that doomsday predictions about environmental deterioration are overblown. Together, these two chapters illustrate how empirical insights are not merely useful for assessing the causal linkages in the environment-conflict relationship, but also for testing the hidden assumptions or preconditions that underlie that alleged association.

The Management of Environmental Conflict

Among the weaknesses of the study of conflict in general is an ignorance of the factors that are associated with its reduction; thus, studies on the causes of war far outnumber those on conflict management or resolution. In most ways, research on environmental security is no different. This part of the book seeks to redress that imbalance in a modest way. Underlying all the chapters in this part is the assumption that environmental concerns are indeed associated with greater conflict (i.e., an empirical relationship exists). Nevertheless, these chapters have important things to say about the environment and how it is managed regardless of the existence or strength of the environment-conflict connection.

If environmental security threats exist, what is the best way that they might be mitigated or managed? One focus is on the states themselves. Numerous scholarly works exist on the so-called 'democratic peace', the idea that democracies are less conflict-prone than other states. A key corollary explored by Manus Midlarsky is the extent to which democratic states are more successful in protecting the environment and therefore in limiting the violence-generating conditions from environment degradation. Looking at several indicators of environmental degradation for a large number of countries, Midlarsky reaches some surprising conclusions about whether democracy is indeed desirable for environmental protection, and may have uncovered an indirect, but significant, caveat to the application of the democratic peace to internal conflict.

Environmental management is not solely the province of states, as international regimes and organizations are playing increasingly prominent roles. Some of these fall under the rubric of international law, but a number of different international institutions might also be called upon to solve international environmental problems. But how do these organizations operate and how effective are they? Rodger Payne explores the regulatory role of one such institution, the Global Environment Facility (GEF) of the World Bank. In particular, Payne evaluates whether GEF can meet the financial, strategic, and political concerns that must be addressed by any supranational effort in the environmental area.

Another way to think about managing environment conflict is to put primary focus on *how* to manage conflict, rather than on the actors who do the managing. In that spirit, David Denoon and Steven Brams apply the framework of 'fair division' (Brams and Taylor, 1996, 1999) to the dispute over the Spratly Islands. The Spratlys represent a good case for analysis in that the dispute over the territory is more than just an environmental one, and therefore its resolution requires a balancing of different considerations and values. Too often, scholars and policy analysts treat environmental concerns in isolation from other elements of a dispute. The 'fair division' approach offers a number of ideas on how seemingly zero-sum problems may be resolved to the satisfaction of all parties.

The preceding three chapters illustrate how various actors can cooperate with respect to environmental issues. Yet does such cooperation actually reduce the likelihood, scope, or severity of environmentally induced conflict? This seems to be assumed by many scholars, but is rarely addressed directly. Ken Conca reviews the empirical evidence that offers some possible answers to this question. Environmental cooperation may have intrinsic benefits, but if it does not help prevent or mitigate violent conflict, then other, more traditional mechanisms of conflict management may be necessary.

The Future of Environmental Security Research

The field of environmental security studies is still largely an emerging one, without the strong theoretical and empirical bases on which to cumulate and integrate knowledge (compare this to the frameworks and evidence available, for example, on the association between power distributions and the outbreak of war). Accordingly, in the final part of the book, we simultaneously look to the past and the future with respect to environmental security research. The focus on the past is concerned with whether the field is moving in the proper direction and whether past studies meet the standards of valid and progressive social science research. On this point, there is considerable disagreement between the authors of the concluding chapters. Gleditsch focuses on the scholarly immaturity of environmental security studies, noting nine major flaws in the conduct of that research. In response, Daniel Schwartz, Tom Deligiannis, and Thomas Homer-Dixon defend the progress and the approach of the Toronto Group against the charges levied by Gleditsch. From this exchange, it is clear that the disagreements between environmental security specialists are serious and are located on a number of important theoretical and methodological dimensions. Although the concluding chapters diverge sharply on their view of past research, there is considerably more convergence between them with respect to the future research agenda on environmental conflict. In this fashion, our book ends with a more optimistic note for the progress that can be made in future studies and offers some directions to achieve that end.

Acknowledgments

Four of the chapters in this book (by Gleditsch, Hauge and Ellingsen, Payne, and Tir and Diehl) were originally presented as papers to a NATO Advanced Research Workshop on 'Conflict and the Environment' in Bolkesjø, Norway, 11–16 June 1996. They were subsequently published in a special issue of *Journal of Peace Research* 35(3), May 1998, on 'Environmental Conflict', guest-edited by Paul Diehl. Also in that issue were the chapters by Midlarsky and Percival and Homer-Dixon. The article by Denoon and Brams was first published in *International Negotiation* 2(2), 1997. The remaining five chapters were especially prepared for this volume, and the earlier chapters were revised. As with the earlier contributions, the new chapters were subjected to external peer review. We are grateful to NATO's Science and Environmental Affairs Division and the Norwegian Ministry of Foreign Affairs for sponsoring the Bolkesjø workshop, which also led to the publication of another volume (Gleditsch, 1997b). PRIO's work on these issues in 1997–1998 was supported by a grant from the United States Institute of Peace. Finally, work on this volume was supported by grants from the Norwegian Ministry of Foreign Affairs and the Research Council of Norway. The earlier chapters have been reprinted by permission of the journals' publishers and we are especially grateful to Sage Publications Ltd. for their generosity. Oddny Wiggen served as managing editor for the volume. In addition, Jaroslav Tir and Hilde Løveid Varvin provided assistance to the project in Urbana, Illinois, and Oslo, respectively. Finally, we would like to express our appreciation to the several dozen scholars who have reviewed one or more chapters for this volume, as well as the friendly and helpful staff at Westview.

Notes

1. Recent literature surveys are found in Lietzmann and Vest (2000), Ohlsson (1999), Rønnfeldt (1997), and Smith and Østreng (1997).

Part I

Environmental Degradation as a Source of Conflict

Chapter Two

The Case of South Africa

VAL PERCIVAL
THOMAS HOMER-DIXON

Introduction

This case study on South Africa was produced for the Project on Environment, Population, and Security at the University of Toronto. The project analysed the causal link between renewable resource scarcities and violent conflict. Researchers sought to answer two questions. First, does environmental scarcity contribute to violence in developing countries? Second, if it does, how does it contribute? The project therefore analysed cases that exhibited both environmental scarcity and violence—cases with a *prima facie* link between these two factors. This method of case selection may appear to prejudice the research in favour of finding a positive relationship between scarcity and violence. However, at the early stages of investigation into links between environmental scarcity and conflict, biased case selection enhances understanding of the complex relationships among variables in highly interactive social, political, economic, and environmental systems (Homer-Dixon, 1996).

We begin with an overview of the theory that guided the work of the project and this case study. Using this theoretical framework, we analyse the relationship between environmental scarcities and violence within South Africa. Although our analysis faced serious limitations in data quality and quantity, the data available suggest that scarcities of renewable resources—in the context of the apartheid system and the transition to majority rule—contributed to pre-election violence within South Africa. First, we examine environmental scarcity within the former homelands, trace its interaction with political, social, and economic factors, and examine the effects of these interactions—primarily migrations to urban areas. Second, we analyse how migrations to South Africa's cities combined with social, political, and economic factors to produce urban environmental scarcity. Scarcity of renewable resources in urban areas and the vast numbers of people moving to and within cities heightened grievances and changed the opportunities for violent collective action. These factors, combined with the transition from apartheid, produced the most devastating levels of violence in South Africa's history.

Theoretical Overview

The context specific to each case determines the precise relationship between environmental scarcity and outbreaks of violent conflict. Contextual factors include the quantity and vulnerability of environmental resources, the balance of political power, the nature of the state, patterns of social interaction, and the structure of economic relations among social groups. These factors affect how resources will be used, the social impact of environmental scarcities, the grievances arising from these scarcities, and whether grievances will contribute to violence.

There are three types of environmental scarcity: (1) supply-induced scarcity is caused by the degradation and depletion of an environmental resource, for example, the erosion of cropland; (2) demand-induced scarcity results from population growth within a region or increased per capita consumption of a resource, either of which heightens the demand for the resource; (3) structural scarcity arises from an unequal social distribution of a resource that concentrates it in the hands of relatively few people while the remaining population suffers from serious shortages.

Two patterns of interaction among these three types of scarcity are common: resource capture and ecological marginalization. Resource capture occurs when increased consumption of a resource combines with its degradation: powerful groups within society—anticipating future shortages—shift resource distribution in their favour, subjecting the remaining population to scarcity. Ecological marginalization occurs when increased consumption of a resource combines with structural inequalities in distribution: denied access to the resource, weaker groups migrate to ecologically fragile regions that subsequently become degraded (Homer-Dixon, 1994: 15–16).

Scarcity and its interactions produce several common social effects, including lower agricultural production, migrations from zones of environmental scarcity, and weakened institutions (Homer-Dixon, 1991: 91). In order for these social effects to cause heightened grievances, people must perceive a relative decrease in their standard of living compared with other groups or compared with their aspirations, and they must see little chance of their aspirations being addressed under the status quo (Gurr, 1993: 126).

High levels of grievance do not necessarily lead to widespread civil violence. At least two other factors must be present: groups with strong collective identities that can coherently challenge state authority, and clearly advantageous opportunities for violent collective action against authority. The aggrieved must see themselves as members of groups that can act together, and they must believe that the best opportunities to successfully address their grievances involve violence.

Most theorists of civil conflict assume that grievances, group identities, and opportunities for violent collective action are causally independent. However, in this chapter, we argue first that grievances powerfully influence the meaning of group membership and the formation of groups and, second, that grievances can shift these groups' perceptions of opportunities for violence. The potential for group formation increases as people identify with one another because of their shared perception of grievance, and the meaning of group membership is influenced by the degree and character of the grievance. In addition, more salient group identity influences the perception of opportunity for group action: it ensures that the costs of violent challenges to authority are distributed across many individuals, and it increases the probability that these challenges will succeed.

Civil violence is a reflection of troubled relations between state and society. Peaceful state-society relations rest on the ability of the state to respond to the needs of society—to provide, in other words, key components of the survival strategies of the society's members—and on the ability of the state to maintain its dominance over groups and institutions in society (Migdal, 1994: 27). Civil society—groups separate from but engaged in dialogue and interaction with the state—presents the demands of its constituents (Chazan, 1994; Putnam, 1993). The character of the state is particularly important; a representative state will receive these demands and react quite differently to a non-representative state such as apartheid South Africa. Grievances will remain low if groups within society believe the state is responsive to these demands. Opportunities for violence against the state will rise when the state's ability to organize, regulate, and enforce behaviour is weakened in relation to potential challenger groups. Changes in state character and declining state resources increase the chances of success of violent collective action by challenger groups, especially when these groups mobilize resources sufficient to shift the social balance of power in their favour (Gurr, 1993: 130).

Environmental scarcity threatens the delicate give-and-take relationship between state and society. Falling agricultural production, migrations to urban areas, and economic contraction in regions severely affected by scarcity often produce hardship, and this hardship increases demands on the state.

At the same time, scarcity can interfere with state revenue streams by reducing economic productivity and therefore taxes; it can also increase the
power and activity of rent-seekers,[1] who become more able to deny tax revenues on their increased wealth and to influence state policy in their favour.
Environmental scarcity therefore increases society's demands on the state
while decreasing its ability to meet those demands.

Severe environmental scarcity forces groups to focus on narrow survival strategies, which reduces the interactions of civil society with the
state. Society segments into groups, social interactions among groups decrease, and each group turns inwards to focus on its own concerns
(Chazan, 1994: 269).[2] Civil society retreats, and, as a result, society is less
able to articulate its demands on the state. This segmentation also reduces
the density of 'social capital'—the trust, norms, and networks generated
by vigorous, crosscutting exchange among groups (Putnam, 1993: 167).
Both of these changes provide greater opportunity for powerful groups to
grab control of the state and use it for their own gain. The legitimacy of
the state declines, since it is no longer representative of or responsive to
society.

Opportunities for violent collective action can decrease, even under conditions of environmental scarcity, when the power of potential challenger
groups is diffused by vigorous horizontal interaction within society and
vertical interaction between civil society and the state. However, if poor
socioeconomic conditions persist, grievances will remain. These grievances
will probably be expressed through an increase in deviant activity, such as
crime. Unless the grievances are addressed, the legitimacy of the government will decrease, society will once again become segmented, and opportunities for violent collective action will increase correspondingly.

Theoretical Application:
Environmental Scarcity in South Africa

Below, we provide evidence for each link of the theoretical framework.
First, we outline the physical geography of South Africa and overview the
degree of environmental scarcity. We present the social effects arising from
this scarcity, such as poverty, rural-urban migration, and declining institutional capacities. We then analyse the link between scarcity, its social effects, and violence by examining the mobilization of group identities and
the opportunity structure for violent conflict.

This chapter analyses environment-conflict linkages in South Africa as
a whole. Moreover, we make specific reference to KwaZulu-Natal because it is one of the most populous and poverty-stricken provinces in
South Africa, and, since the mid-1980s, it has also been one of the most

violent.[3] Because much of the black population in the region is Zulu, explanations of violence cannot be reduced simply to ethnicity. Intra-ethnic divisions—caused in part by the effects of environmental scarcity—produced levels of violence in the region akin to civil war. We outline below the environmental situation in South Africa in general, with particular attention to KwaZulu-Natal.

Physical Geography

The South African eco-system is characterized by land unsuitable for agricultural production, low rainfall, and soils susceptible to erosion. Only approximately 13.5 percent of the land area of South Africa is suitable for crop production. Of this area, only 3 percent is considered high-potential arable land (Whyte, 1995: 43). Approximately 65 percent of the country receives less than 500 mm of annual precipitation, a threshold that is widely regarded by experts as the minimum required for rain-fed cropping (Coetzee and Cooper, 1991: 130). Low rainfall and fragile soils limit agricultural potential. Approximately 60 percent of South African cropland is characterized by low organic matter content. After repeated cultivation, organic matter is rapidly lost and the soil is easily eroded (MacKenzie, 1994: 2).

Of the total area of cropland, 13 million hectares fall within commercial farming areas, while only 2.5 million hectares are in small-scale farming areas in the former homelands (MacKenzie, 1994: 1). This imbalance, combined with other natural resource limits—including weak soils and poor rains—has resulted in extensive environmental scarcities in the homelands.

Environmental Scarcities Within the Former Homelands

Figure 2.1 traces the causes and effects of environmental scarcities in the former homelands. These causal links are discussed in detail below.

Structural Scarcity Under Apartheid: The Political Economy of Apartheid.
The apartheid system institutionalized the uneven social distribution of environmental resources in South Africa, which caused serious structural scarcity for blacks (McGrath and Whiteford, 1994: 49).[4] Approximately 86 percent of the land was owned by the white minority, while the black majority subsisted on 14 percent of the land base (Whyte, 1995: 41). Table 2.1 uses differences in per capita availability of farmland to illustrate the structural land scarcities affecting blacks in South Africa.

Not only did blacks suffer from an imbalanced distribution of the quantity of land, but they also often received the most marginally productive land. Moreover, under the apartheid regime, structural scarcities of land

FIGURE 2.1 Effects of Environmental Scarcity Within the Former Homelands

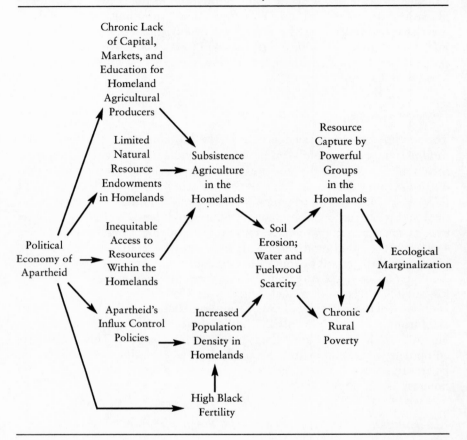

TABLE 2.1 Comparison of Population Densities Within
Rural South Africa, 1991

	South Africa	White Areas	Former Homelands	Natal	KwaZulu
Total Cropland and Pastureland (hectares/person)	4.7	16.22	0.92	5.36	0.68
Total Cropland (hectares/person)	0.75	2.54	0.16	1.1	0.08

Adapted from Development Bank of South Africa (1994: 99).

TABLE 2.2   Comparison of Yields in Crop Agriculture,
Natal and KwaZulu, 1983–1984

	Tons/hectare in Natal	*Tons/hectare in KwaZulu*
Cereals (maize)	2.088	0.826
Legumes (dry beans)	1.011	0.337
Roots (potatoes)	24.015	5.006
Sugar-cane	53.814	28.795

SOURCE: Bromberger and Antonie (1993: 421).

TABLE 2.3   Comparison of Statistics of Cattle Performance,
Natal and KwaZulu, 1987

	Natal *Private Land Tenure (%)*	*KwaZulu* *Communal Grazing (%)*
Herd Mortality	3.9	7.4
Calving Rate	80.0	32.0
Slaughter and Export Rate	25.0	5.0

SOURCE: Bromberger and Antonie (1993: 422).

were often reinforced by stark shortfalls in agricultural inputs, such as capital, fertilizer, veterinary services, and new agricultural technologies. Tables 2.2 and 2.3 compare statistics for crop yields and cattle performance in Natal and KwaZulu, and demonstrate the disparities in agricultural performance for these adjacent regions.

Although the major economic activities in the homelands were livestock and maize production, Table 2.2 shows the maize output in KwaZulu was only 40 percent of the yield in Natal and Table 2.3 shows the mortality rate in KwaZulu is almost twice the rate in Natal. Therefore, residents relied on precarious remittances from mines and other industries outside the homelands for much of their income (Whyte, 1995: 95–96).

In sum, the black population, with little political or economic power in South Africa, was forced to subsist on a severely restricted and eroded land base. Because of the particular vulnerabilities of the South African ecosystem, this structural scarcity interacted with and exacerbated demand- and supply-induced scarcities.

Demand-Induced Scarcity: Population Density in the Homelands.   The estimated population of South Africa in 1995 was 42.6 million, with an annual increase of 970,000. Approximately 28 million people—over 66 percent of the population—lived within towns and cities, while 15 million resided strictly within urban areas (Barnard, 1994: 1). The black population is expected to grow at a 3 percent rate from its current 32 million to 37.2 million by the year 2000, which will be 78.3 percent (up from 74.8 percent in 1991) of the anticipated total population of 47.5 million. Conversely, the white population will stay constant at approximately 5 million, and its proportion of the total population will drop from 14.1 percent to 11.4 percent (Mkhondo, 1993: ix).[5]

The growth of the black population results in more severe scarcity of land and exacerbates the differentials in land availability per capita shown in Table 2.1. Under apartheid, the average population density of the former homelands was ten times the density of rural 'white' South Africa. When labour requirements in commercial agriculture and mining declined, apartheid ensured that black South Africans could not move to cities when they were expelled from rural white areas. Police forcibly moved blacks to the homelands; partly as a result of this forced migration, the population of the homelands grew from 4.5 million to 11 million between 1960 and 1980 (Wilson, 1991: 32).

In addition to this in-migration, the homelands experienced high natural population growth rates. The total fertility rate for blacks from 1985 to 1990 was estimated at 5.12 children per woman (Simkins, 1991: 22). In 1990, Alan Durning observed, 'Black couples . . . have larger families because apartheid denies them access to education, health care, family planning, and secure sources of livelihood—the things that make small families possible and advantageous' (Durning, 1990: 13).

Gender discrimination contributes to these high fertility rates. Research conducted by Cambridge economist Partha Dasgupta shows that women who lack paid employment have less decisionmaking authority in their families. Weak authority, combined with the usefulness of children for labour in subsistence conditions—for collecting fuelwood and water and for herding animals—leads to high fertility rates (Dasgupta, 1995: 40–42). In the former homelands, women are largely responsible for the provision of food, water, and fuel, in addition to caring for children and generating income through activities such as trading forest products. Moreover, legal and cultural barriers deny women the right to own or control natural resources (Deshingkar, 1994: 1). High rates of infant and child mortality also raise fertility rates, because families have no guarantee that their children will survive to adolescence. The infant-mortality rate among black children was estimated at 74 per 1,000 from 1985 to 1990 (Simkins, 1991: 23).[6]

Supply-Induced Scarcity: Soil Erosion, Water and Fuelwood Scarcity. The apartheid regime situated the homelands in fragile environments with thin topsoil not suitable for supporting the level of agricultural production required by their populations.[7] The result has been severe erosion: 'Dongas (erosion gullies) have become small valleys which split the hillsides; soil has given way to a crumbling grey shale, stone-built huts squat in a scene which is almost lunar in its desolation' (Wilson, 1991: 34). Experts estimate that South Africa has lost 25 percent of its topsoil since 1900 and that 55 percent of South Africa is threatened by desertification (Archer, 1994: 5). Approximately 400 million tons of soil have been lost each year for the past decade (Whyte, 1995: 43). Soil quality is also threatened by the overuse of agrochemicals and acid rain which causes soil acidification. The heavy reliance on coal in South African industries and homes contributes to this acid rain (Whyte, 1995: 5–6).

Deforestation is an important form of supply-induced environmental scarcity. By destabilizing soils and changing local hydro-logical cycles, it disrupts key eco-system links (Gandar, 1991: 98). Unfortunately, fuelwood remains the most accessible and inexpensive energy source for many rural and urban blacks, which encourages deforestation. Inadequate energy services force approximately 40 percent of the South African population—approximately 17 million people—to depend on fuelwood for cooking and heating (Whyte, 1995: 62). Estimates place the annual volume of fuelwood consumed at 11 million metric tons (Cooper and Fakir, 1994: 1). In the past fifty years, 200 of KwaZulu's 250 forests have disappeared (Wilson and Ramphele, 1989: 44). A comparison of forest consumption rates with noncommercial forest growth rates shows that all ten former homelands are in a fuel-wood deficit, with supplies expected to be almost depleted by the year 2020 (Gandar, 1991: 98–99). Wood for fuel is perceived as free, and collection costs are seen in terms of women's time, which is generally undervalued. Moreover, 'frequent fires, the high opportunity cost of land, the long time periods for tree growth, and the use of both arable and uncultivated land for grazing all discourage tree planting. Trees can be seen as a threat to crops if they compete for space, water, and labour, and if they are seen to harbour pests' (Peden, 1993: 7).

The scarcity and degradation of water resources is also a problem. South Africa is a water-scarce country: 12–16 million people lack potable water supplies, and 21 million people—half the country's population—lack adequate sanitation (Brooks, 1995: 17). Seventy percent of urban blacks do not have access to running water and are forced to rely on severely contaminated river systems for their daily water needs (Dewar, 1991: 92). The water used by residents in informal settlements tends to have the highest concentration of suspended solids and the highest level of faecal bacterial contamination (Simpson, 1993: 28). The wider health of South African society is at risk as the probability rises in these settlements of epidemics of cholera, gastroenteritis, dysentery, parasitic infections, typhoid, and bilharzia. Pollution from industrial sources and seepage from coal, gold, and other mines threaten the quality of both river and ground water. The level of industrial pollution is particularly severe in the former homelands, where environmental controls were nonexistent.

Resource Capture. As scarcities intensified, powerful groups within the former homelands took control over scarce resources. Rights to communal land were unevenly distributed among homeland populations: up to 80 percent of production came from 20 percent of the farmers who controlled most of the land, and in some areas three or four landholders owned 80 percent of the livestock grazing on communal land. Widespread landlessness existed even in Transkei, the homeland with the best land, where fewer than 50 percent of villagers were allocated a field, and 60 percent had no cattle (Cooper, 1991: 179). These processes particularly affect women: although women comprise 80 percent of the population in rural areas, they have no access to land and no decisionmaking authority over the use of natural resources (Whyte, 1995: 45–46).

Resource capture and environmental scarcities combine to produce devastating levels of poverty. In the 1980s, 95 percent of the black population earned less than $100 per month, whereas 89 percent of the white population earned more. With an average disposable income of only $150 a year—one-sixteenth of the white average—homeland farmers in particular cannot make the long-term investments necessary to protect their land (Durning, 1990: 14). To escape this poverty, the poor move to marginal lands within the homelands and, increasingly, to urban areas.

Social Effects of Environmental Scarcity. We have shown that environmental scarcity has reached alarming levels in many of the former homelands and informal urban settlements in South Africa. Rural areas are unable to support their growing populations: soil is degraded, water resources are inadequate and decreasing in quality, and fuelwood is scarce. Figure 2.2 summarizes the variables and causal relations which we will identify in this section. Below, we describe these interactions in detail.

Poverty and Ecological Marginalization in Homelands. Agricultural potential decreased in the homelands because of growing population densities, water scarcity, and soil erosion. Per capita food production fell; these areas became net importers of food, partly as a result of land degradation and high population growth rates (Durning, 1990: 12–13). The rural black South African population became increasingly unable to sustain itself. As agricultural and forest resources became depleted, people switched to low-

FIGURE 2.2   Environmental Scarcity and Urbanization in South Africa

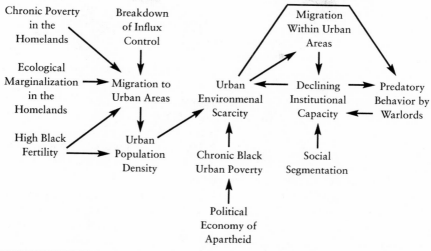

paying jobs in villages and towns. A study of a rural community in Bo-phuthatswana found that such wage labour was the major source of income for more than 90 percent of households; less than 5 percent could make a living from agriculture. Approximately 55 percent of the households studied had no agricultural land at all, and 37.5 percent had too little land to make a living (Boersema, 1988: 113–114).

Finding wage labour became more difficult because of South Africa's serious unemployment problem: formal jobs are available for only 50 percent of the country's population, whites and blacks included (Barnard, 1994: 2). Poverty is therefore endemic within the rural black community (Steyn and Boersema, 1988: 3). In 1993 in KwaZulu, 80 percent of all rural households and 40 percent of urban households were living below the poverty line. The average rural monthly household income was 43 percent below urban income. It was estimated that only 25 percent of the urban population in KwaZulu—and a dismal 16 percent of the rural population—had formal jobs (South African Institute of Race Relations, 1994: 493). Rural poverty, and the hope for a marginally better existence in urban areas, contributes to rural-urban migrations.

Rural-Urban Migration.   Migrations from rural areas to urban and peri-urban areas have increased sharply in recent years (Barnard, 1994: 1).[8] 'Push' factors are difficult to distinguish from 'pull' factors. The former clearly include environmental degradation, unequal access to land, and high population densities within the homelands. Three major pull factors are 'the repeal of the pass laws in 1986, the rapid construction of backyard shacks in formal townships, especially in the Pretoria-Witwatersrand-Vereeniging area, and the increasing designation of land outside the "homelands" as suitable for African residential development' (Simkins, 1991: 23–24).[9] As a result, South African cities are growing at the rate of 3–5 percent a year (Whyte, 1995: 80). According to estimates produced by the World Bank, 20,000 hectares of arable land are lost to urbanization each year (Whyte, 1995: 42). Although the number of blacks moving into cities is estimated to be around 750,000 a year (Lawson, 1991: 47),[10] rural-urban migration rates are disputed, and determining the precise rate will require more research.

However, we can make three generalizations regarding migration in South Africa. First, although most migrants to urban regions are still of rural origin, the percentage is falling. Families arriving in informal settlements increasingly move from closely adjacent communities. Second, the same processes of resource capture and ecological marginalization that take place in the homelands are occurring in urban informal settlements. The concentration of many people on a limited resource base, in the context of weak local government authority, leads to resource capture: 'violence (becomes) entrenched with formation of competing local power structures whose leaders seek to gain and secure power through the control of basic residential resources such as land, home allocations, services, business rights etc.' (Hindson and Morris, 1994: 1). This violence also plays a role in determining migration: people often leave their homes after violence erupts, but their places are quickly taken by migrants desperate for housing (Cross et al., 1992: 43). Third, the combination of this resource capture and environmental problems forces greater urban-urban migration.

KwaZulu-Natal experiences particularly high levels of migration to urban areas; 46 percent of the informal population in the Durban Functional Region (DFR) comes from the surrounding rural districts (Cross et al., 1994: 88–89). Although the population of both rural and urban areas within KwaZulu-Natal is growing, the population growth rate in urban areas is about three times as high as that in rural areas. Moreover, the growth of informal settlements, which now represent more than one-third of the total urban population and more than half of the total black urban population, exceeds growth within formal urban boundaries (Hindson and McCarthy, 1994: 2). Migration from rural regions is largely responsible for these differentials. Nick Wilkins and Julian Hofmeyer note that 'by the mid-1980s it was clear that rural poverty was undermining the system of oscillating migration, and that people were migrating permanently into urban areas. Migrants appear to follow several routes into urban areas, and once there may move several times from area to area' (Wilkins and Hofmeyer, 1994: 109).

Urban Environmental Scarcity. In urban areas, the system of apartheid ensured that black townships were built on sites not useful to the white community. These townships were often overcrowded, short of housing, and located downwind from heavily polluting industries. Infrastructure was inferior, with few services such as electricity and running water (Lawson, 1991: 61). South Africa's economic decline in the late 1980s combined with its infrastructural shortcomings to produce a dire marginal existence for most blacks within urban areas.

The recent influx of migrants has placed natural vegetation under constant attack, as the poor struggle to satisfy their basic needs. A growing population, concentrated in a limited area, coupled with the structural inequalities that deny them access to basic services, such as electricity, running water, refuse collection, and adequate sewage disposal facilities, results in environmental degradation. Overcrowding and poverty means that new residents build their houses from non-conventional materials scavenged from local dumps and public buildings; they use mud, grass, and straw from nearby streams, fields, and hillsides. Trees are cut down for fuel, grasses are used for feeding livestock and thatching, and residents often burn the veld to promote rapid regrowth, which depletes the soil of its humus content. These processes increase soil erosion, which is particularly high during intense rainstorms (Whyte, 1995: 85). Devegetation leads to floods, mud slides, and sinkholes, because informal settlements are frequently in water catchment areas (Lawson, 1991: 54).

An estimated 25 percent of the population of informal settlements have no access to piped water, 46.5 percent have no access to electricity, and 48 percent lack adequate sanitation facilities (Barnard, 1994: 1). Table 2.4 provides statistics on water and electricity services in informal settlements in KwaZulu-Natal and shows the degree to which the population relies on the local environment to provide its daily needs.

As Table 2.4 indicates, 76.2 percent of the population of informal settlements in KwaZulu-Natal rely on springs and streams for their water supply, and 63.8 percent have no electricity supply. Therefore, many urban blacks are trapped between worsening environmental scarcities and inadequate investment in the physical and human capital that might eventually generate alternative employment opportunities. The result is chronic poverty: approximately 40 percent of urban blacks earn incomes below the poverty datum line of R700 per month (Dewar, 1991: 91–92).

TABLE 2.4   Basic Services in Informal Settlements, KwaZulu-Natal, 1994

	Population	*Percentage of Total*
Water		
Only Springs and Streams	229,878	76.2
Taps in Homes	300	0.0
Standpipes	45,434	15.0
Reservoirs	4,800	1.6
None	21,205	7.1
Electricity		
Some Domestic Supply	108,816	36.2
No Supply	191,501	63.8

SOURCE: Hindson and McCarthy (1994: 20).

Declining Institutional Capacity.   Strong community institutions are crucial for managing the social conflicts that inevitably arise from large numbers of migrants. When he received the 1993 Nobel Peace Prize with Nelson Mandela, F. W. de Klerk stated that it was not international sanctions or armed struggle that forced apartheid to change, but instead the movement of millions of people into the cities that created social upheaval and strained community and state institutions (Darnton, 1993: 7). Institutional strength is a function of an institution's financial resources, the adequacy and relevance to community needs of its expertise, and its flexibility in novel circumstances; these factors, in turn, are influenced by the depth of the community's social capital. Community institutions within South Africa were ineffective products of the system of apartheid: they were fiscally weak, unrepresentative of communities, and ill equipped to manage the flow of new migrants.

Uncontrolled influxes of people and the degradation of resources that often ensues can cause social segmentation as subgroups within the community withdraw into themselves to protect their own interests. Segmentation breaks down social networks, weakens community norms, and erodes trust. This loss of social capital, in turn, undermines the ability of institutions to function. In South Africa, segmentation often takes the form of divisions among ethnic groups, among family-based clans, and among the residents of townships, informal settlements, and work hostels.

Marginal urban communities of blacks are often trapped in a downward spiral. Community institutions, already weak in the context of apartheid South Africa, were further debilitated by the processes described above, and unable to provide infrastructure—including sewers, electricity, and running water—to keep residents from wrecking local environmental resources. As people became more dependent on these resources for basic services, and as the resources were thus further degraded, community segmentation increased. This segmentation further weakened essential community institutions, allowed powerful 'warlords' to capture critical resources, and set the stage for outbreaks of violence among competing groups.

KwaZulu-Natal has seen huge influxes of people into its cities. Approximately half the population in the Durban-Pietermaritzburg region now live in informal settlements, lacking infrastructure and basic services (Louw, 1994a: 17–18). According to the Urban Foundation, the region has the largest concentration of informal settlements in the country (Harrison, 1992: 14). These settlements are often run by warlords—local leaders who control their own paramilitary forces and owe 'only nominal allegiance to any higher authority' (Minnaar, 1992: 63). Warlords establish patron-client relations with settlement residents: the residents support the warlord in return for essential resources and services. Paramilitary forces allow warlords to exercise strict control over the right to conduct business and over environmental resources, such as land and water. Resource control multiplies warlord power and wealth, permitting extraction of surpluses in the form of taxes, rents, and levies (Hindson and Morris, 1994: 6–7).

Warlords, in fact, have limited ability to provide their communities with infrastructure. They have no real control over services such as electricity, refuse removal, and roads, since these services—to the extent that they are available—are provided by the local municipality (Hindson and Morris, 1994: 8). They control only their paramilitary forces (often armed by the apartheid state in the pre-election period), the residents in their territories, and the local land and water (including taps into municipal pipelines) that residents depend upon.

Therefore, as resources are degraded within their territories, warlords often try to maintain power by pointing to resources in neighbouring townships and informal settlements, and mobilizing their communities to seize them. 'Squatters are mobilized to fight for access to resources in neighbouring townships, and township youth organize military style units to defend their areas and counter-attack squatter areas' (Hindson et al., 1994: 341). This type of mobilization produced the devastating levels of violence outlined below.

Acute Conflict Within South Africa. Between September 1984 and the end of 1989, an estimated 3,500 people died in political violence throughout South Africa. After Mandela's release in February 1990, violence became pervasive. From that date, until December 1993, political violence killed an estimated 12,000 people—an annual rate more than four times that prior to 1990 (Minnaar, 1994: 1). In 1992 alone, criminal and political violence together produced more than 20,000 deaths (South African Institute of Race Relations, 1994: 296).

TABLE 2.5   Unrest-Related Deaths and Injuries, Natal and Transvaal, 1990–1993

	Natal Deaths	Transvaal Deaths	Total Deaths	Injuries
1989	800*	NA	1,403	1,425
1990	1,685	924	2,609	4,309
1991	1,057	1,197	2,254	3,166
1992	1,430	1,822	3,252	4,815
1993	2,009	2,001	4,010	4,790

*Estimated
SOURCE: Minnarr (1994: 1).

In July 1990, the so-called Reef Township War began in the regions around Johannesburg. Clashes broke out between migrant workers residing in hostels and residents of townships and informal settlements (Minnaar, 1994: 17). In 1992, the annual incidence of violence escalated by 133 percent in the Central Rand, the area immediately surrounding Johannesburg. The area south of Johannesburg saw a increase of 200 percent, whereas the region east of Johannesburg witnessed an increase of 84 percent (Ki and Minnaar, 1994: 26).[11]

Table 2.5 contains totals of deaths and injuries for the former provinces of Natal and Transvaal (the violence occurred primarily in the area around Johannesburg). Table 2.5 does not include deaths from criminal violence, but the distinction between political and criminal motivations is somewhat arbitrary in a politically charged atmosphere, such as that of the pre-1994 election period (Louw, 1994c: 16).

Environmental scarcity is not the sole cause of this violence, yet analysts should not ignore how scarcity has undermined South Africa's social stability. Below, we examine the effect of scarcity on grievances, group segmentation, and opportunities for violent collective action. Figure 2.3 diagrams the surge of violence after 1990 in South Africa. Below, we provide a detailed examination of the relationships that are illustrated in Figure 2.3.

Increased Grievances.   Environmental scarcity reduced rural incomes and helped push many black South Africans into urban areas. The apartheid state depended upon its ties to co-opted local institutions, such as municipal and tribal councils, to maintain order within black communities. These institutions were unresponsive to the needs of the community, and could not address the increasing demands of local residents. The segmentation of urban black communities further weakened local institutions, which often could not deliver basic services to their people and as a consequence lost legitimacy.

FIGURE 2.3   Outbreak of Violence in South Africa

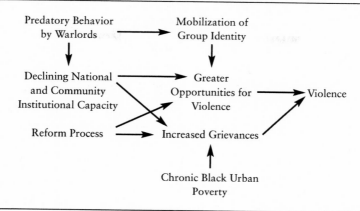

Research conducted on black South Africans' happiness and perception of personal well-being shows that, although levels of happiness have historically been low, grievances escalated during the late 1980s. 'Being black in South Africa was a strong predictor of negative life satisfaction and (un)happiness, even when other background factors were controlled' (Moller, 1994: 27). From 1983 to 1988, the percentage of blacks satisfied with life declined from 48 percent to 32 percent, and the percentage stating they were happy declined from 53 percent to 38 percent (Moller, 1994: 28).

Mobilization of Group Identity.   Group divisions, reinforced and in some instances created by the institution of apartheid, became the basis of politics in South Africa. Identification with one's ethnic group was necessary for survival and advancement within apartheid's ethnically divided political system. These divisions were reinforced by the territorial boundaries of the homelands. When people moved to the cities, they tended to carry their ethnic identities with them. A survey taken just prior to the 1994 election demonstrates the salience of ethnic identity: when asked to name their nationality, 16 percent of blacks replied South African or black South African, while 63 percent gave the name of their tribe (Battersby, 1994: 11). Much of the recent violence in South Africa has been between supporters of the African National Congress (ANC) and those of the Inkatha movement. The Inkatha-based Freedom Party is primarily a Zulu organization, and the ANC's leadership is dominated by members of the Xhosa ethnic group. Thus, ethnic divisions reinforce the political differences between the two groups.

Ethnic groups are not only divided among themselves; they are also divided internally. Environmental scarcity increases the salience of group boundaries, which causes the segmentation of communities. Competition within and among groups grows under conditions of economic hardship and influxes of migrants (Olzak and Olivier, 1994: 2–7). Powerful individuals manipulate group identities within their communities to capture resources, and they distribute resources according to group affiliation to maintain their support (de Haas and Zulu, 1993: 49).

While international attention has often focused on the inter-ethnic conflict between Zulu and Xhosa, the Zulu population itself is cleaved into factions. These cleavages have political overtones and often manifest themselves as conflicts between the ANC and Inkatha. Group divisions were constructed and manipulated by the apartheid state, and the political leaders and warlords on each side. ANC members tend to support political and social change, while Inkatha members support more traditional tribal institutions. The ANC is strong in the townships, while Inkatha draws its strength from informal settlements, often through connections to warlords.

Greater Opportunities for Violence.   After Mandela's release in February 1990, the nature of protest and violence changed, as it became clear that apartheid was about to collapse. The climate of reform made it easier to express grievances publicly. Both the ANC and the Inkatha Freedom Party, led by Mangosuthu Buthelezi and supported by the apartheid regime, were transformed into political parties. The townships went to war with each other as the ANC and Inkatha struggled for political dominance.

In just one month, between August and September 1990, the death count around Johannesburg stood at more than 700, dwarfing the final death toll after four months of the Soweto uprisings of 1976. In the first three months of 1991, more than 400 people died in political violence, 260 of them after the long-awaited and much-applauded Mandela-Buthelezi peace summit. Watching the death count on television and reading about the carnage in newspapers gave the impression that nearly every major South African city, large town, and even outback farming districts was experiencing turmoil more fierce than the 1984–1986 upheavals. More than 7,000 lives were lost in the fourteen months that followed the unbanning of the ANC, and other liberation movements, from February 1990 to April 1991 (Mkhondo, 1993: 48).

The events of 1990 radically changed the opportunities for political violence in South Africa. As the ANC and Inkatha became fully fledged political organizations battling for control of the institutions of power, they mobilized huge numbers of people and substantial financial resources for their political ends. Meanwhile, the apartheid state attempted to control the transition process through its support—both financial and armed—of Inkatha. The ANC and Inkatha mobilized large numbers of alienated and underemployed young men for their political battle. The battle took place within a deeply aggrieved society, brutalized for generations, and well rehearsed in fighting the system of apartheid. It resulted in the worst outbreak of violence in the country's history.

In KwaZulu-Natal, political leaders and warlords on both sides manipulated the conflicts among communities over access to resources, such as land, housing, water, and services (Morris and Hindson, 1992: 158). The large numbers of people moving into and within the KwaZulu-Natal region made the situation worse: migrants contributed to turmoil by increasing demands on resources and straining relations among groups. Disputes over scarce resources within informal settlements were transformed into political battles between the ANC and Inkatha (Morris and Hindson, 1994: 160).

Inkatha came to dominate informal settlements by striking political deals with warlords and manipulating the conservative group identities of many residents who had only recently arrived from rural areas (Hindson et al., 1994: 340). Warlords used the charged political climate to gain protection and favours from Inkatha. The ANC, in turn, promoted a revolt against tradition among Zulu youth, who expressed their opposition to traditional tribal structures through participation in ANC recruitment drives (Louw, 1994b: 21). Divisions between the ANC and Inkatha polarized social relations within townships and informal settlements, mobilizing and politicizing their residents (Louw, 1992: 57).

As a consequence, the region seemed locked into a spiral of violence as conflict created migrants that, in turn, strained social relations in receiving communities: the number of refugees and displacees from violence over the years runs into the thousands. Conflict has arisen when these people either move into new communities or try to return to their homes. This, along with migration of people for economic reasons, puts extra pressure on scarce resources, creating the potential for violent conflict (Louw, 1994b: 21).

Table 2.6 shows how political violence soared during this period in the DFR. After 1990, the use of lethal weapons rose and attacks targeted specific persons, not property or police (Louw, 1993). Deaths in KwaZulu-Natal doubled again in 1992–1993. Between 1992 and the 1994 election, more than one hundred violent events occurred per month, making the conflict in KwaZulu-Natal, and in the DFR in particular, the most sustained in the country (Louw, 1994b: 17). Although violence increased everywhere, the informal settlements became the main zones of conflict. Table 2.6 also shows that—similar to elsewhere in the country—Mandela's release in 1990 substantially boosted violence.

TABLE 2.6   Total Deaths Resulting from Political Violence in the Durban Functional Region, 1986–1992

Area	1986	1987	1988	1989	1990	1991	1992
Total Formal	100	88	186	227	289	151	246
Proportion of Total	70%	63%	50%	44%	36%	34%	30%
Total Informal	43	51	188	288	515	290	566
Proportion of Total	30%	37%	50%	56%	64%	66%	70%
Grand Total	143	139	374	515	804	441	812

SOURCE: Hindson, Byerley, and Morris (1994: 339).

After the election, violence subsided in both KwaZulu-Natal and the region around Johannesburg. Although conflict levels have remained relatively low around Johannesburg, they have risen in KwaZulu-Natal. The lives of people in the province continue to be disrupted by violence that shows little sign of ending.

Conclusion

In this article, we investigate the influence of environmental factors on social and political behaviour in South Africa, and argue that environmental scarcity played a role in generating pre-election turmoil. This analysis of the causes of conflict within South Africa is relatively novel. Much of the commentary focuses on traditional explanations of violence, examinations of the political and economic conditions surrounding the efforts by the National Party to preserve apartheid. According to such accounts, pre-election violence was caused by the competition between the ANC and Inkatha for control of the political arena, fuelled by the National Party's clandestine support of Inkatha. Yet large-scale civil war was averted by the decision of de Klerk and Mandela to engage in peaceful negotiations for the end to minority white rule (Stedman, 1996: 353).

It is impossible to establish the counter-factual argument that, in the absence of severe environmental scarcity, the upsurge of violence in the early 1990s would not have occurred. The data available are simply not adequate for such proof. Moreover, environmental scarcity is always enmeshed in a web of social, political, and economic factors, and its contribution to violence is difficult to disentangle from these other factors. In particular, the apartheid state helped foster much of the violence by fuelling conflict between Inkatha and the ANC. Strong group identities and the transition to democracy also contributed to the violence.

However, analysis that focuses solely on the role of the apartheid state and the tumultuous nature of a democratic transition does not explain the role of factors such as migration, scarcities of resources in black urban communities, poverty, and warlord manipulation of resource access in this violence. Moreover, this traditional analysis does not explain why crime remains high, and why conflicts continue to erupt between communities over access to resources (Fig, 1996).

As we have shown, scarcities pushed up grievances and helped alter opportunities for violent collective action. Therefore, although the role of environmental scarcity is complex, we maintain that scarcity contributed to social instability in pre-election South Africa. In addition, we have argued that analysts must understand the relationship between state and society if they are to understand the complex links between environmental scarcity and violent conflict. During the 1980s and early 1990s, South African society's demands on the state increased as thousands of people migrated to urban areas, while the ability of both national and local institutions to meet these demands decreased. With the decline of local governments, the apartheid regime lost its already tenuous links to society. Society segmented, and powerful groups seized control of resources. These groups married their local conflicts over resource access to the struggle for political control between the ANC and Inkatha.

The election of Mandela changed the relationship between state and society. State legitimacy jumped upwards. The Reconstruction and Development Programme (RDP) recognizes the needs of society, and interactions between state and society are now more constructive and vigorous. The government has established fora around the country to discuss local implementation of the RDP—fora that boost civic engagement and generate social capital. Although scarcities remain severe, levels of grievance have fallen: the proportion of black South Africans expressing satisfaction with their lives rose from 32 percent in 1988 to 80 percent in 1994, while the proportion expressing happiness went from 38 percent in 1988 to 86 percent in 1994 (Moller, 1994: 28).

However, a sharp rise in expectations of change has accompanied this decline in grievances. Blacks have high expectations of the Mandela government. A poll conducted just after the 1994 election shows that 58 percent of the population expect the government to provide ready-built houses and enforce minimum wages, while 71 percent demand that the government provide work to all unemployed. When asked what their reaction would be if their expectations were not met, 20 percent cited violent action, while only 5 percent cited peaceful mass protest (Anon, 1994: 73).

The election of Mandela may have boosted expectations for change, but, for most blacks, objective living conditions remain dismal. Blacks are not happier because their living conditions have changed; rather, they are happier because they think these conditions are going to change. If change is not quickly forthcoming the regime will lose legitimacy, and linkages between state and society will once again weaken. Unfortunately, already severe environmental scarcity makes the process of positive change much harder. Social demands on local institutions continue to expand, and the potential for violence between the ANC and Inkatha remains high.

Nelson Mandela's victory gave hope to many that the ills of apartheid and the violence of recent years would give way to peace and prosperity. Nothing can detract from the accomplishments achieved so far. But without careful attention to the environmental factors that contribute to violence, South Africa may once again be locked into a deadly spiral of conflict.

Postscript

The first version of this chapter was researched and written in 1995, the year after the African National Congress won a majority in the election and Nelson Mandela took office as the president of South Africa. The legitimacy of the South African state rose, and hopes for the future were very high. The Truth and Reconciliation Commission was launched to ensure that the evils of the apartheid era were recognised; forgiven in some cases, punished in others.

Everyone hoped that the violence of the apartheid years would be left behind. Although incidents of political violence declined after the first democratic election, criminal violence rose dramatically. After four years of ANC rule, statistics for crime remain shocking. Every day in 1998 there were 731 house break-ins, 135 rapes, 41 car hijackings, and 68 murders. In total, almost 25,000 people were killed in 1998 as a result of violent crime (Vine, 1999). The grievances that were once expressed through political violence, are now expressed in criminal activity.

The democratic transition was sealed with the second post-apartheid election. On 2 June 1999 the African National Congress won a second consecutive victory, and Thabo Mbeki became the second black South African president. Mbeki addressed high crime rates directly in his inaugural address. 'No night can be restful when millions have no jobs, and some are forced to beg, to rob and to murder to ensure that they and their own do not perish from hunger . . . ' (Mbeki, 1999). Within days of his election, Mbeki announced measures to combat crime and violence, including plans to overhaul the police force. However, the pressures outlined in this paper—migrations, scarcities of resources in black urban communities, and poverty—have not gone away. It is clear that unless these pressures are addressed, violence will continue to plague South Africa.

Val Percival, b. 1970, M.A. in International Affairs, Conflict Analysis (Carleton University, 1995); researcher for the Project on Environment, Population, and Security and The Project on Environmental Scarcities, State Capacity and Civil Violence; currently working with the UNHCR in Guinea.

Thomas Homer-Dixon, b. 1956, Ph.D. in political science (MIT, 1989), director of the Peace and Conflict Studies Program and associate professor of political science at the University of Toronto. Most recent book: *Environment, Scarcity, and Violence* (Princeton University Press, 1999).

Notes

1. Rent-seekers are persons or groups who seek to extract payments from the economy for factors of production that are in excess of what would normally be obtained in a competitive market.

2. Chazan argues that, under conditions of economic strain, both state and society become more insular.

3. Under the new constitution, the formerly white-dominated province of Natal has been integrated with the neighboring Zulu-dominated homeland of KwaZulu to form the province of KwaZulu-Natal.

4. According to its Gini coefficient, South Africa was the most inequitable nation in the world. In 1976, the Gini coefficient based on household income was estimated at 0.68, and in 1991 it was 0.67. The coefficient for the United States is 0.34, and that for Canada, 0.29.

5. Mkhondo obtained these figures from the South African Development Bank.

6. The white infant mortality rate for the period 1985–1990 is 9.0 per thousand (South Africa Statistics, 1992).

7. Land use management practices, not just natural vulnerabilities, must be analysed when soil erosion is discussed: 'Factors such as climate, soil erodibility and topography determine the potential erosion hazard in an area. Nevertheless, the difference in erosion caused by differing management of the same soil is very much greater than the difference in erosion from different soils under the same form of management. Thus cropping and management practices provide the key to controlling soil loss' (Liggitt, 1988: 27).

8. In addition, South Africa has an estimated 7–8 million homeless people drifting from countryside to cities, and also among cities (Barnard, 1994: 1).

9. See also Steyn and Boesema (1988), written before the repeal of the pass laws: 'The rural–urban migration of blacks in South Africa centers around the inability of the rural areas to provide for the material needs of the local people. Structural determinants such as land shortage and the inaccessibility of available land, overpopulation, and the general underdevelopment of rural areas on the one hand, and the attractions of cities and city life such as job opportunities, general infrastructure and facilities on the other hand are relevant in this regard' (Steyn and Boersema, 1988: 134).

10. This estimate was produced by the Urban Foundation.

11. The percentage increases are based on the following figures: Central Rand: 203 incidents to 473; East Rand: 145 incidents to 266; South of Johannesburg: 53 incidents to 160.

Chapter Three

Causal Pathways to Conflict

WENCHE HAUGE
TANJA ELLINGSEN

Environmental Change and Internal Conflict

Since 1945, the world has experienced a clear increase in the occurrence of domestic armed conflict. Up to the mid-1970s, this largely mirrored the growth of independent states in the international system, but from then on the number of conflicts increased faster then the number of emerging states (Gleditsch, 1996: 293). Most domestic armed conflicts during this period have taken place in developing countries, several of them in areas suffering from severe environmental degradation, such as the Horn of Africa and Central America.

During the 1970s and the early 1980s, theories of relative deprivation and of resource mobilization featured prominently in research on conflict causation. During these decades only a few studies, such as one by Nazli

The chapter is part of a joint research programme on the dynamics of conflict at the International Peace Research Institute, Oslo (PRIO) and the Department of Peace and Conflict Research, Uppsala University, funded by Ford Foundation. Wenche Hauge's work has been funded by that project. Tanja Ellingsen's work has been funded in part by the Norwegian Foreign Ministry, and in part by the Norwegian Ministry of Defense. The authors are grateful to these institutions for support of the work reported here and to the editors and referees for comments. An earlier version of the chapter was presented at the 38th Annual Conference of the International Studies Association, 18–22 March 1997, in Toronto, Canada. The dataset used in this chapter is available at: http://www.uio.no/~tanjae/products.html.

Choucri and Robert North (1975), investigated *environmental change* as a cause of conflict. However, with the introduction of the concept of sustainable development by the International Union for the Conservation of Nature and Natural Resources (IUCN) in 1980—a term which gained currency with the Brundtland Report of 1987—there came a rising awareness of the problems created by global environmental degradation. Concern for the environment also fought its way into the security debate. The end of the Cold War and the ensuing search for a new security paradigm helped open up the security debate to new issues. Much has now been written on how to stretch the concept of security to include the environment (Myers, 1993; Westing, 1989). Efforts to link environmental issues to the concept of security have been motivated partly by the need to draw attention to environmental issues (Deudney, 1991). This concern for the environment, whether linked to the debate about sustainable development, environmental security, or to other sources, has inspired new research on the relationship between environmental degradation and conflict—*inter*state as well as *intra*state.

Numerous scholars have concluded that struggle over access to and control over natural resources has been an important cause of tension and conflict (Brock, 1991; Brundtland et al., 1987; Choucri and North, 1975; Galtung, 1982; Gleick, 1993b; Homer-Dixon, 1991, 1996; Homer-Dixon et al., 1993; Lodgaard, 1992; Opschoor, 1989; Percival and Homer-Dixon, 2001; Renner et al., 1991), although there is no consensus on this issue. Several researchers have also questioned the general arguments about the role of resources and environmental factors in conflict (Deudney, 1991; Gleditsch, 2001; Levy, 1995). A major objection is that most of the literature is based on findings from case studies where both stress on the environment and armed conflict are or have been present; this means that no allowance is made for variation in the independent and dependent variables. Homer-Dixon has deliberately chosen a methodology of process tracing in the context of case studies: 'in the early stages of research, *process tracing* is often the best, and sometimes the only way to begin' (Homer-Dixon, 1995c: 8). A further criticism is that most research on environmental degradation and domestic armed conflict fails to take into consideration other conflict-generating factors.

This chapter builds on some of the findings and conclusions from case studies on the linkage between environmental degradation and conflict, but seeks to place these findings in a broader theoretical context of conflict research. Using data covering the period 1980–1992, we statistically test hypotheses on links between environmental scarcity and civil conflict within a multivariate framework and model. To our knowledge, this is one of the first large-N studies within the field of research on domestic armed conflict and the environment.

Existing Literature

Most studies on the linkage between environmental change and domestic conflict focus on the relationship between conflict and degradation and depletion of renewable resources (land, forest, freshwater, fish stocks). However, because rivers and fish stocks, in particular, are resources shared across boundaries, these resources have also formed a basis for studies of interstate conflicts. Research at the intrastate level is mainly qualitative and based on case studies. Two groups have been particularly prominent within this field: the Toronto Group with Thomas Homer-Dixon as its key figure, and the Swiss Environment and Conflicts Project (ENCOP) directed by Günther Bächler and Kurt Spillmann. Both of these groups have produced a series of case studies concerning the relationship between degradation of renewable resources and domestic armed conflict; both conclude that degradation and depletion of agricultural land, forest, water, and fish stocks are the most important types of environmental degradation contributing to domestic armed conflict (Bächler, 1994; Bächler et al., 1996; Homer-Dixon, 1994). Case studies by other researchers have reached similar conclusions (Gleick, 1993b; Swain, 1996).

Bächler and Homer-Dixon use very different theoretical frameworks. In the first of three volumes published by ENCOP, Bächler et al. (1996) discuss the linkages between environmental degradation and domestic armed conflict in relation to theories of over- and underdevelopment, consumption, and modernization. These theoretical approaches are generally supported by a large number of case studies. Homer-Dixon, on the other hand, has developed his own model of how environmental scarcity leads to domestic armed conflict, and applies it consistently (with minor variations) to the case studies. For this reason, the focus of our chapter will mainly be on the theoretical argument developed by the Toronto Group.

Environmental Scarcity

Environmental scarcity is the core concept in Homer-Dixon's work. His model has some parallels in economic theories of the market. The concept of environmental scarcity is composed of three dimensions: supply-induced scarcity, demand-induced scarcity, and structural scarcity (Homer-Dixon, 1994). *Supply-induced scarcity* exists when resources are reduced and degraded faster then they are renewed. *Demand-induced scarcity* is created by population growth or increased per capita consumption. Finally, resources are inequitably distributed when they are concentrated in the hands of a few people while the remaining population suffers from resource shortages. This is referred to as *structural scarcity*.

FIGURE 3.1   Some Sources and Consequences of Environmental Scarcity

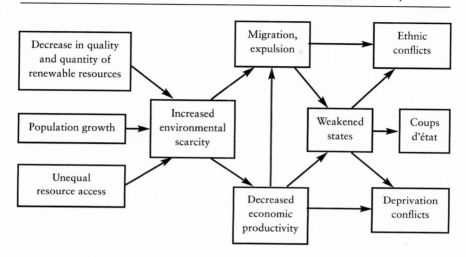

SOURCE: Homer-Dixon (1994: 3).

Increased environmental scarcity caused by one or more of these factors is assumed to have several consequences, which in turn may lead to domestic armed conflict. Important intervening variables between environmental scarcity and conflict are decreased agricultural production, decreased economic activity, migration, and weakened states (Figure 3.1).

On the basis of Homer-Dixon's model, we formulate the following hypotheses:

H_1: Countries experiencing land degradation are more likely to experience domestic armed conflict than countries where land degradation does not take place.

H_2: Deforesting countries are more likely to experience domestic armed conflict than are countries not deforesting.

H_3: Countries with a low freshwater availability per capita are more likely to experience domestic armed conflict than countries with a high freshwater availability per capita.[1]

All these three hypotheses fall within *supply-induced scarcity*. Thus, with reference to the demand-induced scarcity, we formulate a fourth hypothesis:

H_4: Countries with high population density are more likely to experience domestic armed conflict than countries with low population density.

Finally, for the third dimension of the environmental scarcity concept—structural scarcity—our hypothesis is that:

H_5: Countries with high income inequality are more likely to experience domestic armed conflict than countries with greater income equality.

Alternative Approaches

Although support has been found for all of these hypotheses in a series of case studies conducted by the Toronto Group (Howard and Homer-Dixon, 1995; Kelly and Homer-Dixon, 1995; Percival and Homer-Dixon, 2001) these findings are heavily debated and the studies have been subjected to considerable criticism, particularly on methodological grounds.

First, all of the Toronto Group's studies are explicitly selected so that *environmental degradation* as well as *domestic conflict* occur in all of the cases. There is no variation in the dependent variable, or for that matter in the main independent variable, making comparison impossible (Gleditsch, 2001).

Another criticism is that little attention has been given to the relative importance of environmental degradation as a cause of conflict (Gleditsch, 2001; Levy, 1995).[2] Although the Toronto Group pays some attention to the context within which environmental scarcity operates, by referring for example to eco-system vulnerability and in general to the political, social, and economic context, its main focus is on how environmental scarcity affects economy and politics, not vice versa. Part of the problem lies in the concept of environmental scarcity itself, since it includes other factors than actual environmental degradation. Structural scarcity, which concerns unequal distribution of resources (especially land), is mainly a consequence of politics. By disaggregating the concept, Homer-Dixon could have included theories about maldistribution of land and income inequality as a cause of conflict. As it stands, however, the politics of distribution disappear into the environmental scarcity concept.

Theories about the relationship between maldistribution of land and conflict and about income inequality and conflict have a long tradition in conflict research, largely linked to the study of revolution. In a quantitative study of the effects of agrarian inequality and income inequality, Edward Muller and Mitchell Seligson (1987: 443) find that 'agrarian inequality is relevant only to the extent that it is associated with inequality in the nation-wide distribution of income'.[3] They explain the finding with a combination of two different theoretical traditions: relative deprivation (RD) and resource mobilization. RD is based on inequality that creates discontent, but it is the 'vanguard of urban professional revolutionaries' that helps mobilize the discontented urban as well as the peasants, who are more difficult to mobilize (Muller and Seligson, 1987: 427). In contrast, Ranveig Gissinger (1997) found no relationship at all between income inequality and domestic armed conflict. In a survey of studies of income inequality and conflict Lichbach (1989) concluded that these studies point in different directions.

Homer-Dixon and his associates do not refer to any of these theories, although maldistribution of land is an especially important part of the environmental scarcity concept. Nor does he reflect on the fact that environmental degradation is found primarily in developing countries, in the context of disastrous national economies: low gross national product (GNP) per capita, high external debt, strong dependency on export of primary commodities, low levels of industrialization, and poorly developed democratic institutions.

Land distribution, as well as the degradation of land, forest, and water, is linked not only to demographic patterns, but also to economic and political factors. The United Nations Environment Programme (UNEP, 1991: 13) reports that irrigated agriculture tends to expand into rain-fed crop-land. Irrigated agriculture is mostly large-scale agriculture which is used either for domestic consumption or for export. The need for export income often acts to freeze an existing highly inequitable distribution of land, because it is the large-scale agriculture and the large estates which are best suited for export production. Export of cattle is also an important industry, especially in Latin America. This has been part of the problem in Chiapas, Mexico, where the rapid expansion of the financially powerful cattle industry has worsened an already unequal distribution of land, at the expense of peasants and small farmers (Howard and Homer-Dixon, 1995: 18–19). It is usually subsistence farmers and small farmers who are the losers in the subsequent race for good land.

Intensive cash cropping also takes its toll on the soil. Senegal, for instance, took up hefty loans to install refining capacity for a million tons of groundnuts. Today, its soils have become so depleted by groundnut production as to make it impossible to keep production anywhere near the level envisaged (George, 1992). Finally, export of various types of tropical forest has also been viewed as an important source of income for many developing countries.

Third World countries have been heavily indebted throughout the 1980s and 1990s, and income from export has been badly needed for debt repayment.[4] The economic reform programs of the International Monetary Fund and the World Bank have also pressured developing countries to choose strategies of liberalization and export-led growth. The status of these countries' economies may clearly be seen to have affected the environment, for example in the link between debt and deforestation. Of the twenty-four largest debtors in the 1980s, eight never had, or no longer had, forest reserves on a world scale. All of the sixteen remaining major debtors ($10 billion or more) were featured on the list of major deforesters (George, 1992; WRI, 1990).

The work of Homer-Dixon and his colleagues ignores the more direct linkages between economic and political factors and domestic armed conflict. As a consequence, the Toronto Group fails to contribute to a broader understanding of the causal pathway to domestic armed conflict. For example, do democratic regimes pursue a more environmentally sound policy than autocratic regimes?

Nils Petter Gleditsch and Bjørn Otto Sverdrup (1996) found that the effects of democracy are primarily positive when it comes to types of environmental degradation such as deforestation and loss of bio-diversity, but negative when it comes to the emission of climate gases, CO_2 in particular. On the basis of data from around 1990, they argue that political counteraction to the emerging greenhouse effect has not yet taken hold. Midlarsky (2001), on the other hand, finds a significant negative relationship between democracy and environmental performance, using indicators like deforestation and soil erosion, whereas protected land areas show a positive relationship. As Midlarsky (2001: 7) also notes, however, these differences may be explained by sample size and different measures of democracy used. Thus, there does seem to be *some* kind of positive linkage between democracy and environmental preservation.

Most democracies are found in economically well-off countries, which means in the industrialized world. Gleditsch and Sverdrup also found that when they controlled for level of development (using gross domestic product [GDP] per capita and the Human Development Index [HDI] as indicators) the effect of the political system on the environment was reduced (Gleditsch and Sverdrup, 1996: 23). Their study thus indicates that *both* economic and political factors affect the environment, and should not be ignored.

There is also a vast literature studying links among regime types, regime change, democratization, and conflict. Theories on the relationship between democracy and political violence generally lean toward the view that democracies are likely to experience somewhat less violent conflict and rebellion than autocracies and far less than in-between regime types, semi-democracies (Eckstein and Gurr, 1975, Rummel; 1995). We have confirmed this in earlier work using two different data sets for domestic armed conflict in the periods 1945–1992 and 1973–1992 (Ellingsen, 2000; Ellingsen and Gleditsch, 1997). On the other hand, the democratization process itself may generate conflict (Hegre et al., 1999; Huntington, 1991; Jakobsen, 1996).

Another important factor is the level of economic development within a country. Because most armed conflicts during the 1980s and 1990s have taken place in developing countries, it seems self-evident that the level of economic development must be related to domestic conflict. Moreover, in a study of political and economic development in sixty-five countries from 1800 to 1960, William Flanagan and Ernst Vogelman (1970: 14) found that countries with a high level of economic development are less likely to experience domestic violence. This relationship has also found support in our previous work (Ellingsen, 2000, 1997; Hauge, 1997; Hegre et al., 1999). A variant of this view is found in David Rapkin and William Avery (1986), who construct a model in which domestic political instability is produced by sudden shocks and gradual effects originating in world commodity and capital markets. The effects of such instabilities are mediated by levels of domestic economic and political development in Third World countries. In monocultures, for example, or in countries dependent on export income from just a few commodities, falling prices on the world market may have severe consequences for the economy, and thus for the propensity to political instability and domestic armed conflict. Again, our earlier work supports this view (Hauge and Hegre, 1997).

With this discussion of Homer-Dixon's model and of the theories challenging his approach, we have underlined the necessity of testing out Homer-Dixon's findings in a multivariate analysis which includes variables from alternative and/or complementary approaches. In addition to variables indicating degradation of renewable resources and population measures, we would also include indicators of the level of economic development (GNP per capita), regime type, and regime stability in the analysis. Thus, our next hypotheses are:

H_6: Democratic countries, and in particular stable ones, are less likely to experience domestic armed conflict than are countries with other types of political regimes.

H_7: Countries with a high level of economic development are less likely to experience domestic armed conflict than are countries with a low level of economic development.

Since degradation of renewable resources occurs primarily in countries with low economic development and nondemocratic rule we expect to find that:

H_8: Economic development and regime type have a higher explanatory power than environmental scarcity.

Research Design

Our first three hypotheses refer to the relationship between supply-induced scarcity and domestic armed conflict, whereas the fourth concerns demand-induced scarcity, and the fifth, structural scarcity. All of these hypotheses were derived from the work of Homer-Dixon and the Toronto Group. We have expanded the model by including other conflict-generating elements, such as political and economic factors, forming a sixth and a seventh hypothesis. Finally, we posited an eighth hypothesis, on the importance of the various variables relative to each other.

These hypotheses are tested in two different ways. First, in a mixed cross-sectional and diachronic analysis, where we use a logit model based on all country-years in the international system in the period 1980–1992. Here, incidence of domestic armed conflict was the dependent variable. Second, in a pure cross-sectional analysis for the period as a whole, with battle deaths as percentage of the total population as the dependent variable.

Methodology

We use results from two different sets of analyses. First, we want to see whether our independent variables affect the incidence of domestic armed conflict. With a dichotomous dependent variable with only two values in the mixed cross-sectional and diachronic analysis we use a logit model (Aldrich and Nelson, 1984) with country-years as the unit of analysis.

However, several of our independent variables are available for a single year only, and thus remain static throughout the period 1980–1992. Consequently, the usefulness of the country-year approach is questionable. This leads us to run a cross-sectional logit analysis with a dependent variable for the occurrence or nonoccurrence of domestic armed conflict.

Since we are also interested in the severity of conflict, we have performed an additional cross-sectional analysis for the whole period 1980–1992, using a continuous dependent variable: the number of battle deaths as percentage of the total population. Here the unit of analysis is the country.

Because of the different structures of the two methods, the structure of the variables—dependent as well as independent—is also somewhat different. A thorough description of the data would seem to be in place.

Dependent Variables

In the logit model, the data on incidence of domestic armed conflict include both data on civil war collected from the Correlates of War data set as well as domestic armed conflict data collected from Wallensteen and Sollenberg (1997).

The Correlates of War data set (Singer and Small, 1994; Small and Singer, 1982) includes all nations within the international system for the period 1816–1992. Civil war is defined along three dimensions: internality, type of participants, and degree of effective resistance. Small and Singer

(1982: 31–47, 203–222) define civil war as 'a military conflict within a state where the national government is one of the active parties and where both parties in the conflict can and intend to struggle despite any costs'. This definition is quite similar to that used by Peter Wallensteen and Margareta Sollenberg (1997), but whereas Melvin Small and J. David Singer set their lower threshold at 1,000 battle deaths in a single year, Wallensteen and Sollenberg include all conflicts with a minimum of twenty-five annual battle deaths. Their data span the period 1989–1996. However, since most of our data on the independent variables contain information only up to 1992, we restricted ourselves to the years 1989–1992 in this analysis.

The reasoning behind using two different dependent variables is to see whether there are any differences in how our independent variables affect civil war compared with domestic armed conflicts. Homer-Dixon (1995c: 12), for example, has suggested that environmental factors contribute more to minor conflicts than to major ones.[5]

In the cross-sectional analysis, the dependent variable is the number of battle deaths as a percentage of the total population. This information was available only for the civil wars in the Correlates of War data set, so the cross-sectional analysis does not look at minor armed conflicts.

Independent Variables

Supply-Induced Scarcity. Environmental degradation, or supply-induced scarcity, is measured by three different variables: (1) *annual change in forest cover*; (2) *land degradation*; and (3) *freshwater availability per capita*. Data on change in forest cover were collected from *FAO Production Yearbook* (1981–1984). FAO defines forest and woodland as 'land under natural or planted stands of trees whether productive or not, and includes land from which forests have been cleared, but that will be reforested in the foreseeable future' (FAO, 1991: ix). Thus, tree plantations are also included. However, the contribution of the tree plantations to the total balance is small: During 1981–1990, the total forest-plantation area increased annually on average by 2.6 million hectares and the net area by 1.8 million hectares. The net area planted per year, however, was only approximately 12 percent of the area deforested every year (FAO, 1993: x; FAO 1995a).

Originally, the data measured the area covered by forest (in hectares) in each country, each year. On the basis of these figures, we have calculated the annual change in forest cover, relative to the previous year. Thus, deforestation is to be understood as an annual decline in forest and woodland coverage, relative to the figure for the previous year (no matter how small the change is). 'No change' means less than 1 percent decrease in area covered by forest, while an increase is recorded for countries where the area covered by forest actually was extended (for example through forest plantations, because of decline in agriculture or because of climate changes).

Our data on human-induced soil degradation are based on a map of human-induced soil degradation published by UNEP (Oldeman et al., 1991), which refers to four types of soil degradation: water, wind, chemical, and physical degradation.[6] In this chapter, soil degradation is used to refer to all the four types. Our classification of *no* degradation, *low*, *moderate*, and *high* degradation is based on the severity[7] and the extent[8] of all four types of degradation in a country. If the degradation was not severe or affected only a small part of the country, it was considered to be low. If the degradation was somewhat severe and covered a larger area of the country, it was considered to be moderate. If the degradation was severe or covered large parts of the country, it was categorized as high. It has not been possible to obtain data on soil degradation on an annual basis, so all data are based on 1990 estimates and copied for the other years.

Data on freshwater availability per capita were collected from *World Resources* (1986–1995). The variable 'annual internal water resources' refers to the average annual flow of rivers and groundwater generated from endogenous precipitation (*World Resources*, 1994). Data on the variable are based on one year of information for the period 1980–1992, and have been copied for the remaining years of the period 1980–1992.[9] The categorization of the variable follows Shiklomanov (1993).[10]

Information concerning land degradation and freshwater availability is based on a single year of observation. Hence, two of our three measures of supply-induced scarcity remain static throughout the period 1980–1992. As previously mentioned, this reduces the value of an analysis with country-years as the unit of analysis. In the pure cross-sectional analysis, each country is only observed once. The variable measuring decline in forest cover here refers to the percentage decline in forest cover throughout the whole period 1980–1992; that is the percentage of change in forest cover in 1992, relative to the forest cover in 1980.

Demand-Induced Scarcity. Homer Dixon's (1994) demand-induced scarcity is operationalized as *population density*, with data from the *Demographic Yearbook* (UN 1980–1993). Information concerning this variable was available for each year in the period 1980–1992 and is well-suited for the diachronic model. In the purely cross-sectional analysis, the variable refers to the total change in population density (in percent) during the period 1980–1992.

Structural Scarcity. We have operationalized Homer-Dixon's concept of structural scarcity as *income inequality*. A better measure might have been distribution of land, but because of the lack of precise and reliable data on this variable, we had to rely on a perhaps second-best measure. Information concerning income inequality was collected from the World Bank's *Economic Review* (1996). The variable measures the ratio of the top quintile share of income to the bottom quintile share of income.[11] These data were available for one year only and were copied for the remaining years of the period 1980–1992. This also decreases the usefulness of the country-year approach.

Other Conflict-Generating Factors. In order to control for economic and political conditions, and to test hypotheses six and seven, we also included the following independent variables in the model:

(a) The *level of economic development* of a country, measured here as GNP per capita. These data were collected from the World Bank's *World Development Report* (1982–1995). To reduce the huge variations within this variable (from $80 to $37,000), we log-transformed it, so that the variable ranged between 4 (low GNP per capita) and 10 (high GNP per capita).

(b) *Type of political regime* within a country. This information was obtained from Polity III (Jaggers and Gurr, 1995). It includes indices for institutionalized democracy and autocracy, ranging from 0–10, where 10 is the highest score (most democratic or most autocratic). We subtracted the score for autocracy from the score for democracy, yielding a variable varying between 10 (most democratic) and -10 (most autocratic). This variable was categorized into three groups: democracies (6–10), autocracies (-10 to -6), and semidemocracies (-5 to 5).

(c) *Political stability* within a country. If a country had the same type of regime for ten years or more, we characterized it as stable, otherwise as unstable.

Polity III covers the whole period 1800–1993; data on level of economic development were available for each year in the period 1980–1992. Thus, in the mixed cross-sectional diachronic analysis, the variables refer to the country's type of political regime and/or level of economic development in each of the years 1980–1992. In the pure cross-sectional analysis, on the other hand, these variables are based on the average score for the whole period. Earlier studies (Ellingsen, 2000; Hegre et al., 1999) have shown an inverted U-curve relationship between level of democracy and incidence of domestic conflict, hence we used the squared average score. Because our logit model includes the period 1980–1992 with the country-year as the unit of analysis and the *incidence* of domestic conflict as the dependent variable, problems of autocorrelation arise. A country which is in civil conflict in a given year is intrinsically likely to be in civil conflict the next year as well. To reduce the impact of this problem, we have, in line with earlier work by one of the present authors (Ellingsen, 2000), included a variable for whether the country was in conflict in the last year (1) or not (0). An alternative approach would have been to perform the analysis for the *outbreak* of domestic conflict, (i.e., coding the dependent variable positive for only the first year of the conflict), in addition to the *incidence* of conflict, following the pattern of Nils Petter Gleditsch and Håvard Hegre (1997) in their analysis of interstate war. An argument against using outbreak of domestic conflict as the dependent variable is that the years at peace are dependent in exactly the same way: a country which has no domestic conflict in a given year is more likely to have peace in the next year too, compared with a country not at peace in the first year. To control fully for this, one would have to exclude all but the first year at domestic armed conflict and the first year at peace! By including a lagged variable, we correct for both dependencies at the same time.[12]

Finally, findings from Adekanye (1994) indicate that the severity of a conflict is highly determined by a country's military expenditure. Thus, in the pure cross-sectional analysis with the number of battle deaths as the dependent variable, we included a variable measuring military expenditure as a share of GDP. The data for this variable were obtained from the *CIA World Factbook*, CIA (1981–1993) and refer to the average percentage of GDP that a country spent on military items in the period 1980–1992.

Empirical Findings

The Diachronic Study

Table 3.1 shows the beta estimates for each factor in the mixed model. Although we cannot interpret the estimates directly, we can—depending on whether the estimates are positive or negative—say whether they increase or decrease the likelihood of domestic conflict. To be able to interpret the results directly, we must translate the estimates into probabilities, as shown in Table 3.1.

Taking the estimates first, we see that all of the environmental factors—deforestation, high land degradation, low freshwater availability per capita—have positive beta estimates, whether the dependent variable is civil war or armed conflict. This is in line with our hypotheses (H_1–H_3)— the likelihood of domestic conflict is higher in such countries, than in countries with no or less environmental degradation. The same is the case with population density—countries with high population density have a higher risk of domestic conflict than countries with low or even moderate population density (H_4). However, the estimate for decline in forest is significant only for low-level armed conflict. Thus, deforestation may not seem to have any real effect on larger conflicts, only on smaller ones. For smaller conflicts though, the estimate is not only significant, but it is also strongly positive—meaning that deforestation increases the risk of armed conflict substantially. This is interesting, especially since we also see that the coefficients for the two other environmental factors (land degradation and freshwater availability per capita) are stronger for the incidence of armed conflict than for the incidence of civil war. It is tempting to conclude from this that environmental factors are more important in explaining smaller conflicts than larger ones. Could the difference in results be due to different time-spans? A closer examination shows this not to be the case: environmental degradation does not have increased explanatory power after the end of the Cold War, but does have a stronger effect on smaller armed conflicts. This also confirms the expectations in Homer-Dixon (1995c:12). Of the three types of environmental degradation, however, land degradation seems in general to have the strongest effect on the likelihood of domestic conflict.

The estimates for income inequality are also positive—indicating an increase in risk of domestic conflict. However, these results are not significant, and should be interpreted with caution.

GNP per capita has a negative effect on civil war: the higher GNP per capita, the less likely is civil war. This is again in line with our expectations. When it comes to regime type, the results are also as expected—with democracies being the least likely to experience domestic conflict, and semi-democracies being the most likely. Political instability seems also to increase the risk of domestic conflict.

Also in line with our expectations, Table 3.1 shows that if the country was in domestic conflict one year, it is by far more likely to be in conflict the next year, too.

Finally, Table 3.1 shows that both in accounting for civil war and smaller armed conflicts, 'conflict last year' has the highest explanatory power, followed by GNP per capita and land degradation. For civil war, type of political regime follows land degradation, while both deforestation and low freshwater availability are more important than type of political regime in explaining smaller conflicts. Thus, environmental scarcity is indeed less important than economic factors in explaining domestic armed conflict, but—contrary to our expectations—in certain circumstances it is more important than political factors.

In Table 3.2 these estimates are translated into probabilities. The probability of civil war or domestic armed conflict is not particularly high in countries that suffer from only *one* of the supply-induced scarcities—whether deforestation, land degradation, or low freshwater availability. However, as Table 3.2 shows, the risk of minor domestic armed conflicts in these countries is between six and seven times the risk of major conflicts. Moreover, because all these conflict-generating factors are intertwined, it is relevant to inquire into the risk of domestic armed conflict when several risk factors are present within a country. Thus, in Table 3.2 we show the probability (in percent) when risk factors are added to the model one by one. Table 3.2 clearly shows that the propensity for domestic armed conflict increases with an increasing number of risk factors within a country. For example, a poor country suffering from demand-induced, supply-in-

TABLE 3.1   Logit Estimates for Two Indicators of Domestic Conflict

Independent Variable	Incidence of Civil War 1980–1992			Incidence of Armed Conflict 1989–1992		
	Coefficient	Standard Error	N	Coefficient	Standard Error	N
Constant	-5.67*	2.05	107	-4.17*	1.36	39
Domestic conflict last year?						
No			816			281
Yes	5.78*	0.48	77	3.43*	1.12	22
GNP per capita	-0.49*	0.11	893	-0.29*	0.13	303
High						
Low						
Type of Political Regime						
Democracy	·		453			175
Autocracy	0.33*	0.14	270	0.27*	0.12	72
Semidemocracy	0.74*	0.23	170	0.91*	0.39	56
Income Inequality						
Low inequality			168			68
Moderate inequality	0.51	0.89	424	0.49	0.35	134
High inequality	0.61	0.88	301	0.61	0.33	101
Political instability						
No			585			199
Yes	0.27	0.13	308	0.45*	0.17	104
Population density						
Low population density			276			89
Moderate population density	0.18	0.15	423	0.26	0.16	176
High population density	0.35*	0.17	199	0.44*	0.21	38

(continues)

duced, *and* structural scarcity has a 20 percent probability of incidence of civil war and a 45 percent probability of domestic armed conflict. The probability of either type of conflict increases further if the country is a semidemocracy, unstable and with a history of conflict. Because these conditions are part of reality in many Third World countries today, these are truly alarming findings.

The Cross-Sectional Study

As noted, some of our independent variables remain static throughout the period 1980–1992, which reduced the usefulness of taking the country-year as the unit of analysis. We therefore ran a purely cross-sectional analysis for the same period, with the incidence of domestic armed conflict as the de-

TABLE 3.1 *(continued)*

Independent Variable	Incidence of Civil War 1980–1992			Incidence of Armed Conflict 1989–1992		
	Coefficient	Standard Error	N	Coefficient	Standard Error	N
Change in forest						
Increase in forest			197			73
No change in forest	0.05	0.72	278	0.15	0.26	89
Deforestation	0.31	0.51	418	1.08*	0.21	141
Land degradation						
Low land degradation			169			59
Moderate land degradation	0.68*	0.14	402	0.95*	0.31	132
High land degradation	1.38*	0.29	322	1.77*	0.42	112
Freshwater availability per capita						
High freshwater availability per capita			232			78
Medium freshwater availability per capita	0.11	0.18	139	0.26	0.18	46
Low freshwater availability per capita	0.65*	0.18	522	0.95*	0.26	179

Civil War 1980–1992: -2 log liklihood: model chi-squared improvement: 399.329; * $p < 0.05$; N = 893; correctly predicted: 87%. Armed Conflict 1989–1992: -2 log liklihood: 311.414; model chi-squared improvement: 103.316; * $p < 0.05$; N = 303; correctly predicted: 83%. The first category for each variable is the reference group. GNP per capita is a continous variable, and the other variables are categorical. Several models were tested—the one presented here had the lowest log liklihood and therefore provides the best fit. No significant interactions were found.

pendent variable. The results were similar to those presented above and they will not be discussed here.

Although environmental scarcity contributes to the incidence of domestic armed conflict, the severity of such conflicts might be attributable to other factors. Consequently, we ran a pure cross-sectional analysis using number of battle deaths as a share of the total population as our dependent variable. The results of this analysis are reported in Table 3.3.

All but one of the coefficients in the model are in the expected direction. The higher the GNP per capita, the lower the number of battle deaths in civil war. The coefficient for the democracy score reveals an inverted U-curve relationship again as anticipated, and in line with earlier findings (Ellingsen, 1997; Ellingsen and Gleditsch, 1997; Hegre et al., 1999). Moreover, the higher the increase in population density, the

TABLE 3.2 Probabilities (in %) of Domestic Armed Conflict When Risk Factors Are Added

	Incidence of Civil War, 1980–1992			Incidence of Armed Conflict, 1989–1992		
	Deforestation	High Land Degradation	Low Freshwater Availability	Deforestation	High Land Degradation	Low Freshwater Availability
	0.47	1.35	0.66	4.36	8.32	3.84
+High population density	0.66	1.91	0.93	6.60	12.34	5.84
+High income inequality	1.21	3.46	1.70	11.51	20.59	10.25
+Poverty	8.02	20.26	10.91	29.32	45.27	26.70
+Semidemocracy	15.45	34.76	20.43	50.74	67.26	47.50
+Political instability	19.31	41.10	25.16	61.78	76.33	58.66
+Conflict history	98.73	99.56	99.13	98.03	99.00	97.77

Because no countries have all risk factors present, only the probabilities for the most frequent combinations are calculated.

TABLE 3.3   Cross-Sectional Analysis of Civil War Battle Deaths as Percentage of Total Population, 1980-1992

	Coefficient	Sig T
Average military expenditure (% of GDP)	0.33	0.00
Average GNP per capita, 1980–1992	-0.16	0.00
Average type of political regime squared, 1980–1992	-0.05	0.00
Income inequality, 1980–1992	-0.07	0.06
Total change in population density, 1980–1992	0.07	0.02
Total change in forest coverage (%), 1980–1992	0.07	0.02
Land degradation, 1980–1992	0.10	0.00
Freshwater availability. 1980-1992	0.08	0.02

$N = 118$; $r^2 = 0.51$.

greater the decline in forest coverage, the greater the land degradation, and the lower the freshwater availability—the larger the number of deaths. Of these, GNP per capita has the highest explanatory power on battle deaths as a share of total population. All of this is in line with our expectations.

Surprisingly, however, the estimate for income inequality is negative—indicating that the higher the income inequality, the lower the proportion of battle deaths. Although this estimate is not significant at the 0.05 level and, thus, must be interpreted with caution, it is still quite interesting. One possible explanation may be that in countries where income inequality is particularly high, the deprived and, thus, potentially rebellious group(s) simply lack the resources (i.e., weapons) to continue fighting, at least on a large scale. Another explanation may be that the elite exerts massive repression of the deprived group(s), thus suppressing rebellion.

Moreover, although most of the estimates are in the expected direction, all except one are quite small, especially those forming the scarcity concept. Furthermore, before including a variable for military expenditure, the model had an R^2 of only 0.21. The inclusion of this variable increases the R^2 to 0.51. This indicates, therefore, that environmental factors do not necessarily have much influence on how many people get killed during a conflict, even though they contribute to the incidence of such conflict.[13] The relatively weak severity results could possibly be explained by the fact that the cross-sectional analysis includes only the number of battle deaths in civil wars, and consequently all conflicts with battle deaths of 0–999 are treated as the same. Alternatively, the severity of a conflict may be determined by variables such as military capabilities, weapons technology, size of the armed forces, and the duration of the conflict, as well as by various psychological factors, rather than by environmental, political, and economic conditions. In any case, the only variable we have included from this category—military expenditure as a percentage of GDP—turns out to be very important.

Conclusion

Recent case studies investigating the relationship between environmental scarcity and civil conflict have underlined the importance of depletion and degradation of renewable resources, combined with population pressure and unequal distribution of land or income, as sources of domestic armed conflict. In one of the first large-N studies of the relationship between environmental degradation and domestic armed conflict, we have tested these linkages for three different measures of violence and for three measures of environmental scarcity.

Our findings are quite clear: countries suffering from environmental degradation—and in particular from land degradation—are more prone to civil conflict. However, economic factors are far more important in predicting domestic armed conflict than are environmental factors. In general, this also holds true of political factors.[14]

Comparing different measures of conflict, we find that environmental degradation has a stronger impact on the incidence of *smaller* than large armed conflicts. Environmental scarcity has only a small impact on the severity of a conflict, using battle deaths as a share of total population as the dependent variable. The sources of civil conflict are not necessarily closely related to the severity of the conflict. Although environmental scarcity is a cause of conflict, it is not necessarily also a catalyst.

The level of economic development has the strongest effect on the incidence of domestic armed conflict as well as a relatively strong impact on the severity. This highlights the need for further studies of the linkages between economic factors and conflict, a topic given surprisingly little attention to date.

Environmental factors emerge as less important in determining the incidence of civil conflict than economic and political factors. However, our findings relating to environmental scarcity underline the urgent need for a fuller and broader collection of environmental data. Most of the data collected today concern only a few countries or a short time period. This is true even for variables such as deforestation, freshwater availability, land degradation, bio-diversity, and CO_2 emissions. Information about environmental scarcity at the subnational level (e.g. the distribution between different groups) is even more limited. This information could be particularly valuable for understanding the causes and dynamics of conflicts between regional or ethnic groups.

The close linkages between economic, political, and environmental variables indicate that future research should pay more attention to the interaction of these factors. Although a fair amount of work has been conducted on the relationship between poverty and conflict, income inequality and conflict, political regime and conflict, as well as on the relationship between environment and conflict, little work links all four factors. This should be the highest research priority if we are to obtain a more realistic understanding of the causal pathways to conflict.

Wenche Hauge, b. 1959; cand. polit. in political science (University of Oslo, 1991); research fellow, International Peace Research Institute, Oslo (PRIO); current main interest: causes and dynamics of conflict escalation.

Tanja Ellingsen, b. 1970; cand. polit. in political science (University of Trondheim, 1995); research fellow, Department of Political Science, University of Oslo.

Notes

1. The hypothesis on freshwater availability is formulated in a static way, since data on decrease in freshwater availability are not available on an annual basis.

2. The relative importance here refers to the frequency of environmental degradation occurring as a cause of domestic armed conflict globally, compared with other factors, and not its relative weight or importance in any particular domestic armed conflict.

3. 'Relevant' here refers to the statistical effect of agricultural inequality, which is significant only when combined with high income inequality.

4. Some figures for 1993 are illustrative: Uganda 144 percent, Algeria 77 percent, Bolivia 59 percent, Peru 59 percent (World Bank, 1995a).

5. It would be interesting to look at even lower levels of conflict such as riots and protests. Although Taylor and Hudson (1972) and Taylor and Jodice (1983) contain some such data, they do not cover all countries, nor the period in focus here.

6. *Water erosion* is defined as displacement of soil material by water. The GLASOD approach distinguishes between two types of water erosion: (a) loss of topsoil, and (b) terrain deformation. *Wind erosion* is defined as displacement of soil material by wind, with three subtypes: (a) loss of topsoil, (b) terrain deformation, and (c) overblowing (land surface being covered by wind-carried particles). *Chemical degradation* includes three processes: (a) loss of nutrients and/or organic matter, (b) salinization, and (c) acidification and pollution. *Physical degradation* includes: (a) compaction, crusting, and sealing, (b) waterlogging, and (c) subsidence of organic soils (see Oldeman, 1992).

7. 'The severity of the process is characterized by the degree in which the soil is degraded and by the relative extent of the degraded area within a delineated physiographic unit' (Oldeman et al., 1991: 14).

8. Extent refers to geographical coverage within a country's boundaries.

9. The year of information varies from country to country, and in the cases of Egypt and Turkey we had two years of information. For a number of countries, the information dates back before 1980: Djibouti (1973), Ghana (1970), Mauritania (1978), Mauritius (1974), Sudan (1977), Tanzania (1970), Uganda (1970), Zambia (1970), India (1975), Iran (1975), Iraq (1970), Jordan (1975), Kuwait (1974), Lebanon (1975), Malaysia (1975), Oman (1975), Pakistan (1975), Philippines

(1975), Saudi Arabia (1975), Singapore (1975), Sri Lanka (1970), Syrian Arab Republic (1976), Costa Rica (1970), Cuba (1975), El Salvador (1975), Guatemala (1970), Jamaica (1975), Mexico (1975), Nicaragua (1975), Panama (1975), Trinidad and Tobago (1975), Argentina (1976), Chile (1975), Uruguay (1965), Venezuela (1970), Albania (1970), Ireland (1979), Australia (1975). For the other countries the data are based on the latest year available during the period 1980–1992.

10. The categorization into low, average, and high freshwater availability is based on Shiklomanov (1993). The values are given in 1,000 cubic meters as follows: low: 0–5.0; average: 5.1–20.0; high: over 20.1.

11. We recoded this variable into three groups: (0) low inequality (ratio ≤ 5.0), (1) moderate inequality (ratio > 5.0 and ≤ 10.0), and high inequality (ratio > 10.0).

12. Another alternative is to use hazard models, as in Raknerud and Hegre (1997) and Hegre et al. (1997).

13. An additional cross-sectional analysis using number of country-years of civil war as the dependent variable gave similar results.

14. During our final revisions of this chapter the State Failure Task Force published its second report (Esty et al., 1998). Our results are somewhat at odds with theirs. The Task Force has developed a global model of 'state failure', based on data two years in advance of the event, discriminating between states likely to experience major political crises and states likely to remain stable. The procedure of their work was to examine hundreds of factors suggested as theoretically relevant to state crises, among those also soil degradation, deforestation, and freshwater availability, using global data for most of the period 1955–1996.

The Task Force concluded that the most efficient discrimination between cases of state failure and stable cases was obtained from a model with only three factors; the level of material living standards (measured by infant mortality), the level of trade openness, and the level of democracy. However, they did not find any direct, measurable correlation between environmental degradation and state failure. They therefore developed a 'mediated' model in which environmental change had an indirect effect on the risk of state failure, via infant mortality.

Our findings, as presented in this chapter, are referred to in the Task Force report. The Task Force explains the diverging results in the two works by differences in how the dependent variables are operationalized and how the independent variables are used. These differences lead the authors to the conclusion that the models are essentially incomparable. We agree with this, but not with their subsequent point: 'Because the state failure model covers a greater time period and includes trade openness as an explanatory variable, we think its results have more validity' (p. 26). There are several reasons for our disagreement.

First of all, although the state failure model correctly covers a longer time period (1955–1996) than ours (1980–1992), their environmental variables cover only the same time period as ours. Indeed, the same data sources have been used. Information about various types of environmental degradation is not available for earlier years—and one can hardly blame the Task Force for that. Nevertheless, this indicates that the data measuring environmental degradation have been extrapolated in order to cover the total time period 1955–1996, which raises the issue of how accurate their data are. Now, this of course is to some extent also true in our model. The variable measuring soil degradation is based on one year of observation only: 1990. In our view, though, it is less problematic to assume that the extent of environmental degradation remains approximately the same throughout one decade than throughout four decades.

Second, to put revolutionary wars, ethnic wars, adverse regime transitions and genocides/policides all into one big sack labelled 'state failure' is questionable and cannot be fully justified by the fact that there are too few complete state failures to make statistical generalization meaningful (p. 33). In particular, we find it difficult to see how a shift from democratic toward authoritarian rule necessarily represents a case of state failure, especially since nonviolent shifts also are included in this category. In any case, it is difficult to see how genocides and adverse regime changes can be treated as similar phenomena. Moreover, genocide/policide may even be seen as an indicator of a strong state, rather than 'state failure', as in the case of Rwanda. The same can be said about the events in China in 1989.

Finally, the use of the trade openness variable is also very problematic, because of its low validity. Trade openness is measured as the value of exports plus imports as share of GDP (p. 11). Evidently this is a measure of the value of trade, which does not necessarily reflect increases or decreases in the volume of trade. However, changes in the value of trade may reflect a whole series of conditions that are linked as much to the international trade regime as to national regulations. Falls or increases in international prices of important commodities, protectionism in the target country for export, sudden peaks in development aid enabling countries to import more, and trade embargoes are just some of these conditions. The value of trade, as they operationalize it, reflects such a complex series of conditions that it is difficult to draw any conclusions at all. A more precise measure of trade openness would have been some measure of national trade regulations, such as tariffs and non-tariff barriers, or quotas.

Chapter Four

Demographic Pressure and Interstate Conflict

JAROSLAV TIR

PAUL F. DIEHL

A Limit to Population Growth?

Growth in national or global population has often been at the centerpiece of models of environmental degradation.[1] Growing population has been one of the factors thought to exacerbate poverty and starvation, hasten resource depletion, and stifle economic growth (Meadows, Meadows, Randers, and Behrens, 1972). Although the negative impact of population on the environment in such models has been hotly contested (Simon and Kahn, 1984; Singer, 1987), even to the point of questioning whether zero population growth is desirable, discussions about limiting population growth have remained at the forefront of international conferences on the environment (Rio, 1992), population (Cairo, 1994), and the status of women (Beijing, 1995).

Any role that population pressures might play in the initiation and escalation of interstate conflict has received considerably less attention.[2] Within the political arena, population pressures were often cited as a causal factor, in actuality more a pretext, for territorial expansion. The Nazi concept of Lebensraum, based on the ideas of Friedrich Ratzel, argued that Germany needed space to accommodate its growing population. Japan used similar arguments in justifying its invasion of Korea and Manchuria. Yet our

The data set used in this chapter is available at http://www.pol.uiuc.edu/faculty/diehl.html.

analysis of the scholarly literature in the next section does not generally reveal a strong relationship between population pressures and international conflict propensity. Most studies of international conflict concentrate on national characteristics (e.g., military capability, regime type) other than those directly related to population. Even the recent concerns with environmental security (Homer-Dixon, 1991, 1994; Homer-Dixon and Blitt, 1998; Kennedy, 1998) deal with internal conflict resulting from population pressure and resource scarcity rather than interstate conflict.

The purpose of this chapter is to take a renewed look at the relationship between national population pressure and the propensity to engage in international conflict. We are concerned with both static and dynamic population pressure. Static pressure is represented here by a high population density that may lead states to acquire new territory or resources contained in other territories in order to deal with the attendant spatial and environmental problems associated with overcrowding. Dynamic pressure refers to significant population growth, which may put increasing strains on states as they seek to accommodate the demands of its growing population; international conflictual actions may be the product of state attempts to deal with resource shortages and other demographically-induced pressures. We are also concerned with several aspects of conflict involvement by states. Initially, we investigate the propensity of states with different population pressure patterns to become involved in militarized interstate conflict. Beyond mere involvement in interstate conflict, we also investigate whether states with significant population pressures were the ones who initiated that conflict, as the logic of most theoretical explanations suggests. In addition, we explore whether conflicts involving states with significant population pressures are more likely to escalate to war, possibly indicating a separate dangerous effect. Thus, our study considers the population patterns and conflict propensities of all states in the international system from 1930 to 1989.

Several theoretical implications follow from understanding the population-conflict nexus. First, determining if and how population pressures influence conflict is an essential part of constructing a full model of the environmental determinants of security. While resource depletion and other environmental problems may increase international conflict, population pressure may be driving these problems. This is not to say that population pressure is the sole root cause of economic and environmental problems, but it may account for a significant portion. Thus, if population pressure strongly conditions environmental problems, we must view those problems as intervening variables in the causal path to war, rather than as autonomous factors. From this study, we also should be able to assess whether population pressure has a direct effect on conflict behavior, independent of the effects that occur solely through intervening factors. Not considering population pressures in models of environmental security would lead us to ignore incorrectly some important pieces of the causal chain.

Second, much of the scholarly attention in the environmental security literature is directed at internal conflicts or interstate conflict short of some militarized threshold. This study will hopefully allow us to understand more about how population affects militarized interstate conflict. This topic not only receives considerably less attention, but the empirical work offers few definitive conclusions. The results presented below offer some systematic empirical evidence to a field characterized by polemic and anecdotal evidence.

Third, understanding the impact of population pressures also allows scholars to assess the relative impact of national attributes on foreign policy behavior. With the possible exception of national capabilities (although this, too, is usually considered dyadically), scholarly research in the past few decades has concentrated on dyadic attributes (arms races, democratic peace, alliances) or followed the neorealist tradition with a focus on systemic attributes (see Bueno de Mesquita and Lalman, 1988, for a critique). This study is a first step that may suggest a reconsideration of national attributes as important factors in decisions to enter or escalate military conflict.

The study of population pressures and international conflict propensity also has significant policy implications. Even though the increase in global population over the past two decades has been slower than originally projected, the number of human beings on the Earth has grown dramatically. Furthermore, population projections envision significant population increases in the coming years, owing largely to the difficulty of changing individual behavior on a global scale and to the large extant population base (in which even small percentage increases mean millions of new people added to the global population total). With land area fixed and technological adjustments uncertain, we can expect population pressures to increase, especially in Africa and parts of Asia. If those pressures are found to be linked with conflict activity, we might then anticipate an increase in disputes and possibly wars in those areas of the world. For example, it has been suggested (Homer-Dixon, 1991) that scarcity conflicts over water or agricultural land, exacerbated by population pressures, may erupt between Turkey and Syria. Such a prognosis suggests either stronger efforts by the international community to limit population growth or more persistent attempts to deal with resource scarcity and other intervening consequences of population growth.

Before we can address the consequences of a relationship between population pressure and conflict, we must first establish its existence, direction, and magnitude. We begin with a review of the previous scholarly writings and empirical findings. Based on this literature, several hypotheses on population and conflict are presented, operationalized, and tested.

Previous Studies

The study of the relationship between population pressure and international conflict has long historical roots and crosses disciplinary boundaries. Although there is significant theoretical diversity, their orientation can roughly be classified into three sometimes overlapping sets: those based on resource scarcity, those that link population growth and its manifestations to military capability, and quasi-Marxist approaches that look at 'lateral pressure', of which population growth is a significant component. We review each of these three general frameworks, as well as those that reject the assumption that population pressures promote international conflict, and then consider what significant relationships (if any) have been uncovered by the extant empirical literature.

Resource Scarcity

Many of the theoretical arguments that link population pressures to conflict derive from the original work of Thomas Malthus (1798). Malthus postulated the simple, but profound, notion that while food production grew linearly, population increases tended to be exponential. At some point, population would outstrip the capacity of the Earth to feed all the people, passing what has later been referred to as the 'carrying capacity' of the environment. Around this intersection point, international conflict is said to be possible although the exact causal linkages tend to be rather vague. For example, a few of Paul Ehrlich's (1968) scenarios in the classic *The Population Bomb* involve the development of catastrophic military conflict deriving from localized or global food shortages occasioned by overpopulation (see also Ehrlich and Ehrlich, 1991). Daniel Deudney (1991) outlines four scenarios linking environmental degradation to war (water, poverty, power, and pollution wars), any of which could be precipitated or exacerbated by population pressures. A significant segment of Thomas Homer-Dixon's (1991, 1994; see also Homer-Dixon and Blitt, 1998) environmental conflict model stems from population-driven resource scarcities, although he considers civil, rather than interstate, conflict a more likely outcome. Marcel Leroy (1986) links environmentally-induced civil conflict to external, diversionary uses of military force.

Much work in sociology has focused on the link between population pressure and resource scarcity, most often food supply, energy resources, and the like. There is rarely an explicit consideration of international conflict. However, in one of the earliest studies, Warren Thompson (1929) proposed that population pressure was represented by the ratio of resources to people. He argues that the lower the ratio, the greater the population pressure and hence the propensity for national expansion. Thompson does not argue simply that states with greater population pressures are more likely to go to war than those with a more favorable resource-to-person ratio. What matters more is the difference in population pressures between potential conflict initiators and targets as 'a densely crowded people has little or nothing to gain by taking a territory of equally crowded people' (Thompson, 1929: 13–14). Thus, an analyst should look beyond population pressures affecting a given state, to pressures affecting neighboring states that might be the targets of territorial expansion. This would allow analysts to predict if expansion is likely to take place as well as what countries would be the locus of that expansion.

The notion that states will expand to accommodate burgeoning population and acquire living space is found in much of the geopolitical writings in Germany. Karl Haushofer's ideas constituted more of a strategic blueprint or justification for German expansion in the first part of the twentieth century than a theoretical framework for understanding international conflict. (A more theoretical argument for population-driven land expansion in nineteenth-century Europe is given in Merritt, 1995.) He began with the notion that Germany had a separate destiny and was 'incomplete' (Sloan, 1988). He borrowed the idea of Lebensraum from Friedrich Ratzel and believed that space must be expanded to deal with population pressures (Dorplan, 1942). Some of these ideas were said to have influenced Nazi expansionist efforts prior to World War II (Heske, 1987; Sloan, 1988). In more recent variations, states have either worried about the rapid population growth of their neighbors or advocated territorial expansion to accommodate immigrants. A good example is Israel, which has shown fears of the relatively high population growth rates of its Arab neighbors. Moreover, some right-wing politicians have called for an expanded Israel to deal with the influx of Jewish refugees from Eastern Europe.

Despite such political justifications for additional land, the theoretical basis for the connection between increasing population and the need for space is generally weak. The rationales are primarily extrapolations from studies of overcrowding in offices, urban areas, and even among animals. It is not clear whether individual or group behavior can be aggregated to nation-state behavior in this instance (much less whether such animal studies are relevant for humans) and one analyst (Choucri, 1974) explicitly rejects the overcrowding thesis.

Lateral Pressure Theory

Closely related to these sociological approaches on resource scarcity is the 'lateral pressure' model. Although this model is similar to those based on simple resource scarcity, it is given its own category here because it is more broadly-based and occupies a prominent place in the literature on international conflict. Lateral pressure is also related to Marxist formulations of conflict. Marx argued that rising population and the maldistribution of resources in the world led states to fight with one another. Leninist models of imperialism, however, noted that advanced capitalist states experienced market saturation and overproduction and were compelled to expand abroad, acquiring new colonial possession. This seems somewhat contrary to traditional Marxist or lateral pressure models. Market saturation implies too few people to buy goods and overproduction suggests a bounty of resources to support manufacturing.

According to Nazli Choucri and Robert North (1975, 1989) and Choucri, North, and Susumu Yamakage (1992), lateral pressure refers to 'the extension of a country's behavior and interests outside its territorial boundaries (and in some circumstances, the extension of the boundaries themselves)' (Choucri and North, 1989: 289). Several elements drive this expansionism. A growing population is said to create an increasing demand for resources. Combined with advances in technology, the rising demand puts pressure on domestic resources. Lateral pressure within a state makes it likely to expand to where its economic or territorial aspirations collide with those of other pressured states, with international militarized conflict as the result. Those states said to be the most conflict-prone are those with high populations, high technology, and inadequate resources (North, 1984). Thus far, the authors have applied the model to six major powers from 1870 to 1914 and to Japan over the longer period 1878–1987, although they claim broader applicability (Choucri and North, 1989).

Military Capability

The third group of studies linking population to international conflict relies extensively on military capability as either an intervening variable or as a prerequisite for the relationship. Several scholars argue that significant military capability (although the exact threshold is unspecified) is necessary for a state experiencing population pressures to actualize its expansionist needs or desires. Warrem Thompson and David Lewis (1965) cite several cases in which military power was a limiting or facilitating condition for states to expand in order to address population pressures. Helen Hinman (1945) constructed a multiplicative index of population pressure based on how quickly population increased (percentage of families with more than five children) and on the misery factor (mortality before age thirty per 100 persons born). States scoring high on the index (Japan, Germany, Italy, India, China, and Chile in her nine country study) were said to be more war-prone. Yet she observes that adequate military capability is necessary for those states to fight a war, thereby eliminating the latter three states from the list. Her approach would correctly post-dict initiation of conflict in

World War II, although one might question the small sample and the post-hoc analysis.

A second line of research links military capability to conflict proneness and identifies population size as one factor determining how powerful a state is or can become. This work derives from the realist or 'realpolitik' tradition. A large population is often considered a necessary, but not sufficient, condition for a state becoming a major power (Organski, 1958). The small population base of France throughout the nineteenth and twentieth centuries, if not before, is cited as a limiting factor in that country's ability to compete with Germany and other European neighbors. Katherine Organski and A.F.K. Organski (1961) articulate the importance of population in determining a state's power. As a growing population feeds a state's power, that major power can challenge the leading state or hegemon in the international system and a war is likely; the power transition model (Organski, 1958; Kugler and Organski, 1989), in which changing power distributions between rivals may end in war, is illustrative of the argument.

There are several problems with this conception of military capability, both in absolute and relative terms, as an intervening variable between population and war. First, it is not clear whether conflict involvement is primarily or even strongly driven by military or other national capabilities (Gochman, 1989). Second, a large population may be a prerequisite for power (certainly Fiji or Nauru are inherently limited), but the relationship between population and power is probably not linear and additive as is implied. At some limiting point, additional population creates hardships on a state and diminishes its external capacity as resources must be diverted to deal with internal needs; at that point, more population may not make a state stronger, and perhaps might even weaken it (Leroy, 1978). Much of this realist literature was formulated prior to the period of massive population growth, but the problems experienced by India and other states are indicative of the proposition that a state may have too large a population. Third, population is only one of a series of interrelated components of a state's power and it is not clear from these formulations (assuming that such models are even accurate in predicting conflict) what relative explanatory value population has vis-à-vis other concerns such as economic strength, military technology, and the like (a stronger version of this critique is given in Ehrlich and Ehrlich, 1991). Finally, one might even challenge the central proposition that population translates into military capability as easily and directly as postulated (Bobrow, 1984).

The Anti-Malthusians

Previous works on population pressures and international conflict focused on three different ways that the two were linked, but in all cases the assumption was that the relationship was positive. Another group of scholars posit that high population growth will not increase conflict, and may even reduce it; indeed, they deny that growing populations produce negative pressures of any variety. Norman Angell (1936) acknowledges the proposition that wars result from the search for raw materials needed by increasing population. Yet he does not see the relationship as necessary. Resource scarcity is solved by improving access to the resources in question. Territorial acquisition only solves the problem temporarily because the need for resources changes over time and some resources always end up on the wrong side of the border. As an alternative to territorial expansion, Angell proposes lifting trade barriers so that states can gain access to materials peacefully and make use of comparative advantage. Thus, states do not have to fight to gain what they need. Over the past 400 years, international trade has expanded considerably, and concurrently the number of wars fought over territory or commerce issues has declined precipitously. The few resource wars that have been fought over that same time period do not exhibit a clear pattern (Holsti, 1991).

There is a basic problem with the argument that free trade will reduce or eliminate the number of resource-based wars driven by population pressures. Not all factor inputs are easily transferable. For example, skills to use the arable land effectively may be hard to transfer; witness the failure of the Green Revolution in much of Africa to raise the yield of locally grown crops (de Blij and Muller, 1992). Furthermore, even if one argues that trade can theoretically transfer the needed resources, many countries do not always have enough of the right kind of currency to pay for the transfers. Some states, most likely poor ones, will inevitably have little to trade for the resources they need or be so poor as to make the costs of those resources prohibitive. So, even if trade can transfer, say, food, without long term solutions for its more effective production and without a steady source of national income to pay for the transfers, trade can only provide short term mitigations of the problem.

The leading advocate of the school of thought that population increases are not dangerous (indeed they are argued to be desirable) for international peace is Julian Simon (1981, 1996; see also Eberstadt, 1998), who challenges the basic argument that population growth necessarily leads to resource scarcity. Indeed, he argues that most resources are not truly fixed in the economic sense and therefore will not necessarily diminish as the result of a rising population. The ultimate scare resource is human ingenuity. Simon (1989) agrees that population growth can lead to shortages or increased economic burdens in the short run. Yet, he puts great faith in the ability of society to respond to such circumstances by improvements in technology that enhance productivity and efficiency, outstripping the constraints imposed by increasing population. The author does acknowledge that resource considerations once influenced state motives for war, although he argues that they were never paramount. In more modern times, however, he notes that the costs of war outweigh the benefits of seizing and controlling new land areas. Improved transportation, trade, and advanced technology lessen the need for states to seek additional territory for economic gain. Simon dismisses various connections that link population pressures to conflict, including motivations based on expanding agricultural opportunities, acquiring energy resources, promoting greater access to markets, lessening urban overcrowding, acquiring physical capital, and creating a military buffer among others. He posits that as long as population growth stimulates advances in technology (and he assumes it can do so indefinitely), the economic motivation for territorial expansion will diminish; thus, wars driven by population growth may actually be less common in the future. Simon's conception that technology will solve the problems created by population increases is directly in contrast to the lateral pressure model, which assumes a deleterious effect of the interaction of population increases and advanced technology.

There are a number of potential problems with the 'optimist' view in general and Simon's analysis in particular. First, he acknowledges that the lag time between population pressure and the technological adjustment will vary across regions or countries. Even under the best circumstances, this still leaves a window in which pressure might be relieved through conflict; in some cases, this window may be quite wide. Second, technological innovation is not equally distributed in space and all states do not necessarily have equal access to the technological improvements. For example, many of the recent developments in food production are available only to wealthier countries. Thus, the effects postulated by Simon may not apply to underdeveloped countries; his argument is based more on the system or aggregate level and may hide underlying effects among individual or groups of countries. Finally, the assumption that technological advancement will always outrun population growth seems neither sufficiently justified theoretically nor entirely confirmed empirically. Indeed, the multiple and interacting resource scarcities that characterize contemporary and future shortages are more unpredictable and significantly different from previous resource problems so as to call into question any attempts at extrapolating past adaptive efforts into the future (Homer-Dixon, 1991).

Empirical Results

Although there has been a fair amount of theorizing about the connections between population pressures and international conflict, the empirical evidence in support of any of the propositions is scant, in large part because of the limited systematic research available on the subject. Quincy Wright (1965) notes that imperial wars tended to be initiated by countries with more rapidly rising populations. Nevertheless, in his sweeping analysis of all wars until the middle of the twentieth century, he does not find population to be a strong causal factor.[3]

Choucri (1974) analyzed forty-five underdeveloped countries over the period 1954–1972. She studied the relationship of four dimensions of population—size, change, distribution (density, movement, population pressure), and composition (age, segmental divisions)—on the onset of conflict. She reports that size and change played smaller roles than distribution and composition in stimulating conflict, although she noted no specific overcrowding effect. Choucri notes that population factors played a role in thirty-five of forty-five cases, which included wars and lower-order conflicts. Nevertheless, Choucri selects her cases on the dependent variable, and therefore we cannot tell if the conflict-prone conditions she identifies are also present in situations without conflict.

Stuart Bremer et al. (1973) found no significant association between population density or population density change (distribution variables found important by Choucri), and the propensity of states to initiate or participate in wars. They also looked at urbanization as an alternative measure of population pressure and generally found no change in results except for a weak association with war initiation. The sample studied here was European states over the period 1816–1965. Although the results of this study and that of Choucri appear somewhat contradictory, the temporal domains are dramatically different with an overlap of only eleven years. Moreover, their country samples are substantially different. Bremer and his colleagues considered only more developed European states whereas Choucri's analysis was confined to poorer states outside of Europe. From the earlier literature review, we might expect that violence-inducing population pressures would be more prevalent among less technologically advanced countries, in line with Choucri's findings. Furthermore, we might not expect population pressure to have a major influence until into the twentieth century; this would account for the general absence of strong findings on the part of Bremer and his colleagues.

Choucri and North (1975) find some significant empirical support for their lateral pressure model, noting that population growth was a driving force in colonial expansion for major powers prior to World War I. In a case study of Japan, Choucri, North, and Yamakage (1992) also tie technology, resource scarcity, and growing population with conflict behavior. Nevertheless, in a reassessment of their findings, Gary Zuk (1985) explores potential shortages of three key resources (coal, petroleum, and iron ore) among Choucri and North's conflict-prone states prior to World War I and finds either no such shortages or easy access by the states to those materials. He argues that growing national capabilities across several dimensions better account for the conflict propensities of those major powers than does an explanation based on lateral pressure. Furthermore, Ronnie Lipschutz

(1989) concludes that the connection between resource scarcity and war is weak and indirect. Resource concerns, in his view, act more as intervening factors on foreign policy behavior than as direct causal links. Of course, if population pressure primarily affects resource concerns, the former moves even farther away in the causal chain leading to international conflict.

Beyond these broad (quantitative, global, or regional) studies, there are some single-case studies. William Durham (1979), for example, argues that the Soccer War between El Salvador and Honduras was, in part, a product of the population pressures and land stress experienced in each country. Furthermore, some of the more innovative work on environmental security (Homer-Dixon, 1995a) has indicated that population pressure is most likely to produce ethnic disputes and these probably will be mostly internal.

Summing up, previous work on population and international conflict suggests a link between the two phenomena, but there is significant variation beyond this broad consensus. Perspectives vary from those that see increasing population as a threat to international peace and stability to those that welcome burgeoning global population as a precursor to improved technology and the lessening of resource-based conflict. Regardless of the negative or benign view of population pressure, there is some common ground that population's interrelationship with resource availability and military capacity should be considered even if the empirical studies to date are inconclusive. The relationship between population and international conflict may vary over time and may be stronger among less developed countries. In the following section, we develop our own theoretical hypotheses for the relationship between several dimensions of population pressure and several forms of violent conflict.

Theoretical Expectations

Although there is no consensus on this issue, we adopt as a working hypothesis that states experiencing population pressure are more likely to become involved in interstate conflict than states that are not. We do so more to facilitate the investigation than as a reflection of strongly-held beliefs.

There are multiple ways of relieving population pressure beyond territorial expansion; these include such 'substitutable' (Most and Starr, 1989: 97–123) options as family planning programs, levying tax burdens for additional children, and other 'sociological programs'. But such actions may not dampen the propensity of states toward interstate conflict. First, many of the mechanisms to limit population growth are of recent vintage, as the world community did not recognize the population problem until well into the last century and concerted policy efforts at the global level date only to the 1960s and later. Second, most of these efforts take work only over extended time periods. For example, education programs in schools about the benefits of having fewer children will have a significant lag time before socialization is complete and behavior is modified. Such programs do not address the needs of states who must deal with immediate population pressures. Third, even with a diminution of the birth rate, a country with a large population base will still experience significant population pressure. Finally, many of the methods for controlling population pressures run contrary to cultural or religious norms in societies. Along these lines, one researcher (Eberstadt, 1998) seriously questions low-income nations' ability to curb their population growth. Attacking a neighbor for the purpose of either gaining resources or more land may be perceived as a quicker, more effective, and more accepted solution to population pressures.

Before presenting our specific hypotheses, several qualifications or considerations are in order. First, our study is not concerned with the size of a state's population per se, but rather with changes in that size or with its size relative to available space. Previous studies have not demonstrated a strong relationship between simple population size and conflict behavior. Furthermore, it is likely that the relationship between population size and conflict involvement is a function of major power status—major powers have large populations and we know empirically that they are the most conflict-prone states (Gochman and Maoz, 1984). Thus, any relationship between simple population size and conflict is likely to be more incidental and less interesting to our concerns here.

A second consideration is that we do not expect that small degrees of population growth will have much of an effect on international conflict behavior. Population is increasing in nearly all states and most of them are not constantly involved in war or even close to being so. It is relatively easy for societies to adapt to the constraints and problems occasioned by limited population pressure, for instance by government policy or increasing economic efficiency. It is also our expectation that the relationship between population pressures and conflict will level off after reaching some threshold. States can handle only so much conflict and at some limiting point additional population pressures will not produce any greater likelihood of conflict involvement or escalation.[4] In short, the expected relationship between population and conflict can roughly be portrayed by an S-shaped curve.

We turn now to the hypotheses that will form the bases of our empirical tests. We first turn to addressing dynamic population pressures, and therefore the effect of population growth on conflict involvement:

Hypothesis 1: The greater the growth of a state's population, the greater the probability of that state being involved in international militarized conflict.

This hypothesis is largely based on the notion that states with rapidly increasing populations will have little ability to adjust to the resource scarcities and other attendant environmental problems, at least in the short run, other than by international conflictual actions.⁵ We recognize that trade and other actions may be a more efficient mechanism to achieve the same ends, but the first hypothesis allows us to assess whether the conflict option is a frequent choice by pressured states.

Beyond detecting whether states experiencing population pressure will become involved in militarized conflict, we have a special concern with their propensity to engage in the most serious form of that conflict—war. It is conceivable that population pressure may lead to involvement in conflict, but plays no role in the further escalation of that conflict to war. Most of the theoretical work on population and conflict does make a distinction between the initiation and escalation of conflict. On the basis of the general expectations, however, we offer another testable hypothesis:

Hypothesis 2: Given conflict involvement, the greater the growth of a state's population, the greater the probability of that state being involved in international war.

A connection between population pressure and war presumes that such pressure makes states more likely to adopt coercive bargaining tactics in militarized confrontations and perhaps be less amenable to compromise solutions or conciliation efforts; one might presume that the latter would not satisfy the needs of a state affected by a burgeoning population. Although this theoretical justification seems weak and as of yet has no empirical confirmation, it does present the most likely underlying logic for the hypothesis.

A third concern is with the initiation of conflict. Most of the explanations for why population pressure leads to conflict assume that the pressured state will be the one to start the conflict. Whether the motivation is more resources or living space, population pressure is said to induce that state to expand externally. Only in a few instances is there any indication that the population pressured state might be the target of military attack, either because of its weakened state from environmental degradation or in retaliation for excessive polluting of its neighbors (both, at best, indirectly connected to population pressure) (Deudney, 1991). Our third hypothesis offers a corollary to our earlier formulations:

Hypothesis 3: Given a conflict between states, the initiator of the conflict is likely to be experiencing significant population growth.

A significant portion of the theoretical literature emphasizes more than simple growth as leading to conflict. Population must grow past some threshold, and this can vary across states, before any effect is evident. Most of the arguments that stem from claims of overcrowding or notions of Lebensraum derive from this notion; it is not the population growth, but the size of the population vis-à-vis the available space in the country that is problematic. A country with a large population such as Russia may be less constrained or pressured than a much less populous state such as Turkey because of the tremendous differences in land mass; a large land mass can accommodate a growing population and contains, ceteris paribus, more natural resources to meet those needs. Thus, we also consider a static aspect of population pressure, population density.[6] Our next three hypotheses mirror the previous three:

Hypothesis 4: The greater a state's population density, the greater the probability of that state being involved in international militarized conflict.

Hypothesis 5: Given conflict involvement, the greater a state's population density, the greater the probability of that state being involved in international war.

Hypothesis 6: Given a conflict between states, the initiator of the conflict is likely to have high population density.

In testing these six propositions, we must also control for a number of other factors that affect state conflict propensity. Even under the most pessimistic vision, not all interstate conflict is tied to population pressures. States may enter conflict and experience war based on a variety of other influences. In that sense, in any test of the population-conflict relationship we can only expect moderate associations. To correct for some of this bias, as well as to account for variables thought to be important in the relevant literature, we introduce a number of controls. First, we include the geographic opportunity for states to become involved in conflict. States that share a large number of borders or are geographically proximate to other states will, ceteris paribus, be involved in more conflicts and wars; geographic opportunity also is strongly related to the presence of territorial disputes which can be the source of those conflicts (Vasquez, 1995). Beyond geographic opportunity, we also control for the military capability of the states analyzed, with the assumption that powerful states will be more likely to engage in conflicts and wars; military capability is also cited by some scholars as a prerequisite for population pressures to be manifested in conflict. Finally, we control for the level of development of the state. Some studies hypothesize that more advanced states have lateral pressures (Choucri and North, 1989). Furthermore, many advanced states consume greater resources than less developed ones. Of course, other theorists claim that advanced states are the least likely to become involved in population-driven conflicts (Homer-Dixon, 1991). Including this variable may help us sort out the different effects.

Unfortunately, we are not able to include a variable in the empirical analysis specifically devoted to resource scarcity (the closest we come are variables based on level of development and resource consumption noted above and land size, which is reflected in population density). This omission goes beyond data limitations, which are in themselves significant. States and analysts often do not have an accurate estimation of natural resource capacity and therefore potential shortages arising from it. Estimates of energy reserves, for example, have been notoriously inaccurate (Simon, 1996). It may have been preferable to include the perception of a shortage in the analyses, but this would be even harder to measure in retrospect than the actual constraints.

Research Design

We analyze the conflict behavior of all nation-states (for a list, see Small and Singer, 1982) over the period 1930–1989. The end date represents the present limits of our data collection, but the start date deserves some explanation. Prior to about 1930, population doubling time was relatively long. The industrial revolution and advances in health care led to a lowering of death rates and a subsequent explosion in world population. Around 1930 the global population reached two billion; following that date the doubling time of global population significantly shortened (for global population data see, for example, Kegley and Wittkopf, 1995). Furthermore, prior to the early twentieth century, additional territory, in the form of colonial territory, was readily and relatively cheaply available (usually without interstate conflict). Following World War I, however, there were few, if any, portions of the globe that might qualify as *terra nullis* and further colonial acquisition was halted. Thus, states would now likely have to fight other states, seizing or claiming other states' lands, if they wanted to expand. Thus, given the greater population pressures and the limited availability of new territory, if a relationship between population pressures and conflict exists at all, it should be manifested in the 1930–1989 period that we study.

In order to detect conflict involvement, we look first to whether a nation-state was involved in a 'militarized interstate dispute' in the year under scrutiny. Therefore, our unit of analysis is the nation-year. A militarized interstate dispute is 'a set of interactions between or among states involving threats to use military force, displays of military force, or actual uses of military force. . . . these acts must be explicit, overt, nonaccidental, and government sanctioned' (Gochman and Maoz, 1984: 587; Jones et al., 1996). The latest Correlates of War (COW) Project list of disputes is the source of these data. The initiator of the dispute is identified as the state that first undertook the threat, display, or use of military force, crossing the militarized threshold for what might have previously been a much less hostile disagreement.[7] The most severe conflict, war,[8] is identified as an instance in which a militarized confrontation resulted in 1,000 or more battle-related fatalities (Small and Singer, 1982).

For the central independent variables, we rely primarily on the COW Project Material Capabilities Data Set. This data set records the total population of a state for each year in our study. To measure population growth, we look at the percentage rate of change in the total population across the ten years prior to the year under study.[9] Population changes slowly and exhibits slight perturbations on a year-to-year basis and there is not much basis for identifying significant population pressure. Only by considering a broader time frame can we detect high population growth and therefore determine cumulative population pressure on a state at a given point in time.[10] Population density is measured by the ratio of total population to the size of the homeland territory of the state in question. Land size (reported in World Almanac, 1982) reflects the size of the country in 1981; adjustments resulting from territorial changes over the period and reported in Goertz and Diehl (1992) were made to that baseline.[11]

For military capability, we use the COW Project data on military expenditure, expressed in thousands of U.S. dollars. The level of development and resource usage is measured by energy consumption figures in the COW Project capability data set; energy consumption is expressed in yearly thousands of coal-ton equivalents, divided by total population in order to yield per capita figures.[12] Energy consumption is an important indicator for the vital natural resources usage, but it is also an effective indicator of technological advancement and is correlated with GNP.[13] Geographic opportunity is determined by the number of states who share international borders with the given state; borders here are those directly contiguous by land or shared river boundary or within 150 statute miles by water, and are taken from Charles Gochman (1991). Finally, we wish to test to see whether there is an effect based on the major/minor power status of countries, which goes beyond simple military capability. Accordingly, we code states as having either major or minor power status according to the COW classification scheme (Small and Singer, 1982).

The primary method of analysis will be logit analysis, which presents an S-shaped probability distribution consistent with our theoretical expectations about the population-conflict relationship. Logit is also the appropriate technique for dichotomous dependent variables as we are attempting to predict whether a population-pressured country is involved in a dispute or not, or a war or not, for each year in question. We also constructed interaction terms between the population-pressure variables and military capability and energy consumption respectively. This is consistent with some theoretical approaches that postulate that a significant military capacity or advanced technology (or the opposite) is necessary for population pressures to be manifested in armed conflict.

Empirical Findings

Conflict Involvement

In the first set of analyses, we look at the influence of population pressure on conflict involvement. The results in Table 4.1 show the impact of population growth and our other independent variables on the propensity of states to become involved in a militarized dispute in the years under study.

The model as a whole is statistically significant. The model did not overpredict conflicts, in that there were few false positives; that is, significant population growth (as well as high values on the other variables) did not frequently predict conflict when it empirically did not occur. The model did significantly underpredict the incidence of disputes, but this was largely to be expected; as we noted above, population pressures and the other factors are likely not the only causal path to conflict involvement and it was reasonable to expect that many disputes would be driven by other factors.

All variables in the equation have a statistically significant effect on dispute involvement and the coefficient signs are in the expected directions. Population growth has a positive effect on the probability that a state will become involved in a militarized dispute, giving some credence to claims that high population growth can be dangerous. Holding other variables constant at their means, the likelihood of conflict increases 7 percent (an important figure given the low probability of conflict overall) as one moves from very low to very high population growth.[14] As anticipated, states with multiple borders and high military spending are more conflict-prone. We have noted the disagreement in the literature on advanced technology states versus poorer states; our initial results suggest that states with high energy consumption per capita are less likely than other states to participate in militarized disputes.[15] There was no significant interaction effect from the combination of population growth and energy consumption as some lateral pressure models might have assumed.[16] There was a significant positive impact from the population-military capability interaction, suggesting that population pressures combined with capacity to expand do lead to conflict involvement.

We also stratified the analysis into major and minor power clusters. For major powers, no variable was a significant predictor of conflict involvement, either because population pressure does not exert significant influences on the most powerful states or because there is little variation across the relevant variables within the major power subset. The minor power findings mirror those reported in Table 4.1 for the whole sample, suggesting again that population pressures and related variables exercise their greatest influence among the weaker or poorer states in the international system.

In the second set of analyses, we replaced population growth with density and reran the same tests, which are reported in Table 4.2. Despite a statistically significant overall model, population density has no independent effect

TABLE 4.1   The Impact of Population Growth on Conflict Involvement, 1930-1989

Variable	Coefficient	St. Error	Significance
Constant	-1.86	.10	.0001
Population Growth	.01	.003	.001
Military Capability	3.39 (E-8)	1.18 (E-8)	.004
Borders	.17	.01	.0001
Energy Consumption	-.04	.02	.06
Pop. Growth* Energy	-.0003	.0003	.39
Pop. Growth* Military	1.83 (E-9)	6.87 (E-10)	.008

Overall Model Chi Square = 475.35
Significant at $p < .0001$
n = 4,801[a]

NOTE: [a]The number of cases reported is lower than the total number of cases due to missing data.

TABLE 4.2   The Impact of Population Density on Conflict Involvement, 1930–1989

Variable	Coefficient	St. Error	Significance
Constant	-1.63	.07	.0001
Population Density	2.29 (E-5)	8.77 (E-5)	.79
Military Capability	4.72 (E-8)	8.21 (E-8)	.0001
Borders	.18	.01	.0001
Energy Consumption	-.06	.02	.0002
Pop. Density* Energy	-3.5 (E-5)	2.75 (E-5)	.20
Pop. Density* Military	5.55 (E-11)	2.50 (E-11)	.03

Overall Model Chi Square = 491.14
Significant at $p < .0001$
n = 5,734

on the propensity for conflict involvement; that is, more crowded states are not inherently more likely to participate in a militarized dispute. There is also apparently no significant interaction effect from density and energy consumption.[17] Once again, however, the interaction of military capabilities and population pressure (high population density in this case) significantly and positively increases the likelihood of dispute involvement, suggesting that capacity to expand is a prerequisite for population pressures to lead to conflict.[18] Stratifying the analyses by major/minor power status shows that the minor power analyses mirror those reported in Table 4.2 and that all variables are insignificant when focusing solely on major powers.

Escalation to War

The second set of analyses concerns whether population pressure has an impact on the escalation of disputes to war. Table 4.3 gives the results of the analysis of escalation propensity, given that dispute involvement has already occurred.

Although the model as a whole is significant, no single variable is a statistically significant predictor of dispute escalation. The closest to significance is the population growth variable, but like many others in the equation, the sign of the coefficient is the opposite of what might be expected (that is, higher population growth lessens the chances of escalation). Little theoretical logic is consistent with such results. Stratifying the analysis according to major/minor power status results in some minor improvements to the model. For major powers, the energy consumption and borders variables are significant, and perhaps most interesting for our purposes, so is the interaction term of population growth and energy consumption (the greater the interaction, the more likely the dispute will escalate to war). For minor powers, only military spending is a significant predictor of dispute escalation.[19]

Turning to population density as a dimension of population pressure, we again find no strong relationships with dispute escalation (Table 4.4). The model as a whole is not statistically significant and neither are any of the individual variables. These results are not significantly altered when looking at major and minor powers separately.[20] In general, none of the analysis in this section suggest a strong significant relationship between population pressure and dispute escalation.

TABLE 4.3   The Impact of Population Growth on Conflict Escalation, 1930–1989

Variable	Coefficient	St. Error	Significance
Constant	-2.01	.37	.0001
Population Growth	-.02	.01	.07
Military Capability	-5.8 (E-8)	3.71 (E-8)	.12
Borders	-.06	.05	.27
Energy Consumption	-.02	.10	.85
Pop. Growth* Energy	-.001	.004	.75
Pop. Growth* Military	2.05 (E-9)	1.50 (E-9)	.17

Overall Model Chi Square = 14.24
Significant at $p < .03$
n = 1,451

TABLE 4.4   The Impact of Population Density on Conflict Escalation, 1930–1989

Variable	Coefficient	St. Error	Significance
Constant	-2.67	.29	.0001
Population Density	.0001	.0005	.79
Military Capability	-1.5 (E-8)	1.8 (E-8)	.41
Borders	-.03	.05	.53
Energy Consumption	-.03	.06	.59
Pop. Density* Energy	-.0001	.0002	.62
Pop. Density* Military	-9.2 (E-11)	1.2 (E-10)	.44

Overall Model Chi Square = 8.68
Significant at $p < .19$
n = 1,680

Conflict Initiation

Most frameworks that posit a positive relationship between population and conflict implicitly assume that the pressured state will be the one that initiated the conflict. For this analysis, we divided population pressures into high, medium, and low categories.[21]

Table 4.5 indicates that there is little evidence that high population growth states are more likely to initiate militarized conflict. We would not expect that all disputes would be initiated by a population pressured state (again not all conflicts are driven by population), but we would have expected a modest and significant association. Most conflict initiators fall within the middle category of states. Furthermore, high growth states are actually more likely not to be the initiator in a conflict rather than be the state that first threatens, displays, or uses military force. The overall relationship is significant, yet the measure of association reveals a very weak relationship (Cramer's V = .09) between population growth and dispute initiation; furthermore, that association is largely a function of the middle category of population growth and not the high growth category as hypothesized.

The results, in Table 4.6, for population density are no more encouraging. Again, high population states are more likely to be the target of the dispute as opposed to the initiator. The overall relationship between density and conflict initiation is significant, but the association is weak (Cramer's V = .09). In general, there is little evidence that states undergoing significant population pressure are more likely to initiate militarized conflict.[22]

TABLE 4.5   The Impact of Population Growth on Conflict Initiation, 1930–1989 (%)

	Population Growth		
	Low	Medium	High
Constant	73.5	56.1	60.3
Noninitiator	26.5	43.9	39.7
Sum	100	100	100
(n)	117	1,322	116

Chi Square = 13.65
Cramer's V = .09
Significant at p <.002

TABLE 4.6   The Impact of Population Density on Conflict Initiation, 1930–1989 (%)

	Population Growth		
	Low	Medium	High
Constant	58.3	55.0	67.7
Noninitiator	41.7	45.0	32.3
Sum	100	100	100
(n)	742	771	297

Chi Square = 14.21
Cramer's V = .09
Significant at p <.001

Conclusion

Generally, we have found population growth pressure to have a significant impact on the likelihood that a state would become involved in military conflict. The relationship is modest as expected, but seems to confirm the more pessimistic views. It is also evident that significant military capability may be necessary for population pressures to lead to conflict. In other words, problems occasioned by population growth are not always enough for conflict; states must have enough military capability to fight their neighbors for resources or seize new territories. Our results also indicate that low technology countries are more subject to population pressures and conflict involvement than their more advanced peers. This is consistent with some recent ideas on environmental security that the Third World will likely be the locus of population-driven conflicts. In part, it also suggests that some portion of the optimist argument may be correct—advanced technology may mitigate some of the deleterious effects of high population growth. Although there was a positive relationship between population growth and conflict, there was little or no evidence that such growth made states more likely to be the initiator of that conflict or make that conflict more likely to escalate to war.

The findings on population density seem to confirm earlier studies that were unable to link overcrowding to conflict at the nation-state level. There was scant evidence in all three analyses (involvement, initiation, and escalation) that population density exercised any significant impact on state decisionmaking. States do not appear to engage in conflict for the purpose of acquiring new land to support a burgeoning population. The justification of Nazi Germany and other states for expansion appear to be convenient excuses rather than causal mechanisms and, at very least, there is no general pattern of states fighting to acquire more 'living space'; indeed, few Germans and Japanese actually moved into the territories that their countries occupied during World War II (Organski and Organski, 1961). Thus, we conclude that there are substantial limits to the validity of extending overcrowding arguments to the context of interstate relations.[23]

Our study, of course, has a number of limitations. We need to get a better handle on the concept of resource scarcity and incorporate it into our model. Although the scholarly literature makes extensive reference to resource scarcity resulting from population pressures, there is little specification of what resource dimensions are most salient. Should we focus on natural resources or are elements of human resources equally important? Among natural resources, are energy concerns more important than water, air, or minerals? Does this vary by context and how can we identify and assess that relative salience? Even if we had a better conceptual hold of the concept of resource scarcity, there remains the issue of finding a suitable cross-sectional and cross-temporal indicator(s) for it, so that we can assess its importance systematically and empirically.

Future work on population and conflict might also include revisiting some of the theoretical frameworks reviewed in an earlier section of the chapter. Of prime concern is theorizing about the population-conflict relationship that relies on the assumption that the pressured state is the one that initiates the military conflict. Our empirical evidence suggests otherwise, and it is necessary to construct a framework that accounts for states with population pressures to be the target as well as the initiator, or ideally specify the conditions under which each is likely to occur.

Another item for future research would be to move well beyond the concern with growth and density to population concerns that deal with movement of peoples (Homer-Dixon, 1991) and the domestic political effects of population pressures. These elements are suggested in much of the recent literature on environmental security, but they are rarely subject to stringent empirical examination. Attention might also be given to issues of population distribution or demographic transition, rather than merely aggregate population processes. Distributional pressures, such as a burgeoning young population, may be more important than overall population growth. Our findings indicated that less developed states, generally those who have not undergone a demographic transition, were more likely to enter conflict; future research might compare the conflict propensities of underdeveloped states who experience population distribution pressures and those who have successfully induced a demographic transition without industrialization.

Despite our focus on the nation-state level of analysis here, some literature suggests that the difference in demographic growth rates and resource availability between countries are key elements in predicting conflict. Thus, it may be desirable to conduct a dyadic study of the population-conflict relationship among a sample of states that have some inherent potential for military conflict (e.g. neighboring states). Scholars might also focus their attentions on the role that trade and technology might have in mitigating population pressures and resource scarcities. This is suggested in the theoretical literature, but not subject to empirical examination either here or elsewhere.

Finally, studies of population and international conflict would benefit by exploring the interconnection of domestic and interstate conflict. With studies of the democratic peace in particular, the domestic-international nexus has recently received renewed attention in the study of international relations. If population pressures precipitate internal conflict, this may heighten the prospects for internationalized conflict. This causal path was not one considered here, but in light of the most promising work in the environmental security area and recent research on domestic-international conflict linkages, it is worth exploring.

Jaroslav Tir, b. 1972, M.A. in political science (University of Illinois at Urbana-Champaign, 1997); Ph.D. candidate, University of Illinois at Urbana-Champaign. Current main interests: territorial changes and disputes; international and ethnic conflicts management.

Paul Diehl, b. 1958, Ph.D. in political science (University of Michigan, 1983) is professor of political science and University Distinguished Teacher/Scholar at the University of Illinois at Urbana-Champaign. His recent books include *War and Peace in International Rivalry* (University of Michigan Press, 2000), *A Road Map to War: Territorial Dimensions of International Conflict* (Vanderbilt University Press, 1999), *The Dynamics of Enduring Rivalries* (University of Illinois Press, 1998), *International Peacekeeping* (Johns Hopkins University Press, 1994), and *Territorial Changes and International Conflict* (Routledge, 1992). He is the editor of seven other books and the author of more than eighty articles on international security matters.

Notes

1. For a recent review of works linking environmental degradation and conflict, see Kennedy (1998).

2. Another understudied subject is the reverse of this causal relationship, namely the impact of war on population growth and distribution. Although war has some negative impacts on population, compensatory birth waves after a war might mitigate or eliminate the effects in the long run. See Rasler and Thompson (1992) for a review.

3. Of course, during most of the time of Wright's study (prior to 1940), there were probably few cases of rapidly rising populations, a phenomena which is more characteristic of the latter part of the twentieth century.

4. Here, we hypothesize that additional population pressures will not make much difference in terms of added conflict proneness for states that are already highly pressured. How much conflict a state can actually handle before becoming extinct or disintegrated remains unknown.

5. One could also question whether conflict can solve resource scarcity problems, since engaging in conflict itself is costly. Hence, we do not claim that conflict is necessarily the long-run solution to the resource problem, but only that conflict is an alternative that can be used.

6. In this project, density is derived from the total land area of a country. However, future research could attempt to refine this measure by considering different types of land (e.g. deserts, arable land, forests, etc.).

7. The initiator of the dispute is identified by reference to the Correlates of War Dispute Data Set in which one side (Side A) is identified as the initiating one and in which originating parties (those active in the dispute on the first day) are identified. Thus, for us, an initiator is a state on the initiating side (which may include several states) and which is involved from the outset (as other states may join the initiating side over the life of the dispute).

8. Both the list of militarized disputes and wars are obtained from Gochman and Maoz (1984).

9. There is a slight discrepancy in the number of cases for our population growth and population density analyses owing to missing data on either territorial or population size.

10. The results reported below were not substantially different when we look at population change over a five year period.

11. The territorial change data end in 1980. Our estimates of land size from 1982 to 1989 do not reflect any territorial changes occurring during that period. Changes to homeland territory in this period were not substantial and unlikely to affect the results reported below. Following 1989, of course, there were numerous territorial changes and this, in part, influenced our decision to stop our study at 1989.

12. Simple energy consumption figures are strongly correlated ($r > .80$) with military expenditures and therefore including them in the analysis would make interpretation of parameter estimates problematic. Furthermore, energy consumption figures as an indication of technological advancement must reflect the size of the country as population, in part, drives the aggregate level of energy consumption. For these reasons, we adopt the per capita figures for energy consumption, which do not exhibit multicollinearity problems and better represent overall development levels.

13. It was conceivable that the indicators of population, military expenditures, and energy consumption may exhibit multicollinearity and thereby complicate our ability to make valid inferences from the statistical results. We attempted to identify potential problems in several ways. First, simple correlations yielded coefficients all < .30. Regression tests (using combinations of the two variables to predict the third) all produces low R^2 values at .10 or below. Neither of these tests suggest significant multicollinearity problems.

14. The calculation here is based on a comparison of population growth figures at the 10th and 90th percentiles.

15. Tir (1998) reconsiders the impact of interaction between population growth rates and technological development. He argues that technological development can actually alleviate, rather than exacerbate, damaging effects of high population growth. Conversely, underdeveloped states with high population growth rates are most likely to be linked to international conflict. His empirical results confirm that states with high population growth rates and low levels of technological development stand greater chances of international conflict involvement, they tend to be involved in more severe conflicts (including wars), and they have a tendency to be the initiators.

16. The results for the non-interaction variables were largely the same when the interaction terms were dropped from the equation.

17. The interaction term is significant when all but the interaction variables are dropped from the equation. Nevertheless, this is probably a function of the energy consumption component of the interaction term rather than a true interaction effect; when the energy consumption variable is put into the equation, the significance of the interaction term disappears.

18. The results for the non-interaction variables were largely the same when the interaction terms were dropped from the equation.

19. Close to statistical significance (defined here as the .05 level) is the population growth–military spending interaction term, whose sign is positive, consistent with the above analyses on conflict involvement.

20. In the stratified analyses, all variables remained insignificant except for the borders variable in the major power analysis.

21. To make these categorizations, we looked at the empirical distribution and attempted to identify deviant cases from the mean by reference to that statistic and the standard deviation. We also sought to insure that a sufficient number of cases fell within each of the three categories in order to permit meaningful analysis. For the analysis of population growth, high population growth was defined as greater than one standard deviation above the mean (with low growth one standard deviation below the mean). For population density, high density was defined as greater than one-third standard deviation above the mean (with low density one-third standard deviation below the mean). The results reported in Tables 4.5 and 4.6 were not significantly altered when we divided the cases equally among the three categories; that is, our results are not attributable to scaling choices.

22. It is possible that the initiation hypothesis holds, but because of a large number of underpredicted cases (cases in which population pressures did not play a part), this relationship could be hidden.

23. Perhaps one problem with extrapolating overcrowding arguments from animal studies to interstate relations is that such animal studies have only found conflict-producing effects after extremely high population density thresholds; current densities of even the most crowded states are not even close to comparable thresholds.

Chapter Five

Demography, Environment, and Security

JACK A. GOLDSTONE

Violent and Nonviolent Security Issues

Demographic and environmental change can produce security problems of two distinctly different kinds. These have entirely different processes and outcomes and generate rather different sorts of concerns and remedies.

Violent environmental/demographic security (VEDS) issues reflect the impact of demographic and environmental changes on traditional security concerns—that is, ways that demographic or environmental changes increase the risk of violent international or domestic conflicts. To foresee and effectively intervene in those situations, we need to understand the specific pathways by which demographic and environmental factors can lead to political crises.

Nonviolent environmental/demographic security (NEDS) issues reflect changes in population or in the environment that have consequences across international borders that *in and of themselves* produce undesirable outcomes and thus become issues of international security even if they are not likely to produce armed violence. These include emissions that damage the ozone or contribute to global warming; logging, damming, or other development that reduces biodiversity or depletes watersheds by diverting water or increasing erosion and silting across international borders downstream; acid rain or particulate pollution that travels across borders; overfishing of oceans or estuaries that depletes local or global stocks; generation of nuclear wastes or toxic wastes and their transport in international waters or across national borders; environmental damage due to military operations, either collateral damage from conflicts or incidental damage from the operation of bases and routine missions; the spread of harmful biological agents, such as pathogens or perhaps undesirable genetic elements from genetically modified biota; and environmental damage to agrarian regions or other population/resource imbalances that lead to large and unexpected international migrations. In all of these cases, events or decisions in one nation can pose a threat to the quality of life in another nation even if these do not issue in armed violence. Nonetheless, they pose problems for diplomacy and negotiation, and thus fall into the general realm of international political/security concerns.[1]

Security threats are thus far more broadly defined today than they were in the past, when direct military threats dominated security thinking. Indeed, the U.S. Departments of State and Defense and the intelligence community now routinely include environmental security and intelligence in their activities.[2] Yet if environmental security is now a widespread concern, we need to be more careful than ever in examining what falls under this broad rubric, and to avoid mixing up apples and oranges. What processes lie behind *violent* security threats from demographic or environmental changes that increase the risks of war, terrorism, or revolution? And what processes are behind *nonviolent* threats from demographic and environmental changes that in themselves pose threats to the quality of life in multiple nations?

Much of the confusion regarding environmental security has arisen from a failure to clarify and keep separate these two types of threats. Environmental and population changes that increase the risks of violence have been shown to matter almost solely for *internal* or domestic conflicts: ethnic struggles, regional rebellions, or local group conflicts (Homer-Dixon, 1999). By contrast, environmental issues have not played a major role in international violence or wars. Even where one would most often expect it, as in conflicts involving upstream and downstream states disputing their access to water in a transnational water basin, such disputes have been uniformly resolved by negotiations (Lowi, 1999). Minor skirmishes have occurred over fishing rights, and threats have been issued over access to water, but as we shall discuss below, none of these disputes has ever led to international war (Wolf, 1999b).

In regard to increased risks of internal violence, we also need to clarify the distinct roles of population changes and environmental degradation. Although sometimes linked, population change and environmental decay can occur independently, and even move in opposite directions (e.g., population growth can coexist with soil conservation and more intense cropping or tree planting; or careless industrialization can foul the environment even in places with little or no population growth). There is thus no validity to a simple blanket declaration that population and environmental change lead to violent conflict. Progress on demographic and environmental security issues depends on careful specification of what kind and magnitude of population change, and what kind and magnitude of environmental change are generally linked to what kind of conflict (Levy, 1995).

Moreover, the attention given to environmental change as a source of violent conflict can overshadow environmental change as a source of international conflicts that do not lead to violence but that nonetheless have major implications for the prosperity of many nations. For example, the generation of greenhouse gases that contribute to global warming is a source of global conflict, as we describe in more detail below. These conflicts have led to several rounds of negotiations, focused on the Kyoto climate protocols, that seek to impose rewards and penalties on nations for their future carbon emissions. However, if the negotiations do not produce a viable treaty, the outcome would not be violent clashes. Rather, it would be the slow deterioration of the current global climate equilibrium, and perhaps a sudden shift in that equilibrium at some point in the future. Such deterioration and shifts will also dispose of rewards and penalties to various nations, and for that reason greenhouse gas emissions are a major focus of international strategy and negotiations, but they are not closely linked to the threat of international violence or war.

To use a homely analogy, imagine that we live in a house in a stormy climate and a crowded and dangerous neighborhood. We need to preserve the house. To protect against accumulating environmental damage, we need to keep fixing the roof. To protect against aggression from increasingly numerous and perhaps deprived neighbors, we need to keep the doors strong and locked. However, we would appear to be exceedingly mixed-up if we thought that strengthening the roof would protect us against violent threats from the neighbors, or if we thought that having strong locks on the doors would keep us sheltered from storms or floods. Yet that is the kind of confusion we risk in discussing environmental security if we do not make careful distinctions among different kinds of threats stemming from changes in population and changes in the environment, and between threats of violent conflict and nonviolent threats that nonetheless will impose costs and rewards variously on different nations.[3]

Key Findings

After nearly three decades of debate and analysis stemming from Myron Weiner's (1971) pathbreaking study, scholars are beginning to develop much clearer answers to the complex questions regarding how environmental and population changes affect security concerns. Those answers can be summarized briefly in the following propositions, each of which we shall treat in greater detail below:

1) Long-term environmental degradation is not a major or pervasive cause of international wars, ethnic wars, or revolutionary conflicts. Such degradation often brings misery, and can exacerbate local tensions and conflicts in a society, yet such misery does not generally trigger the elite alienation and opposition necessary for large-scale violence to occur. Short-term disasters, however—floods, hurricanes, droughts, earthquakes, and major accidents—can contribute to major political conflicts if elites and popular groups blame the regime for causing, or for a particularly poor or corrupt response to, such disasters. In addition, where environmental resources represent concentrated and scarce sources of wealth (such as prime farmland in the Kenya or Zimbabwe high lands, or hardwood forests in Southeast Asia), then even if those resources are not degraded, conflict over control and exploitation of those resources can be a source of internal violence.

2) Although overall population growth and population density do not generally predict political risks, a number of distinct kinds of demographic changes—particularly rapid growth in the labor force, shifts in the age distribution that create relatively large youth cohorts, a rapid increase in educated youth aspiring to elite positions, unequal population growth rates between different ethnic groups, urbanization that exceeds employment growth, and migrations that change the local balance among major ethnic groups—do increase the risks of violent internal political and ethnic conflicts.

3) Population changes do not directly increase the risks of international wars between domestically stable states; however, because many international wars have their origins in domestic conflicts (e.g., the Iran/Iraq war growing out of Iran's revolution; international wars in West and Central Africa growing out of the collapses of Liberia, Sierra Leone, and Congo/Zaire), in those contexts where population changes produce domestic political crises, the risk of international war is also increased.

4) Certain demographic changes, such as a rise in infant mortality—aside from whatever role they may have as causes—can be powerful indicators of coming political violence.

5) Rapid and large-scale demographic changes, such as a rise in mortality or a sharp rise in migration, can arise as an *outcome* of violent conflicts.

6) In many states, population and environmental changes together *combine* to produce environmental changes with global impact. That is, in countries with large populations and large or rapidly increasing levels of per capita environmental impact (such as carbon dioxide output, forest reduction, natural habitat destruction, and colonization), environmental changes occur with global implications for security.

The Environment and Violent Conflict

Thomas Homer-Dixon provoked a great deal of controversy and concern with his claim that we are 'on the threshold' of an era in which traditional security concerns, for example, armed conflicts, will come frequently, if not primarily, as a result of environmental change (Homer-Dixon, 1991). However, in the years since his warning, the search for evidence behind this claim has provided little support. As Paul Diehl (1998: 275–276) has remarked, the 'many publications from the [Toronto] project have produced largely abstract conceptions of the environment-conflict nexus, with actual cases presented only as anecdotal evidence or as illustrative examples'. After nearly a decade of research, it now seems clear that long-term environmental degradation of the kind that often accompanies development (e.g., soil erosion, deforestation, air and water pollution) has little or no significant role in generating traditional security concerns (Deudney, 1990; Levy, 1995). Detailed cross-national studies have found only very weak relations between environmental degradation and either international or domestic armed conflict (Gleditsch, 2001).

Wenche Hauge and Tanja Ellingsen (2001), in the most comprehensive global test of the environmental-scarcity-leads-to-violence hypothesis with recent data (1980–1992), found that although deforestation, land degradation, and low freshwater availability were positively correlated with the incidence of civil war and armed conflict, the *magnitude* of their effects was tiny. By themselves, these factors raised the probability of civil war by .5 percent to under 1.5 percent! (Hauge and Ellingsen, 2001, Table II: 311). These factors did have a slightly higher impact on the probability of lesser kinds of armed conflict (causing increases in the chances of such conflict by from 4 percent to 8 percent); but their influence paled compared to the impact of such traditional risk factors as poverty, regime type, and current and prior political instability.

Many authors, including Homer-Dixon (1999: 6), have more conservatively approached the issue of causation between environmental change and violence by asking simply whether 'environmental scarcity *can* be an important cause of violent conflict' (emphasis added). Demonstrating some cases in which environmental degradation leading to loss of agricultural potential, as in the South African homelands created by the apartheid regime for native Africans, is linked with violent conflict, does show that there *can* be a connection (Percival and Homer-Dixon, 2001). But this is not the same as showing that there generally will be a connection across a variety of contexts, or that the connection will be important relative to other factors. Evidence for the latter claims has been conspicuously hard to find.

It is true that diminished access to important environmental resources, such as land, forest, or fresh water, is sometimes a grievance among various groups, and that like other grievances—such as increased wage or income inequality, exclusion from government or education, lack of public services, corruption or racism in administration—these can contribute to mobilizing groups for violent rebellions. Of course, the political science literature is quite clear that grievances, in and of themselves, are only tenuously linked to violent conflict (Gurr, 1980; Goldstone, 1994; Tilly 1978), a point that Homer-Dixon and most authors writing on the role of environmental grievances in conflict freely concede. Grievances of many kinds are generally widespread in all societies, especially developing societies, which are often ridden with ethnic hostilities and political and economic inequality. Whether these grievances lead to violence depend on institutional and political conditions for state vulnerability and popular mobilization that have little to do with the causes or contents of the grievances themselves. Beyond this weak connection, however, writers on environmental security rarely ask whether grievances related to environmental resources are more widespread, more severe, or more often the focus of political violence than other grievances.

Hauge and Ellingsen (2001) provide exactly such insight, separating the effects of environmental degradation (deforestation, land degradation, and low freshwater availability) from the effects of high population density, high income inequality, and poverty (measured as low GNP/capita). They find that the risk of civil war (from 1980 to 1992) and of armed conflict (from 1989 to 1992) was fairly high in poor counties with high income inequality, high population density, low cash income, and high land degradation, at 20 percent and 45 percent, respectively. However, the risks of civil war and armed conflict in countries similar with regard to income inequality, population density, and cash income but *without* high land degradation was 19 percent and 37 percent, respectively (Hauge and Ellingsen 2001). Thus high population density, income inequality, and poverty are the major grievances contributing to violent conflict in their data—environmental degradation itself plays a minor, if exacerbating, role. Therefore, they conclude that 'Environmental factors emerge as less important in determining the incidence of civil conflict than economic and political factors' (Hauge and Ellingsen, 2001: 54).[4]

A second thorough and extensive study of the relationships between environmental change and violent conflict (Bächler, 1998) found that though environmental degradation could be a background or triggering factor in ethnic or political conflicts, most such conflicts were local and peacefully resolved by government regulation or negotiations. Whether such conflicts 'pass[ed] the threshold of violence definitely depends on *sociopolitical* factors and not on the degree of environmental degradation as such' (Bächler, 1998: 32; emphasis in original).[5]

A third extensive study, undertaken by an academic Task Force on State Failure sponsored by the U.S. government (Esty et al., 1995, 1998), deliberately sought environmental causes for a wide range of violent conflict events, including authoritarian coups, revolutionary wars, ethnic wars, and genocides. However, after adjusting for the impact of living standards, regime type, and involvement in international trade, *no* direct impact of environmental variables could be found. If environmental change had a causal relationship to political violence, as the authors of this study suggest, it would have to be indirectly, though influencing overall living standards or trade. In other words, only environmental change that was so drastic and far-reaching as to reduce life spans significantly, or to impair international trade in a major commodity substantially, would be likely to increase the risks of violent struggles.

It must be admitted that the range and quality of data on environmental change leaves much to be desired, and the poverty of such data may be one reason for these negative findings. Still, if environmental change were truly a major and pervasive cause of violent conflicts, it seems likely that some large cross-national studies of recent political violence would show more positive findings.

Should we therefore dismiss environment and environmental resources as a cause of conflict? No, although I believe we can be free of the fear that environmental decay will unleash wars and revolutions across the globe. Rather, what research has shown is that although environmental issues do cause international and domestic conflicts, they are of the kind that are *generally settled by negotiation and compromise*, and do not lead to taking up arms.

The reason for that is straightforward. Where the problem faced by two groups, or two nations, is over the degradation or depletion of an environmental resource, war neither solves the problem (it cannot make more of the resource), nor is it an economically efficient way to redistribute the resource (the costs of war almost invariably far outweigh the cost of gaining alternative resources or paying more for a share of the resource). For example, if two nations have a conflict over sharing river water—such as India and Bangladesh over the Ganges (Hill, Ganguli, and Naylor, 1998), Israel and Jordan over the river Jordan (Lowi, 1993b), or Hungary and Slovakia over the Danube (Lipschutz, 1997)—they may threaten violence, but in fact are most likely to produce nonviolent resolution through negotiation or arbitration rather than war (and indeed all of these conflicts led to treaties or international arbitration: Gleick, 1998b). The reason is that for one party to insist on *all* the water would in fact be a casus belli; and to risk a war to simply increase one's access to water is economically foolhardy. Throughout the world, the main use of freshwater (over three-quarters) is for irrigation to produce food. A reduction in water can be compensated either by adopting more efficient means of irrigation (drip rather than ditch); by switching to less water-intensive crops (dry grains rather than rice; tree crops rather than grains); or by importing food rather than producing it. All of these steps, though costly, are far less costly than armed conflict. Thus both for the country with the ability to take more water, and for the country dependent on downstream flows, the issue will be how to use and negotiate use of the resource most efficiently; resorting to war would inevitably be more costly than any gains that could be made from increased access to the resource or costs required to compensate for partial reductions. No nations have ever gone to war strictly over access to water; nor are any likely to do so in the future.[6]

The issue of access to water is therefore not truly a VEDS issue; rather, it is a new sort of issue in which nations face conflicts of interest that, although potentially costly depending on the degree of resource depletion, virtually must be settled by negotiation or arbitration. It is therefore a type of NEDS issue, where the condition or depletion of the environmental resource are *themselves* the main problems to be addressed, not any armed conflicts that may result.

Many other environmental issues take a similar form. Whether it is deforestation or land degradation by overgrazing or erosion or local atmospheric pollution, violent conflict involving nations—or even large subnational groups—is simply not a viable way of resolving the problem. Most environmental degradation is a local and long-term process, in which local residents fully participate. Local residents who have burned forests, overgrazed land, or created pollution generally see these effects as side issues in their own efforts at economic gains, and do not blame their government or others for these environmental changes.

In some cases, as when logging concessions are granted to elites who then rapidly cut forests without regard to the effects of runoff or flooding on farmers in surrounding lowlands, or when exclusive land-use privileges are granted to elites leading to exclusion of indigenous farmers, violent conflicts may indeed arise. However, the conflict is generally aimed at ending the unjust concessionary rights granted to government cronies, rather than at stopping the land use itself. Indeed, if granted the rights to fell forests or farm land, indigenous people will do so with much the same enthusiasm as privileged elites (Terborgh, 1999).

Elites and Violent Conflict

Much of the literature on environmental scarcity and violent conflict has erred in predicting violence because of a fundamental misunderstanding regarding the causes of political crises. It is a profound and repeated finding that the mere fact of poverty, inequality, or even increases in these sad conditions does *not* lead to political or ethnic violence (Gurr, 1980; Goldstone, 1994, 1998a). In order for popular discontent or distress to create large-scale conflicts, there must be some elite leadership to mobilize popular groups and to create linkages between them. There must also be some vulnerability of the state, in the form of internal divisions and economic or political reverses. Otherwise, popular discontent is unvoiced, and popular opposition is simply suppressed. The general assumption that environmental change, because it is so sweeping, *must* lead to large-scale and violent conflicts, is somewhat like a revival of a now discredited aspect of modernization theory, in which political theorists argued that modernization itself was so traumatic that it would inevitably lead to widespread violence and rebellion in countries undergoing industrial change (Feierabend, Feierabend, and Nesvold, 1969; Huntington, 1964; Tilly, 1973).

Political analysts of violent conflict now recognize that the essence of political stability or instability lies in a set of reciprocal relationships: among states in the international system, between states and their society's elites, among elite factions, and between both states and elites and popular groups. When states are fiscally sound, free of severe international threats, and supported by their elites, they are enormously resistant to popular discontent. It is only when states become financially strapped or subject to international pressure, and are deserted by their elites, that popular distress furnishes raw material for mobilizing forces for conflict (Foran, 1997; Goldstone, 1998a).

Oddly, although the environmental conflict literature has conceded that environmental impacts on violence depend on interactions with political and economic structures, this literature has not closely examined the impact of environmental change on states and elites. In fact, most environmental degradation (deforestation, soil erosion, water depletion) takes place *precisely in ways that strengthen states, elites, or the ties between them.* Thus, deforestation often occurs because elites gain concessionary rights from states for timbering; soil erosion and water depletion often involve large-scale agricultural and irrigation projects that benefit states or elites through involvement with international funding agencies or land reclamation. Although exhausting firewood and degrading land often have an adverse impact on popular groups, such changes have little impact on state finances or elite loyalty; they thus have little or no impact on political stability.

In cases where struggles over land or other resources have played a role in regional and ethnic conflict—in South Africa or Kenya, for example (Percival and Homer-Dixon, 2001; Kahl, 1998), the essence of the conflict has been the struggle among elite factions for control of political power, with control of land simply representing one of the prizes that go to the winning faction. Without political struggles that turn elites against the state, or that turn elite factions against each other, large-scale political conflicts are simply unlikely to arise. Although the control of land—like the control of minerals or other resources—may figure in such struggles, the degradation of environmental resources generally is not a significant enough issue to cause major conflicts.

Long-term environmental degradation is thus generally *not* an important source of violent conflict. Whatever popular misery may follow from environmental decay, such decay generally does not erode the loyalty of elites to governments. Indeed, the exploitation of environmental resources more often provides opportunities for states and elites both to profit.

Natural and Man-Made Disasters

Although long-term environmental degradation has not been proven an important determinant of violent conflict, this is not true of short-term and large-scale disasters, such as hurricanes, droughts, floods, earthquakes, and industrial accidents that affect the environment (such as the Chernobyl nuclear power plant accident in the former Soviet Union). A number of studies (Albala-Bertrand, 1993; Drury and Olson, 1998; Shefner, 1999) have shown how political mobilization and unrest are often sharply increased following a disaster. The 1972 Nicaragua earthquake, the 1988 Armenia earthquake, Hurricane Hazel in 1954 in Haiti, and the 1970 typhoon in then-East Pakistan were followed by violent changes of regime. The 1976 Guatemala earthquake and the 1985 Mexico City earthquake were both followed by massive political mobilization. The 1986 Chernobyl disaster, and the secrecy and inadequate protective measures that followed it, are widely credited with undermining elite support for the Soviet government (Haynes and Bojcun, 1990). Of course, not all such disasters have this effect. The 1995 Kobe earthquake in Japan and the devastation of Hurricane Mitch in 1998 in Central America did not produce such unrest. Although A. Cooper Drury and Richard Stuart Olson (1998) have shown that, all other things equal, the larger the disaster the greater the degree of subsequent political unrest, 'all other things' are not generally equal. Thus the context of the disaster matters a great deal.

The key in turning natural or man-made disasters into political turmoil is the responsibility placed on the regime, whether for predisaster causation or postdisaster mitigation. In Mexico and Armenia, the central government, of course, bore no responsibility for the earth-shaking itself. However, these governments *did* draw popular ire for the crumbling of poorly built government-constructed apartment blocks, whose collapse caused the bulk of the fatalities. In Nicaragua, the Somoza regime alienated business elites as well as ordinary urban dwellers by treating the international aid that flowed to Nicaragua in the wake of the earthquake as an opportunity for graft rather than a resource for reconstruction. In East Pakistan, the population turned against the political regime in West Pakistan in response to the perceived indifference and inadequate succor given them by that regime.

An interesting example of the divergent political potentials in natural disasters lies in the 1998 floods in China. The unusual magnitude of the floods was due to the extensive logging that had been supported by the Communist regime; the regime could have taken a great deal of blame for this event. However, the regime responded to the flooding with spectacularly publicized intervention by the army in public relief efforts. These efforts, treating flood mitigation as a patriotic enterprise, actually gained popular support for the regime.

In short, natural disasters provide an opportunity for the regime to display its flaws or to demonstrate its competence. Where the latter is shown, natural disasters can be a cause of increased support for the government; but where the flaws come to the fore, political unrest and violence is a widely observed response.

Population Change and Violent Conflict

In spite of the concentration in the literature regarding the potential for environmental change to cause violent conflict, most environmental change leads to *nonviolent* conflict that is resolved by negotiation. The main exceptions are devastating natural disasters occurring under regimes that display a corrupt or incompetent response.

A somewhat separate judgment, however, must be made for population changes. It is true that overall population growth, or increases in overall population density, do *not* generally lead to violent conflict. But research has shown a variety of instances in which *particular kinds of population changes* are strongly associated with political instability (de Sherbinen, 1995).

For example, if an agrarian population that needs more land to provide for a growing population finds that adjacent land is owned, and even being expanded, for exclusive use by large landowners, conflict is likely and indeed nearly inevitable. Throughout history, confrontations over land between growing populations of peasants and large landholders have prompted rural rebellions in China, Latin America, and Europe. In most such cases, there is no environmental degradation—the land is often being improved by peasants and landowners alike. However, population growth leads to the cultivation of more marginal lands, and incursions by land-hungry peasants into areas also sought by profit-hungry landlords. The result is a combination of pressure on peasant incomes and heightened conflicts with local elites. Conflict of this sort has arisen most recently in Chiapas in Mexico (Whitmeyer and Hopcroft, 1996), but is typical of peasant/landlord relations throughout history, appearing in the French Revolution of 1789, the German Revolution of 1848, the Mexican Revolution of 1910, the Russian Revolution of 1917, and the Chinese Revolution of 1949 (Goldstone, 1991, 1994).

Such rural conflict can be avoided if the urban and industrial economy provides sufficient jobs to absorb an expanding population. However, studies have shown that where urban growth is *not* matched by an increase in economic growth, risks of political turbulence increase (Brennan, 1999). The most recent State Failure Task Force study of political crises in sub-Saharan Africa from 1955 to 1995 found that the risk of crises, other things equal, *doubled* in countries with above-average levels of urbanization but below-average levels of GDP per capita (Esty et al. 1998: 15).

The problem of overurbanization relative to incomes is just one aspect of a more general principle relating population changes to political instability, namely that problems arise when there is a persistent mismatch between employment prospects and the size and nature of the labor force. Thus not only overurbanization, but also overeducation relative to the caliber of available jobs can create political discontent. In revolutionary situations ranging from Tudor England to Enlightenment France, from late Tokugawa Japan to modern Iran and the Soviet Union, political upheaval has been preceded by a surge in the production of youth with advanced education in the context of a relatively limited, semi-closed structure of elite positions (Doyle, 1984; O'Boyle, 1970; Goldstone, 1991, 1998b). The central authorities, who guarded the gates of social and economic advancement, drew elite discontent for a situation in which social mobility was increasingly sought but the paths of mobility were increasingly clogged.

Even without increases in higher education, the rapid growth of youth can undermine existing political coalitions, creating instability. Large youth cohorts are often drawn to new ideas and heterodox religions, challenging older forms of authority. In addition, because most young people have fewer responsibilities for families and careers, they are relatively easily mobilized for social or political conflicts. Youth have played a prominent role in political violence throughout recorded history; the existence of a 'youth bulge' (an unusually high proportion of youths ages fifteen to twenty-five relative to the total population) has historically been associated with times of political crisis (Goldstone, 1999a). In the State Failure Task Force study, the presence of a youth bulge was found to be a major predisposing factor in ethnic conflicts throughout the post-World War II world (Esty et al., 1995); indeed absent such a youth bulge, major ethnic conflicts rarely occurred.

Population movements across, or even within, political borders can also lead to violence. The U.S. Indian Wars of the eighteenth and nineteenth centuries were caused by the expansion of the United States into already-settled Native American territories. The state-assisted migration of Han Chinese into the mainly Uigur-settled region of Xinjiang and into Tibet has led to violent episodes of rebellion in both the latter regions, as their inhabitants struggled to maintain their distinctive identities and control over their territories. The Bantu migrations into southern Africa led to wars throughout the continent, while the movement of peoples, both forced and by choice, across ethnic borders within the former Soviet Union has led to a legacy of ethnic and separatist conflicts (Weiner and Russell, 2000).

The crucial element here is not migration per se; economic migration often leads to substantial benefits for both migrants and the destination country. What appears to matter for conflict are those cases wherein migration leads to clashes of national identity (Teitelbaum and Winters, 1998). That is, where one distinct ethnic group migrates into another area that is considered 'homeland' by another ethnic group, and challenges the dominance of the latter, then conflicts are likely to arise. If these conflicts escalate into contests for political control of the region, then ethnic war and even genocide often results.

To sum up, a number of specific population changes are strongly associated with increased risks of political violence:

A. An expanding agrarian population running up against land that is controlled or being expanded for exclusive use of large landholders.
B. An expanding urban population in an economy that is not providing commensurate economic growth.
C. An expanding population of higher-educated youth facing limited opportunities to obtain elite political and economic positions.
D. A large 'youth bulge'; that is, an expansion of the fifteen to twenty-five age cohort relative to the overall population of a society.
E. The migration of populations into regions already settled by a population with a distinct ethnic or political identity.

Clearly, none of these conditions arise from population growth, or even from specific population changes, by themselves. The conditions that lead to violent conflicts involve population changes in specific contexts that involve blockages to the desires or needs of an expanding population. Thus, if we wish to know in what regions of the globe we are most likely to see population-induced political conflicts, we need to examine both expected population changes and the contexts in which they will occur.

The Risk of Violent Conflict

As we cross into the next century, the world seems to have finally turned the corner on population growth. A combination of increased education for women, national and international support for policies of population planning, and the spread of economic development and accompanying movement along the demographic transition frontier have led to falling population growth rates around the world. Whether among the behemoths—China and India—or among the smaller but rapidly growing nations—such as Saudi Arabia, Kenya, and Malawi—population growth rates have dropped dramatically in the last decade (U.S. Bureau of the Census, 1999: 11).

Yet although population growth rates have dropped around the world, they remain high in some areas. In particular, many nations in the Middle East, Southeast Asia, and central and northern Africa still are growing at nearly 3 percent per year, a growth rate that would lead to a doubling of population in approximately twenty-five years. Moreover, although in most countries the *rate* of population growth has slowed, the absolute number of people being added to the world's population has not; the large number of women of childbearing age in the developing world, carrying the momentum of past population growth, ensure that even while growth rates fall as a percentage of the existing population, the number of new births each year continues to rise. For example, although China's growth rate has fallen to 1 percent per year, China will still grow by 10 to 11 million people per year for the next fifteen years. The world as a whole will add roughly 80 million people per year, or another 960 million (that is, another India) in the next dozen years (U.S. Bureau of the Census, 1999: 12).

Agrarian conflicts thus still arise, particularly in areas that pit growing rural populations against private landlords seeking exclusive rights to large holdings. Where land reform has not corrected the imbalance between large populations holding a minority of the land and small elites holding a majority of the land (or of the best land), population growth exacerbates this imbalance and fuels rural conflict. For example, in Zimbabwe and Kenya, conflict recurs over access to the best farmland, historically farmed by whites and now increasingly controlled by government-sponsored cronies; in Brazil's northeast, violence repeatedly flares between organizations of the landless and large landowners; and throughout Central America and the Andean region of South America, guerrilla warfare (including the Sandinistas in Nicaragua, the Shining Path movement in Peru, and the Revolutionary Armed Forces of Colombia [FARC]) has frequently recurred as a result of conflict between marginalized indigenous farmers and state-supported commercial landlords. In sum, we would expect rural conflicts of this sort to arise wherever the population seeking a living in agriculture is growing rapidly, but most land (or most of the best land) is controlled by a relatively small and privileged elite.

Moreover, because it is not the absolute rate of population growth, but the imbalance between growth in specific sectors of the population and growth of the economy that is crucial to the creation of conflicts, even countries with relatively low growth rates may encounter situations in which population changes contribute to political violence. For example, from 1970 to 1991 in the USSR, when economic growth slowed almost to zero, population growth was also minimal. However, the Soviet Union still encountered four of the five demographic 'risk conditions' noted above, namely an urban population that continued to grow despite minimal economic growth; an overexpansion of young men with a technical higher education, most of whom were relegated to blue-collar jobs owing to party restrictions on entry to the managerial and political elites and a stagnant economy; a large youth bulge in the Central Asian republics; and large-scale migration of Russians into many non-Russian ethnic Soviet republics. All of these factors, plus the environmental disasters of the Chernobyl explosion and the Armenia earthquake, became important in mobilizing the urban and nationalist oppositions whose combination produced the collapse of the Communist regime (Goldstone, 1998b; Urban et al., 1997; Lane, 1996).

It is precisely because of the importance of such imbalances that countries such as Saudi Arabia and China bear watching for political unrest, despite their success in dramatically reducing their rate of population growth. Although Saudi Arabia has dramatically decreased its population growth rate, from 5.2 percent per year in the 1980s to 3.2 percent per year in the 1990s (World Bank, 1996), that is still a rate of population growth that leads to a doubling of population in less than twenty-five years. This rate of growth has produced a large youth cohort, combined with rapid expansion of the labor force and rapid urbanization (urban growth of 7 percent per year in the 1980s and 4 percent per year in the 1990s [World Bank, 1998]). The slow-down of the Saudi economy with the decline in world oil prices portends poorly for absorbing this large number of urban youth into the economy.

China has succeeded in cutting its overall population growth and labor force growth to less than 1 percent per year. But because of its enormous size, this still means finding new jobs for roughly 13 million people per year. Far more important, however, is the shift in China's population from the countryside to the city. Because of the saturation of the agricultural sector, population has been shifting to cities; virtually all of these new job seekers, plus many older agricultural workers, have been seeking urban employment. In an odd anomaly, despite very low overall population growth, China has one of the world's fastest rates of urbanization, at nearly 5 percent per year in the 1980s and 4 percent per year in the 1990s. These rates, combined with China's size, mean that in each decade, approximately 150 million people have been added to the population of China's cities, and are dependent on urban jobs. Until recently, China's enormous rate of economic growth, averaging nearly 10 percent per annum, has allowed China to absorb these job seekers. Yet in 1999, China's economic growth rate dropped as the economy has tipped toward deflation. A sustained collision between diminished economic growth and the tens of millions moving to cities in search of work every year bodes ill for social and political stability.

Therefore, although the marked decrease in population growth in many countries and regions is good news for those concerned about global population, it offers no clear relief for concerns about the security implications of population change. Despite slow-downs in growth, many countries may well experience collisions between their agrarian populations and access to, land, between the expansion of their labor force, educated aspiring elites, urban population, and youth cohorts and the absorption rate of their economies, and—as detailed in other chapters in this volume—between migrants and resident populations that inflame ethnic and regional tensions.

To give a quick overview of regions where such imbalances are most likely to arise, consider that one of the regions with the most rapid population growth in recent years has also been the region with the worst record of economic development, namely sub-Saharan Africa. The two areas with the highest anticipated rates of population growth in the next decade are the Near East (2.4 percent per year) and sub-Saharan Africa (2.3 percent per year) (U.S. Bureau of the Census, 1999: A-4). Although such growth is not itself the crucial issue, it invariably brings rapid labor force growth and increasingly large youth cohorts, and is often linked to rapid urbanization. In fact, urbanization is extraordinarily rapid in sub-Saharan Africa, reaching annual rates in excess of 5 percent per year in many countries. What is truly cause for concern is that these anticipated trends of rapid labor force growth, youth bulges, and dramatic urbanization are combined with the world's lowest rates of economic growth. From 1990 to 1995, average annual growth in *total* (not per capita) GDP in sub-Saharan Africa was 1.4 percent per year, down from an average of 1.7 percent from 1980 to 1990. On a per capita basis, real income has been in decline since 1990. It is this combination of economic contraction with *expansion* in several specific, volatility-inducing, population changes that has helped make Africa a continuing caldron of political and ethnic conflicts.

Looking outside of Africa, urbanization has been slower in most parts of the Near East, although high rates (4 percent per year or more) persist in Turkey, Saudi Arabia, Syria, and Iran. If we look to South Asia, we find a large difference between Pakistan and India. The latter appears likely to face far fewer population/conflict challenges from urban and labor force growth (respectively 2.9 and 1.9 percent per year in the mid-1990s), whereas the condition in Pakistan raises concerns (urban and labor force growth of 4.7 percent and 3.1 percent per year, respectively). However, economic growth has so far been robust in all of these nations (World Bank, 1998). The only areas outside Africa that currently combine high demographic risk factors and low economic growth are Central America and the

Caribbean (Haiti, Nicaragua, even Mexico); the former states of the Soviet Union in Central Asia; and the Palestinian territories of the Gaza Strip and West Bank.

Population changes are most directly linked to domestic political conflicts, but these conditions are also relevant to the international problems posed by genocides and international wars. One major finding of recent genocide studies is that these grisly episodes almost always take place in the context of existing domestic or international violent conflicts (Gurr and Harff, 1994). A second concern is that most international wars in sub-Saharan Africa have arisen as a result of domestic conflicts. Thus the Eritrea-Ethiopia conflict is a legacy of the upheaval that felled the imperial regime in Ethiopia; the Central African conflict involving several nations is a result of the collapse of the Mobutu regime in Congo-Zaire and the internal ethnic turmoil in Rwanda and Burundi; and the west African conflicts that called for a Nigerian-led international expeditionary force arose from internal rebellions in Liberia and Sierra Leone. Other conflicts in Angola and Sudan have sparked more sporadic cross-national intervention. Thus the demographic changes that raise the risks for domestic conflicts simultaneously pose heightened risks of international wars in the region.

To sum up, although most scholarly attention has focused recently on the environment as a source of violent conflict, it appears that the more fundamental threat to international security in the area of violent environmental/demographic security issues lies in a set of specific population changes occurring in the context of limited economic growth. Substantially increased risks of violent political conflict are found when imbalances between population changes and the absorptive capacity of societies arise.

Demographic Change as Indicator and Outcome

Unfortunately, there are literally dozens of nations in sub-Saharan Africa, Latin America (especially Haiti), the Near East, South Asia, and East Asia (especially North Korea) in which past demographic momentum and current population movements are set to produce sustained increases in the labor force, urban populations, educated aspiring elites, or bulging youth cohorts while their economies are threatened with slow growth, setting the stage for political crises. How can we foretell which countries are most likely actually to fall into violent political conflicts?

Part of the answer, of course, lies in tracking economic and political indicators. However, demographic factors have also proven highly useful in models for forecasting political risks. In the work of the State Failure Task Force (Esty et al., 1995, 1998), probably the most comprehensive modeling of risks of a variety of kinds of violent political conflicts in the years since World War II, several demographic variables (including youth bulge, urbanization to development ratio, life expectancy, and adult and infant mortality levels) were found to be useful predictors of political violence, even after allowing for the impact of regime type and such economic factors as international trade relations. In particular, the rate of *infant mortality* was found to be an important predictor of risk in almost all models. This is not because infant mortality itself directly affects political processes. Rather, it appears that infant mortality is the best single tool for assessing the wide variety of factors (average income, income distribution, provision of health care, nutrition) that affect the overall quality of life for individuals in a society. High levels of infant mortality, relative to world averages, indicate higher risks of political crises. Nicholas Eberstadt (1988, 1993) has further argued that in Communist countries in particular, a *rise* in infant mortality—something hardly ever seen, even in the Third World—is a powerful portent of coming upheaval. Such a rise occurred in the Soviet Union prior to its collapse, and now appears to be occurring in North Korea. These demographic changes may serve as a useful 'early alert' of coming security problems.

Finally, it should also be remembered that the relationship between population changes and violent conflicts is not unidirectional. Violent conflicts can also have large and long-lasting impacts on demography. Revolutions frequently bring marked shifts in marriage and birth rates (depending on whether the postrevolutionary period is one of rampant optimism or pessimism), in urbanization (if the new regime sponsors urban development), in education (if the new regime dramatically expands enrollments), and in migration (as the new regime and the violence associated with it may either attract migrants from abroad or send them across borders seeking escape from violence or persecution). Violent conflicts rarely end conclusively; a more common pattern is that cycles of violence succeed one another. Part of the reason for this is that violent conflicts often produce population changes that, in the next generation if not earlier, feed back into the creation of renewed political risks.

For example, in Palestine the preservation of stateless Arabs in refugee camps following the 1967 Israeli-Arab war led, twenty years later, to the growth of a vast, aggrieved youth cohort in the occupied territories, with limited economic prospects. It was this cohort that played a crucial role in the *intifada* uprisings in Gaza and the West Bank. In Central Africa, the movement of Tutsi and Hutu groups across borders as a result of internal conflicts in Rwanda and Burundi led to destabilizing ethnic conflicts in Congo-Zaire, and to renewed and intensified conflicts when new cohorts of formerly exiled Hutus and Tutsis returned to their countries. Unless measures are taken to provide a semblance of economic hope to the populations of present-day Kosovo, Bosnia, Serbia, and Albania, it is likely that the population displacements that have occurred in the recent Balkan conflicts and the weak economic conditions that will face the next cohorts of young men growing up in those regions will produce not a lasting peace, but a renewal of ethnic conflicts. It thus appears that a focus on demographic changes can be helpful both in alerting us to coming security problems and in helping us foresee how these might fuel further problems in the future.

Population Change and International Security

In contrast to violent conflicts, there are other security issues that cannot be dealt with effectively by the deployment of armed force. These are situations in which resources vital to life—such as the atmosphere and freshwater flows—are degraded by actions taken in other nations. We have already mentioned possible conflicts over water supplies from rivers that run through two or more countries as issues that require international diplomatic negotiation. However, as the world's population grows, and that increased population engages in more activities that generate environmental impacts, the total scale of such environmental degradation can threaten the health of ecosystems that sustain life across the globe. Thus, with increasing population and development, this class of security issues is growing. For these nonviolent NEDS issues, both population growth and environmental degradation play critical, interrelated roles.

Water issues are generally bilateral or regional; for these, relatively straightforward negotiations or arbitration are generally able to produce progress toward a settlement. However, a few key issues today are not simply bilateral, or even simply multilateral, but are truly global in scope. For these issues, the actions of a small number of countries pose security threats to *every* other country in the world, regardless of its size or income level. These NEDS issues are truly novel, and pose challenges in the new area of nonviolent global security.

At least three such issues are already evident. One has been the subject of successful global negotiations; one is in the midst of difficult and often deadlocked global negotiations; and one has yet to produce any such negotiations, except on a very limited scale.

The first is the production of ozone-depleting gases. Once it was discovered that the gaping holes in the ozone shield protecting Earth from solar ultra-violet radiation were being caused by human activity, it was fairly clear that action to halt that activity was imperative. If no action were taken, population growth and economic development around the world would soon produce an exponential increase in the use of ozone-depleting substances (mainly freon in cooling systems, but also various solvents and other industrial chemicals) that would expose most of the temperate zones to cancer-inducing radiation. The major producing and consuming nations of ozone-depleting substances thus came together and produced an international agreement—the Montreal Protocol of 1987—that called for the fairly rapid phasing out of those substances. These rather swift and successful negotiations were greatly helped by the fact that the major companies that produced ozone-depleting substances were able to produce safer substitutes that they could continue to sell at a profit. Nor did any nation stand to benefit substantially from violating the protocol. Nonetheless, the Montreal Protocol stands as a model of a globally negotiated solution to a global environmental threat.

The second such issue is the threat posed by climate change, most likely global warming. As with ozone, it has become clear that human activity is altering the atmosphere (Wigley et al.,1998). The burning of fossil fuels releases gases (mainly carbon dioxide, or CO_2) that increase Earth's absorption of solar heat energy. If unchecked, these changes could lead to substantial warming of the planet, with unpredictable effects on weather, crop production, sea levels, and the spread of disease vectors and pests (Brown, 1989; Gleick, 1989; Soroos, 1997a). These effects are no longer speculative: global temperatures have increased markedly in the last two decades; extreme weather events of all sorts (hurricanes, tornadoes, droughts, storms, freezes, floods, El Niño) have become more frequent and severe; the Arctic, Antarctic, and Greenland ice packs have lost tens of square miles to melting, as have glaciers around the world; and plants and animals (from insects to otters) have extended their winter ranges farther toward the poles (Fischer et al., 1999; Pounds, Fogden, and Campbell, 1999). Recent studies of Greenland ice-core samples suggest that global temperatures can shift suddenly and dramatically over the course of a few decades as tipping points are reached (Pollack, 1998).

Although we do not know for certain how much of the current climate change could be reduced or halted by stopping the man-made production of CO_2 that is contributing to it, it seems certain that a further exponential increase in CO_2 production could only accelerate climate change. Stabilizing CO_2 production, and eventually reducing it, is the goal of the current global climate negotiations now being conducted by most nations of the world. The most recent accord reached in these negotiations, the Kyoto Protocol of 1997, calls for reductions in CO_2 production by rich countries, although it leaves open the actions expected of developing nations.

However, these negotiations have constantly threatened to become derailed over the issue of how developing nations will participate in the accords. Population changes and development make this a vexing issue. At the present, the largest producer of CO_2 gases in the world is the United States. In the early 1990s, the United States produced more CO_2 each year than China and India combined. Yet current projections of population growth and economic development in the latter countries suggest a huge increase in their future CO_2 output; by 2010 China and India will be producing 50 percent more CO_2 than the United States (Goldstone, 1999b: 255). What then should be the path for CO_2 reductions? Clearly current reductions are not credible unless they begin with the largest producer, the United States. However, unless China and India bind themselves to a development path that will greatly curtail their burning of fossil fuels, then any reduction achieved by the United States will go for naught, as in a few years the large countries' emissions will continue to escalate global warming. How can India and China—with large populations demanding economic development, which on today's known pathways entails massive increases in energy consumption—bind themselves to constraints on their development? Although one can hope for a minor miracle—for example, a cheap way for India and China to produce the energy they need from wind power and solar cells, thus obviating the need for vast increases in coal or oil consumption—these negotiations still lack a breakthrough that will solve this problem.

A final issue that likely will demand global attention is the preservation of species diversity (Terborgh, 1999). It is already well known that simplified ecosystems—such as parks, gardens, and agricultural fields—are enormously more prone to infection, parasites, and catastrophic species extinctions than are the more varied natural ecosystems. In addition, complex ecosystems harbor millions of species whose role in sustaining the global ecology, or providing specific useful substances, is yet unknown. Thus many scientists suspect that deforestation, particularly in rainforests, or ocean pollution that kills plankton species, may not only drastically affect the ability of the earth to recycle CO_2, but may have unknown effects up or down the ecological scale that would change the balance of species around the world. European nations are also deeply concerned about the potential impact of genetically modified crops and animals upon the quality and diversity of the global gene pool. No global negotiations are yet bent on scaling back activities that reduce the diversity of species, although there have been limited moves in this direction. Controls on genetically modified crops are a subject of discussion in the current round of World Trade Organization agreements. International action has been taken to protect certain 'charismatic' fauna, such as elephants, rhinos, dolphins, and whales, and the United States and many European nations have rather drastic laws aimed at protecting any and all endangered species in their territory. But that is the rub—the majority of the world's species diversity is contained not in the rich societies in temperate climates, but in the poorer societies of the tropics. Their development seems to demand environmental and species destruction (which they are in fact carrying on at a rapid rate). Whether it is a lack of urgency regarding this issue, or a sense that there is no straightforward solution to trading off development in semitropical and tropical nations versus species preservation, it may be some time (perhaps too late) before coordinated international action is taken on this issue. However, as with ozone and CO_2, the fact that the most rapid adverse changes are taking place among countries with the largest populations, and precisely in response to government efforts to settle those populations in more extensive areas and provide them with agricultural incomes, the impact of population growth and population movements is a key element to this problem.

Facing Up to the Real Issues

Discussions of environmental security have been muddied by the confusing multitude of ways in which population, environment, and security have been combined. In fact, environmental issues appear to have very little impact on traditional security concerns, that is, those focusing on armed conflict within and between nations. Population changes, historically and in some regions today (mainly Africa), *have* posed such security concerns. Where demands for access to land or employment, for political participation, and for ethnic or regional political power, have been intensified by shifts in the size and distribution of populations; where urbanization, growing youth cohorts, and the emergence of new aspiring elites have undermined existing political and economic regimes, civil violence has become dramatically more likely.

In addition, there is a substantial set of serious security threats in the future stemming from NEDS issues—issues in which the condition *of the environment itself* is the security threat. Several such issues: sharing of freshwater resources, ozone depletion, global warming, and concerns over species preservation and the global gene pool, have already become evident. The first of these has been the source of numerous bilateral conflicts and treaties; the others (to varying degrees) have become the focus of extended global negotiations aimed at creating treaty regimes. In all these cases, population growth and economic development combine to place the environmental risk on an exponential growth track unless global actions are taken to halt or reverse the trend. Unfortunately, these negotiations often pit the interests of the wealthy developed nations against those of the poorer, but far more numerous, people of developing nations.

To return to the main focus of this volume, it appears that we are on the threshold of a new era in security, but it is not an era in which environmental changes become new sources of traditional security concerns. Scholars who have emphasized the role of environmental change in bringing violent and acute conflicts provided a valuable service in stimulating debate on the relationships among environment, population, and security. However, the initial specification of environmental degradation as a major new threat to stability and cause of violence now appears to be mistaken.

Rather, it is an era in which several specific aspects of *population change*—namely rapid increases in labor force, youth cohorts, urban population, elite training, or migration that produces a collision of ethnic groups—promise to spread recurring political crises when they occur in countries with struggling economies and inflexible or transitional political systems. Indeed, a major reason to fear that such VEDS issues will grow more important in the future is that the vast majority of the world's expected growth in labor force, youth cohorts, urban population, higher education, and cross-ethnic-boundary migration will take place in precisely the countries and regions that have either struggling economies or inflexible or transitional regimes, namely Africa; the Middle East; the Andean region of South America; Central America/Mexico/the Caribbean; Russia and the former Soviet Republics; China; and South and Southeast Asia.

In addition, in countries where *regimes are actively involved in worsening the effects of natural disasters*—whether by taking actions that increase the risk or the toll of such disasters, or by making a corrupt or ineffective response—political upheavals are likely to follow. Population changes and natural disasters, in vulnerable economic and political settings, are thus likely to provide the major VEDS issues for the foreseeable future.

Where long-term environmental degradation emerges as a major security issue is not in prevention of war and managing internal domestic conflicts, but in a new security arena, that of dealing with transnational and global threats *to the environment itself.* Such NEDS issues have already provoked confrontations and international negotiations in regard to water use, ozone depletion, CO_2 production, and the preservation of certain species and controls on genetically modified crops. Such fundamental environmental security issues will take us to new frontiers in science to understand their nature, and—we must hope—to new frontiers in international negotiations and security arrangements to deter and avoid their threats.

Jack A. Goldstone, b. 1953, Ph.D. in sociology (Harvard University, 1981), professor of sociology and international relations, University of California-Davis; Current main interest: long-term social change. Most recent book: *Encyclopedia of Political Revolutions* (Congressional Quarterly, 1999).

Notes

1. This formulation owes much to Nazli Choucri's threefold definition of security as embracing military security, regime security, and structural security, the latter including all threats to 'life-supporting properties—as well as prevailing sources of livelihood' (Choucri, 1997: 180). Others who have been instrumental in expanding our understanding of population and environment security threats include Mathews (1989), Rothschild (1995), Myers (1993), de Sherbinen (1995), and Homer-Dixon (1991, 1999).

2. Relevant offices include the Army Environmental Policy Unit (AEPI), the Directorate of Central Intelligence Environmental Center (DCI/Environmental), and the Department of State Office of Global Affairs. Brief reports on the full range of U.S. government activities focused on demographic and environmental security appear in each issue of the *Environmental Change and Security Project Report* (Woodrow Wilson Center, 1995).

3. Confusion on these issues is rife and yet often unremarked; even skilled analysts have had trouble avoiding vague and ambiguous terms. Thus an outstanding environmental policy scholar, Daniel Esty (1999), in a recent essay refers to 'overseas environmental harms', 'environmental security threats', 'environmental effects on state stability', 'direct environmental threats', and 'direct environmental spillovers' as various ways to link environmental concerns with security. I believe that Esty uses 'environmental effects on state stability' to imply violent consequences of environmental change, and both 'direct environmental threats' and 'direct environmental spillovers' to describe nonviolent threats. But none of his terms has a clear and unequivocal meaning. Moreover they make no explicit mention of population at all, although in his case examples Esty focuses heavily on population-related causes of conflicts. Homer-Dixon (1999), who has perhaps done more than anyone to raise awareness of environmental security issues, focuses almost entirely on threats of violence, leaving the major nonviolent threats to well-being from environmental change (health, climate, fishery/forest maintenance) almost entirely to one side, except as these changes play a role in contributing to local violence. Moreover, Homer-Dixon confounds environmental degradation and population changes by conflating both of them in his umbrella concept of 'environmental scarcity'. Thus, although some analysts (e.g., Bächler, 1998) have been extremely careful in distinguishing among different kinds of environmental and population changes and among different kinds of conflicts, many of the leading authors in this field still use vague omnibus concepts.

4. Even Hauge and Ellingsen, however, are sometimes disposed to the vague conflation of environmental change with other causes of conflict that so often mars otherwise excellent work in this field. For example, at one point in summarizing their analysis, they say 'a poor country suffering from demand-induced, supply-induced, and structural-induced scarcity has a 20 percent probability of incidence of civil war and 45 percent probability of domestic armed conflict' (Hauge and Ellingsen, 2001). However, only the 'supply-induced' scarcity in their model is in any way a reflection of environmental conditions, being measured by availability of freshwater per capita, land degradation, and deforestation. They measure 'demand-induced scarcity' by population density. But since this measure is density relative to national territory, and not to forest or agricultural land, and since, moreover, they have already netted out freshwater availability per capita and soil and forest decay, this measure captures precisely those population effects that are *independent* of environmental degradation. They measure poverty by GNP per capita, and they measure 'structural scarcity' by income inequality. Note that both of these measures rest on the level and distribution of *cash income*, not on the level and distribution of access to environmental resources. They thus more accurately measure failures in industrialization and development, rather than conditions of the environment, and therefore denote a separate set of grievances.

In sum, Hauge and Ellingsen are correct that poverty and income inequality and population density have important effects, and greater effects than environmental decay, in their causal model of violence. But it is an error to suggest that their measures of poverty, inequality, and population density have a relation to 'environmental scarcity', when in fact these are measured wholly independently of environmental conditions, and thus are measures of other grievances.

5. Although Bächler is careful to separate different kinds of conflict and different kinds of environmental problems, his analysis nonetheless rests more on finding a coincidence of environmental degradation with conflict, than with careful analysis of the different causal weights of environmental and nonenvironmental factors. Thus, for example, one of Bächler's major cases of ethnopolitical conflict is the genocidal Tutsi/Hutu civil war in Rwanda, which he associates with 'overuse of land, soil deforestation, and subsistence crisis' (Bächler, 1998: 40). Yet Percival and Homer-Dixon (1998: 218), in carefully examining the Rwanda case for causal mechanisms behind the genocide, discount those factors as important causes. They conclude that 'although the recent violence occurred in conditions of severe environmental scarcity, because the Arusha accords and regime insecurity were the key factors motivating the Hutu elite, environmental scarcity played a much more peripheral role'. In general, environmental degradation is often a symptom of other severe problems in a society—government policies that neglect welfare, severe maldistribution of incomes, aggressive short-term and ineffective development efforts, and corrupt and self-serving elites. Environmental decay may thus often be associated with political breakdown, without being a major cause of that breakdown. Rather, it is one of the consequences or symptoms of the more fundamental problems that lead to political crisis.

6. A recent article providing an excellent survey of water and security issues notes that over 3,600 treaties have been signed over different aspects of international waters, with remarkable elegance and creativity in dealing with water issues; moreover, in the last 3,000 years, 'there has *never* been a war fought over water' (Wolf, 1999a: 2). Lowi (1999: 389) similarly states that 'we have not found, to date, cases in which interstate war derives primarily and predominantly from the depletion, degradation, or inequitable distribution of environmental resources such as freshwater.' See also Wolf (1999b).

Chapter Six

Water and Conflict: Rhetoric and Reality

STEVE C. LONERGAN

Water is far from a simple commodity,
Water's a sociological oddity,
Water's a pasture for science to forage in,
Water's a mark of our dubious origin,
Water's a link with a distant futurity,
Water's a symbol of ritual purity,
Water is politics, water's religion,
Water is just about anyone's pigeon,
Water is frightening, water's endearing,
Water's a lot more than mere engineering,
Water is tragical, water is comical,
Water is far from the Pure Economical,
So studies of water, though free from aridity,
Are apt to produce a good deal of turbidity.

—Kenneth Boulding (1966: 109–110)[1]

Introduction

For several years, numerous statements have appeared in the popular media extolling the possibilities of wars over water. This rhetoric has captured the public imagination and caused much consternation in the intelligence community of various countries, who worry whether water—or other scarce resources—may be a flashpoint for international conflict in the future. In many cases, the comments are little more than media hype; in others, statements have been made for political reasons. Regardless of the source or the reason, it is clear that water is a scarce resource in some regions of the world and that tensions exist—and will likely increase in the future—over water use, water ownership, and water rights. Because water is such a scarce resource in some regions, and because it is the basis for all life on Earth, it is worth examining in detail whether there is a relationship between freshwater supply and conflict.

The purpose of this chapter is to address the following questions:

1. How scarce is water?
2. Has water been a cause of violent conflict in the past?
3. Do shared water supplies increase the probability of violence?
4. Are there other conditions that may trigger conflicts over water in the future?
5. Is it justified to use water as the key example of how environmental degradation and resource depletion can contribute to violent conflict?

The chapter begins with an overview of the role of water in contemporary society, then addresses the questions above by examining three aspects of water: water quantity, water quality, and so-called hydro-politics. It also includes an example from the Middle East, a region where tensions over water are as great as anywhere in the world. Last, there is a discussion as to whether the various processes of global change—environmental, social, and economic—may affect the probability of conflict over water in the future.

How Much Water Is Enough?

The total amount of water in the world is enormous—on the order of 2 million cubic kilometers. But most of it is either too salty for human use or it exists as ice. In reality, less than 0.01 percent of the world's water is available for human use, about 13,500 km^3 on an annual basis, or 2,300 m^3 per person. Is this amount adequate? This is a difficult question to answer, for at least three reasons. First, the demand for freshwater has increased by almost 40 percent since 1950, as a result of increased population growth and increased per capita water use. Since 1900, demand for water has increased at roughly twice the rate of population increase. Second, the supply of freshwater is being adversely affected by pollution. Industrial discharge, saltwater intrusion into aquifers, and human waste disposal are all reducing the amount of freshwater available for human use. And third, the distribution of water is highly variable across Earth's surface. Although water moves easily, it does not move 'cheaply', particularly relative to its present price. Some countries that have enormous water surpluses—like Canada—are moving to prevent all bulk water exports. Added to the unequal distribution of freshwater is the fact that water often flows across political jurisdictions. At present, there are 261 transboundary waterways, presenting at least the potential for international conflict, and sixty-four countries have at least 70 percent of their territories within international river basins (see Wolf et al., 1999, for a detailed description of international river basins). Although international tensions over water seem to stimulate the most media interest, for international organizations and many others there is a greater concern about tensions *within* countries. There are often major variations in terms of water availability within countries, due to both physical reasons and inequitable access. Safe drinking water is essential for development, and the lack of clean water and adequate sanitation facilities take a serious toll on human health, further exacerbating tensions in some regions.

In order to assess how much water is enough, various scales or indicators for water stress and scarcity have been proposed. A commonly used benchmark is that water availability less than 1,700 m^3 per person per year is considered a condition of *water stress*, and countries exhibiting less than 1,000 m^3 per person per year are considered *water scarce* (for all sectors; see, for example, Falkenmark et al., 1989). Others (among them World Bank, 1993, and WHO, 1992) recommend 20–40 lpcd (liters per capita per day)—equivalent to 7.3–14.6m^3—as a minimum for water and sanitation requirements. Peter Gleick (1996) recommends 50 lpcd and notes that in the year 2000, over 2 billion people will live in countries with an average (reported) domestic water use of under 50 lpcd (Gleick, 1998a). A different approach is taken by Leif Ohlsson (1999), who combines hydrological indicators with the Human Development Index developed by the United Nations Development Program (UNDP) into a Social Water Stress Indicator. Ohlsson's proposed indicator—while as problematic as the first two—attempts to combine the biophysical vulnerability to water scarcity and the ability and capacity of a society to respond to such stress. According to these criteria, many countries are experiencing water scarcity or water stress at present, and this number will increase dramatically over the next half century (see Figure 6.1).

Although these benchmarks are widely used, they are not particularly useful. Not only are there various forms of water scarcity, but the level of stress that is imposed on an economy will be a function of many social, economic, and institutional factors, such as efficiency of use, level of national income, and level of agricultural development. Last, there are enormous data problems with respect to water use and availability (Lonergan and Brooks, 1994; Gleick, 1998a). Nevertheless, it is clear that as population grows, the number of countries experiencing water shortages will increase.

FIGURE 6.1   Available Freshwater Resources, 2050

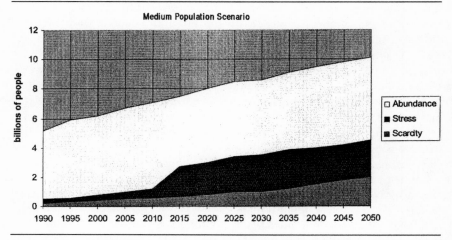

This figure adopts the indicator of water stress and water scarcity proposed by Falkenmark et al. (1989), and assumes no change in the per capita demand for water over time. The population figures are from the UN Medium Population Projection (UN, 1994) and the data on water availability is from WRI (1998).

At present, over two dozen countries exhibit conditions of water stress or water scarcity; by 2025, this number will rise to almost fifty, and by 2050, the number of countries is expected to reach fifty-four, with a total population of over 4 billion persons (Figure 6.1).

Setting aside the problems of data and indicators, there is little question that the availability of freshwater is one of the critical issues of the next millennium. As the International Conference on Water and the Environment noted in Dublin in 1992, 'Scarcity and misuse of freshwater pose serious and growing threats to sustainable development and protection of the environment.'[2]

Increasing Demand for Water

Water availability is severely limited in many regions of the world, and this condition worsen as population grows. Over 20 percent of the world's population presently lacks access to clean water supply and nearly 50 percent lack hygienic sanitation services (WHO, 1996). Although agriculture is by far the largest consumer of water, the growth in demand is occurring in all sectors at a rapid rate (Figure 6.2).

In many countries, competition among water users is increasing, and tensions among various groups in water-short regions are high. Such tensions

FIGURE 6.2   Global Water Withdrawal by Sector, 1900–2000

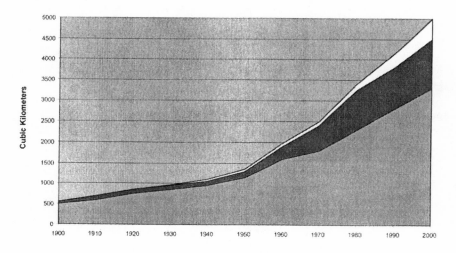

SOURCE: This figure is based on data from Shiklomanov (1993: 20).

are not isolated to developing countries. The summer of 1999 was the driest on record for much of the eastern United States, and tensions rose when one state implemented water conservation measures and surrounding states decided against similar measures. Other developed countries experiencing problems of water supply include the UK, Belgium, Poland, and Singapore.

Perhaps the greatest concern with respect to water scarcity is in the Middle East and Africa. By 2025, forty countries in these regions are expected to experience water stress or water scarcity (out of a total of forty-eight countries worldwide; see WRI, 1998). Water has become a major political issue in the Middle East, and the various peace agreements that have been proposed or signed in recent years all include water as a component. This has led to claims from various sources—attributed (but unsubstantiated) to individuals such as Boutros Boutros-Ghali and former King Hussein of Jordan—that 'the next war in the Middle East will be over water.'[3]

The problem is magnified since sixty-four countries on four continents have over 70 percent of their land area in international river basins, as noted above. In thirteen river basins there are five or more riparian states. This implies at least a potential for water-related disputes between countries.

However, many disputes over water occur within, rather than between, countries. India and China are two countries where competing water users—either separate states or rural-urban users—have argued over water rights and water withdrawals. As water demand in urban areas grows, more is being diverted away from the agricultural sector and to domestic users. This has implications for agricultural productivity and, in a global sense, for food prices. One popular argument is that diverting water from agriculture to domestic uses in China will reduce grain output, and force the country to import grain. In turn, this will increase the price of grain on the world market, and negatively affect smaller developing countries who import grain at present (Brown, 1998).

Countries in the Middle East have experienced similar tensions between the agriculture and domestic sector (Lonergan and Brooks, 1994). Domestic users pay a higher rate than the marginal cost of water, whereas agricultural users continue to be subsidized.

The Problems of Pollution

Coupled with the increasing demand for freshwater has been the degradation of existing supplies and the impacts associated with this. Ninety percent of diseases in developing countries are the result of unsanitary water conditions or water shortages. An estimated 1.4 billion people in the South lack access to safe water, and almost 3 billion people lack adequate sanitation facilities (WHO, 1996). Over 250 million new cases of water-related diseases are reported annually, resulting in over 12 million deaths (Gleick, 1998b). In developing countries, an average of 90 percent of all domestic sewage is discharged into surface waters without any treatment (Nash, 1993). Water can also become saline through poor agricultural practices or saltwater intrusion from the sea. Water pollution may contribute by reducing the amount of freshwater available for use (even with adequate treatment) and also because of its inhibiting effect on development. As an upstream/downstream issue with potentially serious impacts on human health, water pollution may also cause tension within countries and lead to social unrest.

Poor quality freshwater can affect human health in four ways (WHO, 1992; Gleick, 1998b):

1. Waterborne diseases—those transmitted through ingestion of contaminated water, such as typhoid fever and cholera;
2. Water-washed diseases—those resulting from washing, such as certain eye diseases and some types of diarrhea;
3. Water-based diseases—those where the pathogen is dependent on aquatic animals, such as schistosomiasis and dracunculiasis; and
4. Water-vectored diseases—those transmitted by insects that breed in water, such as malaria, yellow fever, and dengue.

These four categories of water-related diseases occur primarily in developing countries, where there is inefficient water supply and wastewater disposal. The solution to these problems is the provision of safe water and sanitation. Water quality improvement is one area where there is reasonable agreement among institutions on both the problem and the solution.

The Distribution of Freshwater. Freshwater is unevenly distributed over space. Even in water-rich regions, availability varies seasonally. In particular, there is a tremendous imbalance between population and rainfall; over two-thirds of the world's population live in regions that receive less than one-quarter of the world's annual rainfall (Gleick, 1993a). On a per capita basis, North America has four times the rainfall of Asia. Although there is much concern with the conflict potential of countries with significant income disparities, the uneven distribution of water is even more of a concern. For example, Iceland has over 600,000 m^3 per capita water availability, whereas Kuwait has less than 75 m^3 per capita (WRI, 1998). There are similar disparities within countries and even during times of the year. In some water-stressed countries or regions, such disparities are exacerbated by seasonal variations. For instance, in India, 90 percent of the rain falls during the summer monsoon season, severely limiting the ability to use what rainfall is available.

The Three Crises

Water scarcity is a function of water supply and demand. Water demand is increasing at an alarming rate in some regions, through population growth and increasing per capita demand. Malin Falkenmark et al. (1989) distinguish among four types of scarcity: *absolute scarcity*, where there is too little rainfall compared with the evaporative demand; *erratic rainfall*, where there are dry spells and droughts that occur irregularly; *soil disturbance*, where there is a reduced permeability of soils, often owing to urban activity; and *population growth*, which is a combination of hydro-climate limitations and population growth per se.

In many water-scarce countries, such as Jordan and Israel, there is no obvious and inexpensive way to increase water supply, and tensions among different water users are likely to result. In other countries, such as Egypt, improvements in water efficiency, moving away from water-intensive crops, or importing water from nearby countries may offer reasonable solutions.

The second crisis is one of deteriorating water quality. Agriculture is the biggest polluter, and increased use of fertilizer and pesticides have contaminated both groundwater and surface water supplies (Falkenmark and Lindh, 1993; Lonergan and Brooks, 1994). Domestic and industrial pollution is increasing as well, and the problem affects both developed and developing countries (WHO, 1992).

Finally, the use of water has a geopolitical dimension. Water moves from upstream to downstream users, and withdrawals and type of use in one location may affect the quantity or quality of supplies downstream. There are also historical, cultural, economic, and social aspects of water use. To some, water is a gift from God, and should not be priced. Others, such as the World Bank, have pushed for full marginal cost pricing of water (World Bank, 1993). The lack of a suitable legal framework for resolving international water resource disputes presents another problem. Sovereignty over international rivers generally invokes one of four doctrines (Correia and da Silva, 1997): absolute territorial sovereignty, which implies riparian states may use water resources in any way they please, even to the detriment of other nations; absolute territorial integrity, which implies that riparian use of a river should not negatively affect downstream riparians; limited territorial sovereignty, which invokes a combination of 1) and 2) within a framework of equitable use by all parties; and community of coriparian states, which promotes integrated management of river basins.

What is a reasonable and equitable use of water resources when more than one riparian is involved? The 1966 Helsinki Rules, adopted by the International Law Association, provided a basic framework of recommendations for international river basins. These were superseded, after twenty-seven years of discussion, by the convention on the Non-Navigational Uses of International Watercourses. The convention was ratified by the UN General Assembly in 1997 (UN, 1997; see also Gleick, 1998b). Despite including sections on cooperation and joint management, the convention is often vague and offers few specifics on water allocations and water rights, which are often key issues in tensions over water (Wolf, 1999b).

Global Warming

Much of the concern with conflicts over water rests on the conditions of increased demand and a constant, or decreasing, supply. One great unknown in terms of its impact on water supplies is what many feel is the major ecological concern of the next millennium: global warming.

Global warming may have significant implications for resource availability, agricultural productivity, and economic output; it may lead to coastal flooding and additional saltwater intrusion into aquifers. In many cases, with adequate prior knowledge, human systems will be able to adapt to a slowly changing climate. However, higher temperatures and, in some regions, less rainfall will lead to less water available. More disruptive to political stability, however, will be the expected increasing magnitude and frequency of extreme events. Extreme events are difficult and costly to prepare for, and may cause major social disruption (IPCC, 1995, 1997). Most concerned will be those regions that are most vulnerable to climate disruptions, particularly areas subject to floods and droughts.

Only a limited amount of work has been done to date in terms of projecting the increased magnitude of extreme events under climate change (IPCC, 1997), but even using past climate variability to estimate temperature and precipitation extremes under a doubling of CO_2 presents sobering evidence of the levels temperature and precipitation could reach. Coastal flooding, a constant problem in much of Southeast Asia, would increase both in terms of flood frequency and the size or level of floods (Parry et al., 1992; Lonergan, 1994). This could cause population displacement and the related problems of environmental refugees. Periodic droughts in arid and semi-arid regions, already a cause of population displacement and conflict, could become more frequent and more long-lasting. Israel has already threatened to abrogate sections of the peace agreement with the Jordanians relating to water because of continued drought in the region (*Jerusalem Report*, 13 March 2000). In the future, countries may be wary of interbasin, international transfer of water if they feel their sovereignty may be threatened as a result of variable climatic conditions.

Water and Violent Conflict

The above description paints a mixed picture of the world's water situation. Increasing demand, degradation of existing supplies, increasing variability in rainfall and longer and more severe droughts, and continued tensions over water use and management all present a dim scenario for the future. Nevertheless, international agreements, joint management efforts, and long-standing multinational institutions such as the Mekong River Commission and the International Joint Commission (between the United States and Canada) give some cause for optimism. Nevertheless, interpreting the above data pessimistically and citing historical precedence, many authors have made reference to potential future water conflicts. Although not inevitable, the various crises noted above make conflicts over water seem likely to occur in the future. But will these conditions of water scarcity lead to *violent* conflict?

The Middle East has been cited as the best example of a region where disputes over water can lead to violent conflict. Particularly important candidates for potential water conflicts are the Nile River, with ten riparian states, the Jordan River, and the Euphrates River (Biswas et al., 1997; Hillel, 1994; Rogers and Lydon, 1994). In the following section, I will refer to examples from this region.

Historically, water has been a target of military activity or water supplies have been damaged as a consequence of military activity. Water supply infrastructure is often the first utility to be disrupted during times of war, and it is an obvious target for terrorist activity. Gleick (1993c) identifies five categories of cause and effect relationships: 1) Resources as strategic targets. 2) Resources as strategic tools. 3) Resources as strategic goals. 4) Resource inequities as roots to conflict. 5) Environmental services and conditions as roots to conflict.[4] One of the first actions of the Arabs after the British left Palestine in 1948 was to cut off the water supply to Jerusalem. The PLO's first terrorist activity after its founding in 1964 was an attempt to sabotage Israel's National Water Carrier. And Iraqi bombing of Kuwait's desalination plants during the Gulf War provides a recent-day example.

Water has also been used as a strategic tool. The most obvious example is the threat by Turkey in the early 1990s to restrict the flow of the Euphrates River to pressure Syria to discontinue its support of Kurdish separatists in Turkey (Vesilind, 1993). Despite assurances to the contrary by then Turkish president Ozal that the country would never hold downstream riparians hostage by restricting the flow of the Euphrates, it is not unlikely, based on this specific threat, that Turkey would be more than willing to use water as a tool to manipulate Syrian policy.

In short, water supply facilities are an obvious target during military activity. In this sense, with water as a dependent variable, water and conflict are related. Cases where water is the cause of, or a major contributor to, conflict (i.e., water as an independent variable) are more difficult to determine. In theory, such a link between water and conflict is possible, but only under certain conditions. Upstream riparians must have the ability to restrict the flow of water to downstream users or, in extreme cases, even make the water unfit for consumptive uses downstream. For this to occur, there must also be an imbalance of military power in the favor of the upstream riparian. In the case of the Nile River, for example, it is doubtful that any upstream riparian would threaten Egypt's stated allocation of 55.5 billion m[3] per year (set as part of the 1959 Egypt-Sudan agreement) for fear of military reprisal from Egypt. On the Euphrates, however, the balance of power rests with Turkey (and its allies). Unquestionably, there have been considerable tensions over the Euphrates River, but, to date, these have not escalated into armed conflict. The lack of empirical evidence linking water and conflict inspired Beaumont's conclusion that 'The likelihood of conflict over water is obviously not directly correlated with per capita water availability' (Beaumont, 1997: 363). However, there is some evidence to the contrary. Wenche Hauge and Tanja Ellingsen (2001) incorporated water as one of three independent environmental variables in their study of the relationship between environmental degradation and armed conflict, and concluded that this relationship (for the period 1980–1992) was positive. However, they also found that the link was stronger between water availability and armed conflict than it was for civil war. The suggestion is that water, and other environmental variables, may be more important in explaining smaller conflicts than larger ones.

Examples where water is treated as a strategic *goal* or where *inequities* over water availability may lead to violent conflict are anecdotal and much less convincing. For example, Myers (1993: 27) argues that 'Israel started the 1967 war in part because the Arabs were planning to divert the waters of the Jordan River system'. John Cooley (1984) and John Bulloch and Adil Darwish (1993) provide historical evidence to support the idea that water was a major factor contributing to the 1967 war. This is in stark contrast to former Prime Minister Begin, who admitted in 1982 that the 1967 conflict was not a 'war of necessity, but a war of choice' (as quoted in Ball and Ball, 1992: 113). There is little evidence—other than hearsay—that water played a major role in the 1967 war. Similarly, Hussein Amery and Atif Kubursi (1992: 56) claim that the invasion of Lebanon by Israel in 1982 was an attempt to access the Litani River and divert it into the Jordan River system. Again, there has never been any evidence that Israel has taken any water from the Litani River.

In the early 1960s, Israel attacked construction attempts by the Arabs to divert water from the Jordan River into Syria. When Israel attempted to build its National Water Carrier in the demilitarized zone, the Syrians brought troops to the border and some shots were fired. Such incidents must be viewed as relatively minor, given the amount of cooperation that has occurred over international water bodies. There is little question, however, that there have been numerous water-related disputes over the past 5,000 years. Peter Gleick (1998b: 125) provides a chronology of these in his recent book. Whether water was ever a direct cause of violent conflict— assuming one can identify a single cause of violent conflict in any context— is a different question. The conclusion of Aaron Wolf (1999b: 262) is telling: 'As near as we can find, *there has never been a single war fought over water.*' However, there have been over 3,600 treaties signed between A.D. 805 and 1984 relating to international water resources, according to FAO (1984), although most of these relate to navigational use of rivers.

Therefore, despite the increased rhetoric, countries seem rarely to fight over water. Unquestionably, there is tension over water, and when Israel publicly announced it was not going to meet the terms of the peace treaty with Jordan (involving transfer of water) because of drought conditions, there was much international furor. But at the international level, cooperation seems to be much more standard than conflict.

Conflict over water at the subnational level, however, seems to be much more likely, as suggested by Hauge and Ellingsen (2001). As Wolf (1999b: 256) notes,

This is not to say there is no history of water-related violence—quite the opposite is true—only that these incidents are at the sub-national level, generally between tribe, water-use sector, or province. Examples of internal water conflicts, are quite prevalent, from interstate violence and death along the Cauvery

River in India, to California farmers blowing up a pipeline meant for Los Angeles, to much of the violent history in the Americas between indigenous peoples and European settlers.

Is there likely to be violent conflict over water in the future? Past experience suggests that this is unlikely. However, John Bulloch and Adil Darwish (1993) claim that the probability of conflict over water is increasing, and population growth, mining of aquifers, deteriorating water quality, and increased economic growth may combine to make water conflicts likely in the future. Despite this pessimism, it remains that fighting over water makes very little sense economically or politically. As Avraham Tamir (1988: 56) noted, 'Why go to war over water? For the price of a week's fighting, you could build five desalination plants. No loss of life, no international pressure, and a reliable supply you don't have to defend in hostile territory'. One attempt to measure both the value of water and the value of property rights in dispute between Israel and the Palestinians has been made (Fisher, 1994). The value (under different scenarios) is less than $200 million (in 1994 U.S. dollars). According to the author, this amount is sufficiently small for nations to negotiate (the assumption being that it is too small to go to war over; Fisher, 1994). Desalination provides another alternative to conflict over water. Although estimates of the costs of large-scale desalination plants in the future vary considerably (see Lonergan and Brooks, 1994), they are still much less than the costs of going to war. Peter Beaumont (1997) is even more explicit about the value of water in various uses affecting the likelihood of conflict. Since 70–80 percent of water is used for low-value crops, then any armed conflict over water will over low-value irrigation water (Beaumont, 1997). Accordingly, there are many other lower cost options available to countries, such as importing food, rather than engaging in conflict. However, it does appear that while interstate conflict over water is unlikely, intrastate conflict may occur under certain conditions. Despite simple economic logic, water is a strategic resource in much of the world, and tensions over water will likely remain.

An Example from the Middle East

The Jordan River basin has often been presented as one of the key examples of where there has been conflict over water—and where there may be water wars in the future. Central to the tensions that exist between Israel and the Palestinians (and neighbouring Arab countries) is the availability of adequate freshwater supplies. There are also significant constraints on the level of agricultural output for the Palestinians owing to a lack of water resources and increased mining and deterioration of the groundwater supply. Admittedly, the situation in Gaza is the result of overpumping by large

Palestinian landowners. In the West Bank, however, inequitable distribution and pricing of water are major issues. The situation has become so extreme that former King Hussein of Jordan is rumoured to have stated that water is the only issue that would lead him to go to war with Israel (Myers, 1993). Despite the recent advances made in the peace discussions, the water issue remains a major stumbling block to a lasting peace in the region.

Virtually all of Israel's freshwater comes from two sources: surface water supplied by the Jordan River, or ground water fed by recharge from the West Bank to one of three major aquifers. There is a long legacy of controversy over freshwater in the region, dating back thousands of years. In the 1950s, there was a proposed comprehensive plan for cooperative use of the Jordan River (the Johnston Plan), but this was derailed by mistrust among the four riparian states (Israel, Jordan, Lebanon, and Syria). Each nation has tended to follow its own water policies since the failure of that agreement, often to the detriment of other nations.

Water has long been considered a security issue in the region, and on numerous occasions, Israel and its neighbouring Arab states have feuded over access to Jordan River waters. As noted above, a number of authors have argued that a major contributing factor in the tensions leading to the 1967 war was the water issue. At the time, Israel was consuming almost 100 percent of its available freshwater supplies. Occupation of the three territories (the West Bank, the Golan Heights, and the Gaza Strip) after the war changed this situation in two ways. First, it increased the freshwater available to Israel by almost 50 percent. Second, it gave the country almost total control over the headwaters of the Jordan River and its tributaries, as well as control over the major recharge region for its underground aquifers. Control of water resources in the West Bank and the Golan Heights is now integrated into Israel's economy and, accordingly, is essential to its future.

Presently, Israel draws over 40 percent of its freshwater supplies from the West Bank alone, and the country would face immediate water shortages and a significant curtailment of its agricultural and industrial development if it lost control of these supplies. Former Israeli agricultural minister Rafael Eitan stated in November 1990 that Israel must never relinquish the West Bank because a loss of its water supplies would threaten the Jewish state (*Haaretz*, 15 November 1990). The growing number of settlements in the region poses an additional problem. The water in the West Bank is now used in a ratio of 4.5 percent by Palestinians and 95.5 percent by Israelis (while the population is over 90 percent Palestinian). The UN Committee on Palestinian Rights concluded in 1980 that Israel had given priority to its own water needs at the expense of the Palestinian people.

To ensure security of the water supply from the West Bank aquifers, Israel has put in place quite restrictive policies regarding Palestinian use of water. Israel's application of restrictions on Palestinian development and use of water not only improves its access to West Bank water, but also extends its control throughout the territory. This inequitable situation with respect to water allocations increases resentment and adds to tensions in the region.

Statistical Evidence

Thomas Homer-Dixon (1991, 1994) hypothesizes that resource scarcity can lead to three types of conflict: *simple scarcity conflict* (where scarcity with result in two nations or groups fighting over the resource), *group identity conflict* (where groups might be displaced from a resource scarce region—environmental refugees—and migrate to another region, causing tension and conflict), or *relative deprivation conflict* (where one group feels deprived of a resource relative to another). The first case seems the most straightforward; resource scarcity among states will result in violent conflict and international warfare. Again, anecdotal evidence is used to support this hypothesis.

It is unquestionably true that water is a scarce—and strategic—resource in many regions. But there is only one statistical study (Toset, Gleditsch, and Hegre, 2000) that focuses on shared rivers and the probability of armed conflict. Their main hypothesis is that everything else being equal, countries that share a river will have a higher probability of conflict than countries not sharing a river (the river can form part of the international boundary, or merely cross the boundary). However, their study does not address the issue of water scarcity directly, so it cannot be considered an appropriate test of Homer-Dixon's hypothesis. In general, their results support the hypothesis that countries with shared rivers have a slightly higher frequency of dispute outbreaks than other sets of countries, yet they are unable to determine whether the disputes are specifically over water.

The Future of Water and Conflict

Problems of water scarcity and water pollution affect human and ecosystem health, and hinder economic and agricultural development. Local and regional problems, in turn, may affect the rest of the world by threatening food supplies and global economic development. The UN Commission on Sustainable Development (UN, 1998) concludes that these problems could result in a series of local and regional water crises, with serious global implications.

The basis for most projections for water conflicts in the future is that with the growth of demand, the decline in freshwater availability (through groundwater mining and pollution), and the adverse health effects from poor water quality, water scarcity will result in violent conflict and water wars. There is little question that water scarcity will be a problem in some regions in the future. Global warming will likely alter rainfall patterns and evapo-transpiration regimes in many regions, and long-term planning for water supply *must* take this into consideration. There is also little question that water will cost more as it becomes increasingly scarce. This will necessitate improvements in water efficiency and possibly the restructuring of economies away from water-intensive sectors. The greatest improvements can be made in the agricultural sector, since irrigated agriculture accounts for almost 70 percent of water use internationally (Gleick, 1998b). As the price of water increases, we are also seeing different distribution systems in operation: water moved by tanker; by long-distance pipeline; and even by plastic bags. We may also see greater use of desalination technology, although to date the cost has been prohibitively expensive, and operations are confined primarily to countries with surplus energy supplies. Importing water—as Singapore does—may become more the norm. And cooperative agreements and preventive diplomacy over shared water supplies will continue to be the dominant scenario.

Two other factors may play a role in water-related tension in the future. First, food imports may be driven by water scarcity. Half the world population will depend on the world food market for their food security (Falkenmark et al., 1989). How poor, water-scarce countries will finance these food imports may become a major issue. Second, there is expected to be increased competition for water: between urban and rural populations; between the agriculture and domestic sectors; and between countries. This competition may be further exacerbated by rapid urbanization in many countries. Nevertheless, many of the problems with water supply in the future can be resolved through cooperative agreements and some degree of economic investment.

Conclusion

This chapter attempted to clarify the arguments for and against water scarcity as a potential factor in violent conflict. It reviewed historical arguments, one statistical study, and the rhetoric on future conditions, and concludes that the probability of international wars over water is low. Historically, there is little evidence that water scarcity has caused violent conflict. However, there are numerous cases where water has been used as a strategic goal or target, as part of military activities. At the subnational level, there have been numerous disputes over water, and it might be the case that probability of violent conflict over water varies inversely with the size (and type) of the political bodies involved. However, there is little question that issues of water scarcity will be at the forefront of the international agenda for decades to come. In some cases, water may even be a contributing factor in international conflict. Uri Shamir, Israeli hydrology professor and a member of the Israeli negotiating team to the Middle East Peace Process, once noted: 'If there is a political will for peace, water will not be a hindrance. If you want reasons to fight, water will give you ample opportunities.'[5]

Steve C. Lonergan, b. 1950, Ph.D. in regional science (University of Pennsylvania, 1981), professor of geography, University of Victoria, British Columbia, Canada. He also directs the Global Environmental Change and Human Security project (see www.gechs.org) for the International Human Dimensions Program on Global Environmental Change. His research focuses on water and security in the Middle East, and he is coauthor of *Watershed: The Role of Freshwater in the Israeli-Palestinian Conflict* (with David Brooks, 1994). His most recent edited volume is *Environmental Change, Adaptation and Security* (Kluwer Academic, 1999).

Notes

1. Reprinted by permission.
2. For the full text of the Dublin Statement, see http://www.wmo.ch/web/homs/icwedece.html.
3. That such quotations cannot be substantiated reflects the state of the media coverage on these issues.
4. See Lonergan and Brooks (1994) for a more detailed discussion of these categories and their application to the Israeli-Palestinian conflict.
5. Personal communication, as cited in Vesilind (1993: 48).

Chapter Seven

Resource Constraints or Abundance?

BJØRN LOMBORG

It is frequently claimed that environmental degradation is one of several reasons for armed conflicts. For example, in a recent Worldwatch paper, it is argued 'the depletion of freshwater resources, excessive exploitation of fisheries, degradation of arable land, and deforestation, among other problems, not only affect human health and well-being and imperil the habitability of some regions, but they are also increasingly understood to play an important role in generating or exacerbating some conflicts' (Renner, 1999: 39).

In general, the argument holds that conflicts arise over scarce resources. The Brundtland report contends that 'nations have often fought to assert or resist control over war materials, energy supplies, land, river basins, sea passages, and other key environmental resources' (Brundtland et al., 1987: 290). The key question is whether environmental degradation leads to resource scarcities and in turn to armed conflict. A large part of the evidence, pro and con, has been collected in this volume.

Nevertheless, the main focus of this chapter is to question the assumption of gloom—the unstated or at least undocumented premise that the environment indeed is getting worse over time, such that we can expect more environmentally induced conflict in the future. The results we see in this volume and other scholarly texts are clearly formulated in a hypothetical fashion: 'If environmental degradation sets in, this will (or will not) cause higher risks of conflict'. There is often a general tendency throughout the entire discussion to *presume* that environmental scarcity indeed sets in

more and more often. Consequently, it is important to look at this unveri-
fied background assumption.

Thomas Homer-Dixon and his associates have carried out a large number of case studies on the connections between environment and conflict
(Percival and Homer-Dixon, 2001, Homer-Dixon, 1999; Homer-Dixon
and Blitt, 1998). They focus on three types of scarcity: *supply-induced* (resulting from environmental degradation and resource depletion), *demand-
induced* (resulting from population and consumption growth), and *structural* (resulting from an unequal resource distribution) (Percival and
Homer-Dixon, 2001).

Here, I shall look at some of the main environmental issues surrounding
the three scarcities. The discussion is based heavily on data from my book
(Lomborg, 1998/2001), which also has many more references. Homer-
Dixon's prime example of the first, supply-induced scarcity is soil erosion,
potentially undercutting the food supply. Similar examples are air and water pollution, which could undermine health, agriculture, or even human
survival.

The second, demand-induced scarcity, covers a wide variety of common
ailments. Again, the food supply is under stress, not only from soil erosion
but also from increased demand. This demand is driven up both by larger
populations requiring more calories and by richer populations wanting better calories from meat, milk, fruit, and vegetables. Other resources, such as
energy, raw materials, and water, will similarly experience higher demands,
both from more numerous populations as well as from richer individuals.

Some of the stresses on nonrenewable resources such as oil could equally
well be placed under the heading of supply-induced scarcity, since their
scarcity is also caused by earlier resource depletion. Likewise, supply-induced erosion could be seen as an outcome of increased population demand,
requiring ever more marginal lands to be farmed. These two categories seem
to be derived by fiat and are not very useful for an analytical separation of
the numerous environmental problems. Only the third, structural scarcity, is
conceptually unambiguous, focusing on the inequality of wealth.

Consequently, in this chapter I will deal with the environmental issues
case by case rather than in terms of the three scarcities. Here, I will look at
the empirical circumstances for the food supply, the threat of erosion, the
question of resources, such as energy, raw materials, and water, and finally
the distribution of wealth. These are the major environmental issues that
constitute the background of much of the debate in this book and elsewhere. And the key question, of course, is whether the environmental
stresses really are growing bigger and bigger.

A large number of environmental issues that cannot be discussed here
due to space restrictions are dealt with at great lengths in *Verdens Sande
Tilstand* [The True State of the World] (Lomborg 1998/2001). Clearly,

there are major environmental challenges in the world. For example, 31 percent of the population in the developing world are without access to clean water and 44 percent without access to adequate sanitation. This causes more than 2 million deaths yearly, and more than 500 million annual cases of severe disease.

The largest environmental challenge that is not discussed in this chapter is the greenhouse effect. Depending on the actual size of climate change, this could have severe, long-term distributional effects, positive for the developed and negative for the developing world. Yet, with its slow, century-scale impact it is unlikely to have any major consequences for conflict within the next few decades. And with the current state of knowledge it is exceedingly difficult to assert with any precision the long-run consequences for conflict.

Food and Hunger

'The battle to feed humanity is over. In the course of the 1970s the world will experience starvation of tragic proportions—hundreds of millions of people will starve to death' (Ehrlich, 1968: xi). This was the introduction of one of the most influential books on hunger, Paul Ehrlich's *The Population Bomb*. More than 3 million copies of the book have been sold.

From the same quarter Lester Brown, who later became president of the Worldwatch Institute and one of the most prominent doomsayers, wrote in 1965 that 'the food problem emerging in the less-developing regions may be one of the most nearly insoluble problems facing man over the next few decades' (Brown, 1965).

There seems to be an underlying assumption in many environmental debates that food production has lost or is losing the race against population. But this belief is wrong. Although there are now almost twice as many of us as in 1961, each of us has *more* to eat, in both developed and developing countries, and fewer people are starving.

Malthus and Hunger

To many it seems evident that more people on Earth must mean less food for each individual. This obvious theory was formulated in 1798 by the English clergyman Thomas Malthus, and made uncannily popular in the 1970s by the best-seller *Limits to Growth* (Meadows et al., 1972). The theory holds that population grows exponentially, while food production only grows linearly, such that population sooner or later will outrun food production.

Malthus's theory is so simple and attractive that it has attracted many reputable scientists. It has been championed by Worldwatch Institute, which annually produces the most widely read environmental tract, *State of the World* (WI, annual). But it does not fit well with data.

The population rarely grows exponentially—actually the rate of population growth has been declining since 1964 (ERS, 1995). The quantity of food seldom grows linearly. In actual fact, the world's agricultural production has more than doubled since 1961, and in developing countries it has more than tripled.

Food for the Masses

Consequently, we now have far more food per member of the population than we used to, even though the population has almost doubled. Figure 7.1 shows that our calorie intake has increased by 15 percent on a worldwide basis, and that developing countries have experienced a dramatic increase of 25 percent.

The calorie figure is, nonetheless, an average, which might conceal a mixture of overeating and starvation. In the first global food survey in 1970, however, the Food and Agriculture Organization (FAO) estimated that 35 percent of all individuals in the developing countries were starving. In 1990, that figure had dropped to 21 percent, and in 2010 it is expected to drop even further to 12 percent (WFS, 1996: 1, table 3). This decline is even more remarkable since it has coincided with a doubling of the population of the developing countries. Actually, the *absolute number* of people starving in the Third World has also decreased. Although in 1971 almost 920 million people were starving, the total fell to below 840 million in 1991. In 2010 it is expected to fall to 680 million. These figures are, of course, still frighteningly high. But over the same period more than 3 billion more people were brought out of starvation.

Prices

At the same time as Earth accommodates ever more people, who require ever more food, food prices have fallen dramatically. The fall in the price of food is a genuine long-term tendency. The price of wheat has declined to one-sixth of the level in the 1840s. The fall in prices has been particularly marked in the postwar period and applied to more or less all major types of food (Figure 7.2). As of this writing, food has never been as cheap.

Since prices reflect the scarcity of a product, foodstuffs have actually become less scarce during this century despite the fact that the population has tripled and demand increased by even more. This has primarily been possible by the so-called Green Revolution, focusing on high-yield crops, irrigation, fertilizers, and pesticides, essentially getting more food out of each

FIGURE 7.1   Daily Intake of Calories Per Capita, 1961–1997

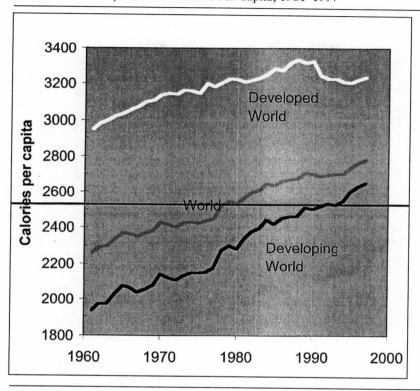

SOURCE: FAO (2000).

hectare of soil. The new varieties have led to a 50 percent increase in maximum yields since 1960.

Improvements in the provision of food per capita have not been evenly distributed throughout all regions. There has been a solid increase in South Asia and Latin America, whereas the Near East and East Asia have experienced a fantastic increase of over 28 percent. Unfortunately, this improvement has not been shared by sub-Saharan Africa. This unfortunate situation is *not* caused by environmental problems—much of sub-Saharan Africa has a large, agricultural potential. The reason is more to be found in societal circumstances. Since decolonisation in the late 1950s, sub-Saharan Africa has been plagued by political and economic instability, where civil and ethnic conflict have been more the rule than the exception. Added to this, the region has been plagued by corruption, inadequate infrastructure, poor education, and politically fixed farm prices, all of which have ham-

FIGURE 7.2   World Bank Price Index for Foodstuffs. 1957–July 1999 = 1

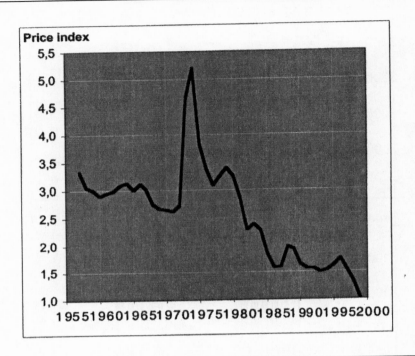

SOURCE: IMF (1999), CPI (1999).

pered agricultural development. In an extremely frank statement, the United Nations Development Program (UNDP) affirms that 'it is not the resources or the economic solutions that are lacking—it is the political momentum to tackle poverty head-on' (UNDP, 1996).

Food in the Future

The record till now is clear—the world is better fed and has fewer starving people. But the question is whether this can go on. It is often argued that the Green Revolution is running out of steam. We are beginning to experience 'a massive loss of momentum', writes Lester Brown (WI, 1994: 179). Growth is slowing and 'either levels off or shows signs of doing so' (WI, 1998: 88). This is true in the sense that global growth rates in yields have been declining for both rice, wheat, and corn, making up almost 50 percent of the world's calorie intake. In the 1970s rice yield annually grew by 2.1

percent, whereas yield growth now is down to 1.5 percent annually, and the figures look similar for wheat and corn (WFS, 1996: 6: Box 1). Should we be worried?

It is useful to subdivide this into three questions. First, does the reduced growth in yields indicate that we are reaching the biological and physiological limits of plant efficiency? Second, what is the effect of possible limits to the ordinary, developing world farmer? Third, does humanity now really need the high growth rates?

An argument is often made to suggest that we are reaching biological limits. For instance, Brown tells us that the American wheat yield has not improved since 1983, and that this indicates an approaching limit (WI, 1998: 82ff). However, the choice of 1983 is crucial to Brown's argument, in that it was the previous top year. The choice of U.S. wheat is similarly decisive, since wheat yields in almost all other regions have been steadily increasing and outcompeting the United States.

Theoretically, there seems to be very little empirical foundation to the idea of impending limits. Tony Fischer, the leader of wheat research in the organization that led the Green Revolution, argues that: 'It is a popular misconception that wheat research has not made much progress since the rapid gains of the Green Revolution during the 1960s'. Actually, since that time 'we have steadily added to the yield potential of wheat at an average rate of about 1 percent per year'.[1] At the same time, the new strains have become more resistant to diseases and more efficient in their use of water and nutrients.

The International Rice Research Institute has announced a prototype of new rice yielding up to 25 percent more than the current modern high-yielding varieties.[2]

Second, it is important to look at the situation of ordinary peasants. By far the largest part of the peasants in the developing countries achieve much lower yields than even the locally best ones. Consequently, there is generally much room for improvement. FAO has specifically examined growth in yields in the developing countries. 'For the developing countries as a whole, the growth rates of per caput agricultural production (all products) have not been generally lower in recent eight-year moving periods compared with earlier ones'. Therefore, the FAO points out that 'in the light of this evidence, it is difficult to accept a position that developments in recent years have marked a turning point for the worse' (FAO, 1995b: 44).

Third, do we need the high growth in the future? Of course, when growth in yield for rice has declined from 2.1 percent to 1.5 percent it could seem troublesome. But at the same time population growth has also dropped from over 2 percent in the 1970s to less than 1.3 percent today, and it will further drop below 0.5 percent within the next fifty years. Consequently, a *smaller* growth in production today can actually give *more* to each individual than what a considerably larger growth could achieve in the 1970s.

In summary, the FAO states that that there is no need to worry about the diminished growth in agricultural production. Basically it 'reflects some positive developments in the world demographic and development scenes': the world population grows ever slower, and inhabitants in more and more countries are reaching a level of food consumption where they cannot eat much more (FAO, 1995b: 5; WFS, 1996: 1: 4.6–7).

Indeed, the FAO predicts that there will be *more* food for *more* people in the year 2010 (WFS 1996: 1, table 3). It is expected that there will be fewer malnourished and that all regions will experience increasing available calories per capita. The same general conclusion is reached by IFPRI, USDA, and the World Bank—and all three predict even lower prices.[3]

Erosion

Another common worry in the literature is 'the degradation and depletion of an environmental resource, for example, the erosion of cropland' (Percival and Homer-Dixon 2001). This fear is based on the fact that when earth erodes owing to the effects of rain and wind, then it loses its nutrients and is rendered less capable of retaining water, consequently leading to smaller yields. Lester Brown has estimated that globally we lose 26 billion tons of topsoil annually (Crosson, 1996). Another, even higher estimate is that we lose upward of 75 billion tons of topsoil annually (Pimentel et al., 1995).

These figures are based on very few and uncertain estimates, primarily from the United States. David Pimentel found in 1974 that the United States lost 30 tons of topsoil per hectare, whereas we know today that the true figure was 12 tons per hectare.[4] His estimate of 17 tons per hectare for all of Europe has turned out—through a string of articles, each slightly inaccurately referring to its predecessor—to stem from a single study of an 0.11 hectare sloping Belgian farmland; the author himself warns against generalization (Boardman, 1998).

More important, Pimentel neglects to discuss the two primary erosion studies, of which one has been sponsored by the UN. The studies seem to indicate that the effect on agricultural production is vastly overstated. There is no doubt that over the last couple of hundred years we have lost more topsoil than what has been created, and that the absolute loss is increasing primarily because of expanding agriculture (Rozanov, Targulian, and Orlov, 1990: 205). Moreover, soil erosion has occurred since the beginning of agriculture and writers of the classical era were already worried about this phenomenon.

The important point here is the effect of erosion on agricultural productivity. Here, there is no one-to-one connection. FAO (1995b: 357) states that the impact of erosion 'on crop yields or production has not been well established in physical terms though there have been many attempts to do so. The relationship between erosion and productivity loss is more complex than previously thought'. FAO adds that much of the soil disappearing simply is deposited further down the slope, valley, or plain, and that the yield loss in the eroded area could be compensated by yield gains elsewhere. It turns out that only very little eroded topsoil moves very far—the last 200 years of water erosion in Wisconsin has moved only 5 percent of the eroded soil all the way into the river (Crosson, 1997a).

The two primary global studies of the effect of erosion on productivity have gone down different paths. The one study has drawn on data from FAO to estimate the spatial extent and productivity effects of land degradation in the world's dry areas that constitute the most vulnerable lands. The annual drop in productivity is estimated at 0.3 percent per year (Crosson, 1996, 1997a,b). The other study, which has been cosponsored by the UN environmental organization UNEP, has asked almost 200 soil experts for their expert assessment on the extent and severity of land degradation in their respective areas, an information that has been compiled into a large World Soil Degradation Map (Oldeman et al., 1991; Buol, 1994: 218ff). About 17 percent of all land is degraded to some extent, but only 0.07 percent is strongly degraded. In total, this erosion has incurred a cumulative loss of 5 percent of agricultural production over the forty-five years from the end of World War II, or about 0.1 percent per year.

The question of soil erosion has to be seen in light of the annual productivity increase of 1–2 percent, stemming from higher-yield varieties, better farming practices, and higher use of irrigation, pesticides, and fertilization. Compared to this productivity increase the effect of soil erosion is so small that it may not justify an extra effort to halt or reverse it. Clearly, many resources are used each year by farmers to safeguard their lands against serious erosion, that is, by fertilizing to avoid nutrient depletion, creating terraces to hold water and soil, and contour plowing and strip-farming. A primary problem is poor peasants who cannot afford to think of tomorrow and consequently overexploit their land today. Today it is technically possible to maintain the content and composition of soil indefinitely under proper agricultural management.

For the United States it is estimated that the total effect of soil erosion over the next hundred years will be about 3 percent. 'By comparison with yield gains expected from advances in technology, the 3 percent erosion-induced loss is trivial' (FAO, 1995b: 119). Soil erosion is primarily a local problem and often a consequence of poverty. However, the present evidence does not seem to indicate that soil erosion in any significant degree will affect our global food production, since its effects both up till now has been and in the future is expected to be heavily outweighed by the vast increase in food productivity.

Energy

We often hear of the imminent running out of oil. For instance, on 11 May 1996 CNN told us that over the next ten to fifteen years we will have a new oil crisis.[5] As the demand for oil increases, and the present oil resources run out, cheap oil will soon be a thing of the past. The party is over. Ahead awaits price increases, economic crises, and long lines at gas stations. Once again, this interpretation does not fit well with the data. There are good reasons to believe that we will not get dramatic price increases, and that we actually will be able to handle our future energy needs.

Limits to Growth

The oil crisis happened because during the 1970s and the beginning of the 1980s the OPEC countries were able to exploit their near-monopoly situation and raise the prices. But it was never an indication of an actual scarcity. There was enough oil and there still is.

Nevertheless, the influential book *Limits to Growth* made the argument that we should have run out of oil before 1992, basically by using the same Malthusian food arguments of exponential growth in demand but with an even more limited supply (Meadows et al., 1972: 58). The revised edition, *Beyond the Limits*, still argued that our resources would run out soon (Meadows et al., 1992: 74 et passim). The first edition might have been somewhat mistaken in the exact prediction of the year of resource exhaustion, but *now* we would soon see the problems cropping up.

Actually, we have long been told that we were running out of oil. In 1914 the U.S. Bureau of Mines estimated that there would be enough oil left for only ten years consumption. In 1930 the Department of the Interior projected that oil would last only thirteen more years, and again in 1951 it was projected that oil would run out thirteen years later (Simon, 1996: 165). As Frank Notestein of Princeton said in his old days: 'we've been running out of oil ever since I've been a boy' (Simon et al., 1994: 325). Again, in 1987 we were told that the oil crisis would return in the 1990s (Ehrlich and Ehrlich, 1987: 222). None of these predictions have come true.

Oil

Here I shall mainly look at the worries about the supply of oil used for energy. With a value of 1.6 percent of global GNP, oil is today the most important and most valuable commodity in international trade. Oil is the most versatile of the three primary fossil fuels. Oil has a high energy content, it is relatively compact, and it is easy to transport.

FIGURE 7.3   Oil Price 1871–1998 in 1998 US$, and
World Production 1882–1997

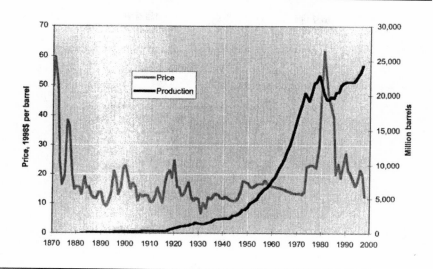

SOURCES: Simon et al. (1995), EIA (1998: table 3.1), EIA (1997: table 11.5), CPI (1999).

How can oil scarcity be measured? Even if we were to run out of oil, this would not mean that oil was unavailable, only that it would be very expensive. Figure 7.3 shows that the price of oil has not had any long-term upward trend despite the strongly rising oil consumption. The price of oil in 1999 was on par with the lowest prices before the oil crisis. Actually, the real price of gas at the pump (the consumer price), even including tax, was never lower in the United States, because most of the price consists of refining and transportation, both of which have experienced huge efficiency increases.

Although consumption has increased, Figure 7.4 demonstrates that we have more reserves than ever before. This may seem astounding. Common sense would tell us that if we have thirty-five years of consumption in 1955, then we should have thirty-four years left the year after or even less since we consumed more oil in 1956 than in the previous year. But Figure 7.4 shows that over time the estimated reserves have been increasing.[6] Although rising oil consumption (with the exception of the 1970s) fits the doomsayers' prediction, the data on the known reserves contradict them, as does the long-term decline in oil prices.

FIGURE 7.4   World Oil Reserves Compared to the Annual Production, 1920

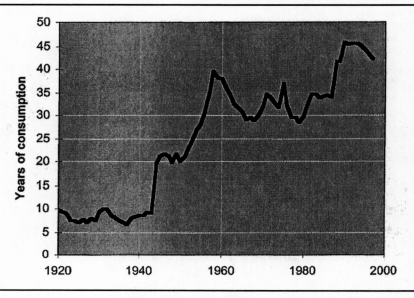

SOURCES: Simon et al. (1995), EIA (1997: tables 11.3, 11.5), EIA (1998: table 11.3). Total reserves until 1944 are only American, since 1944 for the entire world.

The Central Argument

How can increasing oil consumption leave us with greater reserves, not smaller? The answer is found in three central arguments against the limited resources approach:

First, 'known resources' is not a finite entity. We do not *know* all the places with oil, so that we now just need to pump it up. We explore new areas and find new oil. But since prospecting is very expensive, new searches will not be initiated too far in advance of production. Consequently, new oil fields will be continuously added as demand rises.

Second, we become better at exploiting resources. We use new technology to be able to extract more oil from known oil fields, we become better at finding new oil fields, and we can start exploiting oil fields that previously were too expensive or difficult to exploit. An initial drilling typically only exploits 20 percent of the oil in the reservoir. Even with present-day, advanced techniques, using water, steam, or chemical flooding to squeeze out extra oil, more than half the resource commonly remains in the ground unexploited. It is estimated that the ten largest oil fields in the United States will still contain 63 percent of their original oil when production closes down (Craig et al., 1996: 134). Consequently, there is still much to be reaped in this area.

At the same time we have improved our exploitation of each liter of oil— the car gets a better mileage, the heater is more efficient, goods can be produced with less energy. In Denmark electric home appliances have become 20–45 percent more effective over the last ten years (DMU, 1998: 238).

In fact, most developed nations use less energy to produce each dollar, euro, or yen in their national product. Denmark seems to have completely 'delinked' the connection between a higher GNP and a higher energy consumption: Overall, Denmark used *less* energy in 1989 than in 1970 despite a GNP growth of 48 percent during that time (Turner et al., 1994: 45–46).

Third, we can substitute sources of energy. We do not require oil as such, but rather the services it can provide. Most often we want heating, energy, or fuel, and these services can be obtained from other sources. Therefore, we can switch to other energy sources if they were to show themselves better or cheaper. In England around the year 1600 wood became increasingly expensive (owing to local deforestation and poor infrastructure) and this prompted a gradual move to coal. During the latter part of the last century a similar substitution took place from coal to oil.

If we were to run into oil shortages in the short term we might replace oil with other commonly known fossil fuels such as gas and coal. But in the longer run it is quite possible that we will cover a large part of our energy consumption from nuclear power, wind and solar power, biomass, and shale oil.

Other Fossil Energy Sources

Gas is a clean and cheap energy source, but requires a large pipeline distribution system. Gas has had the greatest growth of all fossil energy sources since World War II—production has increased elevenfold since 1950. At the same time, like oil, gas has become *more* abundant. In 1976 we had enough gas for the next fifty-one years at the contemporary level of consumption; in 1996 we had gas for sixty-three years, despite a much higher consumption (BP, 1998).

Historically, coal has been the most important fossil fuel, but after World War II it was partially displaced by oil. Coal can supply us with energy for a long time to come. As with oil and gas reserves, coal reserves have increased in time. In 1978 we had sufficient coal to cover the next 191 years at the 1978 level. But despite a substantial increase in consumption since then, in 1996 we had coal reserves sufficient for the next 224 years.[7] The total coal resources are estimated to be even larger—it is presumed that there is sufficient coal far beyond the next 1,500 years (Craig et al., 1996: 159).

Several other discoveries have also expanded the fossil resources considerably. An increasing amount of attention has been given to tar sands and shale oil. Both contain oil that unfortunately is much harder to extract and consequently more expensive to exploit. In Canada oil has been extracted from tar sands since 1978 and the costs have dropped from $28 per barrel to just $11.[8] For comparison the price of a barrel of Brent oil was $12.37 in 1998, and back up around $20 in mid-1999.

The U.S. Energy Information Agency estimates that today it would be possible to produce about 550 billion barrels of oil from tar sands and shale oil at a price below $30, making it possible to increase the present global oil reserves by 50 percent (EIA 1997b: 37). And it is estimated that within twenty-five years we can produce commercially twice as much as the world's present oil reserves. The total size of shale oil resources is quite numbing. It is estimated that globally there is about *242 times more* oil in shale oil than the conventional petroleum resources (Craig et al., 1996: 159). This stunning amount of energy is the equivalent of our present *total* energy consumption for the next approximately 6,500 years.

Consequently, there's no need for any immediate worry about running out of fossil energy. Parts of the fossil fuels, however, are probably only accessible at a higher price. Still, there is good reason to believe that the total energy share of our budget will diminish—even if we continue to depend solely on fossil fuels. Today the global price for energy constitutes less than 2 percent of the global GNP, and yet if we only assume a moderate continued growth in GNP this share will in all likelihood continue to drop. Even assuming truly dramatic price increases on energy of 100 percent in the year 2030, the share of income spent on energy will still have dropped slightly.

Other Sources

In Lomborg (1998/2001), I discuss many of the other energy issues; here I will just point out the immense potential of solar energy. There are great advantages in using renewable energy. It pollutes less, makes a country less dependent on imported fuel, requires less foreign capital, and has almost no carbon dioxide emission (EIA, 1993: 1). Moreover many of the technologies are cheaper, easy to repair and easy to transport, and are ideally suited for developing countries and remote regions.

Right now, renewable energy makes up very little of the commercial energy production—about 3 to 8 percent, almost exclusively from water power and biomass. In the beginning of 1998, the 'true' renewable energy resources of wind, geothermal, and solar made up just 0.024 percent. This low share is a simple consequence of the renewable sources not yet being competitive with fossil fuels (EIA, 1997b: 85). Up to now most renewable energy projects have been completed with public funding and tax rebates. But price has been rapidly declining, and it is expected that this decline will continue.

The currently most competitive energy source with a wide applicability is wind power. The price today is around 5–6.4 cents per kWh, and although this is more than ten times cheaper than the price twenty years ago, it is still somewhat more expensive than energy derived from fossil fuels (DOE, 1997: 7–3).

But the most important fact is that there is potentially plenty of energy—especially from the sun. The solar energy influx is equivalent to about 7,000 times our present global energy consumption. Even with our relatively ineffective solar cells, an area of 2.4 percent of the Sahara Desert could in principle supply our entire global energy requirement. Although prices have dropped fifty times since the early 1970s (EIA, 1993: 13; Ahmed, 1994: 80), solar cells are not quite competitive, but it is predicted that the price will drop even further and it is expected that by 2030 it will have dropped to 5.1 cents per kWh. Particularly in areas that are far from cities and established grids, solar cells are already profitable.

Summary of Energy

There is plenty of energy. Our reserves—even measured in years of consumption—of both oil, coal, and gas have increased. Today we have oil for at least 44 years at present consumption, at least 63 years' worth of gas, and 224 years' worth of coal. At less than twice the current world price, shale oil can supply oil for the next 220 years at current consumption. All in all, there is oil enough for the next 6,500 years. Moreover, there are many options with different renewable energy sources. Renewable energy resources are almost incomprehensibly large—the sun leaves us with about 7,000 times our own energy consumption.

As the U.S. Energy Information Agency wrote in its latest *International Energy Outlook 1999*:

> Bleak pictures painted of the world's remaining oil resource potential are based on current estimates of proven reserves and their decline in a [typical, theoretical] manner. When undiscovered oil, efficiency improvements, and the exploitation of unconventional crude oil resources are taken into account, it is difficult not to be optimistic about the long-term prospects for oil as viable energy source well into the future (EIA, 1999: 23).

Nonenergy Resources

The concern for running out of resources not only applies to energy but also the vast number of other, nonrenewable resources that we use today. Prices of the vast majority of raw materials have been dropping over the last hundred years. The World Bank's index for the world's twenty-four top-selling nonenergy products shows a general, falling tendency across the century (Leon and Soto, 1995: 16). Over the last 100 years prices have been reduced to a third.

The same picture repeats itself for metals. The IMF index in Figure 7.5 shows how prices since 1957 have dropped approximately 50 percent and that metals in the second quarter of 1995 were cheaper than ever before.

Altogether, raw materials make up at most 1.1 percent of the global GNP. Moreover, a rather limited number of raw materials constitute the vast majority of this expense. The value of cement, aluminum, iron, copper, gold, nitrogen, and zinc constitute 80 percent of the global resource production.

FIGURE 7.5   Price Index for Metals, 1957–July 1999, with Second Quarter of 1999 = 1

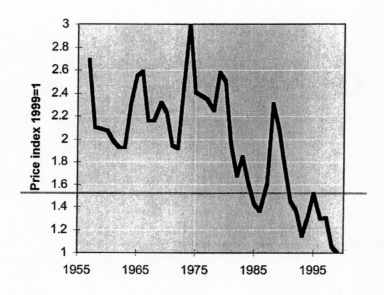

Will We Run Out?

There is no risk of running out of cement (Craig et al., 1996: 340; Hille, 1995: 299). Aluminum is the second most abundant metallic element after silicon—it makes up 8.2 percent of Earth's crust. It is estimated that with the current identified reserves there is sufficient aluminum for 243 years of consumption at the present level. As with oil, gas, and coal, the number of years will not necessarily decline over time, even if we use more and more, because we get better at exploiting existing resources and locating new ones.

In Figure 7.6 we can actually see that for the four most frequently used metals there is no sign of falling years of consumption—indeed, there is a slight upward trend. And this despite the fact that we use ever more of the four raw materials. Aluminum consumption is today more than fourteen times higher than in 1950, and yet the remaining years of consumption have increased from 171 years to 243 years.

Similarly with iron the reserves leaves us with 264 years of consumption at present levels. Figure 7.6 shows that there are *more* years of consumption in 1997 than in 1957 despite the quadrupling of production.

Copper is nowhere as abundant as aluminum and iron. Copper only makes up 0.0058 percent of Earth's crust. Although this is enough for 83

FIGURE 7.6   Years of Consumption of the Four Most Used Metals, 1950

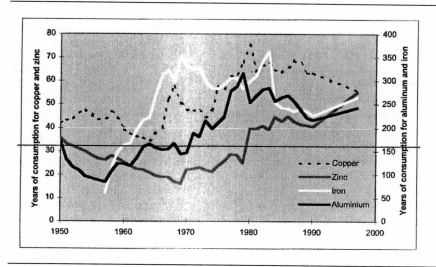

SOURCES: Simon et al. (1995), USGS (1998).

million years of consumption, such a figure is rather fictitious, since we will never be able to extract all the copper. With our present reserves we have enough copper for fifty-six years at present rates of consumption. This figure, however, is still *higher* than in 1950, when we had enough copper left for just forty-two years, despite having consumed about 380 million tons over the period and despite having quintupled consumption. Actually, copper has been found faster than it has been consumed, at least since 1946 (Craig et al., 1996: 273).

Moreover, Earth's crust does not even constitute the most important part of the copper resources. In many places in the deep oceans the seafloor is scattered with small nodules about 5–10 cm in diameter containing manganese, iron, nickel, copper, cobalt, and zinc. It is estimated that the total resources in recoverable nodules are an excess of 1 billion tons of copper, or about the same as the on-land resources (Craig et al., 1996: 273). Consequently, there is at least sufficient copper for a century or more.

Zinc makes up 5 percent of our raw material consumption, and it is mainly used to galvanize steel and iron to prevent rust. Zinc, like copper, is relatively rare—zinc only constitutes 0.0082 percent of Earth's crust, which theoretically is equivalent to 169 million years of consumption, although we could never mine all of it. Nevertheless, we have found much more zinc than has been used, and the number of years of consumption have grown since 1950 from thirty-six to fifty-five years. The demand for zinc has quadrupled since 1950, and yet the price has been dropping slightly.

Nitrogen, Phosphorus, and Potassium

Food production is crucially dependent on three resources—soil, water, and fertilizer. The essential fertilization consists of nitrogen, phosphorus, and potassium, and until the last century this fertilization was mainly achieved with manure. Today, about 6 percent of our raw material expenditure is used on nitrogen, but since nitrogen today is almost exclusively synthesized from air, there is no limit to consumption.

Phosphorus make up about 1 percent of our raw material expenditure. The phosphorus reserves stand at about ninety years at current consumption, but because phosphate rocks look like ordinary shales and limestones, even to experts, we can anticipate discoveries of new, large deposits in the future. Recently, the U.S. Geological Survey announced finding phosphatic crusts and nodules in the continental shelf off Florida containing very large deposits, doubling the phosphorus reserves to about 180 years. Consequently, it is not expected that the availability of phosphorus will become a likely limitation to food production (Craig et al., 1996: 310).

Potassium is the eighth most abundant element in Earth's crust, and there is no cause for concern for this important fertilizer. We spend about 0.1 percent of our raw material budget on potassium. It is estimated that there is at least 357 years of consumption at present levels, and total accessible reserves indicate sufficient potassium for more than 700 years (USGS, 1998).

Moreover, prices on fertilizer have dropped about 40 percent in the postwar period. This is a further indication that fertilizer is not becoming more scarce but rather more abundant.

Conclusion

As should be abundantly clear, we are far from exhausting our raw material resources. The reasons look a lot like the explanations for why we do not run out of oil, gas, and coal: We continuously find new resources, use them more efficiently, recycle them, and substitute them.

Reviewing the forty-seven elements known to have advanced materials applications, studies from the late 1980s showed that only eleven seemed to have potentially insufficient reserves. Today it turns out that for all but three of these, the reserves have become *bigger,* not smaller. The total cost of the last three elements—tantalum, mercury, and cadmium—is about three-millionth of our global GNP.

Moreover, the total economic expense for raw materials is 1.1 percent of global GNP, and 60 percent of our expenses come from raw materials with more than 200 years of consumption left.

Finally, the price on nearly all resources has been declining over the century, and despite an astounding increase in production of a large number of important raw materials they have more years of consumption left than before.

Water

Water is a resource that we often take for granted but that several organizations believe could create trouble in the future.

Global water consumption has quadrupled since 1940 (WRI, 1996: 301). The obvious argument runs: 'This can't go on'. The Worldwatch Institute claims that 'water scarcity may be to the '90s what the oil price shocks were to the '70s'.[9] And a World Bank press release coined the much quoted phrase 'wars in the next century will be over water',[10] even though the actual report being released did not use the word 'war.'

Water is a necessary and wanted resource. But from an economic viewpoint, there is plenty of water as we get richer and better at administering the resource.

FIGURE 7.7   Global Annual Consumption and Per Capita Per Day, 1900–2000

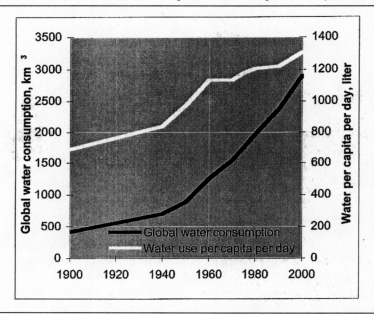

SOURCE: Shiklomanov (1993: 20).

Water in the World

Water is absolutely decisive for human survival. If we are not to exploit the groundwater unsustainably, the question is how much 'new' water we can get each year. The total amount of precipitation on land is about 113,000 cubic kilometers, and taking into account an evaporation of 72,000 cubic kilometers we are left with a net freshwater influx of 41,000 cubic kilometers each year, or the equivalent of 30 cm of water across the entire landmass (Craig et al., 1996: 366–367). This number is equivalent to about 19,000 liters of water for every single person on Earth *every single day*. For comparison, every Dane and every Brit use both directly and through industry and agriculture approximately 500 liters of water per day (WRI, 1998: 304), about 2.6 percent of the possible, global consumption. An American, however, uses about ten times as much water, or 5,000 liters every day.

Looking at the global consumption, each person uses about 1,300 liters per day, or about 6.8 percent of the possible consumption (Shiklomanov, 1993: 20). Over the century, Earth's water consumption has grown from about 400 cubic kilometers to 2,600 cubic kilometers, as is seen in Figure 7.7.

Water consumption per capita has grown from 700 liters a day to 1,305 liters in the year 2000. If this consumption grew at the same rate till the year 2050, with a population of 9.4 billion people, we would use about 5,600 cubic kilometers, or 13.6 percent of the total possible consumption. So what is the worry?

The Central Water Problems

Many countries receive a large part of their water resources from rivers. More than 200 river systems, draining over half of the planet's land area, are shared by two or more countries. At least ten rivers flow through a half dozen or more countries. Most Middle Eastern countries share aquifers (World Bank, 1992: 48; Engelman and LeRoy, 1993). In an international conflict perspective, there are two decisive problems. Are there places where water is a sufficiently scarce resource that battles might be fought? And as the population swells, are these scarcities likely to get worse in the future?

Typically, water scarcity is framed by looking at water per capita, setting cutoff points, and pinpointing water-scarce nations. This approach was prominently advanced in a paper from the organization *Population Action International* in 1993 (Engelman and LeRoy, 1993). The article has since been used countless times (sometimes without explicit acknowledgement). It remains the backdrop for the UN and the World Bank discussion of water scarcity in *World Resources 1996–97*, and it gets prominent references in the standard environmental literature.

Not Enough Water?

Precipitation is not distributed equally. Some countries such as Iceland have almost 2 million liters of water for each inhabitant every day, whereas Kuwait must make do with just 283 liters (WRI, 1996: 306). But when does a country not have *enough* water?

It is estimated that a human being needs about two liters of water today, so clearly this is not the restrictive requirement. The paper from *Population Action International* refers to the so-called *water stress index,* developed by hydrologist Malin Falkenmark, which establishes an approximate minimum level of water per capita to maintain an adequate quality of life in a moderately developed country in an arid zone. She is alleged to have assessed that humans need about 100 liters per day for household needs and personal hygiene, and an additional 500–2,000 liters for agriculture, indus-

TABLE 7.1   Countries with Chronic Water Scarcity
in 1995

	Water, liters per day per capita
Kuwait	283
Libya	304
Singapore	577
Saudi Arabia	697
Jordan	861
Yemen, Rep	982
Israel	1046
Tunisia	1213
Algeria	1447
Burundi	1543
Rwanda	2171
Oman	2445
Egypt	2529

SOURCE: WRI (1996).

try, and energy production. More recent work by Malin Falkenmark (1992, 1993), however, does not even mention any limits beyond the 100 liters per day for personal use.

Since water is often most needed in the dry season, the water stress level is then set even higher; if a country has less than 4,660 liters per person available, it is said to experience periodic or regular water stress. Should the precipitation be less than 2,740 liters the country is said to experience chronic water scarcity.

Table 7.1 shows the thirteen countries in 1995 suffering chronic water scarcity according to the above definition.[11] Are these countries really facing a serious problem? How does Kuwait actually get by with just 283 liters per day? It does not. Kuwait, Libya, and Saudi Arabia all cover a large part of their water demand by desalinating seawater. Desalination requires a large amount of energy (either through freezing or evaporating water), but all of these countries also have great energy resources. The price today for desalinated water is only about $1 per cubic meter, which makes water a more expensive resource, but definitely not out of reach.

Thus, we can have sufficient water, if we can pay for it. *Poverty* and not an absolute resource constraint is the primary limitation. Desalination also establishes a clear upper bound on the weight of water problems in the world. In principle, we could produce Earth's entire present water consumption with a single desalinization facility in the Sahara Desert, powered by solar cells. The total area needed for the solar cells would take up just 0.4 percent of the Sahara Desert.

Also, there is a fundamental problem in looking only at total water resources when trying to assess whether there are sufficient supplies of water. The trouble is that we do not necessarily know *how* and *how wisely* the water is used. Many countries get by just fine with very limited water resources because these resources are exploited very effectively. Israel achieves a high degree of efficiency in agriculture, partly because they use the very efficient trickle watering system to green the desert and partly because the country recycles household wastewater for irrigation. Nevertheless, according to the classification Israel should be experiencing chronic water scarcity.

By far the largest part of all water is used for agriculture—globally, agriculture uses 69 percent, compared to 23 percent for industry and 8 percent for households (WRI, 1996: 306). It is also in agriculture that the largest opportunities for improving efficiency are to be found. It is estimated that many irrigation systems waste 60–80 percent of all water (WRI, 1996: 303; Falkenmark and Widstrand, 1992: 15).

The problem of water waste occurs because in many places water is not well priced. The great majority of the world's irrigation systems is based on an annual, flat rate, and not on charges according to the amount of water consumed (Dinar et al., 1997: 12). Thus, participants are not forced to consider whether it all in all pays to use the last liter of water or not—when you have first paid to be in, water is free. So even if there is only very little private utility from the last liter of water, it is still used because it is free.

This is particularly a problem for the poor countries. The poorest countries use 90 percent of their water for irrigation compared to just 37 percent in the rich countries (World Bank, 1992: 16). Consequently, water will have to be redistributed from agriculture to industry and households, and this will probably imply a minor decline in potential agricultural production (i.e., a diminished increase in the actual production). The World Bank estimates that this reduction will be limited and that water redistribution definitely will be profitable for the countries involved (World Bank, 1992: 16).

At the same time there are also large advantages to be reaped by focusing on more efficient household water consumption. In Manila 58 percent of all water disappears (lost in distribution and stolen), and in Latin America the figure is about 40 percent. Average households in the Third World pay only 35 percent of the actual price of water (World Bank, 1992: 16; 1994: 47). Naturally, this encourages overconsumption. Pricing reduces demand, and consumers will use less water if they have to pay for each unit instead of just paying a flat one-time rate.

Water in the Future

Population Action International (PAI) calculated that 3 percent of Earth's inhabitants today live in nations with water scarcity. In 2050 this number could be 18 percent (Gardner-Outlaw and Engelman, 1997). But this figure is based on the calculation that with more people and constant precipitation, you get less precipitation per person. By definition, this implies that more nations will experience water scarcity. PAI is careful to stress that 'the projections are neither forecasts nor predictions' (Engelman and LeRoy, 1993). Indeed, the projections merely mean that if we do not improve our handling of water resources, water will become more scarce.

But it is unlikely that we will not become better at utilizing and distributing water. The problem is not that there is too little water but that it is used poorly (Miller, 1998: 494). This can be solved by pricing water correctly. Actually, it is likely that a more sensible pricing not only will secure the water supply but also increase the total social efficiency. When agriculture is given cheap or even free water, it often implies a hidden and very large subsidy—in the United States the water subsidy to farmers is estimated to be above 90 percent, or $3.5 billion (Dinar et al., 1997: 20; Cunningham and Saigo, 1997: 431). For developing countries this figure is even larger—it is estimated that the hidden water subsidy to cities is about $22 billion, and the hidden subsidy to agriculture is around $20–25 billion (World Bank, 1994: 121–122; de Moor, 1998, ch. 5).

Conclusion

Adequate pricing actually turns out to be the main issue for water problems. When water is a free resource—as it typically has been throughout the ages—we consume as much as we possibly can (given our private costs). As we become richer and can use more and more water, and as we get more and more people on this planet, we begin to experience limits. To act as if water is free gives rise to problems.

We have to prioritize the use of this resource. Should we use more water to produce extra food, or should we use more water in the cities and force agriculture to become more efficient? Pricing the water ensures the most efficient trade-off.

But when water becomes more valuable, because it is more scarce, it will also mean that nations will become more aware of the distribution of water among themselves. This could imply increased tension and increased focus on water questions. But it is important to realize that first, water resources do not constitute a hard and fixed limit to production. Through pricing it is possible to make water use much more efficient, and place water-intensive productions in water-rich regions through international trade, such as grains.

Second, that water can always be desalinized places an upper limit to the value of water resources—essentially a nation contemplating war over water resources will have to ask whether the gains could be achieved cheaper through negotiation, price incentives, and desalination.

This is perhaps why we have seen very few water wars but many water treaties. Using the International Crises Behavior data set, Aaron Wolf (1999b) has identified seven crises from 1918 to 1994 where water disputes was at least a partial cause. In three out of seven disputes, not a single shot was fired, and none were violent enough to qualify as wars. This should be compared to the more than 3,600 treaties concerning international water resources that have been registered between 805 and 1984.

Ever Greater Inequality?

Another worry, voiced by many, including Val Percival and Thomas Homer-Dixon (2001), is that unequal social distribution can give rise to conflict. Although this is clearly not surprising—an uprising only makes sense if there are possibilities of capturing a profit—the implicit statement seems to be that the social distribution is becoming more unequal and that conflict should consequently get more likely. This seems to be confirmed by the UNDP, stressing that inequality has increased globally (UNDP, 1996: 13).

Most of the available data are at the national level only, so the following discussion will only deal with inter-nation inequality. It would obviously also be very interesting to look at intra-national inequality.

UNDP presents a simple coefficient, which measures the relationship between the richest 20 percent of all nations in the world and the poorest 20 percent. In terms of GDP per capita the ratio in the 1960s was around 30:1, that is, the richest 20 percent earned thirty times as much as the poorest. By 1991 the ratio had increased to 61:1, and in 1994 to 78:1. This is interpreted as showing that 'the global chasm between the rich and the poor widens day by day' (UNDP 1996).

The problem, however, lies in using GDP as a means of comparing nations, because it involves calculations on the basis of international exchange rates. For this reason, translating the Ethiopian birr into dollars says something about what an Ethiopian can buy in the United States, but this comparison is seldom relevant. What is far more important is how much an Ethiopian can buy in Ethiopia. This is measured by the UN index called Purchasing Power Parity, or PPP, that is, what people's money actually can buy.

To an Ethiopian, the difference is enormous: a traditional GDP calculation says that he earns U.S. $100 a year, whereas the PPP calculation estimates his income at $450. This is because Ethiopians earn very little and

FIGURE 7.8   Relationship Between the Richest and Poorest 20 Percent and 30 Percent in the World in Terms of 1985 PPP$, 1960–1990

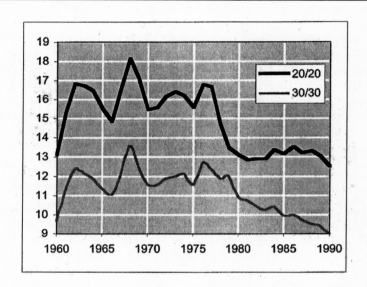

SOURCE: Summers and Heston (1991).

are therefore not particularly well integrated into the world economy. A dollar, then, is very expensive to an Ethiopian, whereas a birr is cheap to an American. It is clear, however, that it is much more reasonable to say that the Ethiopian earns $450 in terms of his own local purchasing power.

The UN actually also relies on PPP to evaluate developments in the incomes of individual countries, and UNDP makes use of it in its *Human Development Index*. So it may seem remarkable that they should choose to use pure GDP for such an important comparison. Figure 7.8 shows that the gap in PPP between the richest and poorest 20 percent and 30 percent in the world has not doubled or even increased—almost the reverse. This is a convincing sign of robust development on the part of even the weakest part of the world toward greater material prosperity.

Even if we look at the standard deviation of the income—to measure the spread—both its log-transformation and the indexed version shows not an increase, but a decline. Thus, when we look at the real income measured in purchasing power, we do not see dramatically increasing inequality, but rather a stable income distribution or perhaps even a development toward a slightly more equal distribution.

Conclusion

In many human endeavors there seem to be a strong tendency to believe that things are getting worse. David Hume asserted that 'the humour of blaming the present, and admiring the past is strongly rooted in human nature' (Hume, 1754: 464). Sal Baron wrote in his book about the history of the Jews that prophets who made optimistic predictions were automatically considered to be false prophets (Simon, 1995b). An Assyrian stone tablet, many thousands of years old, tells us of an obstinate feeling of decline: 'Our Earth is degenerate in these latter days; bribery and corruption are common; children no longer obey their parents; every man wants to write a book, and the end of the world is evidently approaching'.[12]

Often, the discussion of the environment seems similarly to be based on this bleak belief (extensively discussed and documented in Lomborg, 1998/2001). This chapter has focused on some of the important areas singled out by environmentalist writers to see whether the environmental stresses indeed are getting worse or not.

When looking at the food supply, it is evident that not only has stress lessened, in that more people are better fed than ever before, but the evidence also seems to indicate that this trend will continue into the future, making food even more accessible. Likewise, the threat of erosion is largely based on anecdotal evidence, and when we look at the best available, global data, it seems that its effect over the next century will be negligible.

When discussing energy and raw materials, there has always been a tendency to expect a Malthusian exhaustion scenario. However, when we look at the data for oil, coal, gas, and the four most important raw materials (aluminum, iron, copper, and zinc), they exhibit *increasing* years of consumption, despite the enormous increases in annual consumption and the amounts already consumed. Contrary to common sense, there are good reasons to expect that these resources will not get more scarce but rather more abundant with time.

Looking at water, it is clear that what used to be an essentially free resource now has an established cost. In this sense, it has become more scarce. But this need not lead to any significant increase in conflict. Partly, water is by no means a very limited resource and through the pricing of water, great efficiencies can be achieved at fairly low cost. Partly, since desalination sets a clear upper boundary on the benefits reaped from access to free water, it is doubtful that water could be a major objective in the acquisition of foreign resources through war.

Finally, the discussion of increasing inequality, at least as based on national data, seems erroneous. When measuring the purchasing power, inequality has not increased over the last fifty years—rather, perhaps, we have witnessed a slight decrease.

Consequently, although the discussion of environmental stresses and their connection to conflict is clearly an important area of research, it is important to realize that on the main issue areas, resources have not been becoming increasingly scarce but rather more abundant.

Bjørn Lomborg, b. 1965, M.A. in political science (University of Aarhus, Denmark 1991), Ph.D. 1994 (University of Copenhagen, Denmark); associate professor, Department of Political Science, University of Aarhus. Current research interests: Environmental data collection, computer simulation of social dilemmas, and multiparty modelling.

Notes

1. Quote from CIMMYT's web page: http://www.cgiar.org/cimmyt/about/annual94/pushing.htm.

2. http://www.cgiar.org/irri/Riceweb/research/res_issyield.htm.

3. IFPRI (1997), ERS (1997: 4), World Bank (Mitchell and Ingco) described in FAO (1995b: 119) and at http://www.worldbank.org/html/extpb/comq/comq1196.htm. Strangely, Brown quotes FAO to the effect that they project food prices to fall when they state clearly that they will not forecast prices (WI, 1998: 94; FAO, 1995b: 119; Alexandratos, 1997) instead of focusing on IFPRI, USDA, and the World Bank, who all make this prediction.

4. Goudie (1993: 161–162). Pimentel et al. (1995a: 1117) puts it at 17, but the newest estimate from his own source (U.S. Department of Agriculture) shows just 12; Crosson (1995: 462).

5. Http://cnn.com/earth/9605/11/oil.supply/index.html.

6. Part of the increase in the reserve estimates for the OPEC countries in the late 1980s could be caused by the fact that these figures are also used in negotiations for OPEC quotas. This is suggested by CRS (1995) and Ivanhoe (1995: 82). Nevertheless, it is generally estimated that reserves did go up, also in the 1980s (USGS, 1997).

7. Data from *International Energy Annuals*, here from personal communication, Harriet McLaine, EIA.

8. This is also owing to production facilities having been written off (EIA, 1997b: 37).

9. Http://www.worldwatch.org/pubs/ea/lo.html, see also Engelman and LeRoy (1993).

10. Press release, "Earth Faces Water Crisis", 6 August 1995. See also *Middle East and Africa Water Review* 4(1), http://endjinn.soas.ac.uk/geography/WaterIssues/Reviews/0401.html.

11. This is less than the twenty countries that Engelman and LeRoy themselves presented in 1990 (WRI, 1996: 302); the figures from WRI are high because the influx from rivers quite sensibly has been included in the total water resources. These figures have also later been used by Engelman himself (Gardner-Outlaw and Engelman, 1997).

12. Quoted in Simon (1996: 17). See Herman (1997) for a general discussion of the persistent thought of decline in Western culture.

Part II

The Reduction of Environmental Conflict

Chapter Eight

Democracy and the Environment

MANUS I. MIDLARSKY

Conflict, Democracy, and the Environment

As we now know, there is very strong evidence that democracy has a pacific effect on the relations between states. Democracies almost never wage war against each other, certainly not in the post-World War II period (Chan, 1997; Ray, 1995; Russett, 1993; Russett and Starr, 2000). Can democracy yield additional outcomes that minimize other forms of conflict? Specifically, if democracy affects the environment in positive ways, then the minimization of soil degradation, fouling of freshwater supplies, and other forms of scarcity could lessen the tendency toward civil conflict over scarce resources as hypothesized, for example, by Homer-Dixon (1994).

Theoretically, an important intervening variable between environmental scarcity and civil conflict is inequality. The greater the scarcity, the greater the likelihood that some people will possess more of the scarce resource than others. Such inequality at least would exacerbate civil conflict, if not

This is a revised version of a paper presented at the 38th Annual ISA Convention, Toronto, Canada, 18–22 March 1997. The research reported here was supported by United States Institute of Peace Grant no. SF-96-12. I am grateful for the research assistance of Han Jung Kim, and am indebted to the editors and three anonymous reviewers for their comments and suggestions. I am also grateful to Wenche Hauge and Tanja Ellingsen for allowing me to use their data on soil degradation. The dataset used in this chapter is available at: http://www.rci.rutgers.edu/~midlarsk/.

constitute a necessary condition for its existence (Midlarsky, 1988). Economic growth is required to mitigate scarcity and therefore inequality. At the same time, according to the Brundtland Commission (Brundtland et al., 1987), environmental protection requires economic growth, presumably to satisfy the distribution requirements that environmental protection entails. If there is zero growth, then redistribution will necessarily 'gore someone's ox'; someone will have to pay for the protection (Lafferty and Meadowcroft, 1996a; Paehlke, 1996). With economic growth such costs do not necessarily have to be borne by a single group (often the poor). Industries flush with additional funds also would more readily assume the burdens of environmental protection.

Whatever the precise mechanism, Binder (1993; cited in Jänicke, 1996) found that economic growth in the form of gross national product (GNP) per capita is the most important predictor of policy outcomes concerning air pollution controls in thirty-two industrialized countries. Studies by Ringquist (1993) and Khator (1993) found similar effects for the American states; wealthier states tended to enjoy increased environmental protection in comparison with poorer ones. Thus, environmental protection and the mitigation of scarcity, inequality, and the avoidance of serious conflict would all benefit from economic growth that also is strongly associated with democracy. Gleditsch (2001) has an excellent review of some of these issues, as does Gleditsch (1997a).

Democracy clearly is required for the equitable distribution of economic largesse, or equitable redistribution in the absence of economic growth. Without the pluralism associated with liberal democracy (Lafferty and Meadowcroft, 1996b), certain groups may be denied access to the policymaking process, thus making civil conflict more likely at some point in the future. But what if the democratic process does not necessarily operate in the best interests of the environment? Economic growth may operate to enhance both democracy and environmental protection and mitigate the scarcity associated with inequality, thus avoiding severe conflict. But if democracy and environmental protection are not mutually supportive, especially under conditions of economic scarcity, then there may ultimately exist the choice between environmental protection and civil conflict. If small economic gains, or their absence, necessitating redistribution, are subject to democratic pluralism, then simply to avoid serious conflicts, the bargaining process among affected groups and/or their representatives in legislative assemblies might give the environment short shrift. Thus, as environmental issues assume greater prominence, the old 'guns or butter' choice associated with classical economics may devolve into 'environmental protection or conflict mitigation'. If empirical associations between democracy and the environment are positive, then the latter choice may not be especially draconian. The past successful experience of democracies addressing environmental issues may be sufficient to propel them successfully into the future. But, on the whole, if democracy and environmental protection have serious incompatibilities, especially under conditions of slow or negative economic growth, then the choice may be more stark, with environmental protection requiring serious domestic conflict.

Nondemocracies apparently recognized some of the difficulties in maintaining environmental protection in the face of scarcity, inequality, and potential political violence. As a case in point, it may have been the persistent efforts to maintain an approximate equality of circumstance among the population by the Communist authorities in Eastern Europe that, among other factors, prevented mass political violence even as environmental degradation and other forms of widespread scarcity were increasingly experienced by the population. Without such efforts at equalization, political violence would have been more probable and likely would have occurred at an earlier time. The fall of Communism virtually everywhere in Eastern Europe was on the whole a 'velvet revolution', especially in comparison with other historical events of this magnitude.

A major consequence of the end of the Cold War was the realization that the Communist states of Eastern Europe had done a really terrible job of protecting the environment. In their rush to industrialize, in order to compete effectively with the West, the needs of heavy industry were supported to the virtual exclusion of all environmental concerns. This outcome at the Cold War's end effectively confirmed the expectations of those who maintained that totalitarian societies were unresponsive to environmental needs. A corollary to this argument, of course, is that democracies are inherently more responsive to environmental imperatives. The argument and its corollary are now investigated empirically.

This study emerges directly from earlier efforts to examine the influence of the environment on democracy (Midlarsky, 1995, 1999). Variables such as the minimization of the threat of war as the result of many sea borders and abundant rainfall were found to be associated with democracy as measured by the political rights index. Warfare enhances the likelihood of the emergence of autocracies; hence the minimization of the threat of war increases the probability of democracy. Rainfall is associated with the absence of the need for large bureaucratically administered irrigation works that, historically, have been associated with autocracy. The causal arrow effectively is being reversed now in examining the effects of democracy on the environment. The earlier studies emphasized the long-term influence on democracy of the physical environment surrounding human activity. Here, because of the large number of contemporaneous democracies and a vastly increased environmental awareness, we can now examine the impact of democracy on environmental preservation or protection.

Theory

On the whole, with one important exception to be discussed shortly, there is a dearth of empirical research on this issue. Theoretically, the situation is somewhat better. Basically, two positions have been staked out. One, an older set of arguments dating from the late 1960s and 1970s, suggests that individual and free-market behavior associated with liberal democracy is inimical to environmental protection. Under the protection of property rights, both individual persons and, more importantly, corporations, can act willfully, even recklessly, without regard to impact on the environment. Among the prominent have been Ehrlich (1968) and his concerns about the cumulative impact of unlimited population growth, Hardin (1968) and his now famous 'Tragedy of the Commons' wherein rational self-regarding economic behavior can yield collective catastrophe, or some of the more generalized concerns of Heilbroner (1974), especially in regard to the implications of United States foreign economic policy.

In this general view, the emphasis on individual political and economic rights in Western liberal democracies inevitably leads to a devaluation of the community's rights to clean air, water, and other elements of environmental protection that can only come about as the result of collective effort. However, especially in Hardin's critique, the institutions of democracy are largely absent. Furthermore, in modern representative democracies, it is not the individual who governs, although he or she may vote, but the legislative or executive institutions elected by aggregates of individuals that matter. The behavior of such institutions may be different from individual preferences, however aggregated in elections. Corporations also are extremely important as units of analysis, for they are large organizations with considerable economic and political clout that can override the environmental interests of large numbers of people.

The case for a positive relationship between democracy and environmental protection has had strong support. Both President Clinton and Vice President Gore have argued for this association; more recently, arguments in favor of democracy have been systematized by Payne (1995a). These arguments are basically five in number. (1) In contrast to authoritarian states, democracies respect individual rights. Thus, environmentalists are able to freely market their ideas and transform them into environmental legislation. Frequently, the overwhelming weight of information brought to bear by environmentalists may be decisive in influencing public opinion. (2) Democratic governments are inherently more responsive to their citizenry. The necessity to be elected (or re-elected) assures at least a minimal level of accountability to public opinion. (3) Freely flowing information in democracies (in contrast to, say, the USSR) allows for a form of political learning. Open political systems are more likely to learn from scientists and other concerned citizens than are autocracies, even less draconian ones such as

Gorbachev's USSR at the time of Chernobyl. At the same time, their tendencies to identify with each other increase possibilities for the imitation of policies between democracies, including environmental ones. (4) Democratic states tend to cooperate with each other within international environmental agencies. With the recent rapid growth of democracies worldwide, international environmental cooperation has been increasing. Further, transnational pressure groups tend to be far more successful in influencing policymaking in democracies than in nondemocracies. (5) Because all democracies also have free-market economies, businesses in the marketplace can be subject both to environmental incentives and sanctions. The incentives can comprise an enhanced share of the market, if environmentally active groups are satisfied with environmental business practices. On the other hand, if dissatisfied, such groups can attempt to diminish the market share of the offending company directly, or lobby for environmental legislation that might be costly for that corporation.

Yet one wonders if all of the preceding arguments do not constitute an idealization of democracy that ignores the rough and tumble of actual decisionmaking within the legislative and executive branches of government. Corporations and environmental groups can fight each other to a standstill, leaving a decisionmaking vacuum instead of a direct impact of democracy on the environment. Or as the result of budget constraints, democracies may not be responsive to environmental imperatives but to more pressing issues of the economic sustenance of major portions of the voting public. The nuts and bolts of daily democratic governance may turn out to be very different from the ideal.

There are further difficulties in the hypothesized positive relationship between democracy and the environment. First is the problem of potential inequality, always a difficulty in practicing democracy in the absence of draconian redistribution schemes. According to Lafferty and Meadowcroft (1996b):

> Environmental problems are typically experienced as external constraints which frustrate established expectations and which require an adjustment to existing social practices. They threaten a pre-existing structure of entitlements and raise questions concerning distributive justice. While the idea that a cleaner environment will benefit everyone—that green policies are good for both rich and poor, industrialists and consumers—is attractive, in reality environmental problems touch different groups in different ways *[emphasis added]* (Lafferty and Meadowcroft, 1996b: 5).

As intimated earlier, stable democracies cannot long persist under conditions of extreme inequality.

A second concern is the difficulty presented by the globalization of environmental issues. As Paehlke (1996: 28) put it, 'The great danger for both democracy and environment is that, while economy and environment are now global in character, democracy functions on only national and local decision levels and only within some nations.' The problems imposed by the Chernobyl disaster of course constitute an illustration in extremis. But even between democracies there are difficulties imposed by the sharing of a common environment. The acidification of Scandinavian lakes as the result of British industry is but one case in point. Despite the existence of two democratically elected governments accountable to their separate populations, the resolution of such environmental problems between the two countries requires negotiation and treaty making that would not necessarily be accountable to these populations. Even within an international organization such as the European Union, decisionmaking of this type often takes place within a bureaucratic setting, not a democratically elected one. Dobson (1996) provides additional illustrations of the undermining of democracy by environmental necessities.

Finally, a potential remedy for these problems may present its own difficulties. Because the solution to environmental problems may disrupt social relations and inequitably treat certain population groups, suggestions have been put forward to expand the decisionmaking process and include many different groups, both nationally and internationally. O'Neill (1993) has argued for 'associative democracy' wherein environmental decisions are made with the participation of voluntary associations that are not market oriented. A kind of decentralization is achieved in which different associations contribute to decisionmaking in different issue areas, but coordinate eventually through negotiation (Achterberg, 1996a). Specific problems of coordination are discussed by Cohen and Rogers (1992).

Yet, an emphasis on such associations, while containing salutary elements, nevertheless vitiates the importance of representative democracy that lies at the heart of liberal government in the West. In the extreme, of course, forms of corporatism can be practiced that are not congenial to liberal democracy. (Lafferty and Meadowcroft, 1996c, call their version of associative democracy 'cooperative management regimes'.) In an effort to reconcile environmental imperatives with the workings of liberal democracy, there is a real danger that such democracies may be undermined even only slightly, and the slippery slope of corporatism and beyond may not be too far away.

All of these complexities if not inconsistencies between democracy and environmental protection might be more easily managed if there were positive empirical associations between the two variables. If democracy as currently practiced is supportive of environmental protection, then the more extreme versions of these innovative schemes, with their potential dangers, might be avoided. Given this supportive relationship, ethical and legal imperatives for environmental protection, even only within democratic polities, may develop sufficiently to address the international environmental concerns as well.

On the positive side, there is an interesting parallel here between the preceding theoretical development relating democracy to environmental protection, and that concerning the democratic peace (Chan, 1997; Russett and Starr, 2000). Essentially, regime responsiveness, political learning especially as the result of mutual identification, and the tendency toward cooperation in international institutions are thoroughly consistent with similar arguments explaining the absence of war between democracies. Representative institutions that diminish the tendency to rush to war, mutual identification between democracies that might inhibit war between their populations, or the experience of cooperation between democracies in neoliberal international institutions all are consistent with, if not directly parallel to, the arguments for the positive impact of democracy on the environment.

Perhaps most important among these are the arguments for mutual identification and learning. Democracies that cooperate with each other in international neoliberal institutions also may begin to identify with each other and subsequently learn from each other's behaviors. If two or more democracies share a variety of common problems, then they may seek common solutions as a result of repeated interactions. In international settings, mutual identifications may arise such that problems of a political, economic, or environmental nature are solved in similar ways. Especially significant could be a sequential learning process wherein one democracy experiences an environmental problem, solves it, and others, identifying with it, implement a similar solution.

Of further interest is the existence of three distinct emphases that parallel this literature. The emphasis on regime responsiveness here finds an analogue in the use of the political rights index (Gastil, 1988), itself emphasizing freedom of election in studies of democracy (Midlarsky, 1998). The existence of individual rights in democracies is incorporated within an index of liberal democracy (Bollen, 1993). Both of these indexes will be used in the subsequent empirical analyses, as will a third index, Polity III, which emphasizes democratic institutionalization (Jaggers and Gurr, 1995).[1]

The major difficulty in theorizing about democracy and the environment probably arises from the view of democracy as undifferentiated. In this monolithic understanding, perhaps best exemplified by Hirschman's (1981) concept of voice (but used by him judiciously), democracy resides principally in the free political expression by the populace. However, this is only one understanding of democracy which neglects the role of institutions, the particular mode of political expression (or voice), and the extent to which the particular democracy is a liberal democracy. The use of three measures of democracy is designed to obviate this potential difficulty.

It is predicted that elements of the environment are protected better under the conditions of democratic governance. This prediction is consistent with the overall findings of Gleditsch and Sverdrup (1996) that democracy is positively associated with environmental protection using a dichotomization of the Polity III index. The present study differs from theirs in that multivariate analyses will be used throughout in comparison with one such analysis in their study. Additionally, three measures of democracy will be used and in nondichotomized form. Specifically, it is predicted that the more democratic the polity, the greater will be the tendency toward environmental protection. This is a strong form of the hypothesis, for it suggests a monotonic relationship between democracy and environmental protection, in contrast to a dichotomy between democracies and nondemocracies that frequently is used in such analyses. Because the theoretical arguments generally are framed in terms of increasing responsiveness of governments yielding greater environmental protection, a test of monotonicity is appropriate. Further, much less information is lost than in a dichotomous approach.

The Dependent Variables

The dependent variables are six in number, and reflect environmental conditions throughout the world. These are: (1) deforestation, (2) air quality, (3) soil erosion by water, (4) protected land area, (5) freshwater availability, and (6) soil erosion by chemicals. The importance of forests and their precipitous rate of elimination appears to be self-evident. Not only do forests contain rare botanical and zoological species, but apparently are necessary for the maintenance of congenial (to humans) environmental conditions. It is estimated that rapid deforestation could have a significant effect on global warming, not to belabor the more obvious connection between deforestation and increased desertification. Data on deforestation are in the form of the percentage annual deforestation between 1981 and 1990 (WRI, 1996). Air quality, also eminently important, is measured by estimates of carbon dioxide (CO_2) emissions per capita for 1990, from fossil fuel combustion, cement production, and gas flaring (UN, 1996).[2] While these are straightforward data compilations, a similar compilation for soil degradation is more complex and is coded from a map published by UNEP (Oldeman et al., 1991), including four types of soil erosion: water, wind, chemical, and physical erosion. Severity and extent are included for all four types and the data used here constitute an average of the two. Total soil degradation is measured on a scale from 0–3 (0 = no soil degradation, 1 = low soil degradation, 2 = medium soil degradation, 3 = high soil degradation). Initial data analyses were carried out using the codings of Hauge and Ellingsen (2001).

Instead of a single composite value for soil erosion, including all four types, two specific types are presented, namely soil erosion by water and by chemicals. Soil erosion by water represents a human factor, for with the proper infrastructure, it can be controlled by human beings. Chemicals are a unique human contribution to the environment and so should be treated separately. Results for the other two soil erosion forms (physical and wind) are much less related to our environmental concerns and so are omitted.

Protected land area is a variable designed to tap the extent of governmental commitment to the preservation of biodiversity. The establishment and maintenance of parks and preserves is a principal method used by governments to preserve habitats and species. The percentage of land area for 1993 protected in this fashion is found in WRI (1996). Finally, freshwater availability refers to the average annual flow of rivers and aquifers generated endogenously. The data are in the form of water availability per capita (1,000 cubic meters, for 1990; WRI, 1992).

The Independent Variables

The independent variables are indices of democracy plus whatever controls are theoretically suggested in order to obtain conservative estimates of the impact of democracy on the environment. The first measure of democracy is a basic measure of political rights emphasizing freedom of election (Gastil, 1988). The second, explicitly called an index of liberal democracy, has been more recently developed by Bollen (1993). It includes, in addition to the emphasis on political rights, elements of a free political opposition and an effective legislative body. Bollen's index was built upon an analysis of several other indices of democracy, one of which is the Gastil political rights index. It was found to have the highest 'validity' of any of the existing indices examined by him, the lowest systematic or 'method' error, and no associated random error (Bollen 1993: 1220). Finally, a measure that has been used extensively in recent analyses of democracy is the Polity III index (Jaggers and Gurr, 1995). Here, the democracy scale reflects institutionalized political competition among contending groups, institutional constraints on the exercise of political power, and the openness and competitiveness of executive recruitment to serve within the major political institutions.

These are the three measures of democracy. They appear to reflect different emphases in measuring democracy: political rights in the form of freedom of election, a more complex synthesis of three distinct dimensions of democracy called liberal democracy, and an emphasis on the institutions of democracy found in the Polity III index.

Gastil's political rights index is averaged here for the fifteen-year period between 1973 and 1987, effectively an updating of Taylor and Jodice's (1983: 58–61) averaging of the index for 1973–79. The averaging here was accomplished to (1) allow for the correction of errors if they crept in for an earlier year; (2) give a fairly long 'window' of measurement in contrast to virtually all other measures of this type which are given for one year only; (3) allow for greater variability in the dependent variable by adding a decimal point to yearly data that in the data source are given only in single digit form (i.e. 1–7); and (4) provide a median year that is comparable to the Bollen (1993) data. An advantage to the averaging process is found in the potential minimization of systematic error found by Bollen (1993). Random error was found to be nonexistent in the Gastil data set for 1980 and the validity was found to be 93 percent, the highest of all the data sets examined by Bollen, but still leaving 7 percent for 'method' or systematic error (Bollen, 1993: 1220). If judges ratings tend toward bias in one year or two, it is possible that averaging over a fifteen-year period may minimize such method bias because of some compensation against that bias in succeeding years. On the whole, the scores tend toward consistency for most countries during this period and fluctuations, where found, are not extreme.

The average scores are from 1–7, taken to one decimal place, thus effectively yielding a scale from 10–70 (10 = most political rights; 70 = least political rights),[3] comparable although not identical in range and precision to that of Bollen. The scale criteria are given in Gastil (1988: 29–35). Bollen's (1993) liberal democracy index is scored from 1–100 and is an equal weighting of Banks's political opposition and legislative effectiveness measures (Banks, 1971, 1979), and Gastil's (1988) political rights index. The data are given for 1980, the same year as the median year for the political rights index examined separately here. The Polity III democracy scores, chosen for 1980, comprise eleven-point scales constructed from codings on the competitiveness of political participation, competitiveness of executive recruitment, openness of executive recruitment, and constraints on the chief executive (Jaggers and Gurr, 1995: 471).

Controls are introduced to insure proper specification of the multiple regression equations. The first of the controls is that of Gross Domestic Product (GDP) per capita as a measure of economic development for the year 1980 (Summers and Heston, 1988). Multiyear time-lags are introduced to allow for the emergent effects of societal variables on the environment. Here, greater economic development clearly allows for a larger resource base available for environmental protection and cleanup where necessary. This is a potentially important distinguishing feature between countries, whatever their level of democratic development.[4]

Another such variable is agricultural density (for 1983; FAO 1991), which easily can affect all of our measures of the environment. Stresses on water supplies, forests, and soil quality can be affected by the density of persons on arable land. Population growth (UN, 1985: 90) can have similar deleterious effects on elements of the environment examined here.

The amount of yearly precipitation (in total inches; Conway and Liston 1972; Pearce and Smith 1984) is introduced to allow for the effects on water supplies and especially soil degradation. Excess rainfall can be a major factor in stimulating excessive water run-off or even floods that can have significant effects on the retention of topsoil. Even CO_2 emissions may be affected by the amount of rainfall that can possibly limit the burning of certain fuels and consequent gaseous emissions.

Age of the polity (Taylor and Hudson, 1972; Lye and Carpenter, 1987) is introduced to control for maturation effects. Simply, as polities age, they can become more responsive to the public's desires for environmental controls.[5] Newer states may be too concerned with processes of state-building and economic development to pay much attention to environmental concerns. Deaths due to domestic violence (Taylor and Jodice, 1983: 48–51) are introduced in order to control for the presence of violence that in itself can cause environmental degradation as the result of pitched battles in forests, near streams, and on good topsoil, but also as the result of the disruption of protective measures.

Finally, the variable European geographic location (1,0) is introduced in order to control for the widespread organizational infrastructure of the European Union (EU) and its influence on the European continent that can lead to a rapid diffusion of environmental protection, apart from any democratic influences on such protection. As early as March 1973, the European Community (EC) declared its intention to promulgate measures protecting the environment (Moussis, 1995: 184). In 1975, quality standards were laid down for surface water intended for drinking. In regard to air quality, carbon monoxide emissions from motor vehicles were limited in 1970 and sulphur dioxide in 1980, while strong limits for CO_2 emissions were set in 1991. Around the same period, limitations were set on chemical substances discharged as part of industrial waste, and certain natural habitats were given legal protection (Moussis, 1995: 186–195). Thus, for the past quarter century or so, Europe has been a locus of increasing environmental protection extending not only to the member states of the EC and later EU, which were obligated legally, but also to other European states who would emulate the EC members in order to eventually gain entry into the organization. For these reasons, European geographic location as defined by atlases such as Lye and Carpenter (1987) is coded (1,0) in place of membership in the European Union or the older European Community.[6]

The Findings

The results of the data analysis are presented in the form of six tables that contain bivariate and partial correlations as well as regression coefficients (unstandardized) and *t*-tests of significance. The zero-order and controlled associations are included to show any changes that occur between the bivariate and multivariate tests. Values for coefficients of the equations, including the political rights index, are given in the first row of each cell entry, those for the liberal democracy index are given in the second, while those for the Polity III index are given in the third row. Values for the square of the multiple correlation coefficient, and its counterpart adjusted for sample size and other specifics of the analysis, are given in the bottom row of each table. The number of cases in the tables vary as the result of missing data for the dependent variables.

Turning first to deforestation, the results pertaining to democracy appear to be counter-intuitive, at least in regard to the direction of the relationship. In Table 8.1, although the three democracy measures are somewhat negatively associated with this measure of environmental degradation, the partial coefficients are positively associated with it. In other words, the greater the level of democracy, the greater the deforestation, controlling for economic development and the remaining control variables. For two of the democracy measures, political rights and liberal democracy, the relationships are significant at the $p \leq 0.01$ level. Interestingly, the partials are not only reversed in sign, but reveal stronger relationships between democracy and deforestation than the zero-order correlations. On the other hand, the greater the extent of economic development, the smaller the degree of deforestation as might be expected intuitively. A certain level of available funding would be required to maintain forestry control, especially when there are competing demands for funding as in most any society. This relationship holds up well in the partials. European efforts at forestry control dating from the Wilhelmine period in Germany are reflected in the significant negative associations between European location and deforestation exhibited by the political rights and liberal democracy indices.

Only democracy stands out in its positive relationship between the extent of political rights or liberal democracy and environmental degradation. This finding is not likely to be a statistical artifact. The tolerances $(1 - R_i^2$ where R_i^2 is the maximum explained variation in one independent variable by all of the others) are within acceptable limits: not less than 0.21 for the lowest, GDP per capita ($VIF = 4.69$), cf. Kleinbaum et al. (1988: 210). As a further check on possible collinear effects of both democracy and GDP per capita in the same equation, all analyses were run again without GDP per capita. With only one exception,[7] the directionality, although not magnitude, of relationships between democracy and the environmental measures were identical to those reported here. In order to compare this finding with the use of dichotomized variables for democracy, all three measures were dichotomized at their midpoints and the analyses were repeated. In all instances, in this and subsequent analyses, the directions of relationships were identical with the continuous variables, although correlations and levels of significance were lower as the result of lost information in the dichotomization process.

This finding of a positive association between democracy and deforestation is far more likely to be the result of a process overlooked by theorists of democracy, namely the sensitivity of democratically elected governments to the land needs of their populations in many Third World countries. Fearful of being ejected from office by a disgruntled land-poor peasantry,

TABLE 8.1   Regression of Deforestation on the Explanatory Variables

Variable	Correlation (r)	Partial	b	t
Democracy	-0.10[a,b]	0.35	0.27	3.07**[c]
	-0.13	0.29	0.01	2.48**
	-0.19	0.18	0.06	1.49
Agricultural Density	-0.09	0.06	0.001	0.49
	-0.09	0.03	0.001	0.23
	0.15	0.17	0.06	1.35
Population Growth	0.30	-0.10	-0.19	-0.86
	0.31	-0.13	-0.24	-1.06
	0.28	-0.10	-0.20	-0.82
GDP per Capita	-0.41	-0.38	-0.0002	-3.41***
	-0.42	-0.35	-0.0002	-3.03**
	-0.40	-0.33	-0.0002	-2.81**
Log Age	-0.18	-0.01	-0.27	-0.08
	-0.19	0.05	1.41	0.43
	-0.21	0.06	1.51	0.44
Deaths per Capita	-0.05	-0.09	-0.02	-0.73
	-0.04	-0.13	-0.02	-1.04
	-0.05	-0.14	-0.03	-1.15*
European Location	-0.40	-0.26	-1.07	-2.17*
	-0.41	-0.28	-1.21	-2.39**
	-0.41	-0.21	-0.97	-1.74
Precipitation	0.11	-0.04	-0.001	-0.34
	0.10	-0.03	-0.001	-0.26
	0.11	-0.05	-0.001	-0.41
Constant			1.33	0.05
			12.46	0.50
			13.22	0.51

$R^2 = 0.35***$, $R_a^2 = 0.26$, $N = 77$[b]
$R^2 = 0.31***$, $R_a^2 = 0.23$, $N = 76$
$R^2 = 0.29**$, $R_a^2 = 0.20$, $N = 74$

[a]In this table, a positive sign (implied by no indication of sign) denotes a positive impact on a measure of environmental *degradation*. A negative sign means that the variable is associated with environmental *preservation*.

[b]Values given in the first row are for the political rights index, those in the second row are for the liberal democracy index, while those in the third row are for the Polity III index. The same holds true for the multiple correlations at the bottom of the table.

[c]All tests are one-tailed because of the directional hypothesis tested here.

* = $p \leq 0.05$,** = $p \leq 0.01$,*** = $p \leq 0.001$.

elected politicians in Third World countries may accede to the demands for land of a substantial portion of the electorate. This conclusion is reinforced by the higher partial correlation for the political rights index emphasizing voting in comparison with the other two measures. If the preceding arguments are correct, then a measure based principally on voting rights should demonstrate a stronger impact on deforestation than would others based on liberal democracy or democratic institutionalization as in the instances of the Bollen index and Polity III. Even if many of the peasantry in rural locations do not vote, the possibilities for demonstrations, squatting or other headline-commanding behavior might be sufficient to allow deforestation on a massive scale to satisfy the land-poor. In other respects, however, wealthy and European countries exhibit a negative relationship with deforestation. Indeed, the values for European countries are almost uniformly negative in this time-period, implying reforestation activities.

Because of concerns about the impact on the findings of the control for European location, the analyses were also run without this variable. Comparisons revealed no substantial differences with or without the control for Europe other than the loss of percentage variance explained in the latter instance. Similarly, although additional variables altered somewhat the values of coefficients, no substantial differences in findings were obtained when the variables log age and precipitation were omitted from analyses of dependent variables where they might have been less relevant as explanatory factors.

There is an additional possible source of the relationship between democracy and deforestation and pertains to the permeability of Third World democracies to the efforts of large cattle ranchers, farmers, and multinational corporations involved in agribusiness. As members of legislative assemblies in Third World countries or with strong influence upon them, the large-scale rancher or farmer may be in a unique position to control forest resources and initiate deforestation measures for purposes of farming. At the same time, local democratically elected authorities also have forest areas ceded to them by national governments, and these forests then are 'managed' by the local authorities.

Turning to air quality and CO_2 emissions per capita in Table 8.2, we see a similar pattern to that found in Table 8.1. Now all three measures of democracy are significant in their positive influence on environmental degradation as measured by the partials. In this case, however, the zero-order correlations are in the same direction and much higher. The partials are also significant, with one of them at the $p \leq 0.01$ level. As expected, economic development is most strongly associated with CO_2 emissions. A fairly high level of economic/industrial activity would be required to generate high levels of these emissions.

Because of similarities in the findings for the control variables using any of the three measures of democracy, only the values of coefficients emanating from the use of the Polity III index are reported here and in subsequent

TABLE 8.2   Regression of CO_2 Emissions per Capita on the Explanatory Variables

Variable	Correlation (r)	Partial	b	t
Democracy	0.63[a,b]	0.18	0.07	1.69[c]
	0.57	0.20	0.004	1.91*
	0.63	0.26	0.04	2.49**
Agricultural Density	0.20[d]	-0.09	-0.01	-0.81
Population Growth	-0.57	-0.003	-0.002	-0.03
GDP per Capita	0.90	0.84	0.0003	14.39***
Log Age	0.31	-0.23	-3.22	-2.19*
Deaths per Capita	-0.16	-0.05	-0.01	-0.43
European Location	0.47	-0.27	-0.56	-2.60**
Precipitation	-0.24	-0.14	-0.002	-1.35
Constant			-24.36	-2.20*

$R^2 = 0.86***, R_a^2 = 0.84, N = 98$[b]

$R^2 = 0.86***, R_a^2 = 0.84, N = 97$

$R^2 = 0.85***, R_a^2 = 0.84, N = 95$

[a]A positive sign denotes a positive impact on environmental *degradation*, while a negative sign indicates that the variable promotes environmental *preservation*.

[b]Values given in the first row are for the political rights index, those in the second row are for the liberal democracy index, while those in the third row are for the Polity III index. The same holds true for the multiple correlations at the bottom of the table.

[c]All tests are one-tailed because of the directional hypothesis tested here.

[d]Because of similarities in the findings for the control variables using any of the three measures of democracy, only the values of coefficients emanating from the use of the Polity III index are reported here.

$* = p \leq 0.05, ** = p \leq 0.01, *** = p \leq 0.001$.

tables. Age of the country when controlling for economic development, and European location, are significantly associated with reduced emissions. Apparently, older countries and those located in Europe have exhibited an effort to limit their emissions, probably in the case of Europe inspired by the EC and more recently EU requirements. It is interesting to note that the Polity III index based on democratic institutionalization is strongly associated with both the positive impact of democracy on poor air quality and the negative impact of European location. Apparently, it is the aggregation of preferences by democratic institutions that yields both positive and negative effects on air quality. This is in contrast to the effects on deforestation, wherein the individual preferences of people as indicated by the voting rights emphasis of the political rights index (see Table 8.1) apparently are most important in affecting deforestation. The significant negative values of the constant suggest that there may be additional negative influences on CO_2 emissions not considered here.

TABLE 8.3   Regression of Soil Erosion by Water on the Explanatory Variables

Variable	Correlation (r)	Partial	b	t
Democracy	-0.06[a,b]	0.26	0.34	1.56**[c]
	-0.06	0.22	0.01	2.11*
	-0.11	0.16	0.08	1.47
Agricultural Density	0.22[d]	-0.18	-0.08	-1.73*
Population Growth	0.14	-0.16	-0.37	-1.49
GDP per Capita	-0.36	-0.34	-0.0002	-3.40***
Log Age	-0.03	0.11	4.87	1.04
Deaths per Capita	-0.02	-0.08	-0.02	-0.70
European Location	-0.26	-0.23	-1.48	-2.16*
Precipitation	0.08	-0.06	-0.003	-0.56
Constant			42.81	1.22

$R^2 = 0.26***$, $R_a^2 = 0.19$, $N = 97$[b]
$R^2 = 0.24***$, $R_a^2 = 0.17$, $N = 96$
$R^2 = 0.24***$, $R_a^2 = 0.17$, $N = 95$

[a]A positive sign denotes a positive impact on a measure of environmental *degradation*, while a negative sign indicates that the variable promotes environmental *preservation*.

[b]Values given in the first row are for the political rights index, those in the second row are for the liberal democracy index, while those in the third row are for the Polity III index. The same holds true for the multiple correlations at the bottom of the table.

[c]All tests are one-tailed because of the directional hypothesis tested here.

[d]Because of similarities in the findings for the control variables using any of the three measures of democracy, only the values of coefficients emanating from the use of the Polity III index are reported here.

* = $p \leq 0.05$, ** = $p \leq 0.01$, *** = $p \leq 0.001$.

Turning to Table 8.3 and the analysis of soil erosion by water, we once again have a significant negative effect on environmental preservation by democracy. Here, however, the political mechanism probably differs from that involving deforestation in Table 8.1. A principal source of that relationship is probably the unwillingness to deny land to land-poor peasants in democracies or to prevent powerful agribusiness interests from gaining access to forest land, hence the increase in deforestation. Here, the most likely source of the negative relationship is the differential influences on funding in democracies. The stemming of soil erosion is a proactive process requiring physical and bureaucratic infrastructure, and probably large-scale funding, especially after significant deforestation already has occurred. Allowing land-poor peasants to clear forests or logging businesses to engage in such activity is a relatively cheap process for governments. For more expensive projects such as the stemming of soil erosion, peasants in outlying

TABLE 8.4 Regression of Protected Land Area on the Explanatory Variables

Variable	Correlation (r)	Partial	b	t
Democracy	0.34[a,b]	0.16	0.88	1.57[c]
	0.37	0.26	0.07	2.56**
	0.37	0.28	0.62	2.69**
Agricultural Density	-0.004[d]	-0.04	-0.07	-0.37
Population Growth	-0.24	0.07	0.65	0.62
GDP per Capita	0.26	0.01	0.00004	0.12
Log Age	0.34	0.25	48.34	2.46**
Deaths per Capita	-0.08	-0.04	-0.05	-0.34
European Location	0.20	-0.07	-1.89	-0.65
Precipitation	-0.01	0.04	0.01	0.36
Constant			368.05	2.49**

$R^2 = 0.16^*$, $R_a^2 = 0.09$, $N = 100$[b]
$R^2 = 0.21^{**}$, $R_a^2 = 0.14$, $N = 99$
$R^2 = 0.20^{**}$, $R_a^2 = 0.13$, $N = 97$

[a]A positive sign denotes a positive impact on a measure of environmental *preservation*, while a negative sign indicates that the variable promotes environmental *degradation*.

[b]Values given in the first row are for the political rights index, those in the second row are for the liberal democracy index, while those in the third row are for the Polity III index. The same holds true for the multiple correlations at the bottom of the table.

[c]All tests are one-tailed because of the directional hypothesis tested here.

[d]Because of similarities in the findings for the control variables using any of the three measures of democracy, only the values of coefficients emanating from the use of the Polity III index are reported here.

$* = p \leq 0.05$, $** = p \leq 0.01$, $*** = p \leq 0.001$.

areas away from the urban centers of major political activity would have much less influence on the political process of public expenditure than would urban residents or voters simply more centrally located. In making choices among public expenditures in democratically elected governments, the agricultural needs of more remote populations would probably be less favored than the more visible, and possibly cheaper, public expenditures closer to urban populations. A rule of thumb might be: the more visible the public project is to a large segment of voters, the greater is its likelihood of being funded. The stemming of soil erosion, whatever its cost, might not be high on the list of visible public projects, indeed if it is visible at all.

As expected, economic development is negatively related to soil erosion by water, as is being a European country. Interestingly, agricultural density also demonstrates a negative impact on soil erosion by water. The need for farmers and peasants to conserve topsoil probably is a major factor in the diminution of soil erosion by water as the result of agricultural density.

In the analysis of protected land area, we see a departure from the previously consistent findings. It should be noted that this consistency may be due in part to the effect of deforestation on both CO_2 emissions and soil erosion. In Table 8.4, for the first time, there is a positive relationship between democracy and environmental protection. The zero-order relationship is stronger, but the partial relationship still is significant at $p \leq 0.01$ for two of the three measures. Particularly interesting is the apparent institutional mediation implied by these findings. Increased political (i.e., principally voter) rights do not have a significant impact on the percentage of protected land area, but the remaining two indexes, especially the Polity III index, are measures based in large part on the institutions of democracy. Thus, democratic, largely representative institutions are those with positive impact on the protection of forests and habitat preserves. Voters may have a direct negative impact on the environment, especially in land-poor, Third World democracies, as suggested in Table 8.1, but limits may be set by democratic institutions that may allow some deforestation but only up to a point, at which especially valuable, biologically diverse forests may be preserved. This conclusion is suggested directly by the obverse findings of Table 8.4 in comparison with Table 8.1. Here, in Table 8.4, the strongest degree of association between democracy and environmental preservation is found for the institutionally based Polity III index, while in Table 8.1, the strongest relationship between democracy and environmental degradation is evidenced in the political (i.e. voter) rights index. Apparently, the issue of environmental protection generates a tension between voter needs and the perceived necessity for environmental protection by democratic institutions.

Another possible reason for this obverse relationship is the tendency within democratic legislatures for large environmentally destructive measures such as deforestation to proceed only when linked to the preservation of small habitats or parklands.[8] In this process, environmental destruction in democracies shown in Table 8.1 goes hand in hand with much smaller protected land areas in Table 8.4. Consistent with the preceding findings, age of the country is positively related to environmental protection. Once again, however, as in Table 8.2, the constant is significant, suggesting the possibility of more complete model specification.

The last two tables demonstrate no significant partial relationships between democracy and the environment; nevertheless, they are of intrinsic interest. Table 8.5 provides a kind of validation for the overall set of analyses. Variables that are expected to be strongly associated with freshwater availability indeed are associated with it. Agricultural density, of course requiring larger amounts of freshwater, is negatively associated with freshwater availability while GDP per capita, suggesting the wealth required to increase such resources, is positively related to it. European location is sig-

TABLE 8.5 Regression of Freshwater Availability per Capita on the Explanatory Variables

Variable	Correlation (r)	Partial	b	t
Democracy	0.17[a,b]	0.03	0.57	0.29[c]
	0.11	-0.02	-0.01	-0.16
	0.17	0.09	0.69	0.88
Agricultural Density	-0.13[d]	-0.29	-1.86	-2.89**
Population Growth	-0.13	-0.09	-3.17	-0.89
GDP per Capita	0.14	0.28	0.003	2.70**
Log Age	-0.01	-0.10	-61.43	-0.91
Deaths per Capita	-0.11	-0.12	-0.57	-1.15
European Location	-0.06	-0.24	-23.15	-2.33*
Precipitation	0.44	0.48	0.38	5.10***
Constant			-458.43	-0.91

$R^2 = 0.30^{***}$, $R_a^2 = 0.24$, $N = 100$[b]

$R^2 = 0.30^{***}$, $R_a^2 = 0.24$, $N = 99$

$R^2 = 0.36^{***}$, $R_a^2 = 0.30$, $N = 97$

[a]A positive sign denotes a positive impact on a measure of environmental *preservation*, while a negative sign indicates that the variable promotes environmental *degradation*.

[b]Values given in the first row are for the political rights index, those in the second row are for the liberal democracy index, while those in the third row are for the Polity III index. The same holds true for the multiple correlations at the bottom of the table.

[c]All tests are one-tailed because of the directional hypothesis tested here.

[d]Because of similarities in the findings for the control variables using any of the three measures of democracy, only the values of coefficients emanating from the use of the Polity III index are reported here.

* $= p \leq 0.05$,** $= p \leq 0.01$,*** $= p \leq 0.001$.

nificant negatively, suggesting perhaps the greater availability of freshwater resources in water-rich areas such as large portions of sub-Saharan Africa or Latin America. Most importantly, the variable with the strongest expectation of a relationship with fresh water availability, precipitation, indeed exhibits a strong degree of association.

Finally, in Table 8.6 we turn to the analysis of soil erosion by chemicals as the soil erosion most directly induced by human beings. Only one variable has any bearing on this form of environmental degradation, deaths per capita. Apparently, governments in unstable societies are unable to exert sufficient influence on industrial polluters to prevent significant soil erosion by chemicals. Contrary to prediction, the extent of democracy has no relationship with a type of environmental degradation most directly attributable to business or industrial activity. Thus, in the last two tables, we now

TABLE 8.6 Regression of Soil Erosion by Chemicals on the Explanatory Variables

Variable	Correlation (r)	Partial	b	t
Democracy	-0.11[a,b]	0.08	0.14	0.75[c]
	-0.03	0.12	0.01	1.09
	-0.14	-0.02	-0.02	-0.22
Agricultural Density	-0.06[d]	0.01	0.01	0.09
Population Growth	0.16	0.03	0.10	0.29
GDP per Capita	-0.21	-0.12	-0.0001	-1.08
Log Age	-0.06	0.08	5.16	0.79
Deaths per Capita	0.26	0.23	0.11	2.21*
European Location	-0.11	0.03	0.23	0.24
Precipitation	0.05	0.02	0.001	0.19
Constant			41.50	0.84

$R^2 = 0.10$, $R_a^2 = 0.02$, $N = 97$[b]
$R^2 = 0.10$, $R_a^2 = 0.01$, $N = 96$
$R^2 = 0.10$, $R_a^2 = 0.02$, $N = 95$

[a]A positive sign denotes a positive impact on a measure of environmental *degradation*, while a negative sign indicates that the variable promotes environmental *preservation*.

[b]Values given in the first row are for the political rights index, those in the second row are for the liberal democracy index, while those in the third row are for the Polity III index. The same holds true for the multiple correlations at the bottom of the table.

[c]All tests are one-tailed because of the directional hypothesis tested here.

[d]Because of similarities in the findings for the control variables using any of the three measures of democracy, only the values of coefficients emanating from the use of the Polity III index are reported here.

* $= p \leq 0.05$,** $= p \leq 0.01$,*** $= p \leq 0.001$.

have two forms of environmental protection that are not explained significantly in any direction by our three measures of democracy.

These findings should be compared with those emanating from another systematic empirical study of the relationship between democracy and the environment, but with differing results (Gleditsch and Sverdrup, 1996). These comparisons can be made on two variables that are identical in both studies, CO_2 per capita and deforestation. Others, such as freshwater availability and biodiversity, either have different variable definitions, different data sources, and most frequently both differences occurring simultaneously. Regarding CO_2 emissions per capita, when controlling for GDP per capita, Gleditsch and Sverdrup (1996: 23) found a nonsignificant negative relationship between democracy defined as the dichotomized Polity III index and this air pollutant (partial $R = -0.15$). Their universe of countries is substantially larger ($N = 124$) than that found in this study, largely due to the introduction of additional variables and data limitations on the multivariate analyses found here. In a subsequent multivariate test with $N = 108$, approximating the number used here, they found that democracy had a significant negative effect on CO_2 emissions. In this instance, GDP per capita and a human development index (HDI) constructed by the UNDP were included. Given the relatively high correlation between economic development and HDI, as well as the high correlation between economic development plus its square and democracy, the levels of collinearity may be high in this equation.[9] But the major difference is probably due to the necessary omission of Communist countries in the present study[10] because of the absence of such countries in the most highly reputed data source for GDP per capita (Summers and Heston, 1988). The choice between universality of coverage and data quality was difficult, but given the centrality of economic development both theoretically and empirically and the recency of emergence from Communism for these countries resulting in much economic and political flux, their omission was the lesser of the two evils. This major difference between the two studies most probably applies to the deforestation variable as well.

Conclusion

The first and most obvious conclusion is that there is no uniform relationship between democracy and the environment. Three of our indicators, deforestation, CO_2 emissions, and soil erosion by water, demonstrated significant negative relationships between democracy and environmental preservation. Protected land area showed a positive relationship, and freshwater availability and soil erosion by chemicals demonstrated no significant relationship. Of even greater interest, perhaps, is the fact that these relationships ran counter to expectation (Gleditsch and Sverdrup, 1996; Payne, 1995a). Instead of positive relationships between the extent of democracy and environmental protection, as much popular and recent scholarly writings have suggested, the associations found here are principally negative or nonexistent. This should give pause to political leaders such as President Clinton and Vice President Gore who have trumpeted the virtues of democracy in protecting the environment.

A probable impetus to this premature conclusion is the identification of democracy exclusively with Western industrial democracy, wherein here the economic development variable (excepting CO_2 emissions) and to a somewhat lesser extent, European location, demonstrate positive associations with environmental protection. Yet, there are varying degrees of democracy worldwide, and many Third World, only partially developed, democratic polities have relatively large agrarian constituencies to satisfy, thus leading to significant degrees of deforestation, as for example in Brazil. To identify democracy entirely with Europe, North America, and Japan is a mistake; there are other democracies with population needs different from those in the West.

Another apparent mistake is the identification of democracy principally with Hirschman's concept of *voice*. The findings here suggest a more complex reality. Although important, as signified by the relationships disclosed by the use of the political rights index that emphasizes voting rights, nevertheless the political rights index, on the one hand, and the Polity III index emphasizing democratic institutionalization, on the other, at times behaved in an obverse fashion.

European location is another variable which suggests the importance of democratic institutions in limiting environmental degradation. Both CO_2 emissions and soil erosion by water were affected negatively by European location. In the former instance, the Polity III index, which is institutionally based, demonstrated the strongest relationship. But in addition to democratic institutions within countries, the principal institution here is international. The EC (now the EU) established standards of various types, and, even for nonmember countries, provided a model and impetus for conformity to certain standards of environmental protection. Elimination of the European location variable from the regression equations reduced the overall percentages of variance explained, especially for the preceding two environmental indicators. However, eliminating this variable had no substantial impact on the directionality or significance of the measures of democracy in any of the regression equations.

In addition to democracy and European location, economic development also is significant in several of the analyses. Indeed, it largely accounts for the high proportion of the overall variance explained in CO_2 emissions. This implies, of course, that development in general and economic development, in particular, are highly relevant to environmental issues. Yet, even with its inclusion along with the remaining variables, overall percentages of variance explained in the other environmental indicators were not very large. This suggests either that, in addition to the statistically significant effects found here, important variables necessary for model specification were not included, or that there may be significant idiosyncratic explanations of environmental protection that cannot be tapped by systematic investigations of the type represented in this study. Alternatively, large-scale random error in the data also would preclude the explanation of large percentages of the variance in the environmental indicators. Therefore, along with future model-building efforts and careful examinations of data quality, case-studies may constitute an important avenue for future investigations that explore the role of context-specific (country or region) environmental conditions. Studies of this type may reveal the potentially disproportionate impact of large, environmentally important countries such as Brazil or Russia; analyses that obviously could not be undertaken here.

Another caveat pertains to the responsiveness of democracies to problems such as environmental degradation. The currently available data simply may not be able to capture the effects of very recent efforts by democracies to protect the environment. For example, in December 1991, the Council of the European Community outlined a community strategy to limit emissions of CO_2; the goal was to stabilize CO_2 emissions in the community at their 1990 level by the year 2000 (Moussis, 1995: 190). The Clinton and Gore administration has been making concerted efforts to reduce carbon emissions, culminating in the global climate change meeting in December 1997 in Kyoto, Japan. It may take some time for these efforts to bear fruit. Only future studies will be able to ascertain the extent to which past behavior is a guide to the future, or if these recent environmental measures by democracies will reverse the trends disclosed here.

Manus I. Midlarsky, b. 1937, Ph.D. in political science (Northwestern University, 1969); Moses and Annuta Back Professor of International Peace and Conflict Resolution, Rutgers University, New Brunswick (1989–); most recent books: *Inequality, Democracy, and Economic Development* (editor, Cambridge University Press, 1997), *The Evolution of Inequality: War, State Survival, and Democracy in Comparative Perspective* (Stanford University Press, 1999), and *Handbook of War Studies II* (University of Michigan Press, 2000).

Notes

1. While it might have been informative to examine changes in environmental conditions from one time period to the next, the present cross-sectional multivariate analysis of levels is appropriate as a first cut into a considerable amount of data. In the future, changes in the environmental measures might be used as dependent variables to ascertain the extent to which democracies are nonresponsive to environmental threat. Put another way, are environmental conditions improving or worsening as the result of environmental interventions by the world's democracies?

2. Data on CO_2 emissions containing the world flux in carbon from deforestation, reforestation, logging, and changes in agricultural practice (WRI, 1992) could have been used, but these estimates appear to have skewed these data away from the direct contribution of fossil fuel combustion, gas flaring, and so on. The data used here also are consistent with those used by Gleditsch and Sverdrup (1996).

3. Because the direction of greater democracy in the source for the political rights index is reversed from that of liberal democracy and Polity III, the signs in the tables are reversed for this variable in order to establish consistency with the other two measures.

4. The use of this data source presented a difficult choice between data quality and universality of coverage. Because of uncertainties in reporting economic data from Communist countries, Summers and Heston (1988) omitted them from their principal dataset for GDP. Instead, they present a separate table reporting GNP for nine centrally planned countries. These data are not comparable with those for GDP emanating from market economies. As this is the most highly reputed source

for GDP per capita and the Communist countries were undergoing rapid transitions in this time period, their omission was felt to be justified for the purposes of obtaining reliable results.

5. Age of polity is recorded as the year of attainment of sovereignty. Consequently, the directionality of coefficients in the tables was reversed in order to reflect the actual time since independence. The earlier the date of independence, the longer the polity age. Probably even more desirable as a variable would be the age of democracy, but these data are somewhat problematic and probably would require the use of several different measures. First, there are different estimates for the transition to democracy. For example, while Dix (1994: 97) has Turkey emerging to a stable democracy in 1983, Power and Gasiorowski (1997: 153) set the date in 1987. India is given a 1947 date by Dix but 1952 by Power and Gasiorowski, and they further assert that there is a breakdown of democracy in 1975, to be resumed in 1977. As difficult as Third World countries are to pinpoint, there are even problems in specifying the precise dates for older Western polities. Dix has Canada emerging to stable democracy in 1867, while Przeworski and Limongi (1997: 173) specify 1920. The United States is given as 1865 and the United Kingdom, 1918, by Dix, while Przeworski and Limongi have the two dates as 1830 and 1911, respectively. Second, even using several measures of age of democracy, there is the problem of choosing which transition to adopt in cases of multiple transitions. Power and Gasiorowski, for example, provide four dates for Turkey, three for Ghana and South Korea, and two for the Dominican Republic, the Philippines, Togo, Uruguay, and Venezuela. Even choosing the latest transition does not guarantee that this will lead finally to a stable democracy. A data analysis of this type is best deferred to a future study where one would be able to fully concentrate on its intricacies.

6. Because of the absence of data on GDP per capita for the Communist countries in the data source and their consequent exclusion (see footnote 4), European geographical location and European political organizational membership are almost identical in scope.

7. The exception is freshwater per capita in which the political rights index and that for Polity III exhibited significant positive associations with that environmental indicator, with GDP per capita excluded. However, the tolerances for both democracy measures and GDP per capita in the original equations (see Table 8.5) were high enough, ranging between 0.33 ($VIF = 3.00$) and 0.44 ($VIF = 2.27$) so that we can be reasonably confident that the GDP per capita control had a substantive effect, not a statistically artifactual one. In one instance, soil erosion by chemicals, the Polity III index actually had a significant negative association with the dependent variable with GDP per capita removed from the equation. With that control included, as can be seen in Table 8.6, there was no significant association between this measure of democracy and the environmental indicator.

8. I am indebted to an anonymous referee for this suggestion.

9. Evidence of multicollinearity is found in the beta (standardized coefficient) value of -1.31 obtained by Gleditsch and Sverdrup (1996: 25) for GDP per capita. An absolute value of beta above 1.00 is suggestive of this effect.

10. The finding of a linear relationship between GDP per capita and CO_2 emissions ($R = 0.90$) shown in Table 8.2 in contrast to Gleditsch and Sverdrup's (1996: 22) finding of curvilinearity (their linear $R = 0.69$), is suggestive of this important difference in universe composition.

Chapter Nine

The Limits and Promise of Environmental Conflict Prevention

RODGER A. PAYNE

Environmental Conflict

In recent years, a large and growing group of scholars has found that environmental degradation and/or resource scarcities can lead to violent conflict (Homer-Dixon, 1991, 1992, 1994; Klötzli, 1997; Libiszewski, 1997). The focus of this chapter is the possibility of preventing conflicts caused or aggravated by what have been termed 'environmental scarcities'. Of course, prevention of violence and ecological degradation has, for years, been a central goal of researchers working in the field. Thomas Homer-Dixon (1991: 88) indicated a desire to 'help identify key intervention points where policy makers might be able to alter the causal processes linking human activity, environmental degradation, and conflict'. In the same article, he argues against placing 'too much faith in the potential of human ingenuity to respond to multiple, interacting, and rapidly changing environmental problems once they have become severe' (Homer-Dixon, 1991: 103–104).[1] Waiting to act until crises are apparent could prove to be an unacceptably risky approach. Instead, states should act now to mitigate ongoing degradation. If appropriately scaled, prevention strategies can be much less costly in terms of both potential economic savings and reduction in human suffering.[2] Moreover, the exhaustion of certain resources, such as fish stocks or tropical forests, and the devastation related to some kinds of environmental distress, such as eutrophication caused by fertilizer run-off, are nearly irreversible.

Unfortunately, preventing environmental degradation may prove to be an impossible mission, for various reasons. A vast 'doomsday' literature explains several basic and perhaps insurmountable political and economic barriers to global environmental management. To summarize: powerful status quo forces typically preclude action—especially interstate cooperative action—until trouble is imminent. The familiar 'Tragedy of the Commons' (Hardin, 1968) situation illustrates the problem of overcoming individual interest in exploiting the environment. States of the North and South often find very basic material reasons to differ over questions of environment and development. Also, increasingly prevalent and influential private environmental organizations have found themselves at loggerheads with both rich and poor states regarding sustainable development practices. In addition, both states and powerful transnational corporations often overlook negative long-term indicators in favor of short-term profits. To date, global economic development has promoted far more environmental destruction than cleanup (UNEP, 1997: 3). Yet, failure to address ecological problems for whatever reason could prove disastrous, because researchers expect environmentally-induced conflict to 'jump sharply in the next decades as scarcities rapidly worsen in many parts of the world' (Homer-Dixon, 1994: 39).

Given the significance and scale of the political and economic hurdles, forestalling environmentally-caused violence would seem to require unprecedented global policy coordination, and even intervention in particular contexts, to provide targeted assistance for specific 'green' purposes. Such action is not beyond the realm of the imagination, however, as a few recent international initiatives offer some hope. Perhaps the most promising of all was initiated in the early 1990s, when states managed to create a multi-billion dollar Global Environment Facility (GEF) which has attempted to achieve various specific environmental objectives in ongoing development projects. Below, by critically examining the GEF's policies and practices, I explore the broad outlook for environmental conflict prevention. Specifically, I evaluate the prospective ability of an organization such as the GEF to provide meaningful levels of assistance to forestall environmental conflict. Additionally, I focus on the politics of institutional decisionmaking because active participation of poor states and nongovernmental organizations may prove critical to the effectiveness of the GEF or any other similar actor.

Before proceeding, it should be noted that many scholars believe that the link between environmental scarcities and conflict has not been persuasively demonstrated.[3] Nonetheless, the accumulating body of work on the alleged relationship between environment and conflict will here be considered sufficiently persuasive to make prevention a deserving topic of investigation. Of course, the significant economic and health risks associated with degradation and resource exhaustion would make analyzing global ecological assistance a worthwhile task, even if the link between environment and conflict should prove tenuous.[4]

The GEF Case

In 1991, the World Bank, the UN Environment Programme (UNEP), and the UN Development Programme (UNDP) were appointed implementing agencies of a sizable Global Environment Facility. After an initial pilot phase, which included intense negotiations about various 'green' fund proposals at the June 1992 'Earth Summit' (UN Conference on Environment and Development or UNCED) in Rio de Janeiro, Brazil, the GEF was granted permanent independent operational status in 1994. Since then, the GEF has grown in size and scope. During the early 1990s pilot phase, 115 GEF projects worth $730 million were funded in more than 60 states, although up to $4 billion had been pledged. More recently, the fund had $2 billion in its coffers for the three-year period 1994–97, although only about $1.2 billion were spent for all GEF projects through 1996. The fruits of the latest three-year replenishment effort promise more modest growth, with $2.75 billion pledged by March 1998. Over this decade, the GEF has now funded more than 500 projects, worth $2 billion in 120 countries (GEF, 1999).

The GEF has a stated goal of becoming the principal multilateral source of environmental funding, and aims to move other development institutions toward its objectives by adding GEF funds to their projects. Although the agency has encountered fairly typical financial collection problems, the Global Environment Facility is already the world's most important 'green' institution, and is especially significant for the developing world's recipient states.[5]

Of course, neither the GEF nor any other multilateral institution was specifically created to head off environmentally-caused conflict. Nonetheless, given the GEF's promising ecological mission, which is elaborated further below, prevention of violence could well be a fairly direct consequence of its work. Indeed, the connection between environmental degradation and conflict is recognized as important by the agency's leadership. Chief Executive Officer and Chairman Mohamed T. El-Ashry (1995a) has noted that the world faces 'a wide variety of critical environmental threats' including the prospect of 'international conflict over shared water resources'. He warns more generally that 'the potential for conflict over resource use and allocation has been escalating'. By addressing these sorts of concerns, Nicholas Van Praag (1994), the institution's Head of External Affairs, concludes that the GEF will 'help support global environmental security'.[6]

In short, the scope of the GEF's mandate and the vision of its leadership make this relatively new global actor a worthy candidate for investigation of environmental conflict prevention. Focusing on the GEF case is also justifiable because of the insights gained relevant to other related Bretton Woods institutions which affect the global environment, such as the World Bank, the International Monetary Fund, and the World Trade Organization (French, 1995). These and other institutions have been under close scrutiny in recent years and have been pressured by environmental groups and some states to address global ecological concerns. Hypothetically, if sufficient changes occur, these institutions could become good global citizens instead of green outlaws in the eyes of their critics. Already, the World Bank funds numerous dedicated environmental projects and has pursued various institutional reforms (Payne, 1997). The GEF explicitly facilitates this process by attaching approximately two-thirds of its monies to Bank projects. Moreover, a World Bank attorney (Silard, 1995: 653) acknowledges that the GEF is a 'state of the art' organization 'being watched closely' as a potential model institution. Clearly, lessons gleaned from the GEF case are broadly applicable.

Prospects for Environmental Conflict Prevention

In this section, two dimensions of environmental conflict prevention are examined. First, numerous environmental problems must be identified and resolved before they lead to cataclysmic ends. Important economic and strategic problems are already apparent. Second, a variety of political barriers precluding effective global environmental action must be overcome. The following subsections briefly elaborate on various aspects of these issues. Subsequently, I investigate whether an institution like the GEF can overcome these obstacles.

Financial and Strategic Issues

To prevent strife associated with environmental causes, 'conflict-prone' regions or states need to be identified, and their problems addressed in a meaningful and timely fashion. Both the body of case-studies compiled by researchers working on environment and conflict and the relatively high prevalence of all types of inter- and intrastate conflicts in Asia, Latin America, and Africa demonstrate that developing countries are those most likely to suffer violence related to ecological degradation. Since the world's poorest countries face major environmental problems, seemingly without the basic economic wherewithal to address them, meaningfully protecting the environment may well require the commitment of vast external assistance.

Indeed, the absolute level of wealth in some countries may simply be too low to promote ecological goals. Conceivably, internal reallocation of resources could ameliorate some environmental problems in many poor states. Such redistributive policies, of course, pose daunting political, social, and economic challenges which cannot be fully addressed here. However, a partial justification for examining external assistance can be sketched briefly. Homer-Dixon (1995) argues persuasively that resolving resource scarcities may well depend upon an adequate supply of 'social ingenuity', which encompasses (Barbier and Homer-Dixon, 1996: 3) 'ideas applied to the creation, reform and maintenance of institutions', relating to the state, civil society, and markets. Unfortunately, because resource scarcities magnify social conflict and violence, Barbier and Homer-Dixon find that they impede the development of social ingenuity. Elites pursue rent-seeking strategies to preserve their position, and scarce economic capital is spent managing and mitigating crises rather than pursuing long-term adaptation to scarcity. External intervention may well be the best hope for states suffering these problems.

Unfortunately, no one knows how much it would cost to target the environmental problems that are most likely to lead to conflict in the most vulnerable areas. To gain an idea of the external monies required to mitigate a wide range of ecological concerns, consider the financial resources thought to be needed in merely one region, Asia: 'The World Bank estimates that Asia will need $38 billion a year by 2000, or 2–3 percent of the region's gross domestic product, to address environmental problems' (Park, 1995). The funds required globally are truly mind-boggling. At the Earth Summit, the UNCED secretary-general noted that $125 billion annually (Susskind, 1994: 112) would be needed from the North in order for the South to implement Agenda 21, the lengthy environmental action blueprint agreed at the Rio Summit, up to the year 2000. Even if this figure—which is considered by many to be completely arbitrary—is twice that actually needed, the monies required are substantial. The recommended assistance figure is approximately double that currently provided for all aid purposes by the rich states. Moreover, despite the apparent need for vastly greater sums, in recent years many affluent countries have been trimming, rather than increasing, their relief budgets.

Although it is always difficult to find significant cash for development assistance, raising and distributing money may not prove to be the most burdensome problem for global environmental policymakers. Instead, practical strategic concerns may top their agenda. How can conflict-prone regions be identified? Will assistance be forthcoming in advance of environmental calamity? Neither of these questions is easily answered, but the cumulative body of research on conflict and the environment serves as an indicator of high-priority problems and conflict-prone regions.

A comprehensive literature review is obviously redundant, given previous research in this field, but a very brief summary of the main causes of environmental conflict is in order. Recognizing these causes is a strategic prerequisite to any efforts at prevention.

First, states sometimes use violence to assure access to vital raw materials. In addition to oil, case-studies of the Middle East suggest that water shortages or disputes about control can trigger conflict (Gleick, 1993c; Lowi, 1993a). This literature includes much informed speculation concerning the chance for a conflict involving Israel, Egypt, Ethiopia, Turkey, and Syria. Homer-Dixon (1994: 18), however, reports 'little empirical support' for the hypothesis linking renewable resource scarcities to conflict. Second, group-identity conflicts can be provoked by migration of peoples fleeing a degraded or resource-strained environment. India perhaps offers an example of this situation. The poverty and social turmoil suffered by Bangladesh over the past 40 years are related to high population growth rates, severe flooding, and land scarcity. Consequently (Homer-Dixon, 1992: 52; Swain, 1996), millions of people fled to neighboring India, where they have 'triggered serious inter-group conflict' in the state of Assam.

Third, deprivation conflicts can be spurred when the poor find themselves facing the worst effects of deforestation, soil erosion, and pollution of water, soil, and air. People impoverished by environmental calamities tend to become increasingly angry and violent because of their plight. The recent insurgency in the Philippines (Homer-Dixon, 1992), and perhaps the Zapatista case in Mexico, serve as examples. In the Philippines, poor agricultural laborers and farmers could either work unproductive (and ecologically volatile) uplands or migrate to shanty towns around cities. In rural uplands, insurgency movements successfully recruited frustrated peasants for their attempted revolution.

Obviously, with conflict prevention in mind, some objectives should be given higher priority than others. As suggested by this brief list and a burgeoning literature, deforestation, water shortages and flooding, soil erosion, and desertification have been linked to conflict involving one or more states, especially in the developing world.[7]

I will discuss later the GEF's likely distribution of funds for the most important concerns and to the neediest areas. In particular, I examine whether the GEF will be able to prevent environmental conflict given its operational objectives, funding, and political structure.

Political Barriers

In order to collect and distribute funds for environmental purposes, a global institution must first overcome several important barriers to international cooperation. These include traditional impediments to interstate collaboration grounded in state interests, North-South economic and political divisions, and disputes between state and non-state actors over the transparency and accountability of international institutions. This section explains these obstacles.

Clearly, a wide range of environmental problems require genuinely global action. It is now an accepted truism that individual states alone cannot prevent the destruction of the atmospheric ozone layer, head off the so-called 'greenhouse' effect, save whales and many more threatened species, or avoid other 'tragedy of the commons' problems. As a consequence of various barriers to cooperation, collective action problems of this sort may not be resolved. For example, neorealist international relations theorists note that individual state pursuit of relative gains, or power (Grieco, 1990, but see Snidal, 1991), along with the so-called 'free rider' problem, preclude significant interstate cooperation, even on global environmental concerns (Waltz, 1979: 197, 209–210). As states will not readily surrender sovereignty, international institutions that might attempt to regulate state behavior face inherent limitations (Morgenthau, 1985: 328–346).

Fortunately, the most challenging global commons problems do not seem to be high-priority concerns for those narrowly interested in environment and conflict. As noted by Homer-Dixon (1994: 7), climate change and ozone depletion are long-range concerns that should not trigger conflicts in the near term.[8] Obviously, global environmental planners will need to evaluate their concerns regarding conflict partly on the basis of questions of anticipated adverse effects and timing. Most environmental conflicts stem from local or regional problems that are quite immediate and apparent, such as loss of topsoil or clean water supplies. On the other hand, aggregating wealth for the purpose of international disbursement is a collective action problem, subject to the barriers noted above. Thus, to the extent that funding for environmental improvement is critical even to local or regional action, those interested in environment and conflict should be concerned about the difficulty of achieving interstate cooperation.

Another related barrier to global environmental cooperation involves North-South politics. Classic rich-poor divisions undermine the prospects of political cooperation. While the world's most affluent states have the resources to help poorer countries fund environmental protection, securing redistributive policy goals is problematic at best. Yet, as Tariq Hyder, a negotiator for the Group of 77, notes, 'it is now clear that in terms of the global atmosphere and environment, we are all in the same lifeboat. If the developing countries are not given the trade opportunities, debt relief, credit facilities, financial assistance and the technology flows that they require for their development, we all eventually pay the price' (quoted by Jordan, 1994a: 17). Ken Conca (1993: 319) goes so far as to suggest that because of its unilateral ability to pursue unsustainable development, the

South holds 'an effective veto over . . . international environmental protection'.

Effective global cooperation does not merely hinge on the willingness of the North to finance environmental action, or of the South to alter its immediate development plans. Additionally, the North and South often vehemently disagree about the political administration of regimes and/or institutions devoted to development purposes. For example, both wealthy and poor states wish to control decisionmaking procedures in international institutions. This basic 'structural conflict' was explained by Stephen Krasner (1985) who noted that poor states are interested in redistributive goals and wish to control agents authoritatively to make these goals reachable. As a result, they push for decision rules based on 'one state, one vote', as used in the UN General Assembly. At the same time, states of the North want to block extensive redistribution and seek to control agents to prevent this from occurring. Typically, they argue for weighted voting in institutions based on 'one dollar, one vote' (French, 1995: 26), as utilized in the Bretton Woods institutions, the World Bank, and International Monetary Fund.

Several relatively important hurdles must be cleared before effective collaboration can be achieved between North and South. Failure to engage the North means that any proposed solutions will lack adequate financing and perhaps other vital resources, such as expertise. Disregarding the South implies that numerous environmental problems, especially second-order effects such as conflict, will not be addressed. As Joyeeta Gupta (1995: 38) argues, 'in order to deal effectively with global environmental problems, a working [North–South] partnership is a must and mutual distrust needs to be replaced by good faith in each other'. Put differently, the various parties need to recognize and/or construct a generalizable interest in their shared environmental problems (Payne, 1996).

The final political barrier to meaningful global environmental action is the tension between nongovernmental organizations and states. This strain can affect the success or failure of assistance, since research increasingly demonstrates the value of what both scholars and aid officials call 'participation' in the development process: 'A growing body of evidence suggests that for a project to succeed, its planning process must include the people it is supposed to benefit' (French, 1995: 51–52). Yet, NGOs, which are often the best—and sometimes only—representatives of affected peoples, are usually denied direct access to the international institutions created by states. Neither affected individuals nor NGOs typically have much influence over decisionmaking and, in the development realm, are usually denied access even to project information that would otherwise allow them to contribute informed inputs to decisionmaking. Aid recipient states sign confidentiality agreements with international development institutions which virtually assure secrecy in the process.

Over the past two decades, transnational NGOs have attempted to scrutinize numerous World Bank development efforts, but have been slowed by such secretive and aloof procedures. Partly as a consequence of these closed practices, the World Bank is an oft-criticized institution. The Bank has also repeatedly funded unsustainable development and regularly ignored its own environmental standards (Rich, 1994). Apparently, the Bank has been propelled by focused financial imperatives to make loans. In any event, the Bank has arguably magnified its material errors by making decisions without the input of affected parties and by withholding vital project information from potential critics, such as transnational environmental groups. NGOs argue that their exclusion from the development process prevents them from stopping misguided projects or suggesting better alternatives (Gupta, 1995: 40). In short, achieving genuinely sustainable development may depend upon the transparency and accountability of institutions, assured by the free flow of information and multiple inputs into decision-making (Payne, 1995a).[9]

The Global Environment Facility

The Global Environment Facility was specifically designed to fund environmental portions of development projects that would otherwise overlook these dimensions.[10] To that end, the institution's strategic objectives were outlined by CEO Mohamed T. El-Ashry (1995a): 'First, the GEF will seek to minimize the risks of global environmental damage. Second, the GEF will seek to maximize global environmental benefits', presumably by funding environmental cleanup or resource preservation. In the broadest official terms, the GEF will serve as the 'major provider of funds to implement the provisions of the United Nations' action plan on sustainable development, Agenda 21, in developing countries' (Jordan, 1994a: 15). On paper, these stated goals suggest a monumentally important organization. However, in reality, the GEF's agenda is much more narrowly cast. Following the original pilot stage, funds have been targeted at projects in four main areas: those that address global climate change, loss of biodiversity, pollution of international waters, and depletion of the ozone layer. More recently (GEF, 1998a), 'activities addressing land degradation, primarily desertification and deforestation, as they relate to the four focal areas' have also been made eligible for funding.

In regard to global political concerns, the GEF by charter is supervised by an assembly of representatives from all participating countries—165 as of mid-1999. Any UN member is eligible to join. The assembly is responsible for reviewing the general policies of the GEF and meets every three years, although it did not have its first meeting until April 1998. In addition, a council of the GEF serves as the main governing body for all operational issues. By compromise decision, 32 states serve on the council, eighteen from recipient countries (distributed by a predetermined geographic formula in order to represent states from all of the world's regions) and fourteen from nonrecipient donor states. Of the recipient states, sixteen are developing countries and two are states with economies in transition.

The GEF will devote significant resources to preventing environmental destruction in developing nations, thus, some conflicts otherwise triggered or magnified by 'environmental scarcities' might well be averted. As noted in the introductory section, GEF officers certainly see security goals as important to their organization's mission. Indeed, given the GEF's mission and structure, it can be evaluated as both a preventive and cooperative global environmental institution. The following two subsections examine two central questions. First, will the GEF be able to contribute meaningful financial resources in especially conflict-prone regions? Second, can the GEF overcome the significant political barriers to genuine global cooperation?

Financial and Strategic Concerns

The modest resources allotted to the GEF amount to a drop in the bucket of the funds needed to overcome global environmental problems (WRI, 1994–1995: 231). Many tens of billions of dollars annually are needed for that task. Moreover, the GEF's budget compares unfavorably with the economic activity involved in global trade and investment, which undoubtedly have substantial—often negative—consequences for the global environment. For example, the World Bank reported in 1997 that private foreign investment in developing countries totaled over $240 billion in the previous year (Associated Press, 1997). Moreover, since the mid-1980s, developing countries have been transferring over $100 billion annually in debt service to wealthy states. The lowest-income countries spend approximately half their export earnings on debt servicing. These trade, debt, and environment issues are integrally related. Many of the most indebted countries have pursued ecologically destructive practices such as clearcutting, in order to utilize timber and other resources for export. The mobility of global capital makes it possible for transnational companies headquartered in affluent states to instigate such damaging policies.

On the other hand, as the GEF's El-Ashry has noted in defense of his agency, funds from the organization can be viewed as a catalyst for broader environmental action. Additional public and private sector sources of revenues should be attracted to projects that gain attention because of their support from the GEF (El-Ashry, 1995). The parallel is the World Bank, where it is often estimated that a project will receive many dollars for each dollar put up by the Bank. Moreover, because GEF funds are only provided for the environmental portions of specific projects, anyone calculating the total GEF effect on development assistance should arguably include the much larger sums spent on World Bank or other projects that GEF funds often supplement and sometimes make feasible. Because of this incremental cost approach, GEF projects are really only as good as the original development efforts they supplement. As shown below, this can be a major problem.

Rather than diverting monies from traditional assistance programs, GEF funds have from the beginning meant to complement them. This is known as 'additionality' (Susskind, 1994: 18), a term that remains in GEF documents but which seems to be increasingly meaningless for the donor nations that have attempted to get around it. Early indications show that some states have not increased their net development assistance, but have instead merely redistributed their current contributions. Since many affluent nations reduced foreign assistance programs in the post–Cold War era, the GEF seems to be battling other budget-starved entities for increasingly scarce resources. Furthermore, even if a generous economic multiplier is used to calculate the GEF's material effects, the amounts still fall far short of the estimated need for global environmental spending.

The next concern is the GEF's strategic priorities. Are the allocated funds going to conflict-prone regions and issues? To answer this question, it is necessary to examine generally how the budget is spent now and how it will likely be spent in the foreseeable future. Unfortunately, only a broad and speculative review is possible because it is quite difficult to examine the GEF's current environmental record in regard to specific ventures. Most GEF projects are only now moving from the design and planning stages to implementation. As of early 1999, the agency was still only developing indicators for measuring and monitoring progress toward program objectives for its biodiversity and climate change efforts (GEF, 1998). Indeed, Andrew Jordan (1994a: 15) argues that a 'thorough assessment' of most pilot projects, which were funded over the first three years (1991–1994), 'can be made only as the projects reach a sufficient level of implementation, which ... will not occur for another 5 or 10 years'. Because of such limitations, French (1995: 26), who nonetheless provides a partial review of some GEF activities, argues that the 'jury is still out as to how well the [GEF] reforms are working'. A meaningful review may not be possible until early in the twenty-first century.

Nonetheless, a prospective assessment based primarily on stated GEF goals and likely budgets is offered here. Initially, two of the GEF's four strategic priorities are not considered pivotal for those wishing to prevent environmental conflicts in the near term. Climate change and ozone depletion, as noted above, may be important global environmental problems, but these long-range concerns will not contribute significantly to environmental conflict in the short term. Funds for projects mitigating the harms of the greenhouse effect, such as crop damage or coastal flooding, could preclude violence. However, three-quarters of all the ventures in this area involve funding renewable energy sources or energy efficiency and conservation endeavors. Their effects can only indirectly work to prevent conflict, and will be dwarfed unless the developed countries responsible for the overwhelming majority of greenhouse gas emissions alter their own energy policies. Since 1991, the GEF has devoted almost 40 percent of its budget to projects relating to global warming, but only about 5 percent to ozone-related efforts (GEF, 1999). The figures vary annually. Ozone-related project funding was only 1 percent of the budget in the pilot phase, but reached 9 percent in 1995–1996 (WRI, 1994: 23; GEF, 1996). In short, a substantial portion of the GEF budget has gone toward these long-range concerns, although it is expected that GEF ozone projects will be phased out in the next few years.

Initiatives related to the other two agency goals are more promising, particularly when considered in tandem with the recent land degradation objectives appended to the GEF mission. Biological diversity projects have received the largest share of GEF funds since 1991, comprising just over 40 percent of the agency's spending (GEF, 1999). Efforts designed simultaneously to preserve biodiversity and stop land degradation could meaningfully decrease environmental conflict if funds are targeted at critical regions. Especially useful would be projects to slow the pace of deforestation and desertification, problems which can trigger resource deprivation, migration, and other sources of conflict. Unfortunately, some early indications are that the GEF may be doing more harm than good on this front. A few GEF grants for biodiversity protection have been 'attached to larger forestry loans', potentially improving 'the attractiveness of the larger project to make it viable'. The net effect is that a small area of forest is set aside for preservation, but the pristine tract is 'overwhelmed by the destruction caused by the broader project' (French, 1994: 171). Public officials in Congo may have pursued GEF funds for this deceptive purpose, and a proposed project in Laos looks suspiciously similar. These examples highlight the somewhat dubious nature of El-Ashry's economic multiplier claims as well.

With the same caveat concerning the careful targeting of funds, efforts to preserve international waters could affect the risk of conflict in some regions. Since 1991, the GEF has spent approximately 13 percent of its funds on projects involving international waters, though only about 10 percent of all projects are devoted to this program. Will the institution aim its funds where they would be most likely to decrease conflict? According to the officers, it will. GEF CEO El-Ashry (1995b) claims that his agency will 'place priority on addressing . . . four areas of imminent threat'. Specifically, he mentions controlling 'land-based sources of pollution that degrade the quality of international waters', preventing 'degradation of critical habitats (such as wetlands, shallow waters, reefs, etc.)', controlling overfishing and overdrawing of water, and controlling ship-based sources of pollution.

Obviously, if the GEF targets significant funds to areas where states are overdrawing or polluting shared water resources, it could meaningfully decrease the risk of conflict in those regions. For example, the GEF is providing $20 million for a cleanup project involving Lake Victoria in Africa. The lake is bordered by Kenya, Uganda, and Tanzania, supplies water to 10 million people, and provides hundreds of millions of dollars worth of fishing for the three states. However, the World Bank reported in 1994 (cited in American Political Network, 1994) that the water is '"so severely polluted" that the entire lake ecosystem is "on the brink of collapse"'. Worse, the leaders of Kenya and Uganda 'have been fierce political rivals for years' (Wrong, 1996) and the states are historic foes that supported different ethnic groups in the recent conflict in Rwanda. As a further complication, the shoreline Luo people, who reside in both rival states, support the political opposition in Kenya. While forecasting political violence is not the purpose of this article, Lake Victoria does seem to be the kind of project GEF might fund to diminish the risk of future conflict. The situation is not substantially different from others which Homer-Dixon and colleagues have studied.

On the whole, the GEF is a promising global environmental institution, but it remains flawed. Funds available for projects are very modest compared with the substantial global need for environmental improvement. Agent priorities include global goals that are laudable, but do not greatly decrease the risk of environmental conflict in the short-term. Finally, while some funded projects may decrease conflict risks in particular regions—especially in regard to reducing desertification and deforestation and preserving international waters—other projects are quite suspect because of their attachment to larger and environmentally dangerous development plans.

Overcoming Political Barriers

El-Ashry (1995a), perhaps predictably, given his leadership position within the GEF, argues that the institution 'has a key role to play in promoting collective action—both as a facilitator and a funding mechanism'. Moreover, Steven Anderson (1995: 775, 818) writes that the GEF already is a 'successful model . . . for the resolution of global environmental problems'. Yet, as noted above, a number of seemingly intractable political obstacles limit the ability of states to cooperate internationally. In the specific context of global environmentalism, Jordan (1994b: 38) calls disputes between North and South and governments and NGOs '"structural" issues' which 'are so deeply rooted, they will continue to surface in international forums, including GEF'. This subsection will briefly review how such impediments might influence the effectiveness of the GEF.

The first political barrier to global environmental cooperation stems from traditional state concerns regarding pursuit of relative gains and diminution of sovereignty. Already, the GEF has experienced some difficulties in these areas. For an example, consider the GEF requirement that funds go only to projects that serve global environmental purposes, such as stopping the greenhouse effect or ozone-layer depletion, rather than national or regional goals. Of course, this is an especially problematic concern for those seeking to decrease environmentally-induced conflict because these global problems are apparently the least likely to cause conflict in the short term. In any event, rich states have insisted on this requirement as a precondition for their providing additional economic assistance for poorer states. As Gupta (1995: 33) argues, 'the nature of the financial mechanism regime has been heavily influenced by the hegemonic interests of the major donors'. An international relations theorist would note the rich states' reluctance to decrease their relative wealth and power in favor of the poor. These nations have been willing to participate in the institution only if they gain directly, and perhaps disproportionately, from its projects. Put simply, the affluent countries have behaved as if they are far more interested in long-term ozone and climate considerations than short-term improvements in water sanitation or soil conditions in the developing world.

At the same time, because of the various requirements placed on the receipt of funding, developing countries perceive that the great powers, through international institutions, are 'dictating terms and interfering in national policies' (Gupta, 1995: 38).[11] Jordan (1994a: 19) notes that, in the pilot phase, the GEF was clearly a 'donor-dominated operation'. This was because daily financial management was exerted by the World Bank, which is controlled by donors via weighted voting. In recent years, after the initial pilot phase was concluded, the Bank's direct role in the GEF has diminished. Nonetheless, the World Bank remains the institution's trustee, the GEF's secretariat is located within the Bank, and daily operations occur on the Bank's premises (Gupta, 1995: 30). Much of the negative political and economic baggage associated with the Bank has been carried over by critics on to the GEF (Sharma, 1996).

While such concerns have not precluded many states from participating in the GEF (in fact membership has increased substantially even as the World Bank's role has been diminished), they do suggest that individual states might be reluctant to submit specific development projects for GEF review out of concern that their plans would be altered. Depending upon one's point of view, for example, it is 'far from easy' (Jordan, 1994a: 32) to distinguish between global and national benefits, thus, there is ample opportunity for misunderstanding and confusion. A developing country might legitimately worry that its plan to clean up a river that does not flow across borders would flunk the GEF's global benefit standard. It might find itself coerced by funding opportunities to concentrate on a less pressing problem, although one could reasonably argue that improving the waterway would mitigate its several neighbors' fears of a mass emigration of people fleeing a desecrated environment. Even more likely, projects favored mostly by rich nations, such as energy efficiency, could be said to provide both general and specific benefits even though these might be long-term and modest; yet, the early returns suggest these are the easiest projects to fund.

Next, the GEF has in many other ways provided 'a forum and a subject to express the range' of North-South grievances (Gupta, 1995: 41). The mere existence of the institution, with its multi-billion-dollar budget, implies that some basic hurdles to global redistributive politics have been cleared. However, as the preceding discussion shows, the world's wealthiest states have actively tried to limit the GEF's scope to projects with widespread benefits. Rather than funding basic southern sanitation needs, for example, the GEF only funds projects with global dimensions that also help the North.

The GEF has additionally proven a new battleground for rich-poor disputes concerning the arrangement of international institutions. While wealthy states favor weighted voting mechanisms for decisionmaking, developing countries insist upon the one state, one vote procedures that they see as more democratic. On this issue, the GEF has reached a promising compromise. In the words of one scholar (Jordan, 1994a: 32), the restructuring of the GEF during the pilot stage was 'an attempt to balance the competing demands of developed and developing countries'.

It is expected (Jordan, 1994a: 19) that the assembly will be dominated by developing countries because they easily outnumber developed states. Because of the infrequency of its meetings, however, this agent will not be the most powerful within the GEF. The Council of the GEF is a far more powerful body. Meeting every six months in Washington, D.C., the council operates by consensus, but would use a "double majority" voting system to make decisions if members could not agree. In essence, it is modeled on both the UN General Assembly and the World Bank and therefore reflects some concerns of both rich and poor states. All successful votes require both a 60 percent majority of voting countries and the approval of donor countries representing 60 percent of contributions. In other words, northern states have agreed to share some power, but they maintain an effective veto over projects and procedures they might find offensive. The innovation might be more aptly called a 'double veto' since the South has now been granted a mechanism for blocking projects and procedures urged on them by the North.

Will these unique procedures help decrease the risk of environmental conflict? Arguably, they will. In part, this is for the simple reason that greater participation of the South encourages more cooperative outcomes. This is desirable for selecting environmental harms to address and for acting upon those selections. Moreover, sustainable development is apparently encouraged by extensive participation by many actors in genuinely open deliberations concerning global environmental problems and solutions (Payne, 1996). In institutions promoting such discursive practices, agents can intersubjectively identify generalizable interests and jointly construct solutions.

Finally, failure to include NGOs in institutional decisionmaking can be an important barrier to effective environmental action at the global level. Many member countries, especially developing nation recipients, and also the GEF implementing agencies fear that greater NGO access to information and decisionmaking will open them to increased criticism. On the other hand, excluding NGOs increases the risk that they will intensify their pressure-politics tactics and thereby influence donor states to regulate GEF activities more carefully (Fairman, 1994a: 28–29). Moreover, as noted above, to the extent that open access to information and decisionmaking fosters sustainable development practices, then these measures help decrease the risk of environmental conflict.

For its part, the GEF (1998) has proclaimed a 'spirit of partnership with NGOs and community groups around the world'. Indeed, Anderson (1995: 793) calls the cooperation among various state and nonstate actors involved in setting up the GEF 'unprecedented'. Today, NGOs have observer status at council meetings, after having been excluded from participant meetings during the pilot stage (Jordan, 1994a: 32). Five NGO representatives are allowed to interact with other participants in the meetings, while five others view the proceedings from closed circuit television. Moreover, institutional procedures now stipulate that NGOs are to be consulted concerning GEF policy and program issues. According to Jordan (1994a: 31), GEF implementing agencies—namely the World Bank, UNEP, and UNDP—are 'supposed to seek the advice' of NGOs 'for the identification, design, and implementation' of projects. NGOs like the World Wildlife Fund have even 'drawn up complete project proposals that have been adopted' (Anderson, 1995: 790).[12] Perhaps most impressively, procedures (GEF, 1995) designate that 'all GEF-financed projects will "provide for full disclosure of non-confidential information"'. Before rejoicing in these requirements, recall that the World Bank has been criticized for its failure to live up to similar guidelines (Rich, 1994: 306), primarily because even new rules retain borrowers' rights to assert financial confidentiality.

NGOs are also eligible to receive GEF funds. Specifically, they can apply for monies from the special Small Grants Programme (SGP). Disbursements from this account have a ceiling of $50,000 for national projects and $250,000 for regional projects. In total, by June 1998, the SGP had spent $42 million on more than 1,100 projects in 45 countries (GEF, 1998b: 19). Generally, NGOs and grassroots applicants submit very small-scale, decentralized projects. These grants are useful for experimentation purposes, but are obviously limited because of the size and scope of the program. Nonetheless, one of the central roles NGOs often claim for themselves is that they bring new ideas and information to the development debate, thus, their innovative role should not be dismissed lightly. Indeed, World Bank and scholarly studies of participatory development conclude that NGO presence and assistance make projects more likely to succeed, especially in the design stages (see Narayan, 1995).

Because of decades of pressure on international institutions like the World Bank and their donor governments, NGOs are arguably responsible for many of the reforms that now make the GEF both more democratic and accountable (Payne, 1995b, 1997). Nonetheless, many groups around the globe remain critical of GEF operations. As mentioned earlier, particular projects have been condemned, global ozone and climate goals are questioned, and procedures limiting NGO status to observation are criticized (Ong'wen, 1995).

The major concern here is how the NGO-state debate affects environmental conflict. This question is not easily answered. Suffice to say that as NGO participation becomes a normal part of GEF operations, it should be easier to achieve sustainable development. NGOs can identify problem spots, question dubious projects, and involve affected peoples. Even GEF documents (1995) mention the benefits of these practices. As a consequence of NGO involvement, environmental conflict should be reduced. Moreover, NGO participation in quasi-deliberative processes might also help to defuse environmental conflicts by highlighting generalizable interests. Unfortunately, because NGO roles have only recently even been defined at the GEF, I can do little more than speculate regarding the prospective benefits (see Young, 1999).

Conclusion

If ecological degradation, resource scarcity, and related problems are significant causes of conflict, then those interested in preventing global violence should embrace environmentalism. Put simply, sustainable development must be pursued not only to forestall environmental destruction and resource exhaustion, but also to prevent conflict triggered by these causes. Unfortunately, environmentally-caused violence is perhaps most likely to erupt in the world's poorest states which are least capable of pursuing sustainable development without substantial external assistance.

In general, the GEF case reveals a great deal about the prospects for seeking meaningful sustainable development to prevent environmental conflict. First, the evidence detailed above suggests that potentially conflict-prone states or regions might be targeted for aid, but that enormous financial needs and difficult political obstacles diminish the likelihood of meaningful action. Furthermore, although the GEF's institutional innovations may serve as ideals for other organizations, its design limits demonstrate the difficulty in leaping over very basic international cooperation hurdles relating to sovereignty, the power of the North, and the constraints on nonstate actors.

To date, the record suggests that the GEF's ability to help forestall environmental conflict is limited. The pledged $2.75 billion budget over 1998–2000 is superficially impressive, but falls far short of apparent worldwide need. Moreover, many of the monies continue to be targeted at global priorities of the North, such as the greenhouse effect and ozone-layer depletion. While these may be worthy long-term ecological concerns, they are not major causes of ongoing violent disputes. Even when funds are directed at problems that might cause near-term environmental conflict, such as deforestation, some specific projects have been token ecological measures tacked on to worrisome development plans that will cause great harm. Because of the time-lag needed to conduct accurate assessment, it is too early to conduct extensive analysis of GEF project effectiveness.

Politically, the GEF addresses many of the barriers that otherwise inhibit global environmental cooperation. To the institution's credit, many of the reforms were undertaken in response to criticisms levelled at it during the pilot phase (Fairman, 1994b; Sharma, 1996). For example, the South has been given more power in the administration of the GEF than it has ever wielded in Bretton Woods organizations such as the World Bank. Additionally, NGOs have been officially granted virtually unprecedented access to GEF decisionmaking and project information; yet, it remains to be seen whether these reforms are genuine or merely symbolic. Some NGO critics argue that the changes do not go nearly far enough, and they note that recipient states retain final authority over both project decisions and information dissemination.

All in all, the best hope for the current GEF seems to be that it might make a useful, but not extensive, contribution to preventing environmental conflict. The greatest promise lies in efforts to halt land and water degradation and scarcities. These are basic ecological concerns of the developing world, and research to date has identified them as important potential causes of environmental conflict. If the global community can fund projects often aimed at these problems, and simultaneously stimulate some additional public and private expenditures, then it will contribute meaningfully, albeit marginally, to the prevention of violence. Almost certainly, a substantially more effective preventive strategy for addressing 'ecological scarcities' will need to raise and spend tens of billions of dollars and specifically target those funds at regional environmental problems of the developing world. Moreover, developing states, affected peoples, and NGOs will need to have fairly open access to the relevant project design information to provide informed input into the decisionmaking process. Open and accountable institutions which encourage free-flowing information and informed participation could conceivably serve deliberative functions, making it possible to identify generalizable environmental interests and to construct valuable sustainable development practices (Payne, 1996, 1997; Williams and Matheny, 1995).

Rodger A. Payne, b. 1961, Ph.D. in government and politics (University of Maryland, 1989); associate professor, University of Louisville, Kentucky; director, Grawemeyer Award for Ideas Improving World Order; current main interests: transnational environmental politics and the construction of international discourse norms.

Notes

1. Among Homer-Dixon's second-stage policy interventions is the spread of liberal democracy. For a discussion of democracy and the environment, see Payne (1995a).

2. These same sort of arguments are made by those advocating preventive diplomacy (Lund, 1996) and early warning of humanitarian emergencies (Väyrynen, 1996).

3. For example, consider the case-study approach used by most of the researchers. Levy (1995: 56) claims that 'the empirical results of this effort still amount only to a collection of illustrations of violent conflict in which environmental resources played some important role'. He concludes that the environmental causes play 'fairly uninteresting analytical roles' and are often 'secondary or tertiary phenomenon behind more fundamental forces that are responsible for violence'.

4. Similarly, environmental goals may be worth pursuing in conflict situations not caused by scarcities. As the oil fires from the Gulf War demonstrated, conflict can create environmental hazards that should be addressed. GEF funds might well flow toward such problem areas once conflict has run its course. Restoration of a resource base could be an important dimension of post-war recovery.

5. Susskind (1994: 94) calls the expansion and modification of the GEF 'probably the greatest accomplishment' of the Earth Summit. By contrast, Jordan (1994: 35) argues that the GEF is a 'relatively minor player on the international stage'. The latter view is persuasive in part because the GEF budget is minuscule when compared to all global spending devoted to development.

6. El-Ashry (1994: 38) has offered virtually the same words on the GEF helping to 'ensure global environmental security'.

7. Population growth and poverty, also primarily centered in the developing world, have likewise been both directly and indirectly associated with environmen-

tally-induced conflict. However, my focus here is on direct environmental action and avoidance of resource scarcities rather than remedies for broader social ills.

8. Homer-Dixon acknowledges that these problems could contribute to conflict in the long term.

9. The World Bank has recently adopted guidelines which should make it more democratic in practice (Payne, 1997).

10. This so-called 'incremental cost' criterion has been much criticized as an inadequate guide for selecting projects and for shaping GEF strategic priorities. Additional discussion of this issue is offered below.

11. As might have been expected, the most powerful states have made sure that their own sovereignty and power are not threatened by the GEF. In the pilot stage, for example, the USA committed funds to the GEF without putting them in the institution's budget. Effectively, during the Bush administration, the USA provided zero funding for the GEF Core Fund (Anderson, 1995: 799). This maneuver allowed the USA to be the only state to maintain control over all its GEF-related monies. Additional wealthy states, such as Japan and Switzerland, also have limited access to some of their contributions.

12. All projects, regardless of sponsor, must be approved and endorsed by recipient governments (Island Resource Foundation, 1995).

Chapter Ten

Fair Division in the Spratly Islands Conflict

DAVID B. H. DENOON
STEVEN J. BRAMS

The security issues in East Asia commanding the most attention today are: the continuing uncertainty on the Korean penninsula, antagonism between Beijing and Taipei, and competing claims of sovereignty and economic jurisdiction in the Spratly Islands in the South China Sea.

Concern that North Korea might acquire nuclear weapons put Pyongyang in the international spotlight during the 1990s, and negotiations have yet to resolve this problem. Growing hostility in the Taiwan Strait dominated political commentary in 1995–1996, when China attempted to disrupt the Taiwanese presidential elections by testing missiles off the Taiwan coast. Yet attention may well shift southward in the next few years as the significance of the Spratly Islands is more widely understood.

Many observers have speculated about potential offshore oil in the Spratlys region (Chen, 1993: 247). In light of this potential, there has been an extensive debate about China's military intentions and capabilities in the area (Gallagher, 1994). The intent of this article is to broaden that discussion and explain the strategic significance of the issue; show that neither the current working groups nor the rules of the Law of the Sea Convention are likely to resolve the problem expeditiously;[1] and

---

An earlier version of this chapter was published as Denoon and Brams (1997).

demonstrate how a new fair-division procedure could facilitate negotiations and possibly resolve the dispute among the claimants to the Spratlys.

Background

There are more than 230 islands and reefs in the Spratly group, clustered in the South China Sea in the shape of a parallelogram, between the Philippine Island of Palawan and the southeastern coast of Vietnam. There are six claimants to all or part of the Spratlys (see Map 10.1 below).[2] Four of them—Vietnam, the Philippines, Malaysia, and Brunei—are members of the Association of Southeast Asian Nations (ASEAN); the remaining two claimants are China and Taiwan.

Since the Taiwan government (Republic of China) and the government of the People's Republic of China (PRC) both still assert there is only one China, the PRC's and Taiwan's claims currently overlap. We will not speculate on how their differences may be resolved in the future. Instead, we will treat them as a single Chinese claim. This is a reasonable simplification because, at the workshops sponsored by Indonesia and at the Senior Officers' Meetings (more on these later), China and Taiwan have had separate representatives but have coordinated their positions in advance.

Most of the Spratly islands and reefs are tiny; none is over a mile in length (Garver, 1992: 1015). It is also important to note that many of the reefs are not above high tide and therefore do not qualify under the Law of the Sea treaty (LoS) for a twelve-mile territorial sea (U.S. Department of State, 1995: 6).

China did not occupy a single Spratly Island until March 1988, when it clashed with Vietnam and took over Fiery Reef.[3] Yet the PRC claims the *entire* chain on the basis of early exploration and historical visits by Chinese naval and fishing vessels.

Vietnam bases its claims on French administration of the Spratlys and its subsequent occupation of selected islands (mostly by the South Vietnamese). The Philippine claims result from the actions of Tomas Cloma, a Filipino, who asserted rights to the entire region in 1956 on the grounds that the islands were unoccupied. Malaysia has made much more limited claims, based on occupancy and LoS rules for extension of its continental shelf. Brunei claims no islands but a defined territorial sea, based on LoS. We present in Table 10.1 a detailed summary of these competing claims and their historical origins.

World attention was drawn to the Spratlys in March 1988 when China sank three Vietnamese vessels and killed at least seventy-five Vietnamese soldiers and sailors in the process of seizing Fiery Reef (Chang, 1990). This clash followed an earlier incident in 1974, when China fought with South

MAP 10.1   Conflicting Malay and Chinese Claims

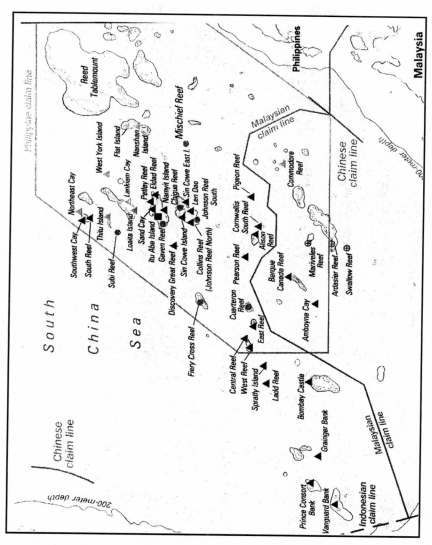

SOURCE: Interviews in Tokyo, Beijing, Kuala Lumpur, and Jakarta.

TABLE 10.1 Spratly Island Controversy

	1st Claim	1st Occupation[a]	Nature of Claim	Number of Islands/Reef Occupied Today
PRC/Qing Dynasty[b]	1887	1988 (6)	Historical Contacts + Treaty w/France	7
Taiwan/KMT	1930s (protesting French occupation)	1956 (1)	1952 Taiwan Treaty w/Japan + same basis as PRC	1
Vietnam[c]/*France*[d]	1933	1933 (9)	French administration of the region	
North Vietnam	1956–1975		Recognized Chinese claims	
South Veitnam	1956	1974 (6)	Reassertion of 1951 San Francisco Treaty claims	
United Vietnam	1978	1975 (6)	Historical use/occupancy	25
Japan	1939	1939–1951 (entire)	Relinquished control in 1951 San Francisco Treaty	0
Philippines[e]	1971	1968 (1)	*Res. Nullius*	8
Malaysia	1979	1988	Islands + continental shelf	3
Brunei	1992	none	Continental shelf + fishing zone, amended to EEZ	0

[a]The numbers in parentheses in the "1st Occupation" column are the numbers of islands initially occupied.

[b]The 1887 treaty between France and China divided the Gulf of Tonkin, giving all islands east of the meridien 108° 3' to China. The treaty did not cover the South China Sea, but China has claimed the treaty implied their control east and south of the Gulf of Tonkin.

[c]In 1958, China published its first Law of the Sea proclamation, extending its claim to the entire South China Sea. In 1992, the National People's Congress issued a new law covering the Senkakus, Paracels, and all the Spratlys.

[d]The Vietnamese first affirmed sovereignty over the parcels in 1816, but their claim to the Spratlys derives mostly from French occupation.

[e]In 1956, Tomas Cloma, a Philippine businessman, claimed a parallelogram-shaped area in the Spratlys, which he called Kalayaan (Freedomland). He based his claim in the concept of *Res. Nullius*, i.e., ownership because the area was previously unoccupied in 1971, the Philippine government followed this with an official claim for all of Kalayaan (which includes all of the Spratlys except Spratly Island). In 1978, the Philippine government "annexed" Kalayaan to Palawan Province.

SOURCE: Interviews in Tokyo, Beijing, Kuala Lumpur, and Jakarta.

Vietnam and expelled Saigon's troops from the Paracel Islands. Following China's occupation, Deng Xiaoping, leader of the Chinese Communist Party, told Philippine president Corazon Aquino, during her state visit to Beijing in 1988, that the entire South China Sea was Chinese territory. Deng said China's position on the Spratlys had three components: Beijing (1) had sovereignty, which was nonnegotiable; (2) would assure free passage for aircraft and ships; and (3) was willing to participate in joint ventures with other nations to develop the oil and gas deposits.

This rigid stance by China sparked major concerns in Southeast Asia. Each of the ASEAN claimants felt their interests were being dismissed and, worse, that China was clearly willing to use force to get its way.

By 1990 Indonesia, with assistance from Canada, was trying to defuse tension over the Spratlys.[4] The Indonesians set up a workshop series that included researchers and officials from all the claimants as well as outside specialists. These workshops gradually evolved into two tracks of discussions: an extensive series of technical working groups, focusing on such issues as mapping, scientific research, and ecological issues; and the Senior Officer's Meetings (SOMs), at which government representatives discuss more sensitive subjects, including sovereignty.

In 1992 China took two unilateral actions which, again, upset the ASEAN countries. In February, the Chinese National People's Congress passed a revised Territorial Sea Law, which made sweeping claims of Chinese sovereignty over many areas clearly in dispute.[5] Some observers saw this mostly as an attempt to bring Chinese law into conformity with the revised LoS Convention (Wang and Pearse, 1994), whereas others saw it as a brazen attempt to legitimzie Chinese unilateral moves (Kim, 1994). In addition, in June 1992 authorities in Beijing announced that they had let an oil concession to Crestone Energy Corporation, a small Denver-based firm, for exploration and development in the Wan-an Bei 21 (Vanguard Bank) sector off the Vietnamese coast. The WAB-21 site was in the center of several conflicting claims by other countries. The manner of the announcement was interpreted as a sign of Beijing's willingness to rebuff ASEAN claims.

These Chinese moves caused such a furor within the region that, in July 1992 at the ASEAN Summit Meeting's Post Ministerial Conference (which included observers from Beijing), China was pressed into agreeing that no more violence would be used in settling Spratly Island issues; and questions of sovereignty would be postponed until there was an appropriate climate for settlement.

Still another flap developed in January 1995 when it was discovered that Chinese People's Liberation Army troops had removed Philippine markers and set up an encampment on a tiny coral outcropping, known as Mischief Reef. Although Mischief Reef had not been occupied by Filipinos, and no force was used, the location was hitherto Philippine and clearly within

Manila's 200-nautical-mile Exclusive Economic Zone (EEZ). This produced a very heated reaction within ASEAN, leading in April 1995 to ASEAN representatives at the Hangzhou SOM taking a unified stand against China's actions. Subsequently, China took a softer diplomatic tack in dealing with ASEAN governments over the Spratlys, but it reinforced its structures on Mischief Reef in 1998 and continued to send its fishing boats into Philippine waters near Scarborough Shoal in 1999 (Dolven and Holland, 1999: 28).

In May 1995, the U.S. Department of State issued a formal statement on the Spratlys, saying that 'freedom of passage was a fundamental interest of the U.S.' and urging all the parties to avoid further use of force (Shelly, 1995). Responding to the resentment engendered by its actions, the Chinese government decided on a conciliatory move. In July 1995 at the ASEAN Summit in Brunei, Foreign Minister Qian Qichen announced that China would attempt to resolve the Spratlys dispute using 'recognized international law', including the 1982 LoS Convention.

Currently, there appears to be a period of moderate calm. However, this may be deceptive, because there has been, essentially, a stalemate in the Indonesia workshops, and no progress in the SOMs since the Hangzhou standoff. China's approach has been to concentrate on bilateral discussions, especially with Vietnam and the Philippines, and to avoid bargaining through ASEAN.

Many analysts see China caught in something of a bind. On the one hand, Beijing places a high premium on preserving its autonomy and avoiding concessions that will limit its future actions. Yet China's need for foreign capital and technology requires adhering to international norms (Yi, 1994). Attempts at maintaining this balance may explain the oscillation between a confrontational style and a more diplomatic one.[6]

The Need for a Resolution

A peaceful and stable resolution of the Spratlys claims is important for several reasons. First, the *pattern of violence* makes many observers speculate: Are the 1974 and 1988 incidents a prologue to a larger conflict?

Second, *freedom of passage* is critical not only to countries in the region but also to all major trading nations. Approximately 25 percent of world shipping moves through the South China Sea, so it is vital that no hostile nation control the shipping routes (Grunawalt, 1993). Similarly, the area is critical for military sea lanes, because fleets moving from the Pacific to the Indian Ocean need to transit the South China Sea. Moreover, if one nation dominated the area, it would have a chilling effect on the ASEAN region (Shambaugh, 1992). Thus, specialists have been working on how best to ensure that freedom of passage is guaranteed. Should it be through bilateral or multilateral treaties? Or is a better path the creation of a broader regional security organization?

Third, the *complexity* of this issue is such that no single institution in the region has been able to deal satisfactorily with all aspects of it. The workshops and the SOMs have been a useful venue for low-keyed discussion, and the ASEAN summits have provided visibility for the topic. But there is little doubt that one of the principal motivations for proceeding with the ASEAN Regional Forum (ARF) was to create a setting wherein China could not only participate but also hear the concerns of its neighbors (Tasker and Schwarz, 1994: 14–15). Hence, a central question is: Will ASEAN, China, or outside major powers be able to handle this dispute in a way that strengthens regional cooperation, or will the area's rivalries exacerbate this conflict?

The Basic Issues

There are four principal issues that underlie the stalemate over the Spratly Islands, which can be summarized by the following questions:

1. Who has *sovereignty* over the islands and surrounding waters?

2. How will the *economic potential* of the Spratlys region be developed?

3. How will *freedom of passage* be guaranteed?

4. What form will *regional security* take?

Sovereignty[7]

Sovereignty is the central problem, with maneuvering on it delaying progress on the other three issues.[8] Although it might be possible to reach some kind of agreement on regional security arrangements and freedom of passage without resolving sovereignty, a precise delineation of national ownership would make dealing with all the other issues far simpler.

It was not until the economic potential of the Spratlys and surrounding areas was recognized that the scramble for claims broke out. This process was accelerated by the negotiations over UNCLOS III, which heightened the salience of continental shelves and EEZs. Because the seabed between the Spratlys does not hold promising formations for hydrocarbons, it is the islands themselves that have become key pieces, in a game of strategic positioning, for gaining access to the surrounding areas and continental shelves.

The legal basis for *Chinese* claims rests on three grounds: discovery, occupation, and repeated assertion of ownership (Chang, 1991). It has been established that Chinese sailors surveyed parts of the Spratlys during the Eastern Han dynasty (A.D. 25–220), and that Chinese fishermen and traders frequented the area up until the 1600s (Shiying, 1993). Discovery, however, does not confer ownership unless there is relatively continuous occupation, coupled with strong protest should one's nationals be expelled.

Most of the Spratly islands and reefs are not large enough to sustain human habitation, so it is not surprising that China failed to occupy them continuously. This might not have been critical except for the fact that several colonial powers did hold sway in the South China Sea. Moreover, their successor governments (Vietnam, Malaysia, and Brunei) see no good reason to cede ownership to China (Jie, 1994).

Although there are overlapping claims among the ASEAN countries, the Southeast Asian nations are not a military threat to each other. This is why the dispute has generally been posed as one of China versus ASEAN. Although China repeatedly asserted its claims, beginning in the 1930s, they were broad and often undefined, thus limiting their significance under international law. In fact, many observers believe that China's claims to the Spratlys (and thus 200-nautical-mile EEZs spreading outward from the islands) would not be sustained in the International Court of Justice (ICJ).

This does not mean, however, that the ASEAN claims are necessarily stronger (Haller-Trost, 1994). As noted in Table 10.1, *Vietnam* holds the most islands of all the claimants. It is the successor state to France, which surveyed, periodically occupied, and established an administrative region covering both the Paracel and the Spratly Islands.[9]

Nonetheless, there is an enormous hole in Hanoi's claim. During the period 1956–1975, North Vietnam 'recognized China's claims to the Spratlys'; legally, the reunited Vietnam is the successor state to North Vietnam. Although diplomats from Vietnam now assert that this concession to Beijing was made under duress—to get assistance during the Vietnam War—this weakens Hanoi's current claim.

The *Philippine* claim is even more dubious. No international legal experts have taken the Philippine claim to all the Spratlys seriously. Nevertheless, the Philippines now occupies the same number of islands as China, and its occupancy has been for a longer period than Beijing's. It is important to note that, despite the Manila Treaty (which obligates the United States to defend the Philippines from attack), the United States has never supported or taken a formal position on the Philippine claims in the Spratlys.

The *Malaysian* claim stems not from historic ties or long-term occupancy but rather from its interpretation of the LoS Convention. During the 1970s, the Malaysians were active participants in LoS negotiations. Recognizing that their continental shelf extended far into the South China Sea, Malaysian forces occupied three reefs (Swallow, Ardasier, and Mariveles) and then made the unprecedented argument that the 200-nautical-mile EEZ gave them sovereignty over these additional sites within their EEZ.[10] (See Map 10.1 for their locations.)

The Malaysian claim has not been tested in any court yet, but its logic is the converse of what the UNCLOS III drafters expected. The drafters envisaged that countries would have a right to control the resources in the sea, and on the seabed out to 200 nautical miles from their 'baselines' of undisputed territory. What the Malaysians have done is to claim that the EEZ actually gives them the right to claim additional territory within the EEZ. If the Malaysian tactic is legally accepted, then it would complicate the Spratlys problem (and other marine development issues as well).

Brunei has taken a lower-keyed approach and does not claim sovereignty over any of the Spratlys. However, it does claim an EEZ of 200 nautical miles, extending northwest from its land territory. Brunei's EEZ covers the waters and seabed surrounding Louisa Reef and Rifleman Bank, which are occupied by Malaysia, but it does not include a claim on the land areas. Brunei expects to manage the fisheries and seabed resources without contesting Kuala Lumpur's control of the land.

In sum, the tangle of sovereignty claims makes clear that no country has *both* an unassailable legal basis and continuous occupancy to support its Spratly claims. Furthermore, none of the countries occupying an island/reef seems likely, voluntarily, to relinquish it, at least without some form of compensation or broader political settlement. Also, if China were actively to pursue Foreign Minister Qian Qichen's suggestion that these competing claims be resolved on the basis of international law, there would certainly be years, possibly decades, of litigation.

Development of Economic Potential

Although imbroglios over the fisheries suggest the long-term marine potential of the Spratlys is significant (Murdo, 1995; Chanda,1995), there is little doubt that the main economic potential of the region is in hydrocarbons. By 1976 there had been enough seismological work done on the South China Sea to indicate the possibility of oil and gas finds (Park, 1978). Nevertheless, before accurate estimates of hydrocarbon reserves can be made, there need to be two additional steps: exploratory drilling and construction of 'appraisal wells'. Except for the Wan'An Basin, these additional steps have not been completed, so present estimates remain highly speculative.

In this environment, there has been an unfortunate tendency for some observers to assume the finds will be massive. In July 1995, Beijing's *People's Daily* referred to the South China Sea 'as the second Persian Gulf'

(Haus and Chanda, 1995). Moreover, some Chinese specialists have asserted that the potential for the entire South China Sea is as great as 130 billion barrels of oil (or the equivalent in natural gas) (Salameh, 1995–1996: 139).

These estimates seem grossly overstated. In the Wan'An Bei area, Crestone's geophysical data indicate the prospect of two fields with reserves of roughly 1 billion to 1.5 billion barrels of oil (Johnson, 1995). In other areas that are within 200 nautical miles of the Spratlys, there are estimates of three sites with up to 24 billion cubic feet of gas. Although these levels of potential deposits are impressive, we will not know when and to what extent these resources will be economically viable for development until the appraisal wells are completed.

Many economists assume China will become a major energy importer in the next century (Wu and Fesharaki, 1994). However, because building deep-sea platforms can cost as much as $1 billion per site, it would be optimistic to assume that the disputed South China Sea locations will be developed before sovereignty is resolved. Also, given low oil and gas prices in the 1990s, the major oil companies were not rushing to develop high-cost, deep-water deposits.

Freedom of Passage

In one sense, this is the most straightforward of the issues in the Spratlys conundrum. At present, no country is proposing to restrict air or sea passage through the Spratlys. Three different Chinese leaders have affirmed that the PRC will not impede passage.[11] In addition, the world's preeminent naval power, the United States, has explicitly stated that freedom of passage must not be interrupted. These commitments would seem to settle the subject. So why does the issue keep resurfacing?

Even if the Chinese and American avowals are firm, the stakes are enormous. For *commercial* traffic, if movement through the South China Sea were restricted or unsafe, it would mean taking a much longer alternative route from the Indian Ocean to the Pacific Ocean, probably through the Lombok Strait. This would be slower, longer, and more costly. It would be more expensive for two reasons: the distance traveled would be greater and, if there was the perception of higher risk in the Spratlys region, insurance rates would rise.

Freedom of passage is vital for *military* purposes as well. UNCLOS III has very clear language covering the conditions under which vessels can transit territorial waters in 'innocent passage' (Hollick, 1995). For example, submarines must travel on the surface and show their flag. Surface combatants must maintain an unthreatening stance and are, to some extent, vulnerable, because they cannot maintain full combat readiness. (In addition, aircraft must request permission to transit airspace.)

The bathymetric features off the Spratlys are such that submarines could easily hide in some of the waters around the islands and reefs. Hence, countries like Japan and Singapore, which depend on seaborne trade for their existence, are very concerned that passage not be impeded. Japan's concern is with Chinese naval ambitions (Shambaugh, 1992), whereas Singapore has reservations about even its ASEAN neighbors' intentions. Senior Minister Lee Kuan Yew (1995) articulates this position: If ownership of these atolls means territorial waters with 200-nautical-mile economic zones, there will be no more open seas. The South China Sea will be divided into a mosaic of little lakes for six or five different owners.

There is a related issue which currently complicates the freedom-of-passage question. At the December 1995 ASEAN Summit, the ASEAN heads of government agreed to establish a Southeast Asia Nuclear Weapons Free Zone (NWFZ). The intent was to create a zone in which neither ASEAN nations nor foreign powers would use or threaten to use nuclear weapons. In the definition of the NWFZ, the communiqué included not only the sovereign territory and waters of the ASEAN states but also their EEZs and continental shelves. Since most of the Spratlys region would be within the EEZs or on a continental shelf of an ASEAN nation, the NWFZ concept would, in addition limit outside powers and their ability to extend deterrence in the region.[12] This is currently unacceptable to both China and the United States. Hence, although freedom-of-passage questions are not the central ones in the Spratlys dilemma, they are important and could become critical over time.

Regional Security

Leaders in most of the ASEAN countries see the dispute over the Spratlys as a test case of regional solidarity in the face of Chinese pressure on the region. Their immediate objective is to avoid any legal judgment or political settlement that would legitimize a substantially increased Chinese presence in Southeast Asia. The goal of these leaders is to develop some kind of security structure, perhaps by treaty, that makes ASEAN more self-sufficient militarily, especially since Russian power has faded and the United States presence has ebbed somewhat in the region.

This means dealing with two related questions: Externally, what policies will the Chinese pursue? Internally, what kind of security structure will work best, given the heterogeneity of interests and different historical experiences of the ASEAN countries? Although neither of these issues can be fully addressed here, it is worth noting how broad the range of opinion is on the subjects (Denoon and Frieman, 1996).

Some analysts argue that Chinese leaders were shocked by the results of the Persian Gulf War and, though they have no intention of pursuing expansionist policies, are committed to developing a modern, high-tech military (Shulong, 1994). Others see China as fundamentally redefining its interests, with plans to use its new 'Active Defense Strategy' as the first step toward projecting its political-military power throughout Southeast Asia and into the mid-Pacific (Huang, 1994). Still others see China as taking a more global approach, based on *Realpolitik* that combines increased international influence with military power rooted in a 'limited deterrence' capability (Johnston, 1995–96).

There is no question about the fears that China has created by its threats to fight for the Spratlys (Associated Press, 1995). Strategic studies institutes in Southeast Asia are already planning how to respond if there are further military skirmishes in the Spratlys (Agence France Presse, 1995), and uncertainties about the post–Cold War security picture have led to a sharp increase in ASEAN defense expenditures (Ball, 1993–1994).

Given uncertainty over Chinese directions, the search for a viable 'security architecture' has become a quietly discussed but ever-present topic in Southeast Asia. A variety of approaches has been suggested,[13] but all, to date, have foundered over who is to guarantee what? Since there is no immediate military crisis, and no nation wants to appear to be 'containing China', these discussions have been rather theoretical. However, were there to be a major military clash in the region, the latent interest in developing a more tangible alliance would quickly become manifest.

Previous Approaches

Study Groups and Dialogues

The Indonesian 'South China Sea Workshops' have played an important role in regularizing discussion between China and the ASEAN countries. In addition, the workshops have facilitated the creation of the Technical Working Groups and often laid the basis for communiques at ASEAN ministerial meetings. The workshops have met annually since 1990 and have agreed on both principles and topics to be explored.[14]

The principal advantage of the process so far has been the informal and unpolemical nature of the discussion (Stormont, 1994). But this has been offset by the fact that the central problem, sovereignty, has been put aside. This means that the technical groups can proceed only so far without knowing who will control which parts of the Spratlys.

President Fidel Ramos of the Philippines has urged United Nations intervention in the dispute, whereas other observers have suggested focused bilateral discussions (Shephard, 1994). However, there is a growing sense among ASEAN foreign policy makers that the study group and dialogue process will make little progress without more political direction.

Proposals to Defer Settling Sovereignty

This is the option the Chinese government prefers, and it has certain advantages. If resolving sovereignty will take years or even decades, then it might be worthwhile to develop the most promising sites as soon as possible. Indeed, there are a number of instances where joint development is already proceeding, even between countries in potentially explosive relationships. For example, Chevron has negotiated an arrangement between Beijing's China National Offshore Oil Corporation (CNOOC) and Taipei's China Petroleum Corporation (CPC) to explore and develop sites north and east of Taiwan. Similarly, there has been cooperation between Vietnam and Cambodia, and even China and Vietnam, on limited sites (Valencia and Miyoshi, 1986: 225, 244).

Although this appears to be a pragmatic way to finesse sovereignty, the most promising undeveloped sites in the South China Sea are in such deep water and so far from markets that they will require enormous investments to be made profitable. Few investors will take such risks unless competing claims on the terrain have been settled.

Proposals to Allocate Sovereignty

There has been a plethora of proposals for how to allocate sovereignty in the Spratlys. Oversimplifying, they have been based on two different principles: allowing states to extend their EEZs and squeezing down the size of the disputed area to a small 'doughnut hole', or constraining EEZs to certain shapes and creating a relatively large central area that could be managed by an international development authority representing the six claimants.

The first idea was proposed informally by the Indonesians as a way to clarify questions of sovereignty and to minimize debate about procedures. Although the 'doughnut' solution has the merit of simplicity, it would give the bulk of the seabed to the countries nearest the Spratlys, greatly limiting the areas that China would receive. Not surprisingly, Beijing rejected the idea.

The second approach has been presented in several variants by Mark Valencia, Jon Van Dyke, and Noel Ludwig (1995). It has considerable intrinsic appeal, because bargaining would shift from the messy claims of who is entitled to what real estate to the allocation of shares in a development authority. Specifically, to get China to give up some of its claims for a fixed or indefinite period, Beijing might be offered a major say (e.g., a veto) in decisions of the authority.

Although this approach has political advantages, there are two main drawbacks: investors are likely to be leery of a multinational authority; and Beijing may prefer to have a naval presence in Southeast Asia to protect its sovereignty rather than share this control with others. The international-authority concept is certainly worth pursuing, but the political and managerial difficulties of making it work are daunting.

Limitations of International Law

International Law

Because none of the claimants to the Spratlys has both solid legal justification and continuous occupancy as grounds to assert sovereignty, a court or arbitration panel would have to weigh the relative merits of de jure claims versus de facto possession. In a case as complicated as this, with six direct claimants and several concerned outside parties, there is no apparent way to reach a fair decision. International law does allow judges to use 'equity' as a basis for delimiting claims, but this is a highly subjective criterion; its use would certainly be challenged by any party that thinks its interests were not well served (McHugh, 1985).

A second problem with applying international law is that the International Court of Justice is, by its very nature, composed of jurists with different philosophies. Even experts in dealing with the ICJ often have trouble predicting how it will rule. For example, one of its leading figures, Shigeru Oda, opposes the trend, incorporated in UNCLOS III, of expanding EEZs to favor the rights of littoral states over other maritime users (Vicuna, 1989). These uncertainties in predicting results from ICJ rulings lend credence to charges of arbitrariness. Although there is the very real possibility that elements of this dispute may be brought to the ICJ, many potential litigants shy away from using the ICJ as a dispute-resolving mechanism.

The Law of the Sea Convention

UNCLOS III has very elaborate dispute-settlement provisions. Although some issues require 'compulsory, binding dispute settlement', maritime boundary disagreements were specifically left to various means of nonbinding conciliation. Consequently, various international forums could be convened to work on the Spratlys dispute, but the parties would not be bound to heed their recommendations. Hence, it is not surprising that Lee Cordner (1994: 61) concludes: 'The prospect of the law of the sea providing the key to resolution of the [Spratly] dispute is limited, even though each of the protagonists variously refers to the 1982 United Nations Convention on the Law of the Sea to support its claims'.

We concur with this view and suggest that the disputants will, ultimately, need to look elsewhere if there is to be timely resolution of their claims.

Why seek a negotiated settlement now? The ASEAN claimants have several reasons to desire a negotiated settlement: (1) they want to proceed unhindered to develop the hydrocarbon resources; (2) they are concerned that China will attempt to negotiate bilaterally with each of them, thus vitiating the temporary solidarity created by the initial Mischief Reef incident; and (3) China will be a more formidable party to negotiate with in the future insofar as her economic growth continues.

Many observers think it is in China's interest to delay settling the Spratlys dispute. No Chinese political leader wants to be known as the one who negotiated away 'Chinese territory'. Few in Beijing are likely to champion the cause of settling with the ASEAN claimants, even though Zhang Zemin seems to have gained firm control of the political leadership after Deng Xiaoping's death. Moreover, if the top Chinese military does plan to develop a power-projection capability, dominance of the South China Sea will be an important objective that would be inconsistent with compromising now.

Nevertheless, there are some factors that might tip the balance in Beijing toward negotiation: (1) China's rapid economic growth will soon necessitate increasing energy imports, which could be reduced if the hydrocarbons in the Spratlys region could be developed quickly; (2) Chinese assertiveness in the South China Sea frightens its neighbors and legitimizes the continuing U.S. military role in East Asia; and (3) China's handling of its other border disputes is rendered more difficult if Beijing takes a rigid stance on the Spratlys.

Thus, we see it to be in the *long-run* interests of both China and the ASEAN claimants to achieve an equitable settlement in the Spratlys. If the Indonesia Workshops are stalled and the LoS is not capable of resolving sovereignty disputes, it is time to consider other approaches.

Adjusted Winner

The following procedure by which two people divide a cake, parts of which they value differently, is well known: one person (A) cuts the cake into two pieces, and the other (B) gets to choose one piece. This procedure assures that each person will get at least half the cake if A cuts the cake 50–50 (as he or she values it), and B chooses his or her preferred piece.

This approach to fair division goes back to antiquity, receiving mention in, among other places, the Hebrew Bible, Hesiod's *Theogony*, and Aesop's *Fables* (Brams and Taylor, 1996, 1999, ch. 1). More relevant for our purposes, cut-and-choose was incorporated in the 1982 draft of the LoS Convention. That draft specified that countries having the technology and capital to mine the seabed must, using this procedure, share the desirable locations for extraction.

More specifically, if a country is capable of and wants to mine the seabed, it must propose a division of the location into two tracts. Then an international mining company, called Enterprise—representing the interests of the developing countries through the International Seabed Authority—chooses the tract it prefers. The country proposing the arrangement receives the remaining tract. In this manner, parts of the seabed are preserved for commercial development by the developing countries, which, in the absence of Enterprise, could not otherwise afford to mine the seabed.

One difficulty of applying cut-and-choose to the Spratlys is that there are more than two players. This difficulty can be sidestepped if we regard the conflict as, for the moment, one between China and ASEAN (with ASEAN being considered as a single player).[15]

We think this view is realistic as a first step in resolving the overall dispute. China is by far the largest single claimant, against which the ASEAN countries have formed an implicit coalition. Although the Southeast Asian countries now control most of the Spratly Islands, the ASEAN political leaders are aware that China's power and influence are likely to grow over time, so bargaining now (and as an ASEAN group) has advantages. Later we shall indicate how the ASEAN countries might, internally, settle their own competing claims.

There are three major problems in applying cut-and-choose to the China-ASEAN dispute over the Spratlys (we henceforth assume the cutter, A, is male and the chooser, B, is female:

1. *Inequitability.* The chooser, B, has an advantage, insofar as she can generally obtain her preferred piece when A is forced to make a 50–50 division in terms of his preferences. By contrast, an *equitable procedure* ensures that each player not only receives at least 50 percent of the goods to be divided but also gets exactly the same amount above 50 percent as the other player.

2. *Inefficiency.* Assume A likes only the vanilla portion of the cake, and B likes only the chocolate portion, but A does not know this. Then A, to ensure himself 50 percent whichever piece B selects, must divide the cake into two halves. Each of these halves must include one-half the chocolate and one-half the vanilla, making the division exactly 50–50 for both participants. On the other hand, an *efficient procedure* (in the economist's parlance, 'Pareto-optimal') is one which gives an allocation which cannot be improved upon for both players. In this case, the efficient outcome would be to give all the vanilla to A and all the chocolate to B.

3. *Lack of Sharing.* Cut-and-choose does not allow for sharing part of the cake, whereas a sharing procedure allows for some level of sharing (not necessarily 50–50). In the case of the Spratlys, this would translate into joint jurisdiction and/or development of some of the islands, especially those in which both sides have a more-or-less equal level of interest and where both can benefit from sharing.

The aforementioned problems with cut-and-choose are solved by a new fair-division procedure called Adjusted Winner (AW). Under AW, each side is given 100 points to allocate among the goods to be divided, although AW permits the claimants to have unequal entitlements. For example, if one claimant is entitled to twice as much as the others, this can be reflected in the AW calculation (to be described shortly). We suppose here that China and ASEAN are equal claimants, which seems to us a reasonable starting point. Nevertheless, this supposition could be changed, subject to agreement by the parties.[16]

In the Spratlys dispute, the 'goods' we propose are five groups of islands and adjacent maritime areas in different parts of the South China Sea: North Central, South Central, East, South, and Southwest (see Map 10.2). This division into zones simplifies the allocation problem to one of more manageable proportions than giving each side, say, 1,000 points to allocate over 230 islands and reefs.

How China and the ASEAN countries would allocate their points depends upon the goals they seek to maximize. We posit three alternative goals for China (C1, C2, and C3), and two for the ASEAN countries (A1 and A2), to illustrate AW.

Scenarios for China Based on Goals it May Wish to Maximize.

C1. *Political cooperation.* China seeks to establish firmly its sovereignty in the region but minimize antagonisms with the ASEAN countries. In C1, China gives priority to gaining control of the zones closest to China, North Central and South Central—by placing 40 and 30 points, respectively, on these—and moving less assertively on the East, South, and Southwest zones by bidding only 10 points each for these.

C2. *Military prominence.* China seeks to secure bases in the North Central, South, and Southwest as a means to project its power throughout the entire region. Accordingly, Beijing places 30, 30, and 40 points, respectively, on these three zones but no points on the South Central and East zones.

C3. *Economic gain.* China seeks to control the zones with the most promising hydrocarbon deposits (the South and, especially, the Southwest) by placing 30 and 50 points, respectively, on them. It reserves 20 points to try to gain control of the more proximate North Central zone.

Scenarios for ASEAN Based on Goals it May Wish to Maximize.

A1. *Political cooperation and economic gain.* ASEAN avoids intruding on the zones closest to China while making strong bids for the South and Southwest, which have the greatest economic potential, by placing 40 points each on these. A modest bid for the East (20 points)—which China was willing to give up on completely in two of its three scenarios—is also a feature of this scenario.

MAP 10.2   Spratly Islands as Zones

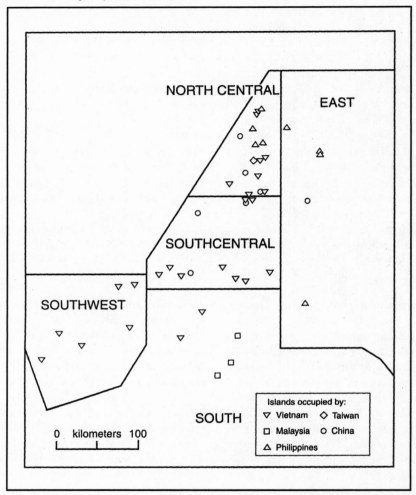

SOURCE: Adapted from U.S. department of State Map #B01010. March 1995. Contained in *The Win-Win Solution*, by Steven J. Brams and Alan D. Taylor, (1999) p. 134.

A2. *Concentration of control.* ASEAN cedes political control in the North Central and economic control in the Southwest to China. By concentrating its points on the South Central, East, and South—with allocations of 30, 30, and 40 points, respectively—ASEAN tries to force China into noncontiguous zones, thereby impeding China's political-military control over the entire South China Sea.

TABLE 10.2   Scenarios for China and the ASEAN Countries

	China			ASEAN	
Region	Political Cooperation	Military Prominence	Economic Gain	Pol. Coop & Econ. Gain	Concentration of Control
North Central	40	30	20	0	0
South Central	30	0	0	0	30
East	10	0	0	20	30
South	10	30	30	40	40
Southwest	10	40	50	40	0
Total	100	100	100	100	100

These scenarios for China and ASEAN are summarized in Table 10.2. Pairing off each of China's three scenarios with ASEAN's two scenarios gives six combinations. We have applied AW to each.

To illustrate how AW works, we apply it to (C2, A1). AW begins by awarding each zone to the player that places the most points on it. China 'wins', initially, on North Central (30 to 0); there is a tie on South Central (0 to 0); ASEAN wins on the East (20 to 0) and the South (40 to 30); and there is a tie on the Southwest (40 to 40). Ignoring the ties for the moment, China wins on one zone, worth 30 points, whereas ASEAN wins on two zones, worth 20 + 40 = 60 points.

AW awards ties, initially, to the biggest winner, which is ASEAN with 60 points. (If both parties won the same number of points initially, then ties would be broken randomly.) This gives ASEAN 60 + 40 + 0 = 100 points, compared with China's 30 points, which is inequitable.

To ensure equitability, AW has the party that receives the most points initially give back points to the side with the lower total, which is China. The criterion for givebacks is to start with the zone that has the lowest ratio of winner-to-loser points. Observe that the ratio 40/40 = 1 on the Southwest is lower than 40/30 = 1.33 on the South.[17] Nevertheless, if ASEAN were to give back all of the Southwest to China, then China would have 30 + 40 = 70 points and ASEAN only 20 + 40 = 60, so this giveback is too much to create equitability.

It is easy to show that, if ASEAN gave back seven-eighths of its 40 points, or a total of 35, and kept the remaining 5, then ASEAN would have

$20 + 40 + 5 = 65$, and China would also have $30 + 35 = 65$, making the allocation equitable. We determine the giveback by solving for the fraction x of ASEAN's 40 points that China, which has 30, would have to receive to give it the same number as ASEAN, which has 60 (ASEAN would retain the complementary fraction, $1\text{-}x$). Setting China's point total equal to ASEAN's (assuming this giveback), we have

$$30 + 40x = 60 + 40(1-x),$$
which yields $x = 7/8$.[18]

The AW allocations for the six combinations are given in Table 10.3. In all except (C1, A1), there is an *equitability adjustment*, whereby one side receives a certain fraction, and the other the complementary fraction, of one zone. This fractionalization of zones ensures not only that the allocation is equitable but also that it is efficient. In fact, AW produces a unique allocation that is equitable, efficient, and *envy-free*, which means that neither side would prefer the other side's allocation to its own and so would not envy the other side.

Because the equitability adjustment always occurs on the one zone that the two sides value most equally, it has the strongest claim for being the zone over which the two sides share control. In our first example, (C2, A1), this zone was the Southwest, to which both sides allocated 40 points. The fact that China ends up with 7/8, or 87.5 percent, of it is because China was the initial loser overall and needs this percent of the Southwest to catch up with ASEAN.

Practically speaking, what might such sharing mean? One answer is that the islands in the Southwest could be divided in the ratio of 7:1, but then

TABLE 10.3 Winners and Partial Winners for Six China-ASEAN Combinations

Region	(C1, A1)	(C1, A2)	(C2, A1)	(C2, A2)	(C3, A1)	(C3, A2)
North Central	C	C	C	C	C	C
South Central	C	5/6C, 1/6A	–	A	–	A
East	C	A	A	A	A	A
South	A	A	A	3/7C, 4/7A	A	3/7C, 4/7A
Southwest	A	C	7/8C, 1/8A	C	8/9C, 1/9A	C
Points (for each party)	80	75	65	82.9	94.4	82.9

C = China; A = ASEAN. The number following each letter indicates the one (of three) possible goals of China and the one (of two) possible goals of ASEAN.

there is the question of who is entitled to which islands. This question would be especially difficult to answer if there were hydrocarbon deposits near some islands but not others. Alternatively, the two sides could negotiate a production and revenue-sharing agreement, based on this ratio.[19]

Except for the zone on which there is an equitability adjustment, each side would gain complete sovereignty over all islands in the zone it wins. This is not to say that joint development agreements would be ruled out, and might even be attractive, if a promising field overlapped two zones.

The winners and partial winners in Table 10.3 show that each side benefits substantially under AW. Depending on the combination of bids, both China and ASEAN realize between 65 and 83 percent of their objectives. Even in the worst case, (C3, A1), each side gets almost two-thirds of the zones *as it values them*. Moreover, because AW is efficient, there is no other allocation of the (C3, A1) combination—or any other combination—that would give *both* sides more points than shown in Table 10.3.[20]

For all the parties to have confidence in the procedure, its skillful administration by an unimpeachable neutral party would be essential. We shall not discuss administrative issues here, but they should be relatively easy to resolve.

Although we have concentrated on the China-ASEAN AW results, various fair-division procedures applicable to more than two players could be used among the four ASEAN claimants (Young, 1991, 1994; Moulin, 1995; Brams and Taylor 1996). There are clear natural divisions within ASEAN: the East for the Philippines, the South for Malaysia and Brunei, and the Southwest for Vietnam. Of course, these allocations would depend on the outcome of the China-ASEAN division, on which each of the ASEAN claimants would have input.

One final question remains: How should one deal with the three other major issues involved in the dispute—freedom of passage, economic development, and regional security? As with the sovereignty issue, we think AW could be used to determine who wins, relatively speaking, on what issues, but these could also be settled in other ways.[21]

Freedom of passage is probably best dealt with through a multilateral treaty. China has repeatedly affirmed that it supports freedom of passage, while the U.S. Seventh Fleet is the current guarantor of it. As long as sovereignty is satisfactorily resolved, the economic development issues are attenuated, except for the zones that must be shared. In that case, AW could aid in determining production and revenue-sharing arrangements.

Establishing a security agreement for the region involves many uncertainties, including the following: Which nations will be involved? What is to be guaranteed? What enforcement and dispute-resolution methods are most appropriate? What administrative structures need to be established? We believe AW might also be helpful in allocating roles and responsibilities for regional security arrangements.

Of course, the process of developing security cooperation would be facilitated if there was confidence in the solution AW produced on the sovereignty issue. If amity is not created, then no formal allocation mechanism can be the glue for a regional security pact.[22]

Conclusion

The argument of this article can be summarized by the following seven propositions:

1. None of the legal or other claims to the Spratlys is decisive. Although there is some merit to the claims of all six parties to the dispute, all claims can be challenged.
2. The workshops sponsored by Indonesia have been useful, but they were designed mainly to deal with technical questions and also to create a climate such that cooperation between China and the ASEAN countries would be encouraged. They are not an adequate forum for resolving sovereignty issues.
3. The LoS Convention may be helpful in determining certain legal questions, but its rules were not established to settle sovereignty disputes. LoS suggests two principal routes for resolving sovereignty disputes: conciliation or arbitration, which seem to have limited promise, and hearings before the International Court of Justice, which the PRC has said it will not accept.
4. The most promising areas for oil and natural gas deposits are in the southern and southwestern parts of the South China Sea. Because these areas have deep waters and are a long distance from major markets, it is highly unlikely that these deposits will be developed until sovereignty questions are resolved.
5. To avoid continued tension on the Spratlys and to provide an adequate basis for development of the hydrocarbon resources, it is in the interest of both China and the ASEAN countries to resolve the sovereignty dispute.
6. All parties to the Spratlys dispute can benefit from a fair settlement. The dispute has remained intractable because there is no clear notion of what is 'fair', especially in light of different legal and extralegal claims, including forced occupation of some of the islands.
7. Adjusted Winner provides a promising way to reach closure on a settlement.

Our AW scenarios for China and ASEAN are meant to be illustrative, because we do not know exactly what priority each side would attach to different goals. We think the goals we postulated are plausible, but it is likely, especially for ASEAN, that the actual bidding strategies might reflect a blend of the goals we identified.

This blending, of course, would produce different allocations. However, our main purpose is not to say what the 'true' valuations of China and ASEAN are, but, rather, to suggest a *methodology* for reaching a fair settlement.

Thus, our analysis does not stand or fall on substantive disagreements about point allocations or the goals that underlie them. In our opinion, this methodology, in producing equitable, efficient, and envy-free agreements, is a very substantial improvement over cut-and-choose.

The Asian economic crisis, which started in July 1997, has affected the Spratlys dispute in several ways: the ASEAN countries have been reeling from their economic difficulties, making it harder for them to build up their military capabilities. At the same time, China has been skillful at exploiting those ASEAN weaknesses through offers of economic aid and subtle efforts to keep the ASEAN governments from forming a unified position for negotiating with Beijing. Despite China's blatant expansion of its facilities at Mischief Reef, the Philippines was not successful at getting any unified ASEAN action to criticize or constrain the Chinese at the December 1998 ASEAN Summit in Hanoi (Denoon and Colbert, 1998–1999). These developments reinforce our view that AW is a neutral and speedy means to deal with a very volatile situation.

We do not argue that AW is the only satisfactory way to resolve the Spratlys dispute. We do think, however, that the various approaches currently being tried could greatly delay a settlement, aggravating the conflict. Perhaps more important, AW and its extensions encourage the parties to see the process as a bargaining and sharing one, rather than one whose solution is dictated by a court or imposed by an outside power.

David Denoon, b. 1945, is associate professor of politics and economics at New York University. His most recent books are *Real Reciprocity: Balancing U.S. Economic and Security Policies in the Pacific Basin* (Council on Foreign Relations, 1993) and *Ballistic Missile Defense in the Post Cold War Era* (Westview, 1995).

Steven Brams, b. 1940, is professor of politics at New York University. His two most recent books, coauthored with Alan Taylor, are: *Fair Division: From Cake Cutting to Dispute Resolution* (Cambridge University Press, 1996) and *The Win-Win Solution: Guaranteeing Fair Shares to Everybody* (Norton, 1999).

Notes

1. The formal title of the most recent agreement, completed in July 1994, is the United Nations Convention on the Law of the Sea III (UNCLOS III). To simplify matters, we will refer to the convention as simply LoS.

2. The word 'claimant' is used here rather than 'countries', because Taiwan has a long-standing claim but is not an independent country. Also, since all the claims include territorial waters, when we use the term 'Spratly Islands' we mean 'Spratly Islands and surrounding waters'.

3. Taiwan occupied one Spratly Island, Itu Aba, between 1947 and 1950 and then, continuously, after 1956.

4. Indonesia chose to play this role because it was not a claimant in the Spratlys area. Although the Natuna Islands, where Exxon plans a $35 billion natural gas investment, are inside the Chinese 'dashed-line' of claims, it has been widely reported that Indonesia has been given assurance by China that Beijing will not contest Jakarta's rights to develop the Natuna fields.

5. In addition to the South China Sea, which the 1992 Law claimed as unquestionably Chinese, the law also said the Senkakau (or Diao yu-tai) Islands—occupied by the Japanese—were indeed Chinese.

6. China continues to build structures in the Spratlys even on reefs that are not above mean high tide ('Concrete Claims', 1995: 14).

7. 'Jurisdiction' is the right or power to administer an area, whereas 'sovereignty' includes both the power to administer and being recognized as the lawful government. Most of the claimants in the Spratlys area have jurisdiction over assorted islands, reefs, and surrounding waters; few have internationally recognized sovereignty.

8. If the United Kingdom, France, the Netherlands, and the United States had been concerned about the Spratlys before World War II, there probably would have been a precise division of ownership. Similarly, if it had been a pressing issue at the time of the 1951 San Francisco Peace Treaty with Japan, there might also have been some sort of settlement of the sovereignty issue.

9. The Paracel Islands are approximately 300 miles north of the Spratly Islands.

10. The additional Malaysian claims are for Amboyna Cay, Banque Canada Reef, and Commodore Reef. Vietnam controls Amboyna Cay and Banque Canada Reef, whereas the Philippines controls Commodore Reef.

11. Deng Xiaoping in 1988 in Beijing, Li Peng in 1990 in Singapore, and Qian Qichen in Brunei in 1995.

12. The ASEAN NWFZ Treaty would limit nuclear deterrence in the region because the wording forbids a nuclear nation to threaten another *from within* the NWFZ, or to threaten a target inside the NWFZ *from outside* the zone.

13. See, for example, McInnes and Rolls (1994); Bundy, Burns, and Weichel (1994); and Selin (1994).

14. The main principles are that there will be peaceful negotiation over sovereignty, but that sovereignty negotiations will be postponed until the timing appears propitious. The topics are: joint development projects, navigation and communication systems, search-and-rescue operations, marine science research, control of drugs, pollution protection, and international legal questions.

15. We use the term ASEAN here, even though Singapore and Thailand are not claimants and it is uncertain on what terms Indonesia would be involved.

16. See Brams and Taylor (1996: 70; 1999: 76) for an illustrative calculation using unequal entitlements.

17. The other winner-loser ratio (on the East), 20/0, is infinite, so its ratio is obviously the largest. The ratio for the other tie (South Central) 0/0, is undefined, but it does not matter—as far as points are concerned—because neither side put any points on it. In fact, to avoid dividing by 0, AW specifies that each side must put a minimum of 1 point on each zone. However, we have ignored this requirement here to emphasize the fact that each side might be willing to cede control of a zone completely in order to maximize the number of points it puts on other zones.

18. If the initial allocation of points to the parties is very lopsided, then the winner might have to give back not just a fraction of one zone but an entire zone and then, possibly, some fraction of another zone. Indeed, in combination (C1, A1), the initial point allocation is 70 points to China and 100 points to ASEAN. By giving back the East, which has the lowest winner/loser ratio (20/10 = 2, compared with 40/10 = 4 each for the South and Southwest), ASEAN decreases its point total from 100 to 80, whereas China increases its total from 70 to 80. Hence, only the give-back of *all* of the East creates equitability in this case. Also notice in this case that what the initial winner, ASEAN, loses (20 points) is not what the initial loser, China, gains (10 points) in the giveback. There will be equality in the giveback only if there is a tie in the points that the two sides allocate to the zone, as was true in our earlier example (C2, A1).

19. To facilitate such negotiation, a neutral party administering AW might tell the two sides that there was a relative winner, getting seven-eighths, and a relative loser, getting one-eighth, but not which side was the winner. Then both sides would be asked to formulate two agreements, specifying what the seven-eighths winner and the one-eighth loser would each receive whoever won. Only after these agreements were reached would the parties be told which side was the winner and which side the loser.

20. To be sure, AW, like any allocation mechanism, is potentially manipulable if one side knows the other side's point allocation. However, as shown in Brams and Taylor (1996, ch. 4), there are safeguards one can build in against manipulation. For example, a less manipulable procedure, called Proportional Allocation (PA), is one alternative that either side could invoke if it believed the other side had received advance information about its bid—and was trying to exploit it. Although strategically more robust than AW, PA is not efficient. In the case of (C2, A1), for example, each side would obtain 62.9 points under PA rather than the 65.0 it receives under AW. Moreover, under PA, every zone would have to be shared, making the sovereignty problem less tractable. In practice, AW would be extremely difficult to manipulate to one's advantage. Indeed, if one side tried to do so, but its guesses about the other side's allocations were only slightly off, it could end up hurting itself badly. Consequently, we think each side would have a strong incentive to make sincere allocations, keyed to its own goals.

21. So far AW has been applied only retrospectively to international disputes. These include the 1978 Panama Canal Treaty between the United States and Panama (Brams and Taylor, 1996, ch. 5; Raiffa, 1982, ch. 12); and the 1979 peace treaty between Egypt and Israel, as it was negotiated at Camp David in 1978 (Brams and Togman, 1996; Brams and Taylor, 1999). We believe that AW can be

applied prospectively, as well, to a broad range of current territorial and nonterritorial disputes, as illustrated herein.

22. If current approaches to the Spratlys dispute continue to produce stalemate, the tension between China and the ASEAN countries may reappear, leading to a desire to exclude China from Southeast Asian security planning.

Chapter Eleven

Environmental Cooperation and International Peace

KEN CONCA

From Conflict and Insecurity to Cooperation and Peace?

Global ecological interdependence has uncertain implications for peace and conflict. Clearly, unchecked environmental degradation is not a recipe for social harmony. A large literature on environmentally induced conflict documents cases where environmental problems appear to play a role in triggering or exacerbating intergroup violence. As environmental degradation worsens, such cases are likely to become more common in occurrence and broader in scope.

But environmental problems also create incentives for cooperation and collective action. The past few decades have seen an explosion of international environmental agreements, ranging from narrow bilateral accords to ambitious attempts at global governance. We have also seen the deepening of linkages between national environmental bureaucracies, significant envi-

The author wishes to acknowledge the helpful comments of Matthew Auer, Charles Breiterman, Douglas Blum, Geoffrey Dabelko, Nils Petter Gleditsch, Allison Morrill, Marcus Schaper, Antoinette Sebastian, Ashok Swain, Larry Swatuk, Stacy Vandeveer, Erika Weinthal, Kenneth Wilkening, and three anonymous reviewers.

ronmental reforms in many intergovernmental organizations, and an explosion of transnational networking among environmental organizations and social movement groups.

The cooperative potential surrounding environmental problems suggests that the discussion of environmentally induced conflict and ecological insecurity has overlooked what may be a critically important corollary. If environmental degradation can trigger violent conflict, then perhaps environmental cooperation can be an equally effective catalyst for reducing tensions, broadening cooperation, fostering demilitarization, and promoting peace. If so, then ecological interdependence could be seized upon as a catalyst for promoting peaceful cooperation and collective human security, and the availability of these benefits would become a powerful argument for intensified environmental cooperation.

Whether environmental cooperation can have such peace-enhancing effects is unclear, in part because what we know about environmental cooperation is largely divorced from considerations of peace, conflict, and security. A large and rapidly growing literature now exists on the conditions required for environmental cooperation.[1] But this literature has had little or nothing to say about linkages between environmental cooperation, peace, and conflict. Welfare gains, domestic and transnational political pressures, the strengthening of environmental norms, and the political use of knowledge are taken as the main instigators of cooperation, with little or no attention paid to the violence potential of environmental problems. Research on environmental cooperation has also had little or nothing to say about the *consequences* for peace or conflict. Much of the literature defines the 'effects' of such cooperation in a narrowly ecological sense (Bernauer, 1995); when the dependent variable has included political effects, the main focus has been on domestic realignments or the apparatus of the state rather than interstate or transnational relations (Young, 1999).

Similarly, research on environmental conflict has tended to skirt the issue of environmental cooperation. Studies of environmentally induced conflict typically end with generalized recommendations for environmental cooperation as a way to forestall such conflict. But this work nearly always lacks a careful analysis of the specific mechanisms required or of the pathways to the desired outcome of peaceful dispute resolution.

The growth of knowledge about environmental conflict and environmental cooperation as two separate and unconnected strands of inquiry has meant that important questions *linking* conflict and cooperation have gone unexamined. Does environmental cooperation in fact reduce the likelihood, scope, or severity of environmentally induced violence? Can the potential for environmentally induced conflict be an important spur to cooperation? Can environmental cooperation catalyze broader forms of peaceful interaction? If peace is thought of as a spectrum ranging from the absence of violent conflict to the inconceivability of such conflict, does environmental co-operation push states and societies further along that spectrum? We know that there are welfare gains and ecological benefits to be had from international environmental cooperation, but potential benefits in the form of reduced international tensions or an increasing improbability of violence have gone largely unexamined.

Given the lack of investigation, answers to whether environmental cooperation has positive spin-offs for peace remain conjectural. This chapter reviews several strands of scholarly research in international relations that suggest possible answers, or at least hypotheses: deductive and game-theoretic studies of the possibilities for cooperation under anarchy; empirical research on the implications of interdependence for international peace and conflict; studies of the process of interest formation and the role of norms in shaping perceptions of national interest; and research on the growing role of nonstate actors, transnational coalitions, and 'global civil society' as agents of governance. My reading of this literature suggests that there is, in fact, good reason to think that carefully designed initiatives for environmental cooperation can create specific, tangible political opportunities to build more broadly peaceful international relations. Environmental problems are certainly not the only opportunities to seek these gains, but they often have specific properties that make them a particularly rich set of opportunities.

In evaluating the deductive case for environmental peacemaking, two separate hypothesized pathways will be discussed. These are referred to as 'changing the strategic climate' and 'strengthening post-Westphalian governance'. 'Changing the strategic climate' refers to ways in which environmental cooperation might alter processes of strategic bargaining between governments, change the perceived costs and benefits that shape this bargaining, enhance confidence in the benefits of cooperation, or lessen prevailing barriers to collective action. At this level the discussion focuses in particular on realist models of interstate interaction, because the problem of peacemaking is most substantial under that set of assumptions. The second pathway, labeled 'strengthening post-Westphalian governance' refers to more broadly transformative effects, not only between governments but across societies. Here the emphasis is on ways in which environmental collaboration might affect the institutionalization of new norms of cooperation, alter state and societal institutions, or create or affect trans-societal linkages. It should be stressed that, in both cases, the idea of 'peace' actually consists of several dependent variables that might be affected by environmental cooperation. There are perceptual dimensions that include trust, certainty, and confidence; structural dimensions involving the costs and benefits from different forms of interaction and the institutional settings within which those costs and benefits are realized; and, at least in the second pathway, constitutive dimensions related to collective identity and the normative fabric within which those interactions occur.

Environmental cooperation does not occur easily or automatically. Serious conflicts of interest or perception often thwart cooperation, and difficult barriers to collective action remain even when interests and perceptions converge. Nor can it be claimed that all forms of environmental cooperation will have similar peace-enhancing effects; it is not difficult to identity counterexamples, such as the forcible creation of 'wilderness' through the expulsion of local or indigenous peoples (Peluso, 1993; Guha, 1997; COICA, 1998). Rather, the argument is that environmental problems frequently have properties—ranging from technical complexity, uncertainty, and longer time horizons to the particular types of interdependencies they create—that may lend themselves to peace-enhancing types of cooperation. If so, then the link between environmental cooperation and peace becomes as important a topic for investigation as the link between environmental degradation and violence.

Environment, Conflict, and Insecurity

The 'ecological security' debate has overlapping empirical and normative components. As discussed elsewhere in this volume, empirically oriented work has focused primarily on environmental change as a potential cause of violent conflict. The findings of this work have been mixed. On the one hand, several cases have been identified in which natural resource depletion, ecosystem disruption, and other forms of environmental degradation appear to be linked to various types of intergroup conflict (Homer-Dixon, 1994, 1999; Homer-Dixon and Percival, 1996; Bächler et al., 1996; Bächler, 1998). These studies suggest that environmental change is best understood as a potential catalyst for conflict rather than a sole or direct cause, triggering or exacerbating conflicts along existing social cleavages such as ethnicity, class, or region, and that these conflicts can in turn spill over to more widespread violence. Quantitative studies have provided some support for this hypothesis, although generally finding a stronger link to conflict for political and economic variables such as regime type, openness to international trade, or quality of life indicators than with environmental variables (Hauge and Ellingsen, 2001; Esty et al., 1998). The long and complex causal chain, in which many steps are posited to lie between environmental cause and conflictual outcome, may explain why environment-conflict relationships have shown only weak or second-order associations.

Spurred in part by this research, a more explicitly normative debate has emerged on the question of whether and how to incorporate environmental 'threats' into security policies. This debate has been highly polarized between, one the one hand, traditionalists with an unreconstructed vision of national security, and on the other hand, more transformative approaches that advocate reorienting societal resources, delinking the idea of threats from specific enemies, and generally 'greening' and demilitarizing security discourse, policies, and institutions (Dabelko and Dabelko, 1995). Both poles in this debate have been criticized as ambiguous, vague, and contradictory (Deudney, 1990; Finger, 1991; Conca, 1994; Dalby, 1999). A narrow security-state frame of reference ignores the poor fit between military tools and environmental 'threats', the enormous ecological toll of war and war preparation, and the obstacles to effective environmental cooperation created by the zero-sum logic of the national-security state. The more transformative vision of environmental security has also been subjected to intense criticism. Critics point to a naive faith that 'engaging' security institutions on environmental matters will 'green' security policy rather than militarize environmental policy. There is also a troubling tendency to wield the concept of security in a way that is at once both vague and all-encompassing. The powerfully evocative but poorly specified concept of 'development', which has become a vehicle for so many contradictory agendas, offers a cautionary tale about this sort of terminological redefinition (Escobar, 1995). And the specific pathways by which 'ecological security' will not only reduce environmental triggers of conflict but also transform the zero-sum logic of the national security state too often remain unclear or implicit.

What this debate has *not* provided is a clear strategy for environmental peace. Such a strategy would need to work on at least two different levels: It would have to create minimum levels of trust, transparency, and cooperative gains among governments strongly influenced by a zero-sum logic of national security, also laying the foundation for transforming dysfunctional institutions and practices reflecting a zero-sum logic of national security in directions conducive to peaceful coexistence and cooperation. Both tasks are necessary. Stabilizing intergovernmental relations without promoting institutional transformation runs the risk of merely reinforcing the zero-sum, statist logic of national security while implementing short-term mitigation of environmental problems. On the other hand, seeking to transform institutions and ignoring the need for stable interstate relations risks being ineffective, irrelevant, and perhaps even counterproductive.

Can environmental cooperation have these peace-enhancing effects? Admittedly, such claims are difficult to test. One could measure environmental cooperation through participation in international environmental agreements and look for a correlation between such participation and peaceful international behavior. This could mean that environmental cooperation helps to build peace—but it could just as easily mean that peace is a prerequisite for environmental cooperation, not a result. Also, it is generally recognized that governments are willing to enter into formal international agreements when the costs of doing so are low, that many environmental accords lack significant binding power on states, and that many forms of environmental cooperation are not codified in formal agreements. These facts make readily available indicators such as ratification of environmental treaties or participation in international environmental regimes poor measures of meaningful cooperation (Downs, Rocke, and Barsoom, 1996).

Despite the difficulty of showing an empirical connection, there is a good deductive foundation for the idea that environmental collaboration can promote some of the conditions necessary for peace. The remainder of this chapter presents a review of several strands of the literature on cooperation theory, in an attempt to generate hypotheses about the peace-enhancing spin-offs of environmental collaboration. The chapter begins with the problem of changing the bargaining dynamic among governments and then shifts to the broader problem of institutional transformation and trans-societal relations.

Changing the Strategic Climate

According to the Carnegie Commission on Preventing Deadly Conflict (1997: 25) 'Violent conflict results from choice—the choices of leaders and people—and is facilitated through the institutions that bind them'. The discussion that follows is by no means comprehensive in its treatment of the various factors that shape choice in a particular setting of interstate interaction. It focuses instead on selected dependent variables that may be affected by environmental cooperation, which in turn have been identified by various strands of cooperation theory as enhancing the prospects for peaceful interaction. These dependent variables include the properties of *uncertainty* surrounding interstate relations, the nature of *reciprocity* in actions between states, and the *time horizon* governments consider in their international dealings. Considering each of these potential leverage points in turn:

Reducing Uncertainty

Uncertainty is often a barrier to international cooperation. Keisuke Iida (1993) draws a useful distinction between two types of uncertainty, strategic and analytic. Strategic uncertainty exists because actors have incomplete information about each other's attributes, preferences, and intentions. Analytic uncertainty results from incomplete understandings of cause-and-effect relationships in a particular system, domain, or issue-area.

Neither analytic nor strategic certainty is always necessary for international cooperation, of course. Actors may perceive gains from cooperation despite very different causal understandings. And cooperation would rarely occur if it required full knowledge of the preferences and intentions of other actors. Nevertheless, uncertainty, conflicting understandings, and the knowledge struggles that result can be debilitating barriers to cooperation, for at least two reasons. First, opportunities for mutual gains from cooperation may go unidentified. Second, opponents of cooperation can use knowledge conflicts to cast aspersions on the motives of the other side, to argue for a wait-and-see stance in the face of uncertainty, or to offer vague proposals for further research as an alternative to concrete action. Disputes over the verifiability of arms-control agreements provide a classic example, with opponents of arms control invariably exploiting the uncertainty argument in all of these ways.

In the environmental realm, both strategic and analytic uncertainty are pervasive, and both have inhibited international cooperation. Analytic uncertainty surrounds the harmful effects of environmental problems, the severity of such harm, the impact of environmental policy measures, and even basic ecological cause-and-effect relations. These forms of uncertainty render the benefits of cooperation more difficult to demonstrate and provide a powerful tool for opponents of cooperation. The U.S. government used analytic uncertainty surrounding the causes and consequences of acid rain to delay action for more than a decade on Canadian claims of transboundary damage from acid precipitation (Zehr, 1994). The Montreal Protocol[2]—widely hailed as one of the most successful environmental accords and touted as a model for international cooperation—required more than a decade to sort out conflicting knowledge claims about causal mechanisms in ozone depletion, the extensiveness of damage to the ozone layer, and the severity of human health consequences (Haas, 1992; Litfin, 1995).

The effects of strategic uncertainty in inhibiting cooperation can be seen in the deep suspicions governments often voice about the hidden economic and political motives of actors with whom they disagree on specific environmental policy initiatives. The Montreal Protocol was nearly derailed by the mutual suspicions of U.S. and European negotiators that the other side's regulatory proposals were merely veiled efforts to create competitive economic advantage (Benedick, 1998). Many Brazilians, including elements of the military, have dismissed international pressures to halt deforestation in the Amazon as merely the latest attempt to control development of Brazil's natural-resource wealth (Conca, 1995a). Russian support for environmental protection in the Caucasus has been interpreted by the region's newly independent, post-Soviet states as an effort to slow the development of independent regional energy resources and part of a Russian bid for continued regional hegemony (Blum, 1999).

The combination of strategic and analytic uncertainty can turn environmental policy debates into intensive knowledge struggles. The technical complexity, limited knowledge base, incomplete information, and inherent uncertainty surrounding an issue merge with suspicions about underlying intent—with the result being a political struggle over the definition of what is true. The international debate on climate change provides a good example: disagreement over the certainty of key scientific hypotheses has combined with deep suspicions about the motives of various actors on this high-stakes issue, resulting in an intensive knowledge struggle at the heart of the political debate. In this atmosphere of rival knowledge claims, even seemingly straightforward attempts to quantify the greenhouse-gas emissions of different countries can provoke an international furor over the best way to portray responsibility (Agarwal and Narain, 1991; WRI, 1992: 209).

But the same uncertainty, technical complexity, and rival forms of knowledge that make environmental cooperation difficult may also provide opportunities to create new cooperative knowledge. Taking advantage of these collaborative opportunities might reduce both strategic and analytic uncertainty in ways that enhance the prospects for regional peace and security. With regard to analytic uncertainty, environmental collaboration often gives governments a better understanding of the extent of their economic and ecological ties. Environmental cooperation typically requires the pooling of national data to construct a larger transboundary or regional picture of the problem, creating opportunities for cooperative knowledge ventures. As cooperative knowledge deepens, new opportunities for mutual gain through cooperation are often revealed.

Asymmetries in information or in knowledge-generating capacities can also create opportunities for mutual gain. National science establishments are likely to have different levels of expertise across the various types of science that must be integrated to understand a particular problem; technological capabilities in environmental monitoring, testing, and data analysis are also likely to vary, usually in proportion to national scientific strength in a given field.

Environmental collaboration may also offer opportunities to reduce strategic uncertainty. When viewed in traditional security terms, environmental collaboration can provides governments with a relatively low-stakes arena in which to begin to establish a pattern of greater clarity and transparency regarding their interests and intentions. States in Northeast Asia, for example, have fallen into a pattern of regular consultations on regional environmental problems emphasizing regional collective goods, despite being unable to do so on traditional security concerns (Schreurs and Pirages, 1999). Joint ventures in knowledge creation can institutionalize practices of information exchange, as well as making it harder to support accusations that science is being politicized for national gain.

Finally, there may be important synergies between reductions in analytic and strategic uncertainty. A deeper base of shared knowledge can enhance the ability of governments to monitor and verify, thereby increasing transparency and reducing suspicion. Conversely, these reductions in strategic uncertainty can support efforts to reduce analytic uncertainty, by making previously secret or sensitive information available to researchers, environmental advocates, and interest groups in society.

Promoting More Diffuse Forms of Reciprocity

Reciprocity can be defined as replying in kind to another's actions. There is substantial evidence that reciprocity is a key element of international cooperation. Drawing on insights from game theory, Robert Axelrod (1984) identified the reciprocal 'tit for tat' strategy—cooperating when the other party has cooperated, and defecting from cooperation when the other party has defected—as an effective way to promote cooperative behavior. (Questions remain about the robustness of this strategy across different payoff structures and settings; see Bendor and Swistak, 1997.) The value of this form of reciprocity is that it consistently alters the other party's incentives in the direction favoring cooperation, by rewarding cooperative behavior and retaliating against defections from cooperation. Without reciprocity, cooperative systems can easily break down when there are potential short-term gains from cheating or otherwise abandoning cooperation.

The problem with reciprocity in international relations is that a shortage of political currency often limits cooperation to barterlike situations, in which reciprocity is immediate and direct. It can be very difficult to displace reciprocity across time, because mutual mistrust and suspicion often prevent governments from exchanging current actions for future promises. It also can prove difficult for governments to displace reciprocity across political space by linking separate issues, accepting as payment an action in a far-removed policy sphere. The difficulties many governments have faced when they seek to link trade relationships to progress on human rights or weapons proliferation provide examples.

The difficulty in creating these more diffuse forms of reciprocity can severely limit the number of opportunities for international political cooperation, just as a strict barter economy imposes drastic limits on the scope of potential economic transactions. As Robert Keohane (1984: 129) points out, what is needed is a form of political credit:

> In purely simultaneous exchange, neither party has to accept obligations, rules, or principles, since the exchange is balanced at every moment. There is never a 'debt' or 'credit'. . . . This sort of perfectly balanced reciprocity provides an unsatisfactory basis for long-term relationships [in international relations].

Thus cooperation theorists have placed great importance on the idea of diffuse reciprocity—that is, reciprocating in ways that may be displaced in time or space—as a way to expand the number of situations in which cooperation can be sustained.

The potential value of environmental cooperation lies in the fact that it typically demands diffuse, but not too diffuse, forms of reciprocity. Specific environmental problems typically involve upstream/downstream relationships or other asymmetries in the distribution of responsibilities and consequences. Even in the classic case of a 'commons' or common property resource, it is rarely the case that all actors bear identical responsibility for environmental damage or that the resulting losses will be distributed in a purely symmetrical fashion. These asymmetries tend to create situations in which different actors bring very different types of goods to the bargaining table; the basis for cooperation tends to be more complex than simply asking each actor to contribute in the same way and to accept the same benefits.

Diffuse reciprocity is also common in environmental cooperation because the costs and benefits of cooperating tend to be displaced in time. Costs will typically be incurred in the short term so as to provide a future stream of benefits. Thus, even if the basis for cooperation is a simple transaction in which downstream victims purchase the compliance of upstream polluters, the transaction is more like a joint venture than a barter arrangement or cash payment for services rendered.

On the other hand, the varying actions demanded by shared environmental problems are not so diffuse as to make effective reciprocity impossible. Quite the contrary: when viewed not as isolated problems but rather as part of a set of regional ecosystemic relationships, pollution and environmental degradation offer many rich opportunities for reciprocity. On a regional scale, for example, actors are typically joined in many overlapping ecological interdependencies simultaneously, and states that are upstream in one case may well be downstream in another (as is often the case with states that share both watersheds and airsheds, for example). In other words, even though individual problems will often have a stark upstream/downstream character, who is upstream and who is downstream will vary substantially across the range of environmental problems joining particular states. This enhances the possibility of linking narrow sets of environmental problems into more robust, multidimensional commitments to environmental protection. In other words, governments contemplating environmental cooperation have little choice but to gamble on diffuse forms of reciprocity on specific issues—but in doing so they are likely to be able to take advantage of many potential counterbalancing linkages.

This combination may be an important difference between ecological and economic interdependence. The main instruments of economic interdependence are trade and foreign investment, each of which presents a different problem regarding reciprocity. Trade is reciprocal by definition, in that something of value is exchanged for something else of value. But trade-based interdependence is difficult to sustain both politically and economically if reciprocity becomes too diffuse. Large trade deficits can become sources of tension and discord, as U.S.-Japanese relations demonstrated in the 1980s. Stable trading relationships therefore tend toward direct and immediate, as opposed to more diffuse, forms of reciprocity. Foreign investment presents the opposite problem, in that reciprocity tends to be so diffuse as to produce widespread perceptions of no reciprocity at all. Governments may make tangible concessions on taxes, wages, or regulatory standards to attract foreign investment, in exchange for anticipated future benefits of employment, technology transfer, and multiplier effects. In other words, trade tends toward a form of reciprocity that is insufficiently diffuse to be a strong confidence builder, whereas foreign investment tends toward such diffuse forms of reciprocity as to raise questions about whether it is genuinely reciprocal at all.

The greater tendency toward diffuse reciprocity probably makes robust environmental cooperation more difficult to establish than trade-based interdependence. But it also suggests that effectively established environmental cooperation could provide important opportunities to institutionalize diffuse reciprocity—opportunities that may not be as abundant in economic forms of interdependence.

Lengthening the Shadow of the Future

It is widely accepted that international cooperation is more likely when actors perceive themselves to be part of an ongoing relationship that promises regular future benefits. It can be shown that a longer 'shadow of the future' can transform situations in which actors face seemingly intractable barriers to cooperation. In the classic metaphor of the so-called prisoners' dilemma, for example, it can be shown that the gains from cooperation can overcome the strong incentives for defection when actors see themselves as locked into regular future interaction with no end in sight (Axelrod, 1984; Oye, 1986). The logic behind this observation is straightforward: The temptation to defect from cooperation becomes less if the stream of future benefits from cooperation becomes larger. The value of establishing and maintaining a cooperative reputation increases in settings where actors expect repeated interaction, because defections are likely to hurt future cooperation.

It is often argued that environmental diplomacy has been inhibited by the relatively short time horizon that most governments take into account; it has often been difficult to get actors with primarily short-term concerns of profit and power to focus on a longer-term agenda. An important corollary of this proposition may also be true, however—that environmental problems can be used as a way to shift the frame of reference from a series of disconnected, short-term interactions to a more continuous focus on a longer time horizon. A longer shadow of the future exists when actors pay more attention to the future, when they value it more relative to the present, and when they expect to engage in sustained interaction with one another. Environmental collaboration can affect all three of these dimensions in ways that may turn discrete and disconnected forms of interaction into ongoing relationships that promise regular future benefits.

One way in which environmental collaboration can lengthen the shadow of the future is simply by forcing actors to think about it. The buildup of environmental problems is often a creeping, incremental process, with the harmful consequences of environmental degradation often emerging in delayed and nonlinear fashion. Ecosystems may show few or no effects of change until their buffering capacities are depleted, with change difficult or impossible to reverse once these effects are unleashed. The incremental accumulation of effects and the danger of crossing irreversible thresholds can force actors to think in anticipatory ways and to frame policy responses in preventive terms. The payoff structure of most environmental problems also tends to shift actors toward a more forward-looking orientation. Rather than creating immediate and reciprocal benefits from exchange (as in the case of international trade), environmental cooperation tends to provide public goods that will pay a stream of future benefits on a joint investment made today.

A second way in which environmental collaboration can lengthen the shadow of the future is by changing society's discount rate. Environmental economists have made a persuasive case that the depletion of natural capital should be an explicit part of national income accounts (WRI, 1998: 191–193). Environmental ethicists have raised an analogous point about the impact of environmental degradation and resource depletion on the rights and opportunities of future generations (Weiss, 1989; Rothenberg, 1993).

Finally, environmental collaboration can lengthen the shadow of the future if it establishes particularly dynamic forms of cooperation that promote long-term relationships and sustained interaction. Effective environmental management is information-intensive; it demands that data be collected, exchanged, and interpreted on a regular basis. The uncertainty surrounding many environmental problems can lead to innovative institutional practices that promote ongoing relationships. The international bargaining over the problem of ozone-layer depletion, for example, dealt with the problem of uncertainty and a changing knowledge base by formalizing a requirement to revisit the accord's provisions in light of new findings (Weiss, 1998). This commitment created a dynamic process that kept governments focused on the issue and strengthened the agreement over time.

Strengthening Post-Westphalian Governance

The discussion thus far, in its heavy reliance on interstate cooperation theory, has been grounded in a fairly traditional international-relations perspective that assumes the centrality of governments, the separateness of societies, the fixed character of national interests, and the rationality of choice. These assumptions take as fixed several key properties of the international system: the territorially sovereign character of states, the consolidated national identity of their peoples, and the hegemony of authoritative governments as the dominant behavioral agents.

Yet a growing body of research has shown this frame of reference to be, at best, incomplete. The dominant trend in contemporary international relations theory is to expose these allegedly fixed properties of sovereignty, territoriality, national identity, and governmental authority as fragmented, incomplete, and often tenuous social constructions—the reproduction of which is never easy, often violent, and in many cases becoming more difficult (Biersteker and Weber, 1996; Kuehls, 1996). Research on migration processes, gender dynamics, and indigenous peoples reveal national identity to be not a fixed and immutable property of national populations, but rather a constructed and often tenuous mechanism of social control (Heisler, 2000; Tickner, 1993; Wilmer, 1993). Studies of intervention and postcolonialism have exposed the contingent, partial, and fragmented character of state sovereignty (Weber, 1995; Doty, 1996; Inayatullah and Blaney, 1996). Research on the role of advocacy networks, international knowledge communities, and transnational social movements challenges the notion that states are the preponderant actors in international relations (Keck and Sikkink, 1998; Lipschutz and Conca, 1993; Wapner, 1996). Even the fixed, essential character of territory becomes questionable in a world of border-straddling ecosystems, transboundary pollutant flows, and deterritorialized global commons (Kuehls, 1996). In such a world, to stake environmental peace on strategic bargaining among governments is to make increasingly unwarranted assumptions about their ability to deliver.

A second problem with a narrow frame of reference on the unified state as rational chooser is that states themselves are often at the heart of the problem of insecurity (ecological or otherwise). Just as territory, national identity, authoritative government, or sovereignty cannot be viewed statically, as the fixed properties of states, anarchy cannot be understood as a fixed property of the international system (Ruggie, 1983). Far from being an immutable fact of international life that justifies militarized responses to the inevitable security dilemma, anarchy is, to quote Alexander Wendt (1992), 'what states make of it'. And what modern states have too often made of it is a domain of violence and insecurity that becomes a self-fulfilling prophecy in interstate dealings and a justification for violence and repression in the domestic sphere. If so, it is not enough to render unrecon-structed national security states less wary and suspicious of one another, important though that task may be. A broader transformation of the zero-sum logic of the security state itself is also required. This means transform-ing institutions of governance and forging healthier, cooperative trans-soci-etal relationships.

In other words, in this formulation the focus shifts away from the per-ceptions of state elites and the structure of their interactive games to focus instead on the constitutive character of states, the normative fabric of inter-national life, and the increasingly dense array of trans-societal linkages. Does environmental cooperation soften rigidly exclusionary and narrowly territorial notions of sovereignty that stress states' rights over their respon-sibilities? Can environmental cooperation create the political "space" for new types of political mobilization with implications for personal and group identities that transcend national loyalties?' (Hayes and Zarsky, 1994). Does environmental cooperation push governments in the direction of more legitimate, open, and accountable forms of authority? Clearly, the answers to these questions will be contingent on the specific form that envi-ronmental cooperation takes. One can imagine initiatives that have the ef-fect of softening sovereignty, transnationalizing identity, and democratizing governance, just as one can imagine initiatives that have the opposite effect.

The question of system transformation raises a series of theoretical and empirical challenges that lie far beyond the scope of this chapter, and per-haps beyond the grasp of current knowledge. The discussion that follows, therefore, is quite preliminary and by no means comprehensive. It examines four mechanisms by which certain forms of environmental cooperation might push an important dependent variable in a post-Westphalian direc-tion. These mechanisms include the creation of new forms of interdepen-dence, the fostering of new norms, the deepening of transnational civil soci-ety, and the transformation of governmental institutions in the direction of greater transparency and democratic accountability.

Creating New Forms of Interdependence

It is close to an article of faith among liberal theorists of international rela-tions that interdependence is a force for peace and stability in world poli-tics. John Oneal and Bruce Russett (1997) summarize the classic liberal ar-gument, first articulated by Emeric Cruce in the early seventeenth century: 'Trade created common interests and increased the prosperity and political power of the peaceful, productive members of society'. This statement re-flects the emphasis on economic forms of interdependence, and trade in particular, that pervades the theoretical literature on interdependence. It also illustrates that the link between interdependence and peace has traditionally been based on two arguments. First, interdependence is said to create opportunities for mutual gain across national borders. This, it is argued, gives states a stake in peaceful cooperation and raises the costs of war to an unacceptable level.

The second and more transformative part of the interdependence argument involves domestic politics, with interdependence said to broaden and decentralize the distribution of power in society. According to the original formulation of the interdependence model by Robert Keohane and Joseph Nye (1977), a key property of interdependence politics is that interstate interaction occurs across multiple channels, with various domestic subgroups and transnational actors (businesses, bureaucratic organs of the state, interest groups, and so on) playing an increasingly important role in shaping national policies. The claim that interdependence promotes peace assumes that these actors will use their rising political influence to prevent the disruption of these transnational ties, at the same time reducing the danger that foreign policy is controlled by a 'warrior class' in society.

More recently, a third argument has been added, that interdependence is a structural determinant of international cooperation. Motoshi Suzuki (1994) presents evidence that higher levels of interdependence make it easier for states to balance the relative-gains strategies of states seeking a disproportionate advantage. If so then the tendency to value relative gains over absolute gains should attenuate as the level of interdependence increases, removing an important impediment to cooperation.

Efforts to demonstrate a link between interdependence and peace have focused overwhelmingly on *economic* forms of interdependence and, within that domain, primarily on international trade. Susan McMillan (1997) identified twenty studies testing the claim that interdependence, measured in terms of trade, inhibited violent conflict. She found that a majority of these studies supported the hypothesis. In a broad review of the literature, Oneal and Bruce Russett (1997) found fairly strong evidence to support the trade/peace hypothesis. They identified several studies showing that the importance of trade to a country's economy is inversely proportional to involvement in international conflict or a propensity to initiate war. They also point to evidence of the particularly pacifying effects of trade among contiguous states (where conflict is generally most frequent); that trade appears to inhibit militarized disputes even when controlling for the fact that conflict patterns and expectations about conflict may shape the growth of trade flows; and that both trade relationships and economic openness are strongly associated with peace in dyadic relationships among contiguous states or involving great powers (the cases most likely to lead to war), even when controlling for a wide range of potential confounders such as alliances or regime type. Ranveig Gissinger and Nils Petter Gleditsch (1999) find more complex effects of an open economy, with higher levels of trade associated with domestic peace but also with effects of income inequality that can lead to political instability in poorer countries.

But what of *ecological* interdependence? Obviously, environmental problems themselves constitute a form of interdependence: In a world where pollution respects no borders, states are increasingly sensitive and vulnerable to each other's polluting activities. One could argue that, to the extent that it reduces these mutual sensitivities and vulnerabilities, environmental cooperation constitutes a lessening of interdependence. But a more important effect of environmental cooperation may be to create important and potentially powerful new interests supporting transnational cooperative arrangements. Business interests coalesce around the provision of environmental technologies, clean-up services, monitoring, and so on. Nongovernmental organizations evolve from pressure groups into supporters of, and even participants in, international agreements, in some cases even taking on the role of service providers or data collectors. Transnational NGO networks established around a particular problem can deepen and broaden their ties by tackling new issues. The result is to create a new set of stakeholders in continued cooperation, much as the trade-based interdependence model envisions exporters in country A and importers in country B forming a transnational coalition for peaceful relations. One way this process might work is through the process of 'tote-board diplomacy' described by Levy (1993) in the case of Europe's Long-Range Transboundary Air Pollution Convention.[3] Rather than creating strong and binding rules, LRTAP emphasized consensus building on sources of the problem. This created informational resources that could be used to generate not only external but also domestic pressure on noncomplying or nonparticipating states.

A second potentially important effect of environmental collaboration is that it can galvanize a domestic base of support very different from the typical coalition of actors supporting economic interdependence. The polarizing effects of economic globalization have created broad constituencies, across a wide range of societies and ideological stances, that are increasingly wary of the toll of economic interdependence on community, employment, and democracy (Broad and Cavanagh, 1999; Markoff, 1999). The result of these concerns is a growing transnational coalition opposed to the particular form of interdependence at the heart of the liberal internationalist agenda, namely international trade and investment.

Under these circumstances collaboration may provide an important political opportunity to change or balance the form that interdependence takes and broaden the coalition in support of it. In domestic political terms, therefore, one of the crucial questions is the nature of the constituency engaged by emerging forms of environmental cooperation. More generally, it is crucial to map the linkages between emerging patterns of ecological and economic interdependence at a time when both are deepening.

Fostering New Norms

Relations of peace or conflict are embedded not only in material circumstances but also through internalized norms. Martha Finnemore (1996) identifies and traces a historical process of social construction in the definition of 'national interests' (see also Katzenstein, 1996; Risse-Kappen, 1995). Behavioral norms, or 'shared expectations about appropriate behavior', are part of an international structure of 'meaning and social value' that helps states determine their interests:

> States do not always know what they want. They and the people in them develop perceptions of interest and understandings of desirable behavior from social interactions with others in the world they inhabit. States are socialized to accept certain preferences and expectations by the international society in which they and the people who compose them live. (Finnemore, 1996: 128)

One of Finnemore's historical case studies, focused on the International Red Cross and the Geneva Conventions, reveals war as a 'highly regulated social institution whose rules have changed over time' (1996: 69)—illustrating that socialization mechanisms are at work even on matters related to the high politics of violent conflict and state survival.

Emanuel Adler (1997) has argued that norms related to peace and conflict can be internalized at the supranational level. Building on Karl Deutsch's concept of a 'pluralistic security community' and Benedict Anderson's concept of the nation as an 'imagined community', Adler argues that we are seeing the emergence of new identity constructs whose borders are defined not by territorial state boundaries but rather by shared norms of peaceful conflict resolution and 'dependable expectations of peaceful change' (Adler, 1997: 255; see also Adler and Barnett, 1996).

The question is whether environmental cooperation can help to spur these processes of national socialization and transnational community-building. One potential avenue is through evolving practices and norms of sovereignty (Conca, 1995b). Karen Litfin (1997) suggests that responses to environmental problems contribute to the 'reconfiguration' of sovereignty by reworking norms of state autonomy and state legitimacy. One possible pathway to such reconfiguration is through renewed emphasis not just on state rights but also state responsibilities embedded in the principle of sovereignty (Wapner, 1998). Another avenue may be a norm of the environment as the 'common heritage' of humanity (Weiss, 1989). Although much of the discussion in this domain has been at the global level in the sense of focusing on an ethic of planetary responsibility, there may also be effects at the regional level if such norms translate into a 'good neighbor' ethic.

Asking whether environmental cooperation fosters such normative changes means examining several possible pathways. Finnemore (1996: 3), though not focusing specifically on environmental issues, stresses the role of intergovernmental organizations as agents that 'socialize states to accept new political goals and new values'. Peter Haas and Ernst Haas (1995; see also Haas, 1991) also focus on intergovernmental organizations, in this case as laboratories for the development of effective knowledge-based adaptations through processes of organizational learning. Stacy VanDeveer and Geoffrey Dabelko (1999), examining Baltic environmental cooperation, point to a process in which transnational norms related to environmental protection become codified through national environmental legislation. Paul Wapner (1996), in a study of transnational environmental advocacy organizations, stresses a different pathway, grounded in the dissemination of an 'ecological sensibility' across an ever-wider swath of society.

Alternately, it may be these various forms of environmental institutionalization are best understood as effect rather than cause; John Meyer (1997) and other 'world-society' theorists have suggested that the proliferation of international environmental institutions is the expression of the globalization of underlying norms of Western scientific rationalism and Weberian bureaucratic administration. Moreover, one can readily imagine forms of international environmental cooperation that reproduce and rigidify traditional norms of sovereign separateness. Perhaps one of the best indicators in this regard is whether cooperation is restricted to the traditionally 'international' domain of transboundary pollutant flows and transnational commons issues, or whether it also develops to the point of embracing questions of local/domestic resource management and incorporating a more holistic perspective of integrated ecosystems, natural cycles, and environmental services.

Building Transnational Civil Society

Along with a few other issue areas—notably including human rights, grassroots development, the status of women—environmental problems have been at the forefront of arguments that we are seeing the emergence of a transnational or even global civil society (Keck and Sikkink, 1998; Lipschutz, 1992, 1996; Potter, 1996; Princen and Finger, 1994; Wapner, 1995, 1996). This perspective is rooted primarily in liberal democratic theory, which presumes that a myriad of social, cultural, and other forms of collective interaction are an important counterbalance to the concentrated power of state and market institutions in society. Scholars applying the concept of civil society to the transnational sphere have stressed as driving forces the effects of economic globalization, the communications revolution, and the deepening of state authority crises in the face of challenges such as environmental degradation. The result of these processes has been to create a thinly institutionalized but growing transnational civil society, manifest primarily as networks linking local nongovernmental organizations and social-movement groups with genuinely transnational, 'sovereignty-free' actors (Rosenau, 1990).

The potential significance of these transnational networks is twofold. First, they can greatly empower previously marginalized groups to have a voice in policy decisions, in both domestic and international fora. For local community organizations struggling against problems as diverse as the construction of large dams, the destruction of forests, or the stripping away of traditional land rights, transnational networking has been an increasingly important resource for community empowerment. These changes in power relations can provoke social conflict and violence, to be sure. But as resource use intensifies and environmental degradation worsens, creating space for the disparate and dissident voices of stakeholders is increasingly acknowledged as a prerequisite for effective international cooperation (Susskind, 1994).

A second peacemaking effect of transnational networks may lie in the realm of identity. As Adler suggests, 'There is much evidence in the social psychology literature that cooperative behavior between individuals is mediated by the perception of membership in a common category' (Adler, 1997: 264; see also Kelman, 1997). If a common category is to be forged embracing principles of sustainability and shared responsibility, it seems at least as likely to emerge from trans-societal linkages as from interstate bargaining. Wapner (1996) argues that transnational environmental organizations are important international political actors because of their capacity to go around, above, or below the state to shape directly the values, preferences, and collective choice mechanisms of large numbers of people.

Whether the result is also to loosen the traditional moorings of political identity remains unclear. James Rosenau (1990) refers to a 'skill revolution' in world politics at the level of the individual, leading more people to assess governmental legitimacy in terms of governmental performance—thereby creating crises of authority for many if not most governments. It is also not clear whether newly emergent identity formations move in the direction of shared interests and responsibilities across borders. As Larry Swatuk (1997: 128) suggests in the context of Southern Africa, a wide range of differing identity constructs may emerge from such crises of the state:

The feelings of alienation from and abandonment by the state on the part of the majority of the region's peoples, exacerbated in some cases by the negative impacts of structural adjustment, have given rise to sub- and supra-national redefinitions of 'security' and 'community': from Islam and ethnicity to crime networks and cooperatives.

Transforming State Institutions

It was argued above that states are often part of the problem of violence and insecurity, in that they tend to internalize norms of secrecy, separateness, and conflictual zero-sum relations. Thus one of the key questions about environmental peacemaking is whether environmental cooperation fosters the transformation of the state, and in particular of military institutions, away from these orientations.

Environmental issues offer many opportunities to engage traditional security institutions in new forms of cooperation. The military and intelligence organs of the state often wield assets in the form of technology, expertise, and information that can be useful in addressing environmental problems. In many settings the quest for a post–Cold War mandate has left security institutions open to at least discuss new missions and budgetary justifications. And the drumbeat of concern about environmentally induced conflict has placed environmental issues on the military agenda in a wide range of settings.

Some advocates of 'environmental security' have suggested that these opportunities can be seized upon to break down the culture of secrecy that pervades interstate relations in the security domain (see for example Stern, 1999). Drawing security institutions into environmental discussions may institutionalize new norms of information sharing, institutional accountability, and cooperation, while making such practices less mysterious and threatening to the institutions themselves. Kent Butts (1999), for example, points to the reformist value of military-to-military ties dealing with environmental themes. Others have argued that a more likely outcome is the militarization of environmental policy under the guise of greening security policy (Deudney, 1990; Finger, 1991; Conca, 1994).

The U.S. experience with efforts to redirect spy satellite activities toward environmental monitoring illustrates both the potential and the obstacles of this high-stakes game of institutional transformation. As Litfin (1998: 196–197) suggests,

> Military agencies still control the lion's share of high resolution satellite imagery and are reluctant to share it with others. As the militaries of the Cold War superpowers come under pressure to redefine their mission in a post-Cold War era, they have become involved in environmental research. For decades, the security forces of both superpowers did a good deal of inadvertent environmental research, which scientists are now eager to acquire.

In a study of the U.S. experience, Ronald Diebert (1996: 29) remains skeptical about institutional transformation:

Despite the intuitive appeal of this logic . . . the actual scope of the refocusing that has occurred has been relatively small. While gathering momentum with each successive year, the deeply pervasive secrecy of U.S. intelligence agencies guarantees that any potential mission adjustments or 'outside' intrusions into intelligence activities and priorities are met with a blanket of suspicion and institutional inertia.

Diebert also describes a trend toward the merging of environmental and military reconnaissance systems under a single umbrella, as in the U.S. National Reconnaissance Office or in Brazil's $1.4 billion Amazonian surveillance system, raising troubling questions of institutional and informational control (see also Conca, 1997).

Conclusion

There are no guarantees that international environmental cooperation will continue to expand at either the global or regional level, nor can it be said that such cooperation will automatically spill over to promote broader forms of peace and comprehensive security. But there is a theoretical foundation for the claim that environmental cooperation can promote and enhance peace. In the short run, environmental cooperation could create positive externalities for international peace and human security by improving the climate of strategic interaction and political bargaining. In the long run, it could be an important way to strengthen the institutionalization of post-Westphalian forms of governance, by creating new norms, deepening and broadening positive transnational linkages, deepening the development of international civil society, and transforming institutions of the security state. At the very least, there may be a link between environmental cooperation and peaceful international relations that is at least as strong as the link between environmental degradation and violent conflict.[4]

This premise harkens back to ideas of the early post–World War II era, including the claims of so-called 'functionalists' such as David Mitrany and integration theorists such as Karl Deutsch. Mitrany argued that the growth of routine international cooperation would gradually promote cooperation in ever more conflictual areas; 'low politics' would gradually intrude on the domain of 'high politics' (Mitrany, 1966, 1976; Haas, 1964). Deutsch (1952, 1963) argued that an increase in international transactions would produce an increase in value compatibility and mutual trust across societies, resulting in support for closer ties and, eventually, political integration (see also Deutsch et al., 1957; Inglehart et al., 1996).

Critics suggested that these claims were naive, citing as evidence the limits to East-West cooperation during the Cold War. Daniel Deudney (1993: 285) describes a common criticism of Mitrany's functionalist view:

Realist critics claim that states which were antagonists in high politics would not allow extensive low politics collaboration. Indeed, the realists argued, the spillover occurred in the opposite direction to that predicted by Mitrany: economic and welfare collaboration would be retarded by high politics conflict between states. Mitrany was 'unrealistic' to think that economics and welfare would ever be allowed to operate autonomously of the high political sphere. Thus the low politics of collaboration between long-time antagonists France and Germany after World War II presupposed the American-led military unification of Western Europe. And the high political conflict between the United States and the Soviet Union greatly impeded substantial welfare and economic collaboration between the blocs.

The same process may inhibit environmental peacemaking. In other words, the very problems of suspicion, mistrust, and uncertainty that environmental cooperation is meant to overcome may serve to inhibit environmental cooperation in the first place. Lothar Brock (1991: 414) surmises that 'At present, ecological cooperation is a dependent variable that reflects the state of overall relations more than it influences these relations'.

Nevertheless, there are at least two rejoinders to these pessimistic conclusions. First, as Deudney and others have suggested, it may be that functionalism was dismissed too soon. Environmental problems may be the first test case in which the stakes are high enough and the logic of cooperation strong enough to promote the sort of positive, cooperative spillover that Mitrany envisioned. Unlike the coordination of international postal service or air-traffic control, environmental problems may be serious enough to compel governments to take greater chances on international cooperation—even when an overarching security logic for cooperation, such as that which facilitated European integration, is absent. Second, the ideological and strategic hostility of the Cold War probably represents an extreme case. To dismiss environmental confidence building because it failed to end the Cold War—or for that matter, because it cannot transform relations between Israel and Palestine or India and Pakistan—would be to let short-term evidence from a few particularly hard cases cause us to abandon prematurely a useful strategy for enhancing peace. Both on a global scale and in regions as diverse as post–Cold War Northeast Asia, postrevolutionary Central America, postapartheid Southern Africa, and post-Soviet Central Europe, states and societies are in the process of sorting out new security relationships in the wake of a particularly turbulent period of change. Where they are not locked into patterns of confrontation and conflict, but rather groping toward new relationships under conditions of great uncertainty about the future, the catalytic potential of environmental cooperation may be more apparent and more substantial.

Whether environmental problems lead to widespread violence or antici-patory initiatives to create cooperative, comprehensive, human security de-pends on several factors. These include the rate, distribution, and intensity of transnational environmental degradation; the perceptions actors hold of the problems and opportunities inherent in environmental change; and the ability of governments and other actors to design effective institutions that overcome barriers to cooperation. But it will also depend on our ability and willingness to seize upon the inescapable fact of our ecological interdepen-dence as a catalyst for building a more peaceful international order.

Ken Conca, b. 1959, Ph.D. (Energy and Resources Group, University of Califor-nia, Berkeley, 1992); associate professor of government and politics, University of Maryland (1998–); assistant professor (1993–1998). Most recent books: *Green Planet Blues: Environmental Politics from Stockholm to Kyoto* (with Geoffrey D. Dabelko; Westview, 1998*), Manufacturing Insecurity: The Rise and Fall of Brazil's Military-Industrial Complex* (Lynne Rienner, 1997).

Notes

1. Haas (1990), Keohane and Levy (1993), Clapp (1994), Litfin (1994), Mitchell (1994), Sprinz & Vaahtoranta (1994), Young (1994; 1998), Haas, Keohane & Os-trom (1995).

2. Montreal Protocol on Substances that Deplete the Ozone Layer. *International Legal Materials* 26: 1541; entry into force 1 January 1989.

3. Convention on Long-Range Transboundary Air Pollution. International Legal Materials 18 1442; entry into force 16 March 1983.

4. I am grateful to an anonymous reviewer for this observation.

Part III

Environmental Conflict: A Future Research Agenda

Chapter Twelve

Armed Conflict and the Environment

NILS PETTER GLEDITSCH

War, Resources, and the Environment

After the end of the Cold War, resource and environmental issues have come to the forefront of the study of armed conflict and security. According to a recent study from NATO's Committee on the Challenges of Modern Society, 'NATO looks increasingly at threats from non-traditional sources' and applies a 'new and broader security concept' that 'recognises that security and stability have political, economic, social and environmental elements' (Lietz-mann and Vest, 1999: 1). And the German minister of environment argues that 'global environmental degradation . . . as well as the depletion of renewable resources . . . and non-renewable resources . . . are increasingly seen as major contributing factors to conflicts' (Trittin, 2000: vii).

Earlier versions of this article were presented at a NATO Advanced Research Workshop 'Conflict and the Environment' at Bolkesjø, Norway; a meeting of the NATO Committee on the Challenges of the Modern Society Pilot Study Meeting on Environmental Security in Ankara; the Fifth National Conference in Political Science at Geilo, Norway; at the 38th Annual Conference of the International Studies Association, Toronto; and at the 1997 Open Meeting of the Human Dimensions of Global Environmental Change Research Community at Laxenburg, Austria. I gratefully acknowledge financial support from the United States Institute of Peace, the Norwegian Ministry of Foreign Affairs, and the Research Council of Norway. For assistance I thank Tanja Ellingsen, Norunn Grande, Håvard Hegre, Cecilie Sundby, and Bjørn Otto Sverdrup. Finally, I am grateful for comments from fellow editor Paul Diehl and two anonymous referees, as well as Scott Gates, Dan Smith, and a number of participants at the various conferences.

Arguments about resource scarcity as a cause of violence are not new in peace research. Pioneers like Quincy Wright (1942/65: ch. 32) and Lewis Fry Richardson (1960: ch. 7) discussed them under the general heading of economic causes of war. But the end of East-West rivalry, which completely dominated international relations for over 40 years, has permitted such factors to appear more clearly.

In this line of argument, the prime resource seen as worth fighting for is obviously *territory*, as in the conflict-filled expansion of European settlers in North America or the border conflicts between China and several neighbors. A more recent variety of territorial conflict concerns the *economic zone* on the continental shelf, a traditional matter of dispute between countries which are neighbors over water and which may raise tiny islands to monumental importance because of their consequences for boundaries at sea. Thus, there are no less than six claimants to all or part of the Spratly Islands in the South China Sea (Denoon and Brams, 2001), and the use of force cannot be ruled out. Another valuable resource is *strategic raw materials*. The strategic importance accorded to Indochina in the 1950s was justified by U.S. president Eisenhower—in the statement that made famous the 'domino theory'—with reference to the importance of raw materials such as tin, tungsten, and rubber.[1] Some such raw materials are closely tied to arms production, others are simply seen as essential to the economy. A third is *sources of energy*, the most obvious example being oil supplies from the Persian Gulf, a factor in several recent conflicts. A fourth is *water*, with widely expressed fears that irrigation or dam projects may result in a water shortages downstream and eventually to serious upstream-downstream conflicts (Gleditsch, 1997b: section E). A UN study has identified over 200 major river systems shared by two or more countries, many of them subject to unresolved disputes (Renner, 1996: 60). A fifth resource is *food*, including grains and fisheries. Disagreements regarding shared fisheries resources have occasioned numerous confrontations between fishing vessels and armed vessels of coastal states, including three 'Cod Wars' between Iceland and the United Kingdom in the period 1958–1976 (Bailey, 1997). Increasing food prices can give rise to domestic violent riots; at the international level, food sales have been used for strategic leverage (de Soysa and Gleditsch, 1999: 79f).

The traditional Malthusian argument is that the combination of population growth and high resource consumption per capita produces resource scarcity. Thomas Malthus made this argument in relation to the supply of food. A similar argument can be made in relation to other resources, but food still retains pride of place because of its importance to human survival. The modern variant of this argument is that excessive use will deplete the resource base and produce environmental destruction, which in turn makes for even greater scarcity. The more unequal the resource distribution, the greater the number of people affected by scarcity; affluence and scarcity can coexist in the system. The final link in the causal chain is that

FIGURE 12.1   A Simple Model of Environmental Conflict

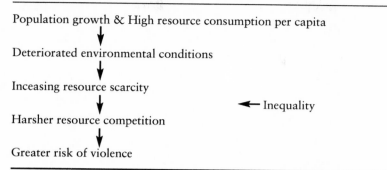

harsher competition for resources will increase the chances of violence. I have formalized this argument in Figure 12.1.

Not everyone who writes on resource and environmental conflict would include all the elements of this causal chain or put the emphasis in the same place. Biologists frequently single out population growth as the key causal factor; environmentalists tend to start with environmental degradation; and critics of capitalism tend to emphasize excessive consumption in the First World and the need for the First World to restrict its consumption if the Third World is to be allowed to catch up. There is not necessarily any contradiction between these positions, but they stress different parts of the causal chain.

Thomas Homer-Dixon and associates in one of the most widely recognized modern formulations use a tripartite division of scarcity (Percival and Homer-Dixon, 2001): *supply-induced* (corresponding to environmental deterioration), *demand-induced* (resulting from population growth), and *structural* (due to inequality).

Despite numerous pronouncements on the relationship between conflict and the environment, there is no consensus on the links in this causal chain. Several writers have questioned the overall argument. Daniel Deudney (1991, 1999), Julian Simon (1996), and Bjørn Lomborg, (1998, 2001) have listed a number of problems with the notion of increasing resource scarcity.[2] First, it ignores human inventiveness and technological change, both of which have vastly increased agricultural yields and the rate of resource extraction from raw material lodes. Modern industry produces highly processed goods, which require intensive use of capital, technology, and energy, rather than raw materials like minerals. Secondly, the pessimistic argument also overlooks the role of international trade; most scarcities are local rather than universal. Third, raw materials can be substituted, so being dependent on a particular resource today is not the same as being vulnerable tomorrow if the supply lines should be choked off. Fourth, in the event of increasing scarcity,

prices are likely to rise, leading to greater economizing, and further technological change, trade, and substitution. In fact, these processes have been sufficiently effective in recent decades for raw materials prices to fall even
though global consumption of natural resources has increased. Thus, while
the international bestseller *The Limits to Growth* (Meadows et al., 1972)
predicted imminent scarcities in a number of minerals, such as copper, the
trend since then has in fact been in the opposite direction.

Even in the event of scarcities which could theoretically be overcome by
imperialist behavior, the major powers have learned—from Vietnam,
Afghanistan, and a number of other wars in the Third World—that subdu-
ing a resisting population, however technologically backward, is a very
costly affair.

On the basis of an overall 'cornucopian' view where the human being is
the most essential resource, Simon (1989) argues that, rather than further-
ing war, population growth is likely to end it. Instead of armed conflict,
Deudney argues, conflicts over resources such as water may lead to joint
exploitation of the resources and a network of common interests. Similarly,
resource scarcity based on environmental degradation would encourage
joint efforts to halt the degradation. Marc Levy (1995) also argues that environmental degradation is unlikely on its own to be a major cause of
armed conflict; further, that it is not a national security issue for the United
States, and is even unlikely to prove interesting as a research area unless
seen in conjunction with other causes of armed conflict.

Many of the more balanced statements on environmental factors in conflict are rather cautious about drawing causal links. Arthur Westing (1986:
6), for instance, concludes only that 'what the ultimate cause or causes of
war might be defies simple explanation'. Lothar Brock (1991: 410) con-
cedes that the importance of natural resources as a source of conflict is easily exaggerated, citing Ronnie Lipschutz and John Holdren (1990: 121),
who argue that despite Eisenhower's famous 'domino' statement and numerous other policy pronouncements, the problem of access to resources
has not 'really played such a central role in shaping US foreign and military
policy in recent decades'. The same holds for other nations, Lipschutz and
Holdren argue, although resources have frequently served as rationaliza-
tions for public consumption 'in support of policies with much more elaborate origins' (Lipschutz and Holdren, 1990: 123).

In spite of the strong cornucopian counterattacks, the neomalthusian argument linking resource scarcity to conflict, is stated with considerable
force, as when U.S. Vice President Al Gore declares the fate of Earth to be
hanging 'in the balance' (Gore, 1992). Michael Renner of the Worldwatch
Institute asserts that resource depletion is 'increasingly understood to play
an important role in generating or exacerbating some conflicts' and that if
'climate change becomes a full-blown reality' it will 'translate into a sharp
increase in human conflict' (Renner, 1999: 39–40). The object of this article

is to examine the research foundations for such claims. I begin with a brief summary of systematic research in this area and go on to discuss nine common theoretical and methodological problems in the extant literature. Finally, I outline some priorities for future work in this area.

Systematic Research

Neither in the environmental literature nor in studies of the causes of war or civil war has there been much systematic research (quantitative or comparative) on the relationship between conflict, resources, and environmental factors. For example, the comprehensive *Handbook of War Studies* (Midlarsky, 1989) does not list 'ecology', 'environment', 'land', 'raw materials', or 'water' in its index, although there is a chapter on 'lateral pressure' (Choucri and North, 1989). Within the Correlates of War project, an early article finds some support for the idea that population pressure may be a factor in war initiation (Bremer et al., 1973); but generally environmental factors do not seem to have attracted much attention from the largest modern research project on war. Most of the relevant studies are of quite recent origin.

A number of studies summarized in Jaroslav Tir and Paul Diehl (2001) have related two indicators of population pressure, *population density* and *population growth*, to conflict and violence. Both are measures of demand-induced scarcity in Homer-Dixon's terms. They do not measure resource scarcity or environmental degradation directly. But they may provide an indirect measure, in that a high value indicates a high or increasing *load* on scarce resources. Tir and Diehl reviewed an extensive literature in which there was little theoretical or empirical consensus beyond the suggestion that there was a link between the population variables and international conflict. In their own empirical study of all nations for the period 1930–1989, they conclude that there is a significant but fairly weak relationship between population growth and interstate militarized conflict and war, but that population density has no effect.[3]

Territory is undoubtedly the resource that has been studied most extensively in the context of conflict. Several quantitative studies have underlined the role of territorial issues in armed conflict. For example, Kalevi Holsti (1991: 307) concludes that among interstate wars in the period 1648–1989, territorial issues were by far the most important single issue category. Reanalyzing Holsti's data, John Vasquez (1993: 130, 1995: 284) finds that between 79 percent and 93 percent of interstate wars over the five time-periods involve territorially-related issues. Paul Huth (1996: 5) in a study of territorial disputes from 1950–1990 characterizes this issue as 'one of the enduring features of international politics'. The territorial explanation of war also fits in with the finding that most interstate violence occurs between neighbors (Bremer, 1992) or between proximate countries (Gleditsch, 1995). One may question why such conflicts occur—because neighbors are more easily available for conflict than other states, because of friction in their day-to-day interaction, or because of disputed boundaries or territories? However, Vasquez (1995) presents a strong case for the territorial explanation.

The question of 'water wars', i.e. armed conflicts resulting from scarcity of freshwater particularly between upstream and downstream states (Lonergan, 2001), has recently come to be subjected to some systematic study. Using data from the International Crisis Behavior project, Aaron Wolf (1999b) finds that water issues rarely feature in international crises since 1918, but that water sharing is very frequently the subject of interstate cooperation. Hans Petter Wollebæk Toset, Nils Petter Gleditsch, and Håvard Hegre (2000) find that sharing a river increases the probability of dyadic militarized conflict (over and beyond simply being a neighbor), but not by a very wide margin. They are unable to conclude whether the increased probability of conflict relates to water scarcity or the fluidity of river boundaries.

An empirical investigation of resource imperialism by Mats Hammarström (1986, 1997) examined how interventions in the Third World by three major Western powers (France, UK, and the USA) in the period 1951–1977 might be accounted for by the presence of economically and militarily essential minerals in the less developed country. Hammarström found that the importance of the less developed country as a supplier of minerals did not affect the likelihood of intervention from the USA and the UK, and affected it only slightly in the case of France. This finding also held for the subset of countries within the sphere of influence of the major power, for the subset of minerals upon which the major power was extremely dependent, and for regions rather than individual countries.

While the study of war has been dominated by the question of interstate conflict, most wars in the post–World War II period have been internal wars, and this trend has continued after the Cold War. The literature using single cases to study the effects of environmental degradation is mostly concerned with civil war and other internal violence. In this field, there is even less comparative and quantitative work here than in relation to interstate conflict. Peter Wallensteen and Margareta Sollenberg (1999: 599 ff.) show that in slightly more than half the conflicts in the first decade after the Cold War, the basic incompatibility concerned territory rather than government. The chapter by Wenche Hauge and Tanja Ellingsen (2001) stands out as unique in trying to integrate environmental degradation into a more general model of civil war and test it in a large-N mode. They conclude that environmental degradation does stimulate the incidence of conflict, but less so than political or economic variables and that the severity of such conflicts is better accounted for by military spending.[4] Phase II of the *State Failure Task Force Report* (Esty et al., 1998) differs from the Hauge and Ellingsen study in that it generally found the environmental variables not to be significant. But direct comparison is impeded by the more complex dependent variable used in the state failure study. Finally, in a study of desertification and conflict, Turi Saltnes (1998) found a bivariate relationship between the spread of deserts and internal armed conflict in the period 1980–1990. But this relationship largely evaporated when she controlled for political and economic variables.

Many economists who have studied the economic effects of natural resources have drawn rather pessimistic conclusions, arguing that an abundance of resources often lead to rent-seeking and predatory behavior. Based on this literature and his own empirical research, Indra de Soysa (2000) argues that resource abundance in LDCs is more likely to lead to civil war (given circumstances otherwise favorable to violence than resource scarcity).

On the whole, then, quantitative studies of resource and environmental issues indicate that these do seem to play a role in interstate as well as intrastate conflict. However, the influence of such variables is less dramatic than frequently assumed in the political debate, it is mediated by other factors, and it may even at times have the opposite effect of what the environmental literature posits—abundance leading to fighting, scarcity to cooperation.

Nine Common Problems

Apart from the role of territory in interstate armed conflict, and to some extent the demographic factors, there is very little systematic research on the effects or resource or environmental factors on armed conflict. In the absence of solid evidence, the field has been left wide open to speculation and conjecture. Thus, in debating population pressure, even serious academics are driven to support their respective positions in the US debate by referring to the sparsity of population that anyone can observe out of an airplane window (Bolch and Lyons, 1993: 27) or the obvious overpopulation which is evident when one drives in a major city at rush hour (Ehrlich and Ehrlich, 1996: 211). Such low standards of evidence make it difficult to assess the state of the art. In what follows, I will concentrate on work with more solid claims to seriousness. Even within this literature, however, there are many problems. This article discusses nine of them, in no particular order. Obviously, not all of the problems apply to every piece of writing—the critique is directed at the literature broadly speaking.

Resource Scarcity or Environmental Degradation?

Virtually *all* resources are 'scarce'—to some degree, at some times, or in some places. By definition, scarcity leads to 'conflict' in the sense of conflict of interest. Indeed, it is only a small extra step to argue that *all* conflicts of interest derive from scarcity.

Environmental degradation may exacerbate conflicts of interest over resources because it reduces the quantity or quality of the resource in question. Pollution of a river, for instance, reduces the quality of the water; but it can also be interpreted as reducing the quantity of clean water, and therefore contributing to increased scarcity. Similarly, air pollution in a city degrades the quality of the air and changes an unlimited public good (clean air) into a scarce one.

Stephan Libiszewski (1992: 2) argues that simple resource conflicts are very common, but that the concept of *environmental* conflict calls for a more restricted use. The latter he defines as a conflict caused by a human-made disturbance of the normal regeneration rate of a renewable resource (Libiszewski, 1992: 6). Thus, a conflict over agricultural land is an 'environmental conflict' if the land becomes an object of contention as a result of soil erosion, climate change, and so on, but not in the case of an ordinary territorial or colonial conflict or an antiregime civil war aiming at the redistribution of land. Nonrenewable natural resources (such as oil) are not integrated in any ecosystem. Their depletion may lead to economic problems, but they are not in themselves environmental problems, so conflicts over such resources should *not* be considered environmental conflicts.

Libiszewski's distinction between those conflicts which result from simple resource scarcity and those which result from environmental degradation is useful, but is not reflected in most of the literature on environmental conflict. When, for instance, Homer-Dixon (1991, 1994) refers to 'environmental scarcity', the terminology itself muddies the waters. In the following, within the bounds of the practical, I will try to distinguish between simple resource conflicts and environmental conflicts. However, I find it more difficult to follow Libiszewski in linking environmental conflict to the concept of an ecosystem, with its questionable overtones of balance and equilibrium.[5]

The distinction between simple resource scarcity and environmental degradation does raise some problems. Today's simple scarcity may well be the result of environmental mismanagement in the past. The lack of forests around Madrid may be seen as a fact of nature today, but can be interpreted as a result of excessive ship-building in the sixteenth century, and thus as an old case of environmental degradation. Most, if not all, territorial conflict can be seen as the result of past population policies (or a lack thereof) which have permitted groups to multiply beyond what their traditional territories could support. As far as the present is concerned, Libiszewski's distinction sets a useful standard. However, not all conflicts of interest lead to overt conflict behavior, and fewer still to the use of force.

Definitions and Polemics

The term *environmental security* was launched to place the environment on the agenda of 'high politics' (Lodgaard, 1992: 115). If one adopts a broad conception of security as 'the assurance people have that they will continue to enjoy those things that are most important to their survival and well-being' (Soroos, 1997a: 236), it can be plausibly argued that serious environmental degradation can indeed threaten security. This would be particularly true if the most serious warnings about global warming or holes in the ozone layer turn out to be correct, but even more traditional environmental concerns like air and water pollution can kill more people than smaller armed conflicts or even wars. Politically, then, it makes sense to give such issues very high priority. Like common security, structural violence, or sustainable development, environmental security made a good slogan—so successful that the U.S. Department of Defense now has a position called 'Deputy Under Secretary of Defense (Environmental Security)', the NATO Science Committee has sponsored several workshops on environmental security (Gleditsch, 1997b; Lonergan, 1999), and NATO's Committee on the Challenges of Modern Society has conducted a large study on the same topic (Lietzmann and Vest, 1999). Defense establishments in many countries in NATO and among the cooperating partner countries in East and Central Europe are rushing to acquire a green image by improving their environmental performance.

But political success does not necessarily make a slogan into a workable research tool (Græger, 1996). Merging two objectives like security and environmental protection into a joint term does not give us new theoretical or empirical insight into whether the two are mutually supportive—or in competition. Those who on the basis of the broad definition of security deliberately disregard the question of armed conflict are in a sense on fairly safe ground.[6] But most of the literature cannot resist the temptation to bring the danger of armed conflict back in, as a consequence of environmental degradation (Gleditsch, 1997b; Lodgaard, 1992). Indeed, why else would armed forces and military alliances be so interested in environmental security?

On this point, the critical literature (Deudney, 1990; Levy, 1995) does not take us much further. In part, this literature engages in similar definitional exercises in order to prove the futility of the concept of environmental security. In addition, it demonstrates theoretical and empirical problems in the writings on the environment and security. Some of the critical points are well taken, but if they do not end up in an alternative or improved research design, they are of little help.

Overlooking Important Variables

Conclusive proofs that human activity could shift the average global temperature by, for example, five degrees, would be a very important finding. No climate researcher would argue, however, that human activity is the one and only determinant of global temperature. Anyone who correlated emissions of greenhouse gases with temperatures recorded monthly would seem

patently ridiculous, since the effect of human activity is likely to be completely swamped by long-established seasonal variations. In the social sciences, such caution is often thrown to the winds. Far too many analyses of
conflict and the environment are based not only on bivariate analysis but
also on overly simplistic reasoning.

The greatest weakness in this respect is that much of this literature ignores political, economic, and cultural variables. When writers on environmental conflict refer to the '214 shared river systems' or 'water scarcity'
generally as potential sources of violent conflict (Gleick, 1993c: 79–80),
they rarely distinguish between rivers which run through poor, undemocra-
tic, politically unstable countries ridden by ethnic tensions, and rivers running through stable and affluent countries. It is tacitly assumed that resource conflicts have a high potential for violence, regardless of the
countries' political system or economic orientation. Since democracies
rarely if ever fight one another (Gleditsch and Hegre, 1997; Russett, 1993)
and since they rarely experience civil war (Hegre et al., 1999) there is no
reason to believe that they will suddenly start fighting over resource issues
between themselves, or internally, any more than over other issues. Moreover, if it is correct that democracies generally display more benign environmental behavior than do nondemocracies,[7] then democracies are also less
likely to generate the kind of extreme environmental degradation which
may be assumed to generate violent conflict. Thus, democracy may have a
double effect in preventing armed conflict over the environment: it generates fewer serious problems, and it provides other means of conflict resolution once these problems have arisen.

Most work on environmental conflict does not discuss how regime type
may influence such conflict. For example, in many of the case studies published by Homer-Dixon and his associates, there are general references to
'key social and political factors' (Percival and Homer-Dixon, 1995: 3), to
corruption, weakened legitimacy, resource capture by elites, and so on.
However, words such as 'democracy' or 'autocracy' do not occur in the
model. The work by Homer-Dixon and his associates is more sensitive to
political variables than many other studies in this field, and their work frequently hovers around the idea that democratic procedures might have
something to do with the level of conflict. But their work never states
clearly whether democracy matters, and in what way. In view of the extensive theoretical and empirical literature relating the degree of democracy to
civil violence in an inverted U-curve (Hegre et al., 1999; Muller and Weede,
1990;) a democracy variable (and its squared term) should have been included explicitly.

Many of the militarized interstate disputes between democracies have
been over resources—or more specifically over one particular resource, fish
(Bailey, 1997; Russett, 1993: 21) At sea, boundaries between states are not

yet well settled, and even where they are established by law or by custom, they are not visible. The fluidity of any sea boundary makes it more conflict-prone than an established land boundary. Moreover, fish stocks straddle national boundaries and migrate across them with the seasons, with no concern for the consequences for human conflict. It is not surprising, then, that international fisheries should be ridden with conflict. However, even if fisheries conflicts between democracies may involve some use of force or threats to use it, such conflicts rarely, if ever, escalate to the point where human life is lost. Since 'war' is usually defined as a conflict with more than 1,000 dead (Small and Singer, 1982; Wallensteen and Sollenberg, 1997), terms such as 'cod war' or 'turbot war' (Soroos, 1997b) are misnomers. Moreover, these conflicts usually involve one private party (a fishing vessel) against representatives of another state (a ship from the Navy or Coast Guard). When such conflicts occur between democracies, the two states take particular care not to engage in force or threats of force between their own representatives. Thus, as far as the militarized part of the conflicts is concerned, these disputes are not really 'interstate'.

A similar point holds for economic variables. Poverty is one of the strongest predictors of civil war (Collier and Hoeffler, 1998; Hegre et al., 1999). Moreover, economically highly developed countries rarely fight one another (Hegre, 1999; Mueller, 1989). Economic development is also closely related to environmental performance. While economic development does tend to exacerbate certain environmental problems (such as pollution and excessive resource extraction) up to a point, the most advanced industrial economies also tend to be relatively more resource-friendly. The rate of emissions of environmentally harmful products increases initially with growing wealth, but the environmental damage tapers off at high levels of development. For some noxious emissions (such as SO_2) there is a significant decrease at very high levels of economic development, because rich countries can afford to acquire modern technology and also because their decisionmakers put a higher premium on a clean environment.[8] Hence, pollution, resource depletion, and resource competition are likely to be less fierce domestically as well as externally among the most highly developed countries. For example, highly developed countries have very strong economic motives for not fighting over scarce water resources; instead, they use technology to expand the resources or find cooperative solutions in exploiting them. Poor countries generate more local environmental problems, which in turn may exacerbate their poverty and which is also conducive to conflict. The three types of environmental degradation studied by Hauge and Ellingsen (2001)—deforestation, lack of freshwater water, and soil erosion—are all negatively correlated with development.

Much of the environmental literature ignores these relationships between economic development, environmental degradation, and conflict or por-

trays environmental degradation mainly as a function of excessive development in the rich countries. In the work of Homer-Dixon and his associates,
the link between poverty and environmental degradation is explicitly discussed. But they tend to interpret poverty as an 'intermediate effect' between environmental scarcity and conflict (Homer-Dixon and Blitt, 1998:
223, 227).

A third set of variables which need to be included in analyses of environmental conflict relate to ethnic, linguistic, and religious fragmentation. Although the overall role and importance of such cleavages in generating conflict is disputed (Ellingsen, 2000; Henderson and Singer, 2000), it is striking
that most of the societies that Homer-Dixon and his associates have examined for the effects of environmental disruption (such as Chiapas, Gaza,
Pakistan, Rwanda, South Africa, see Homer-Dixon and Blitt, 1998) are
highly divided. In the South African case, in particular, it seems very likely
that the effects of the environment are swamped by the effects of racial seg-
regation.

In general, the environmental security literature gives an appearance of
trying to reinvent the wheel. Instead of developing models from scratch, analysts might have been better served by incorporating resource and environmental variables into existing models of conflict.

Untestable Models

While there is much single-factor reasoning in the literature, some work
goes to the opposite extreme. The work of Homer-Dixon (1991, 1994,
1999) employs a very complex theoretical scheme, where four basic social
effects of environmental disruption (decreased regional agricultural production, population displacement, decreased economic productivity, and
disruption of institutions) may produce scarcity conflicts, group-identity
conflicts, and relative-deprivation conflicts. This model has been reproduced in various forms in a number of publications from the Toronto
Group (such as Percival and Homer-Dixon, 2001), and by others (e.g.
Hauge and Ellingsen, 2001).

The complexity of these models makes them very hard to test. The rebellion in Chiapas (Howard and Homer-Dixon, 1995) is explained by seven
(mostly economic) independent variables acting through nine intervening
variables and one additional independent variable. Violence in Gaza (Kelly
and Homer-Dixon, 1995) involves an explanatory scheme of eight independent and intervening variables, which in turn draw on a six-variable
scheme for explaining three kinds of water scarcity and a ten-variable
scheme for explaining the increasing level of grievance against the Palestine
National Authority. Whether in a large-N or a comparative case study
mode, such a comprehensive scheme would be very difficult to test. Empiri-

cal testing is not helped by the imprecise labelling of many variables, such as 'health problems'. Neither is it helped by a research design in which the number of variables well exceeds the number of units. Similar problems can be found in the work of Shin-wha Lee (1996), in otherwise interesting case studies of Sudan and Bangladesh.

Of course, single-factor reasoning and overly complex models are generally not found in the same studies. In a literature divided between these two modes of analysis, however, there is little room for modestly multivariate analyses and of a gradualist approach to model-building. This is not an argument against the aspiration to develop large and complex models, like those used in macroeconomics, some of which have also been applied to environmental problems (Nordhaus, 1994). But such models must be built gradually, with more limited modules being put to the test first.

Selection Bias

Qualitative and quantitative research serve the same logic of inference, although their styles are different (King, Keohane, and Verba, 1994: 3). In the literature on the environment and armed conflict, the case study has been by far the dominant approach. Homer-Dixon (1991: 83) criticized earlier writing on this topic as 'anecdotal' and has lambasted the work of a well-known environmentalist (Myers, 1993) as being 'marked by an almost complete absence of empirical rigor and theoretical structure' (Homer-Dixon, 1999: 184). His own major contribution to the literature is a number of carefully documented case studies analyzed on the basis of a detailed theoretical scheme. Case studies from Homer-Dixon's project include Chiapas, Gaza, Pakistan, Rwanda, and South Africa (Homer-Dixon and Blitt, 1998). A number of case studies have also been reported by the Environment and Conflicts Project and successor projects at the Swiss Federal Institute of Technology (Bächler, 1999; Bächler et al., 1996).

Levy (1995: 56) argues that Homer-Dixon's case studies offer 'more anecdotes, but not more understanding'. This charge may be overly harsh, but cannot easily be dismissed. All of these studies are single case studies of 'environmental scarcity and violent conflict'. They offer no variation on the dependent variable,[9] thus violating an important principle of research design, whether the approach is qualitative or quantitative (King et al., 1994: 108). Regardless of the accuracy of the historical description and the excellence of the theoretical model, these studies fail to provide an empirical basis for comparison. In the Toronto Group's study of Chiapas, for example, 'weak property rights' is a factor in creating 'persistent structural scarcities' which in turn contributes to the outbreak of rebellion (Howard and Homer-Dixon, 1995: 23). But in order to evaluate the causal nature of this link, we need to examine cases *without* conflict, many of which will certainly also be characterized by weak property rights. Only when we know that conflict occurs more frequently in the former group, can we even begin to think about causal links.

A plausible justification for studying cases selected on the dependent variable is that such an approach is justified in the early stages of a research program (Homer-Dixon, 1999: 182). Process tracing of single cases can help researchers 'to identify key contextual factors and scope conditions pertinent to their hypotheses' (Homer-Dixon, 1999: 182). Homer-Dixon has conceded that 'these hypotheses should be tested using a broader range of methodologies, including cross-national statistical analysis, counterfactual analysis, and carefully controlled comparisons of cases varied on both the dependent and independent variables' (Homer-Dixon, 1999: 182). Almost any methodological limitation can be justified at an exploratory stage. The problem arises if the project does not move on to the next stage, but instead concludes on the basis of the exploratory case studies that 'environmental scarcity causes violent conflict' (Homer-Dixon, 1994: 39).

Another justification for the single case study approach is that 'biased case selection enhances understanding of the complex relationships among variables in highly interactive social, political, economic, and environmental systems' (Percival and Homer-Dixon, 2001; Homer-Dixon, 1996). This seems to imply that environmental problems are more complex than other social (or for that matter physical) phenomena that researchers study. No justification is given for this view. I would argue, on the contrary, that any social system is as complex as the theory developed to study it. In other words, the complexity is in the mind of the beholder rather than in the phenomenon itself. If this is an 'extraordinarily strong constructivist position' (Schwarz et al., 2001), so be it.

A third, and more recent justification for single-case study is that it is particularly suitable for discovering causal *mechanisms,* as distinct from causal *effect* (Schwarz, Deligiannis, and Homer-Dixon, 2001). As Gary King, Robert Keohane, and Sidney Verba (1994: 85–87) argue, the identification of causal mechanisms can build support for a theory and can create new causal hypotheses for investigation. However, if we are only interested in causal mechanisms and not in establishing causal effects, we are in effect making statements of the following type: 'If environmental degradation is related to conflict (which we don't know), this is how it seems to work'. Such statements are of no more use to the policy community than to academics seeking to expand our knowledge base.[10]

Even quantitative studies on resources and war on territorial conflict sometimes suffer from similar selection problems. Both Holsti (1991) and Vasquez (1993) derive their findings concerning the territorial basis of armed conflict from an examination of the *issues* involved in the armed conflict. However, they do not examine situations which did *not* escalate to armed conflict to see if also they contained unresolved territorial issues. Huth (1996), in a study of territorial disputes, does not include territorial claims which are not expressed publicly (Huth, 1996: 24, 239). For example, the question of the Finnish territories conquered by the Soviet Union in the Winter War of 1939–1940 could not be raised during the Cold War due to Finland's somewhat precarious position. Thus, if one wanted to test a hypothesis about conditions under which territorial disagreements are completely suppressed, Huth's data set would not be suitable.[11]

In examining only cases of conflict, one is likely to find at least partial confirmation of whatever one is looking for, unless there are very clearly specified criteria for the threshold level of the independent variable assumed to lead to violence. No society is completely free of environmental degradation, nor is any society completely free of ethnic fragmentation, religious differences, economic inequalities, or problems of governance. From a set of armed conflicts, one may variously conclude that they are all environmental conflicts, ethnic conflicts, clashes of civilizations, or products of bad governance. Indeed, conflicts like the internationalized civil war in Ethiopia from the mid-1970s have been described in most of these terms. Only by adopting a research design where cases of conflict and nonconflict are contrasted can the influence of the various factors be sorted out.

Reversed Causality

It is well established—and in a sense not very surprising—that modern war wreaks havoc on the environment (see, e.g., Arthur Westing, 1990, 1997; de Soysa and Gleditsch, 1999: 56–65). The Vietnam War brought this issue to public attention, although earlier large wars had also caused destruction of vital infrastructure and generated other negative environmental effects. More recently, the prospect of a 'nuclear winter' pointed to the prospect of the obliteration of human activity on the Northern Hemisphere as a result of the environmental effects of a nuclear war. For instance, Sagan and Turco (1993) maintained that a global nuclear war could lead to a worldwide fall in temperature of 15–20 degrees centigrade. Even more optimistic scenarios than this could put the earth's climate back to the most recent ice age. These environmental effects could be worse than the direct impact of nuclear war such as blast, fire, and radioactive fallout. Similarly, the campaign to abolish landmines has focused public attention on the long-term environmental effects of a weapon long after its military utility has gone.

This war-environment relationship is sometimes confounded with the possibility that environmental degradation *causes* armed conflict and war. For instance, in arguing for a link from the environment to violent conflict, Johan Jørgen Holst (1989: 126) points out that five of the six countries on the UN list of countries most seriously affected by hunger had experienced civil war (Ethiopia, Sudan, Chad, Mozambique, and Angola). However, it is highly probable that the violent uprising contributed to the hunger, or even that starvation was used as a weapon of war in some of these conflicts. Thus the most important causal link is very likely the opposite of that indicated by Holst.

Anthony McMichael (1993: 322) suggests a slightly more complicated relationship as a positive feedback process: 'environmental destruction and resource scarcity promote war which, when it breaks out, further increases environmental destruction and resource depletion'. However, a somewhat different feedback process seems more likely:

War → environmental destruction → resource conflict → exacerbated armed conflict.

This process starts from a well-documented relationship rather than from a more conjectural one. It also contains in the endpoints the process of violence repeating itself over time, which has been found to be highly significant in studies of interstate war (Raknerud and Hegre, 1997) as well as civil war (Hegre et al., 1999). Of course, if the process were to continue indefinitely, these two feedback cycles would be identical and the world would have entered a process of accelerating deterioration and violence. Studies of interstate war and civil war indicate that violence is repeated, but not necessarily with increased intensity. Perhaps it may be thought of as an echo, weaker than the signal it reflects, and petering out in the end. Thus, it does matter whether the process starts with war or with environmental degradation.

Using the Future as Evidence

Homer-Dixon, and many other authors in this area, have stressed the *potential* for violent conflict in the future. There is a lack of empirical study of armed conflicts in the past as well as a lack of explicit theorizing for if and why resource scarcities should have a higher violence-generating potential in the future than in the past. Much of the literature deals with conflicts of interest involving *potential* violence rather than with actual violence. For example, no one is really arguing that any armed conflict in the past has occurred mainly because of water issues. To argue that water has been a main issue in the many conflicts in the Middle East, and specifically in the wars between Israel and its neighbors, would be to seriously underestimate the explosive ethnic and territorial issues in the region (Lonergan, 1997: 383). The argument is often in terms of *future* wars which may happen. In *Silent Spring*, arguably the most influential environmentalist book ever published, Carson (1962: ch. 1) described in the past tense 'a town in the heart of America' hit by mysterious diseases caused by the excessive use of pesticides, but in fact this was 'a fable for tomorrow'. Similarly, when Paul Ehrlich (1968: 11) started *The Population Bomb* with a statement that 'The battle to feed all of humanity is over', went on to state as a certainty that hundreds of millions of people would starve to death, and then discussed the political consequences, they were arguing from future empirical 'evidence' which in fact turned out to be wrong. While they now hold that the principal problem 'of course' is not acute famine, but malnutrition (Ehrlich and Ehrlich, 1996: 76), they also argue that there is every reason to think that the limits to the expansion of plant yields is not far off (Ehrlich and Ehrlich, 1996: 80) and liken the human race to animal populations which grow beyond their carrying capacity until they 'crash' to a far lower size (Ehrlich and Ehrlich, 1968: 67). These are hypotheses based on controversial theory and debatable extrapolations, rather than 'data' to confirm their predictions.

In principle, the future may always differ from the past. Despite whatever painstaking empirical mapping we may have made of past wars, future wars may run a different course. Environmental organizations and other advocacy movements are prone to argue that we are now at a turning-point in human history and that patterns from the past may no longer hold in the future. In saying this, one may easily slip into prophecy. 'There will be water wars in the future' is no more a testable statement than the proverbial 'The End of the World is at Hand!', unless terms such as 'the future' and 'at hand' are clearly specified. In an effort to make pessimistic environmental predictions more precise (and to prove them wrong) Simon repeatedly challenged his opponents to place bets on resource issues. Three environmentalists took him up on this in 1980 and predicted that the price of a basket of five metals would rise over a ten-year period. Simon, who thought they would decline, won the bet (Myers and Simon, 1994: 99, 206).

Civil War and Interstate War

Since the end of World War II most wars have been internal rather than interstate (Gleditsch, 1996: 294). Although the number of domestic armed conflicts, whether the smaller ones or the larger conflicts conventionally called 'wars', has declined slightly after the end of the Cold War (Wallensteen and Sollenberg, 1997), they remain much more numerous than international armed conflicts. This pattern is unlikely to be broken in the near future.

Homer-Dixon's work is explicitly related to domestic conflicts, and Tir and Diehl (2001: 319) argue that most studies of population pressures and war focus on internal conflict. Yet, much of the reasoning about the prevalence of scarce resources as a factor in war is built on lessons from the study of interstate war, as my literature review above indicates. Both at the theoretical and empirical level, the study of interstate conflict has been conducted largely separately from the study of civil war. Some factors are similar, but one cannot easily generalize from one to the other. An obvious difference is that many theories of war at the interstate level are related to the absence of any overarching system of power, i.e. what realists call international anarchy. At the domestic level, war is often related to revolt against excessive state power or its abuse. Many issues which stimulate armed conflicts at the interstate level may be too weak to force a break *within* a society held together by a central authority. Theories linking environmental degradation to violence therefore need to be quite specific concerning whether they are addressing domestic or interstate violence.

Levels of Analysis

Studies of war require precision about the unit of analysis. For example, in studies of democratic peace, it is frequently assumed that if democracies do not fight one another, then there will be more peace as the fraction of democracies grows. I have shown elsewhere (Gleditsch and Hegre, 1997), that this holds true only under certain conditions. Under a plausible set of assumptions, an *increase* in the number of democracies is more likely to lead initially to an increase in the frequency of war in the system. Only later, after the degree of democracy is above a certain level, will further democratization decrease the probability of war. Similarly, we cannot automatically generalize theories and empirical evidence concerning resource and environmental factors from one level to another without committing a level-of-analysis fallacy. Below, follow three hypotheses about interstate armed conflict using the same independent and dependent variables, but at different levels of analysis:

(1) *System level:* In a world with high resource constraints, there will be more interstate conflict.

(2) *Nation level:* Countries with high resource constraints are more likely to be involved in conflicts with other countries.

(3) *Dyadic level:* Countries with high resource constraints are likely to be involved in conflict with countries with an ample supply of the same resource, and even (but to a lesser extent) with other countries with the same resource constraints.

Although these three hypotheses are derived from the same kind of thinking, the one does not logically follow from the other. If we assume that the overall frequency of interstate war is regulated mostly by systemic factors (such as the balance of power), or that states' propensity to war is largely determined by national characteristics like regime type or wealth, resource factors may still determine the *direction* of warfare (i.e. dyadic war). Thus, even if resource scarcities are relevant for 'who fights whom', that is not equivalent to saying that global resource scarcity determines the overall level of armed conflict. This levels-of-analysis problem is not, to my knowledge, dealt with at any length in the relevant literature, which freely jumps between the dyad, the nation, and the system levels with regard to theory as well as empirical evidence.

The Way Ahead

The nine problems discussed above add up to a fairly pessimistic assessment of the state of the study of environmental causes of conflict. Even leading studies in the field come up against fairly elementary problems in theory construction or empirical testing. Critical studies, like those of Deudney and Levy, are valuable in pointing out some of these problems. But their critique—like my own—will serve to advance the field only if it stimulates more satisfactory research.

Systematic cross-national study by social scientists of any aspect of the environment is in its infancy. As noted, a good deal of work has been done on the relationship between economic development and environmental degradation. In some recent work (Gleditsch and Sverdrup, 1996; Midlarsky, 2001) attempts have been made to relate indicators of the environmental performance of nations to their regime characteristics. The conclusions from these two empirical analyses are at some variance with one another. Generally, the study of political predictors of environmental degradation lags far behind the study of economic factors.

There is even less rigorous work using environmental degradation as a predictor to conflict. The studies by Jaroslav Tir and Paul Diehl (2001) and Wenche Hauge and Tanja Ellingsen (2001) are relevant and representative of a tradition in theoretically-grounded empirical research on armed conflict, based on cross-national (and, to a more limited degree, cross-temporal) data for a large number of nations. Both these analyses place the analysis of resource and environmental variables squarely within a multivariate perspective. Both studies do indeed find an effect of such variables—population growth in one study; deforestation, land degradation, and low availability of freshwater in the other. Since all these predictor variables are traditionally associated with poverty, this raises the issue if the association between conflict and environmental load (as in the Tir and Diehl study) or conflict and environmental degradation (in Hauge and Ellingsen's work) may be primarily an underdevelopment problem. Highly developed (or even 'overdeveloped') countries also have environmental problems (traffic noise, industrial pollution, etc.) but there is no evidence that such environmental issues generate armed conflict, internally or externally. In this sense, perhaps environmental conflict should be analyzed mainly as a development issue? At least this is an avenue worth further exploration.

The study of territory and war is ahead of any other field of inquiry relating resources to violent conflict. However, even where territory is shown conclusively to be a significant factor in armed conflict, the question remains whether the territory itself is at issue, or the resources that may be found on it. For more precise theorizing about the link between resources and conflict, we need to understand which resources are decisive. Some resources are probably too trivial to fight over, while oil might be seen as economically essential. The territory itself might be seen as important to the identity of a people and the symbolic function might be more important than any material value. In a study of modern border disputes, Robert Mandel (1980: 435) hypothesized that ethnically oriented border disputes would be more severe than resource-oriented ones because ethnic issues seemed less tractable, more emotional, and less conducive to compromise. He was able to confirm his hypothesis in a study of interstate border disputes after World War II, using data from Robert Butterworth (1976). To extend the concept of 'resources' to include ethnic affiliation or the symbolic value of 'the land of our fathers', would be possible, but strained.

In general, those who have researched the general patterns of war have been much more concerned with alliances, power configurations, and other elements of realist theory (and more recently with democracy, economic interdependence, and other elements of liberal theory) than with environmental factors. It is possible, of course, that this is because environmental factors simply do not play much of a role in warfare—but one would feel more confident of this conclusion if environmental hypotheses had at least been tested. Another explanation for the relative neglect of these factors could be that the environmental boundaries of state policy have not been central to the grand political debate until quite recently. Moreover, most research on international conflict has focused on national, dyadic, and systematic *attributes* for understanding international behavior, whereas the *issues* involved in conflict have generally been ignored—including, presumably, environmental issues (Diehl, 1992).

A striking feature of the existing empirical studies is the problem of gathering valid and reliable data on the environmental behavior of nations or smaller geographical units. Environmental accounting is miles behind national economic accounting. The three indicators of 'supply-induced scarcity' used by Hauge and Ellingsen, are not very highly correlated ($0.08 < r < 0.22$). The data reliability may be low, but perhaps the three indicators tap different dimensions of environmental performance. Moreover, the Hauge and Ellingsen study is limited to a fairly short time period (1980–1992), mainly due to data limitations. In order to move forward in relating environmental studies and the study of armed conflict, we need major improvements in systematic data collection—a Correlates of War project for the environment.

Nils Petter Gleditsch, b. 1942; Mag.Art in sociology (University of Oslo, 1968); research professor, International Peace Research Institute, Oslo (PRIO) and editor of *Journal of Peace Research;* professor of political science, Norwegian University of Science and Technology, Trondheim; most recent books in English: *The Peace Dividend* (coeditor, North-Holland, 1996), *Conflict and the Environment* (editor, Kluwer, 1997).

Notes

1. Statement made by President Eisenhower in a press conference on 7 April 1954, cf. *Public Papers of the Presidents of the United States.* Eisenhower, 1954: 382, quoted from LaFeber (1980: 163). For other statements by US policymakers in the same vein, see Kolko (1985: 76), who finds such references to raw materials to be 'integral to American policy considerations from the inception'.

2. For other general broadsides against environmental pessimism, see Maddox (1972), Bolch and Lyons (1993), Bailey (1995), and Easterbrook (1995). Recent responses are found in Ehrlich and Ehrlich (1996), and Schroll et al. (1999).

3. A point which may modify the relevance of these relationships in the future is the declining fertility in many countries, which will contribute to easing population pressure (Gleditsch, 2000).

4. While it may be premature to assign precise causal weights with any certainty (in this sense, I agree with Schwarz et al., 2001), we can hardly shirk our responsibility to try to assess whether some factors are very important while others are rather marginal.

5. Libiszewski speaks (1992: 3) of 'a dynamic equilibrium oscillating around an ideal average'. Whether such equilibria exist in anything but the short term, seems questionable. At least it is implausible that only human intervention can change them. Otherwise, it would be difficult to explain the disappearance of the dinosaurs and other animals long before human beings were numerous enough to have much influence on the global environment, or even before human beings existed. Or should we see the emergence of the dinosaurs, as well as their subsequent disappearance, as part of an 'ideal' or 'baseline' world?

6. There is still a danger of conceptual slippage, by including all manner of environmental problems in the concept of environmental security, and not just those which are serious enough to be treated on a par with war destruction. This development is reminiscent of the fate of the concept of structural violence (Galtung, 1969), which was so successful in the short term that it came to include any social ill—and eventually self-destructed.

7. As argued by Payne (1995), Gleditsch and Sverdrup (1996), and Gleditsch (1997a); Midlarsky (2001) is more skeptical.

8. Dietz and Rose (1997) provide a brief survey of recent writings. Cf. also Lomborg (2001).

9. Nor, for that matter, do they provide any variation on the independent variable, but that is not necessarily a problem in the research design, cf. King, Keohane and Verba (1994: 137).

10. Schwartz et al. (2001) refer to the recent discovery of a causal mechanism for why aspirin works as a pain-killer, citing Garavito (1999). However, there is noth-

ing in that article to suggest that the problem of why aspirin relieves pain was solved by detailed process-tracing of a single patient whose pain had been relieved in this manner. While hypotheses about causal mechanisms may be generated in mysterious ways, establishing their empirical validity requires systematic study of many cases.

11. Another problem, peculiar to the literature on territory and armed conflict, is that regardless of the issue which started the conflict, the contestants need a territorial base to deploy force of any size; even guerrillas need some sort of safe haven. Thus, armed conflicts, domestic as well as international, at least when they escalate to a certain size, become conflicts over territory even if territory was not the most salient issue from the start.

Chapter Thirteen

The Environment and Violent Conflict

DANIEL M. SCHWARTZ
TOM DELIGIANNIS
THOMAS HOMER-DIXON

Introduction

Nils Petter Gleditsch (2001) has written a widely noted critique of recent research in the new field of environmental security. He focuses in particular on research that examines how environmental stress might lead to violent conflict, often singling out the work of the team led by Thomas Homer-Dixon of the University of Toronto (henceforth referred to as the Toronto Group). Gleditsch identifies a number of specific 'problems' of theory, conceptualization, and methodology in the Toronto Group's and other scholars' work. In this chapter, we respond to these concerns and propose avenues for future research.

Methodological issues underpin Gleditsch's critique, and we therefore deal with them in detail. Gleditsch asserts that much environment-conflict research—including, by implication, that of the Toronto Group—is methodologically unsound and fails to qualify as systematic research. He contends it violates the rules of conventional, quasi-experimental methodology. This perspective is his starting point for identifying many of the specific problems in the Toronto Group's work. As a result, he disregards the detailed findings of the Toronto Group, the Swiss-based Project on Environment and Conflict (ENCOP), and other research projects that do not meet his standards of evidence. We argue that Gleditsch's proposed approach is a methodological straightjacket that would, if widely adopted, severely constrain research in the field. We also show that the case-study method used by the Toronto Group has epistemological qualities that complement quasi-experimental methods.

In the first section, we deal with some of the conceptual and theoretical 'problems' identified by Gleditsch and discuss his selective critique of the literature on the relationship between environmental scarcity and conflict. Gleditsch's critique does not address the validity of the specific findings that emerged from ENCOP and the Toronto Group. Instead, he treats these projects with a broad brush, at times associating them with other, less rigorous, research. The second section examines underlying methodological issues. The final section of the chapter looks forward and suggests avenues for future research on the environment-conflict nexus.

Conceptual and Theoretical Issues

Gleditsch identifies a number of common 'problems' with the literature on environmental stress and conflict. This section responds to conceptual and theoretical criticisms aimed explicitly at the Toronto Group's research. The order of our points below does not strictly match Gleditsch's.

Employing a Comprehensive Definition of Scarcity

Disputes among scholars about how to conceptualize environmental stress have long hindered research on the links between this stress and violent conflict. Essentially, these are disputes about the delineation of the independent, or causal, variable. Gleditsch's criticizes Thomas Homer-Dixon's concept of *environmental scarcity*—which integrates supply, demand, and distributional sources of the scarcity of renewable resources—suggesting it 'muddies the waters', although he fails to explain why.

Following Stephan Libiszewski, Gleditsch adopts a distinction between conflicts that result from 'simple resource scarcity' and those that result from 'environmental degradation' (Libiszewski, 1992). Unfortunately, however, Libiszewski's distinction is a wholly inadequate starting point for research on the environmental causes of violence. First, as Gleditsch himself acknowledges, the two categories are not causally separate: degradation of an environmental resource, like cropland or freshwater supplies, can cause a straightforward scarcity of that resource. Second, degradation of an environmental resource is only one of two possible sources of a decrease in a resource's supply. Degradation refers to a drop in the quality of the resource, but cropland, freshwater, and the like can also be depleted, which means the resource's quantity is reduced. If we restrict our analysis to conflicts caused by degradation of environmental resources, we will omit a main source of the reduced supply of these resources in many poor countries around the world. Gleditsch provides no justification for such a restriction.

Third, environmental degradation, the phenomenon Gleditsch wants us to emphasize, is exclusively a supply-side problem. Any hypothesis linking environmental degradation to violence is linking, essentially, the reduction in the resource's supply to violence. If we want to explore the causes of violence, however, a resource's *absolute* supply is not interesting. What we should investigate, rather, is the resource's supply *relative to*, first, demand on the resource, and, second, the social distribution of the resource. The relationships between supply and demand and between supply and distribution determine people's actual experience of scarcity, and it is these relationships that, under any sensible hypothesis, influence the probability of violence. This is the reason that we include demand and distributional aspects in our definition of environmental scarcity.

Fourth and finally, focusing on environmental degradation alone tends to lead researchers to overlook or neglect key interactions—such as the processes we call *resource capture* and *ecological marginalization*—among supply, demand, and distributional pressures (Homer-Dixon, 1999: 73–80). *Resource capture* occurs when the degradation and depletion of a renewable resource (a decrease in supply) interacts with population growth (an increase in demand) to encourage powerful groups within a society to shift resource access (that is, to change the resource's distribution) in their favor. These groups tighten their grip on the increasingly scarce resource and use this control to boost their wealth and power. Resource capture intensifies scarcity for poorer and weaker groups in society. *Ecological marginalization* occurs when unequal resource access (skewed distribution) combines with population growth (an increase in demand) to cause long-term migrations of people to ecologically fragile regions such as steep upland slopes, areas at risk of desertification, tropical rain forests, and low-quality public lands within urban areas. High population densities in these regions, combined with a lack of knowledge and capital to protect the local ecosystem, cause severe resource degradation (a decrease in supply) (Homer-Dixon, 1999: 177). Resource capture and ecological marginalization are often intimately interlinked, with one leading to the other.

Some might argue that by including distributional issues in our definition of environmental scarcity, the Toronto Group makes the concept so broad as to be useless, because conflicts solely over resource distribution are thereby classed as environmental conflicts.[1] The argument is misguided. Uneven distribution never acts on its own; its impact is always a function of its interaction with resource supply and demand. In practical terms, resource distribution is important because the resources people want (that are, in other words, in demand) are in finite supply. Indeed, the Toronto Group found in its research that problems of declining resource supply and rising resource demand were always intimately entangled with uneven resource distribution.

For these four reasons, an exclusive focus on environmental degradation in environment-conflict research unreasonably restricts and distorts the scope of the research and misses crucial aspects of the environmental challenges facing the developing world. It is better, we believe, to acknowledge explicitly that the fundamental issue is one of scarcity of renewable resources and that any treatment of this scarcity should encompass the exhaustive set of scarcity's sources: decreases in supply, increases in demand, and changes in distribution. These three facets of scarcity are thus incorporated in the Toronto Group's tripartite definition of scarcity.

Challenging Simonesque Optimism

At a more fundamental level, Gleditsch questions the very idea that humanity is facing increasing environmental scarcities. His critique seems to be guided by the assumption that the links between environmental scarcity and violence are overstated, because humanity shows astonishing capacity to adapt to scarcities. Markets stimulate human inventiveness and commerce that open up new sources of scarce resources, encourage conservation, and create technologies that allow substitution of relatively abundant resources for scarce ones. These adaptive processes certainly operate in many cases, as we have previously noted (Homer-Dixon, 1995b, 1999: 31–35, 107–132). But Gleditsch does not acknowledge that societies often fail to adjust adequately to scarcity, with poverty, migrations, and institutional failure the result. Environmental scarcities unquestionably have profoundly debilitating effects on some economies, societies, and social groups.[2] Just because humans are remarkably adaptive in some cases does not mean that they are always adaptive.

Gleditsch seems particularly influenced by Julian Simon's thesis that, based on the historical record, human societies can bring to bear on their resource scarcities sufficient ingenuity to prevent any decline in well-being over the long run (Simon, 1996). But Simon's arguments are too simplistic for three reasons. First, he tends to project the truly extraordinary improvements in human well-being over the past two centuries linearly into the future, without much questioning or reflection. Yet if we look back further than 200 years, it is clear that human affairs have been marked by many nonlinear events—sudden, sharp changes in economic and social behavior—some of which have had decidedly negative effects. The progress of the last two centuries is not the only evidence we should use to estimate our trajectory into the future.

Second, when Simon analyzes trends in human well-being, he usually uses highly aggregated data, such as statistical averages for all of humankind. Yet when these data are disaggregated—that is, broken into sub-categories—Simon's optimism is less persuasive. For example, although both the percentage and absolute number of hungry people have fallen globally in the last twenty years, Latin America, South Asia, and especially Sub-Saharan Africa have not seen reductions in the absolute number of hungry people.[3] Third and finally, close study of specific cases shows that societies do not always generate the ingenuity they need when and where it is needed (Lele and Stone, 1989). Although environmental and demographic stress often drives up the requirement for ingenuity in poor countries, a number of factors—including market failure, inadequate human capital, and political competition over scarce natural resources among powerful groups—can impede the flow of ingenuity (Homer-Dixon, 1999: 107–132).

Bringing Nature into Social Theory

Gleditsch's skepticism about the seriousness of environmental scarcities is the starting point for a key element of his critique of the environment-conflict literature. He argues that the literature overstates the impact of environmental scarcities on violent conflict and, in the process, ignores other, perhaps more powerful, political, cultural, and economic causal variables. By deemphasizing environmental scarcities, Gleditsch correspondingly emphasizes other variables.

This approach implies that environmental stress may be no more than an intermediate or intervening variable between dysfunctional political and economic institutions and conflict. Thus, Gleditsch asks if environmental conflict may be primarily an underdevelopment problem, because environmental degradation or load is strongly correlated with poverty. He seems to argue that conflict in developing countries is best explained by social causes, not by the physical influences of the natural environment. In the process, like many scholars of comparative development, Gleditsch marginalizes the physical circumstances of human society as explanatory variables; he appears to consider them to be, at most, secondary causes of social behavior. When it comes to violent conflict, they are merely aggravators of already existing social stresses.

If this is his position, Gleditsch is making a classic endogeneity mistake: he is claiming that environmental problems are a consequence of, and endogenous to, the broader social system and that, therefore, any conflict caused by environmental problems is ultimately caused by social factors.

It is unquestionably true that social variables must be central to any adequate explanation of human conflict, whether in rich or poor countries. The Toronto Group discuss at length the political, economic, and cultural factors that interact with environmental scarcity to cause violence. The so-

cieties most vulnerable to environmentally induced violence are those simultaneously experiencing severe environmental scarcity and various forms
of institutional failure (especially failures of states and markets) that hinder
social adaptation to the scarcity. The key role of social variables must
therefore be acknowledged. Nevertheless, this requirement does not mean
that physical variables should be made fully endogenous to the social system and, consequently, turned into relatively uninteresting secondary
causes of social conflict and stress.[4]

As Homer-Dixon (1999: 16–18, 104–106) has noted, there are three reasons why environmental scarcity should be considered at least partly an exogenous factor in social behavior and conflict and why, therefore, environmental scarcity deserves research attention in its own right.

First, environmental scarcity is not only influenced by social variables
such as institutions and policies, it can itself affect these institutions and
policies in harmful ways. This is the case when shortages of a renewable resource, such as cropland or forests, motivate elites to seize control, through
either legal or coercive means, of the resource's remaining stocks (a process
the Toronto Group has labeled *resource capture*). In other words, we
should not assume that social variables are completely independent and external starting points in the causal chain; it turns out that they can be affected by environmental scarcity, sometimes negatively.

Second, the degree of environmental scarcity a society experiences is not,
as it turns out, wholly a result of economic, political, and social variables,
like failed institutions and policies. It is also partly a function of the particular physical characteristics of the society's surrounding environment.
These characteristics are, in some respects, independent of human activities. For example, the vulnerability of coastal aquifers to salt intrusion from
the sea and the depth of upland soils in tropical regions are physical
'givens' of these environmental resources.

Third, once environmental scarcity becomes irreversible—as when most
of a country's vital topsoil washes into the sea—then the scarcity is, almost
by definition, an external influence on society. Even if enlightened reform of
institutions and policies removes the underlying social causes of the
scarcity, because the scarcity itself is irreversible, it will remain a continuing
burden on society. Scholars and policymakers must take into account the
independent causal role of environmental scarcity if they are to understand
and respond to many important cases of civil violence around the world.[5]

Identifying Key Variables

Gleditsch claims that the Toronto Group and other researchers overlook
important variables such as regime type and democracy. Yet, the Group's
full model does integrate regime-type variables into its analysis of the social

and economic effects of environmental scarcities. In the scholarly literature on the origins of revolutions and civil violence, the variables of *opportunity structure* and *state capacity*, which are central to the Toronto Group's model, are recognized as integral aspects of regime type (Goodwin, 1997; Tarrow, 1994; Skocpol, 1979). Furthermore, in his recent work, Colin Kahl (1998) explicitly builds on the Toronto Group's model to further our understanding of how regime type affects the links between environmental scarcity and violence.

More specifically, however, Gleditsch's suggestion that the Toronto Group is blind to the importance of regime type is, on close reading, actually a call for the inclusion of a *democracy* variable in environment-conflict models. We agree with Gleditsch that a more explicit focus on democracy could be beneficial—as long as analysts are careful in their use of 'democracy'. As Homer-Dixon has argued, 'the term *democracy* is used too loosely by lay commentators and experts alike. It commonly encompasses an extraordinarily variegated set of social phenomena and institutions that have complicated and multiple effects on the incidence of social turmoil and violence' (Homer-Dixon, 1999: 182).[6] Gleditsch deserves credit for advancing environmental conflict literature along this important theoretical path. If future research can address the difficult issues surrounding the precise definition and operationalization of democracy, important findings may yet emerge.

Using Historical Evidence

Finally, Gleditsch claims that the Toronto Group's model about the links between environmental scarcity and conflict is profoundly flawed, in part because it is founded on inferences about future scarcities. Gleditsch (2001) asserts that 'Homer-Dixon, and many other authors . . . have stressed the potential for violent conflict in the future' without providing adequate empirical evidence of past or present linkages between environmental scarcities and violent conflict.

Gleditsch is mistaken that the Toronto Group uses 'the future as evidence' to substantiate its claims that there are links between environmental scarcities and conflict. In the process of developing its model, the Group has undertaken more than a dozen detailed historical case studies. These include studies of the Chiapas rebellion, the Rwandan genocide, violence between Senegal and Mauritania, civil conflict in the Philippines, and ethnic violence in Assam.[7] The historical analyses in these case studies were informed by the rich literatures on the causes of revolution, insurgency, and ethnic strife. Taken together, they are a foundation for the Toronto Group's larger theoretical model about linkages between environmental scarcity and violent conflict. None of the hypotheses in this model depends on events yet to come; rather, the model is informed by events that have already taken place.[8]

To support his claim that the Toronto Group uses the future as evidence for its model, Gleditsch takes issue with commentators who argue that water scarcity in the Middle East could lead to armed conflict in the future. Without referring to any research in particular, but having identified the Toronto Group by name in the beginning of the paragraph, Gleditsch concludes that this is a hypothesis based on 'controversial theory and debatable extrapolations, rather than "data" which may confirm the prediction'. Gleditsch thus conflates the findings of the Toronto Group with largely unsubstantiated claims by other writers regarding the potential for conflict over water resources.

The specific findings of both the Toronto Group and ENCOP are certainly worthy of detailed consideration in any discussion of links between environmental scarcity and conflict. In this case, Gleditsch did not to refer to the Toronto Group's thinking on the consequences of water scarcity. Had he done so, he would have noted a number of interesting hypotheses worthy of testing. Homer-Dixon argues that the world is not about to witness a surge of water wars. 'Wars over river water between upstream and downstream neighbors are likely only in a narrow set of circumstances', Homer-Dixon writes. 'The downstream country must be threatening to restrict substantially the river's flow; there must be a history of antagonism between the two countries; and, most importantly, the downstream country must believe it is militarily stronger than the upstream country. . . . There are, in fact, very few basins around the world where all these conditions hold now or might hold in the future' (Homer-Dixon, 1999: 139). The Toronto Group's research on water scarcity is, in fact, at odds with sensationalist claims about water wars. On this point, we agree with Gleditsch.

Finding Our Way in the Wilderness

Underpinning many of Gleditsch's criticisms are deeper methodological issues pertaining to the conduct of social science inquiry. Gleditsch claims, for instance, that the Toronto Group fails to select cases appropriately, neglects to investigate the possibility of reverse causation, devises untestable models, overemphasizes the complexity of ecological-political systems, and lacks the tools to weight causal variables. These criticisms can only be understood in the context of Gleditsch's unduly narrow perspective on what constitutes systematic research.

In this section, we first show that process tracing within single cases should be an integral part of systematic research in the social sciences; this method complements more conventional quasi-experimental approaches. Drawing a distinction between *causal effect* and *causal mechanism*, we then show why Gleditsch's criticisms of the Toronto Group's research—as identified in the previous paragraph—are unfounded. We also recap some of the key findings of the Toronto Group that Gleditsch overlooked as a result of his methodological bias. In short, we show that there are more than a 'few lights in the wilderness' to guide future research into the relationship between environment and conflict.

Conducting Systematic Research

Gleditsch asserts that little systematic research has been conducted to date on the link between environmental scarcity and violent conflict. By systematic research, he seems to mean either experimental or quasi-experimental analyses.[9] Gleditsch additionally contends that past research into the links between environment and conflict consisted merely of exploratory case studies that failed to demonstrate causal connections.

In our opinion, Gleditsch has an overly circumscribed view of what counts as systematic research in the social sciences. Many social science methodologists have long recognized that systematic research includes not only experimental and quasi-experimental methods, but single-case methods as well.[10] Highly influential studies in the social sciences—such as Graham Allison's *Essence of Decision* (1971) and Arend Lijphart's *The Politics of Accommodation* (1975)—have used single-case studies to build and test theories.[11]

At issue in this debate over the merits of the case-study method are fundamental ontological and epistemological questions pertaining to the nature of causation. Among competing views on how causation can be demonstrated, philosopher David Hume's arguments remain influential.[12] Hume asserted that causation could be demonstrated only by showing a high degree of covariance between types of events, which he termed *constant conjunction*. Hume's notion of constant conjunction underpins experimental and quasi-experimental methodologies in the social sciences; many researchers, including Gleditsch, appear to believe that it also vitiates the single-case method. Nevertheless, Alexander George and Andrew Bennett (2000) show convincingly that Hume's notion of causality underpins not only experimental and quasi-experimental methods but the single-case study method as well. George and Bennett note that Hume recognized three 'sources of causality', only one of which was constant conjunction. The other two were *temporal succession* and *contiguity*. George and Bennett argue that although constant conjunction is related to what methodologists term *causal effect*, temporal succession and contiguity are related to *causal mechanism*. The causal effect of an explanatory variable is defined by George and Bennett as 'the change in probability and/or value of the dependent variable that would have occurred if the explanatory variable had assumed a different value'. Causal mechanism, on the other hand, is defined as 'the causal process and intervening variables through which causal or explanatory variables produce causal effects' (George and Bennett, 2000). Both causal effect *and* causal mechanism are therefore essential and complementary facets of causality. Although the experimental and quasi-experimental methods aim to gauge causal effect, they say little about causal mechanism. The single-case method, conversely, helps reveal causal mechanism, but gives little indication of causal effect. In short, neither the experimental and quasi-experimental nor the single-case method is sufficient to demonstrate causation with any finality. It is equally evident, however, that the single-case method is a necessary tool to demonstrate causation.

An example from the natural sciences illustrates the distinction between causal effect and causal mechanism. Although the correlation between smoking and cancer has been known for many years, only within the last five years have researchers pinpointed exactly *how* smoking engenders cancer. That is, the causal effects were already known, but until recently the causal mechanisms remained unknown. The recent identification of these mechanisms has put the tobacco industry on the defensive, because they now find it harder to retreat to the claim that scientific proof is lacking.[13]

Noted philosopher of science, Rom Harre, provides a second example from the natural sciences, which illustrates the potential hazard of drawing conclusions from causal effect without also investigating causal mechanism. Suppose we are studying plant growth. The experimental method can tell us that plant growth requires light in the presence of heat; but it will not tell us if light and heat are accompanied by a third variable that is the real cause of plant growth. Harre (1985: 40) notes that to resolve this kind of dilemma, 'we need to investigate the mechanism of growth, the process by which a plant synthesizes new material'. Only when we understand the process of photosynthesis can we be sure that light (in the presence of heat) is in fact the cause of plant growth. In short, without an understanding of *how* light stimulates growth, we risk drawing false conclusions. Thus, Harre (1985: 40) concludes: 'In practice we never rest content with laws for which there are no explanations'.

The distinction between causal mechanism and causal effect is also cogent for the social sciences. Timothy McKeown (1999: 172–174) notes that only by distinguishing between causal effect and causal mechanism can one begin to understand why Allison's *Essence of a Decision* and Lijphart's *The Politics of Accommodation* had such momentous impact. Both seriously challenged long-standing theories. Allison's analysis of decisionmaking during the Cuban missile crisis undermined the notion of the state as a unitary, rational actor. Lijphart's analysis of politics in the Netherlands challenged prevailing ideas about the impact of political cleavages. The important processes that these authors identified in their case studies would have been overlooked in a statistical analysis. McKeown asserts these case analyses had a large impact precisely because they highlighted *how* events unfolded by identifying their causal mechanisms.[14]

Several leading philosophers of science have made similar points. Wesley Salmon (1984: 121), for example, argues in favor of explicating causal mechanisms: 'The mere fitting of regularities into patterns has little, if any, explanatory force'. Andrew Sayer (1992: 106–107) states that 'what we would like . . . is a knowledge of *how* the process works. Merely knowing that C has generally been followed by E in not enough: we want to understand the continuous process by which C produced E . . . ' Finally, Abraham Kaplan (1964: 329) asserts that 'we see better *why* something happens when we see better—in more detail, or in broader perspective—just *what* does happen'.[15]

George and Bennett note that the distinction between causal effect and causal mechanism has prompted a debate among methodologists about which of these two sources of causality is more important. Although some analysts suggest that causal effect is logically prior to the identification of causal mechanism (King, Keohane, and Verba, 1994: 86), others insist that causal mechanism is ontologically prior to causal effect (Yee, 1996: 84). George and Bennett dismiss this controversy, arguing that 'causality involves both causal effects and causal mechanisms and its study requires a diversity of methods, some of which are better adapted to the former and some to the latter' (George and Bennett, 2000).

The reluctance of George and Bennett to confer priority on either causal effect or causal mechanism, however, does not suggest that the identification of one should not precede the identification of the other in terms of the practical task of puzzle solving in the social sciences. Indeed, when a research program is in its early stages and the underlying theory is still largely undeveloped, focusing first on causal mechanisms is probably the best strategy. Once researchers have discovered these causal mechanisms and elaborated the theory, they can then begin to estimate causal effects.[16] Thus George and McKeown (1985: 34–41) emphasize the role that single-case methods (involving process tracing) can play in the development of theory.[17]

With this methodological underpinning, the Toronto Group set out to perform a series of case studies of the causal links between environment scarcity and conflict. Although the possibility of such links had been recognized by previous scholarship, theory was rudimentary. Using a process-tracing approach, the Toronto Group conducted over a dozen case studies to better understand the causal mechanisms that might connect environmental scarcity to conflict. The results produced by the Toronto Group reflect the methodology used. The Group does make nomothetic claims about causal mechanisms. For example, Homer-Dixon (1994: 39) says explicitly that 'environmental scarcity causes violent conflict'. But the Toronto Group has been careful to avoid making such claims about causal effects. Nowhere in the Group's research reports are there any claims about the power of environmental scarcity relative to other potential causes of conflict.[18]

Without undertaking research into causal mechanisms, estimates of causal effect are far less illuminating, for two reasons. First, researchers will not know which potentially confounding variables they should control in their statistical tests. Second, researchers may overlook key processes and causal relationships that are hidden in the data. In quasi-experimental methods of social science, it is impossible to control all variables that may affect the dependent variable under study; therefore, researchers must pick and choose their control variables carefully. Process tracing helps identify those particularly worthy of control.[19] Also, process tracing reveals variables and causal patterns that may not emerge from statistical analysis. For instance, the patterns of ecological marginalization and resource capture, which were discovered by the Toronto Group using process tracing, are not obvious and would undoubtedly have remained hidden from statistical analysis. The Group's research suggests, however, that quasi-experimental and statistical methods should now be used to investigate these patterns.[20] This more inclusive understanding of systematic research helps us address five further concerns raised by Gleditsch about contemporary environment-conflict research: selection of cases on the independent and dependent variables, failure to consider that the dependent variable may in fact be an important cause of the independent variable, a propensity to develop untestable models, overemphasis on the complexity of ecological-political systems, and an inability to gauge the relative power of environmental scarcity as a cause of conflict.

Selecting Case Studies

Following Marc Levy (1995) and Carsten Rønnfeldt (1997), Gleditsch contends that, because the Toronto Group chose to study cases in which both environmental scarcity and violent conflict were known a priori to exist, it violated a fundamental principle of research design that applies to both qualitative and quantitative analyses. Consequently, Gleditsch asserts, the Group has produced nothing more than anecdotal evidence to support its hypotheses.

Gleditsch's approach to research design appears to hinge on the assumption that causality is little more than causal effect. Causal mechanism is regarded as less important or is simply not considered at all. Although we agree that researchers must allow for variation on both the independent and dependent variable if they want to estimate casual effect, we contend researchers will find such an approach less helpful in identifying causal mechanisms. If causal mechanism is believed to be an integral aspect of causality, then selecting case studies on the independent and dependent variable is hardly an egregious error in research design. Indeed, in order to understand whether there are causal links between environmental scarcity and violent conflict—and, if there are, *how* these variegated links work—it will be sometimes necessary to select cases in this manner. The Toronto Group therefore intentionally selected cases in which environmental scarcities and violent conflict were known a priori to exist (Homer-Dixon, 1999: 169–176). The Group then used process tracing to determine if the independent and dependent variables were actually causally linked, and, if they were, to induce from a close study of many such cases the common mechanisms of causality and the key intermediate variables that characterized these links.

A related objection to selecting cases on both the independent and dependent variables is that the researcher might, as a result, overlook possible confounding variables and spurious relationships. The researcher might, for instance, believe that data show a causal link between variables A and B, a link that fits the researcher's hypothesis nicely. But the researcher might fail to look for variable C, a variable that is linked to both A and B and is a cause of both. For example, environmental scarcity might appear to be a cause of conflict, but, in reality, not be a cause, if poverty is actually a cause of changes in both these variables. This concern, however, is misplaced, because vigilant case-study researchers should detect such situations. Harry Eckstein (1975: 125–126) contends that such researchers can test 'countertheories'—that is, theories about other likely causes of changes in the value of the dependent variable.[21] Just as the quasi-experimental researcher must anticipate variables to control, the case-study researcher must anticipate potentially spurious causal mechanisms.

Investigating Reverse Causation

A distinction between causal effect and causal mechanism helps us address Gleditsch's concern that violent conflict (the dependent variable in most research in this field) may in fact be an important cause of environmental scarcity (the independent variable). Gleditsch claims that environment-conflict researchers have neglected this possibility of reverse causation and have similarly failed to consider the possibility that environmental scarcity and violent conflict are related to each other in a positive feedback loop—that is, a vicious circle.

We do not deny that conflict may exacerbate environmental scarcity, but this possibility was not the focus of the Toronto Group's research. Nevertheless, we would argue that process tracing offers an excellent way to discover reverse causality, because it unearths causal mechanisms. It allows researchers to trace causal mechanisms that unfold over long periods of time and thereby to investigate the impacts of past conflicts on subsequent environmental conditions. An approach that focuses on causal effects, however, cannot reveal reverse causation as easily. Although simultaneous equations can be used to model reverse causation, and although quasi-experimental methods, using lagged variables or congruence procedures, can be used to span time, a far more intuitive approach is to focus on causal mechanisms, because they will tell the researcher exactly *how* past conflicts exacerbated environmental scarcity.

Moreover, the quasi-experimental method can produce ambiguous results when attempting to differentiate between cause and effect. Consider the following example: when a barometer falls, deteriorating weather is likely to follow. The falling barometer clearly does not cause the weather to deteriorate, even though it precedes the change in weather. Thus, we can not distinguish cause and effect. If we understand the mechanism that causes the barometer to fall, however, we understand that cause and effect can only be differentiated once weather conditions *prior* to the barometer's fall are controlled (Miller, 1987: 34).

Constructing Testable Models

Although Gleditsch contends that much of the environment-conflict literature to date is overly simplistic, he asserts that the Toronto Group is guilty of just the opposite mistake—that is, of developing overly complex models that are not testable. We believe that Gleditsch contradicts himself here by demanding a strict adherence to conventional research design and simultaneously calling for an incremental and modular approach to theory building. Conventional research design forbids the omission of variables that are correlated with the key independent variable. Such an omission creates what Gary King, Robert Keohane, and Sidney Verba (1994: 168–176) term *omitted variable bias.* Many of the variables considered by the Toronto Group are correlated with the key independent variable of environmental scarcity. If Gleditsch is suggesting that we drop these variables out of the equation in the name of testable models, he is also suggesting that we contravene a fundamental canon of conventional research design. Because the Toronto Group did not adopt such a research design, however, this internal contradiction does not directly concern us. Nevertheless, Gleditsch's preference for less complexity is disturbing. If environmental scarcity were either a necessary or a sufficient cause of conflict, it would be possible to reduce our model's complexity. Of course, environmental scarcity is neither a necessary nor sufficient cause (there are few, if any, such causes of conflict). If, therefore, researchers are to make a nomothetic claim about the relationship between environmental scarcity and conflict, environmental scarcity must be what John Mackie (1965) terms an *INUS* condition: it must be an *insufficient* but *necessary* component of a condition that is itself an *unnecessary* but *sufficient* cause of conflict.

Discovering INUS conditions is the goal of the case-study researcher. For environmental-conflict researchers, this entails unearthing the myriad and variegated ways in which environmental scarcity interacts with other social, economic, and political factors to engender conflict. We do not mean to suggest that a process-tracing approach eclipses the important goal of parsimony. Rather, by focusing on relevant causal mechanisms, process tracing helps the environment-conflict researcher determine the boundaries of the sufficient condition. Without a clear picture of these boundaries, simply dropping variables in the name of parsimony becomes a haphazard affair. Once these boundaries have been defined, however, estimating causal effects becomes a more precise procedure.

Dealing with Complex Systems

According to Gleditsch, the Toronto Group claims that ecological-political systems are more complex than strictly social or physical systems. He goes on to argue that this claim is unwarranted because 'any social system is as complex as the theory developed to study it' (2001). In other words, the complexity is in the mind of the beholder, rather than in the phenomenon itself. Actually, the Toronto Group does not argue that ecological-political systems are more complex. They argue simply that these systems are, intrinsically, exceedingly complex. No doubt many social, biological, and physical systems are just as complex or even more complex (although some unquestionably are not).

The problem of complexity exists in the real world. It cannot be wished away by assuming that it resides only in the mind of the researcher. Gleditsch's extraordinarily strong constructivist position on this issue (a position that resonates with Berkleyian idealism) is indefensible both empirically and philosophically (Rescher, 1998). Researchers in a variety of fields increasingly acknowledge the reality of complexity and are developing powerful theories to understand complex systems. These theories raise serious questions about conventional (often mechanistic) explanations of social phenomena and about the conventional methodologies used to study these phenomena (Cowan, Pines, and Meltzer, 1994). Rather than denying complexity's existence, Gleditsch and other social scientists should explicitly acknowledge the problems it creates for their research and try to develop methods—such as those focusing on causal mechanisms—for dealing with it.

Weighting Causal Variables

Gleditsch implies that process tracing within single-case studies does not allow researchers to gauge the relative weights of causal variables. He suggests that the quantitative analysis by Hauge and Ellingsen (2001) is one of the few attempts to test systematically the relationship between environmental scarcity and conflict. These researchers, he notes, did find a statistically significant relationship between environmental degradation and violent conflict, but they concluded that economic and political variables were more important than environmental variables. Thus, Gleditsch implicitly accepts the notion that independent variables can be assigned weights that indicate their relative causal power. Gleditsch, of course, is hardly alone here. Causal weighting is widely considered to be the ultimate goal of statistical analyses, and the lack of ability to weight variables using single case studies is considered this method's foremost drawback.

The practice of causal weighting, however, has its problems. Elliot Sober (1988) contends that the standard statistical technique of analysis of variance (ANOVA) does not actually yield causal weights. Rather, it identifies the *difference* that various causes can make in an observed effect. Ascertaining the difference, Sober maintains, is distinct from ascertaining a causal weight. Similarly, Richard Lewontin (1976) argues that, although causal weighting may be appropriate when the relationships among variables are additive, it is misguided when the relationships are interactive. Lewontin contends that analysis of variance produces uninterpretable results when dealing with interactive variables.

If environmental scarcity is one component of a sufficient condition, as argued above, then environment-conflict researchers are not dealing with additive relations among causal variables. Rather, these relationships are interactive. Environmental scarcity, for example, interacts with a society's ability to supply social and technical ingenuity. If the society can supply abundant ingenuity in response to its environmental problems, then severe social disruptions will probably be avoided; if it cannot, then negative outcomes, including conflict, are much more likely.

Interactivity is hardly limited to the relationships among variables in ecological-political systems. Most social systems exhibit interactivity among variables. That so many researchers treat the relationships among variables in social systems as additive does not reflect the reality of these systems. Rather, it reflects misguided attempts by researchers to avoid dealing with the reality of the *complexity* of these systems.

Suggestions for Future Research

In Gleditsch's final section, he asserts that 'critique will serve to advance the field only if it stimulates more satisfactory research'. Although we do not agree that all work on environment and conflict has been unsatisfactory, we do agree that debates in the field, such as the one we are engaged in here, can provide the spark for new research agendas. In this spirit, we draw on the above remarks to make some suggestions for future work. These suggestions fall in five categories: filling data gaps, operationalizing key variables, specifying contextual factors, dealing with complexity, and encouraging methodological pluralism.

Filling Data Gaps

We agree with Gleditsch that serious data gaps impede research on the links between environment and conflict. There is a particular lack of good data on the extent and degree of soil, water, and forest degradation in developing countries; data on resource distribution and resource-use practices are also poor. The field therefore needs a more systematic and rigorous approach to data collection. Because this research crosses so many disciplinary boundaries, systematic data collection must involve intimate collaboration with experts in a wide range of disciplines, including soil science, hydrology, forest ecology, and the political economy of community resource use.

In our efforts to improve the foundation of data on which we build our environment-conflict research, however, we must recognize that not all good data are quantitative: process tracing of single cases, in fact, generates thick descriptions of environment-conflict linkages—descriptions rich with *qualitative* data. The work of the Toronto Group has already produced a substantial body of qualitative data that can be used by future researchers. More local case studies are needed, which build upon research done to date, and test and refine existing hypotheses at the local level.

Operationalizing Key Variables

If environment-conflict researchers want to estimate causal effect, it is essential that they include in their analyses key variables identified by environment-conflict research. In order to include these variables, efforts must turn toward their operationalization.

The Toronto Group has identified a number of variables that play a pivotal role in the link between environment and conflict. For instance, as noted above, the quantity of ingenuity a society supplies in response to environmental scarcity can play a key role in determining its ability to adapt to that scarcity. The supply of ingenuity, then, is an independent variable that should be included in any statistical analysis attempting to measure the causal effect of environmental scarcity on conflict. Operationalizing this variable, however, is not a straightforward task. Researchers need an adequate measure of ingenuity. Other variables identified by the Toronto

Group that should be included in any complete statistical analysis—and that therefore require operationalization—include state capacity and social segmentation, as well as the aforementioned processes of resource capture and ecological marginalization (which can potentially be represented as single variables).

Specifying Contextual Factors

Empirical research has now identified some causal processes linking environmental scarcity and violence. Nevertheless, much more work remains to be done to determine precisely the intervening and interacting variables—the contextual factors—affecting the strength of these processes. Under what circumstances, exactly, do these processes unfold? In the following, we refer to some of the specific findings of the Toronto Group, and suggest some contextual factors worthy of further investigation:

1) By setting in motion processes of resource capture and ecological marginalization, environmental scarcity often increases the wealth gap between elites that take advantage of the opportunities scarcity offers and marginal groups that suffer the brunt of scarcity. How does the degree of state autonomy affect these two processes? To what extent would better defined and enforced property rights reduce the predatory behavior of elites?

2) The multiple effects of environmental scarcity increase demands on the state, stimulate intraelite behavior, and depress state tax revenues. Such pressures can weaken the administrative capacity and legitimacy of the state. How does institutional design affect state capacity in the presence of these pressures? How do international economic forces both aggravate and mitigate these pressures?

3) Narrow distributional coalitions (i.e., coalitions of rent seekers that work to redistribute the economy's wealth in their favor) often block institutional reform—including reform of markets, property rights, judicial systems, and the state's resource-management regimes—essential to reducing environmental scarcity or alleviating its harsh effects. To what extent does scarcity provoke such behavior? Can a robust civil society counteract the obstructionist behavior of these narrow distributional coalitions?

Dealing with Complexity

At the methodological level, we need to explore how causation works at the interface between the physical/ecological and social worlds. Environment-conflict research brings us face to face with some of the most intractable issues in philosophy of science, specifically whether causal generalizations describing the social world have the same status as those describing the natural world. Because systems in both these domains are fundamentally complex—characterized by huge numbers of components, causal interactions, feedback loops, and nonlinearity—environment-conflict researchers can gain insights from complexity theory. We urge greater receptivity to the concepts and findings of this rapidly developing field.

Encouraging Methodological Pluralism

In order to deal with the research challenges described above, we encourage our colleagues to accept a degree of methodological pluralism. The various methods available to us make up a diverse set of arrows in the quiver of social scientists, and we should choose the arrow most likely to hit our target. Statistical and quasi-experimental methodologies are needed to identify correlations and causal effects; process tracing of single cases is needed to specify causal mechanisms. These two general approaches should not be used in isolation from each other; rather, we should try to exploit the synergies that are possible when they are used in parallel by collaborating researchers. For instance, statistical analysis can identify outliers and anomalous cases that deserve focused attention using process tracing. In turn, process tracing can identify key interacting variables and scope conditions that should be incorporated into statistical tests of the environment-conflict hypothesis. Methodological pluralism, however, is not a license for shoddiness. Researchers should be held to high standards of evidence and analysis, and research programs should have sound ontological and epistemological foundations.

Daniel M. Schwartz, b. 1970, Ph.D. candidate, political science, University of Toronto. Current main interests: causal weighting, causation, and environment and conflict. He has written on environmental terrorism in *Journal of Peace Research* (1998) and on environmental conflict for United Nations Environment Programme (1999).

Tom Deligiannis, b. 1967, Ph.D. candidate, political science, University of Toronto; current main interest: environmental stress and conflict in Latin America.

Thomas Homer-Dixon, b. 1956, Ph.D. in political science (MIT, 1989), director of the Peace and Conflict Studies Program and associate professor of political science at the University of Toronto. Most recent book: *Environment, Scarcity, and Violence* (Princeton University Press, 1999).

Notes

1. This objection was raised by an anonymous reviewer of this chapter, as well as by Dessler (1999: 100–101).

2. The literature supporting this claim is so vast it cannot be summarized. An excellent survey can be found in World Bank (1992). See also Midlarsky (1999) who provides compelling empirical evidence on the intimate connections between scarcity (including resource scarcity), inequality, and social conflict. Dasgupta

(1993) provides an economic analysis of the effect of resource scarcity on communities in the developing world. Good and relatively current surveys of the state of the environment in China and India, which together constitute about 40 percent of the world's population, are Smil (1993) and Repetto (1994).

3. Recent data from the Food and Agriculture Organization (FAO, 1999a) shows that the percentage of undernourished in all three regions has either remained steady (Sub-Saharan Africa) or fallen (South Asia and Latin America). However, the absolute number of undernourished over the past thirty years has either grown (Sub-Saharan Africa and South Asia), or remained relatively stable overall (Latin America). See also FAO (1999b).

4. Daniel Deudney (1999a) has recently coined the phrase social-social theory for theories that presume social events have only social causes; he uses nature-social theory for theories in which natural variables play a significant causal role.

5. The claim that environmental scarcity can be, in part, an exogenous variable, should not be confused with the claim (which we do not make) that environmental scarcity can have a direct impact on conflict. We argue that the link between environmental scarcity and conflict is most often indirect. Nevertheless, environmental scarcity can still have an exogenous impact on the social conditions that eventually lead to conflict.

6. For an excellent treatment of the variegated nature of democracy, see Collier and Levitsky (1997).

7. Several of the Toronto Group's historical case studies are reproduced in Homer-Dixon and Blitt (1998).

8. ENCOP similarly relied upon a large number of historical case studies during the course of the project research. These case studies are published, along with their theoretical findings, in a three-volume work (Bächler et al., 1996).

9. He discusses statistical analyses and controlled-case comparisons in particular, but quasi-experimental methods could also include counterfactual analyses and congruence procedures.

10. See, for example, Campbell (1975), Dessler (1991), Eckstein (1975), George (1979), George and Bennett (2000), George and McKeown (1985), Yee (1996), and McKeown (1999).

11. This point is made in McKeown (1999: 172–174). Nonexperimental methods have also been widely used in the natural sciences (see McKeown, 1999: 174, and Eckstein, 1975: 114–115).

12. Hume was, in fact, highly skeptical of our ability to show causation. His analysis of causation was meant to ascertain the bare epistemic facts that undergird our intuition of causality.

13. See Grady (1996: 3). A similar distinction between causal effect and causal mechanism has implications for other areas in the natural sciences as well. For instance, although scientists have known for nearly a century that aspirin relieves pain, it is only within the last few years that they have discovered the causal mechanisms behind this pain relief. (See Garavito, 1999: 108).

14. Although qualitative quasi-experimental methods, such as the comparative case study, can also detect causal mechanisms, the single-case method is often a more efficient means of discovering these processes. Moreover, because control is extremely difficult to achieve in the comparative method, it is questionable if causal mechanisms can be more accurately detected than with the single-case method.

15. Kaplan also argues that descriptions, which are often differentiated from explanation, may themselves be explanatory, 'because the "how" may provide a "why" and not just a "what"'. One notable criticism of this approach is made by Kincaid (1994: 117), who argues that causal mechanisms can always be discovered at deeper levels (e.g., at psychological or even neurophysiological levels). King, Keohane, and Verba make a similar point (1994: 86). We believe this criticism ultimately fails, however, because a researcher must always conduct their research at a chosen level of analysis, and the causal mechanisms they seek should correspond to the level of analysis of their research. Moreover, if deeper causal mechanisms are discovered and if they support the theory, then the theory will only be more robust.

16. Research is sometimes sparked by a preliminary correlation analysis that offers a promising avenue for further research (e.g., the Democratic Peace). Nevertheless, we maintain that a full-blown statistical analysis of these preliminary findings would benefit greatly from case-study research into causal mechanism. The research process, then, should be viewed as an *iterative* one, with quasi-experimental and case-study methods complementing one another.

17. Although the logic for separating the testing and building of theories in quantitative methodologies is sound, Donald Campbell (1975: 178–193) shows that this partition is not necessary in case-study research. Campbell convincingly demonstrates that the problem of ex post facto hypothesizing is overcome in the 'pattern matching' methodology—from which process tracing was conceived—because this procedure opens the possibility that an hypothesis initially generated by a particular case could subsequently fail to be supported by the same case. Also see Collier (1993: 115).

18. Although Homer-Dixon (1994) does not refer explicitly to causal mechanism, the underlying approach taken throughout the article consists of an explicit attempt to discover these processes. It is therefore reasonable to assume that the nomethetic claim made is this article refers to causal mechanisms.

19. The common mistake among researchers is to omit a variable that should be controlled in a statistical analysis. This can result in what statisticians refer to as a Type I error, where the null hypothesis is true but the researcher decides that it is false. However, it can be equally dangerous to include a variable that should not be controlled. This can result in a Type II error, where the null hypothesis is false but the researcher decides that it is true. Nancy Cartwright (1979: 429–432) points out that an 'irrelevant' control variable can always be found that annuls or reduces a true relationship. Therefore, to avoid both Type I and Type II errors, we suggest that researchers use process tracing to determine the appropriate control variables.

20. A parable recounted by Diana Baumrind (1983: 1297) illustrates why research into causal mechanisms can be invaluable in discovering control variables. 'The number of never-married persons in certain British villages is highly inversely correlated with the number of field mice in the surrounding meadows. Marital status of humans was considered an established cause of field mice by the village elders until the mechanism of transmission were finally surmised: Never-married persons bring with them a disproportionate number of cats relative to the rest of the village populace and cats consume field mice. With the generative mechanisms understood, village elders could concentrate their attention on increasing the population of cats rather than the proportion of never-married persons'. Clark Glymour et al. (1987: 19–21) oppose Baumrind's 'generative' account of causality. They argue that in fact

'never-married persons *do* cause variation in field mice, even if the causation is indirect, and nothing in the story prevents the use of covariance analysis on uncontrolled samples to discover that the intervening variables is the density of cats'. But this belies the process that social scientists use to discover control variables. Without an investigation of the causal mechanisms, it is doubtful that the density of cats would have been included in a statistical analysis.

21. Although it is not possible for case-study researchers to consider all possible spurious relationships, neither is it possible to include all possible confounding variables in a statistical model. David Dessler (1997: 101) adopts this approach when he suggests that environment-conflict researchers 'Test causal claims not against the *null hypothesis* but against rival substantive accounts of political violence in the cases analyzed'.

Bibliography

Achterberg, Wouter. 1996a. 'Sustainability and Associative Democracy', in Lafferty and Meadowcroft, eds. (157–174).

Adekanye, J. 'Bayo. 1994. 'Military Dimensions of Africa's Debt and Adjustment Problems, North/South Coalition', *Information Bulletin* 2(2): 32–49.

Adler, Emanuel. 1997. 'Imagined (Security) Communities: Cognitive Regions in International Relations', *Millennium* 26(2): 249–277.

Adler, Emanuel, and Michael Barnett. 1996. 'Governing Anarchy: A Research Agenda for the Study of Security Communities', *Ethics and International Affairs* 10: 63–98.

Agarwal, Anil, and Sunita Narain. 1991. *Global Warming in an Unequal World.* New Delhi: Centre for Science and Environment.

Agence France Presse. 1995. 'Analysts See Chance of Small Skirmishes in Disputed Spratlys', *International Herald Tribune,* 21 April: 4.

Ahlburg, Dennis. 1998. 'Julian Simon and the Population Growth Debate', *Population and Development Review* 24(2): 317–327.

Ahmed, Kulsum. 1994. *Renewable Energy Technologies: A Review of the Status and Costs of Selected Technologies.* Technical Paper (240). Washington, D.C.: World Bank.

Albala-Bertrand, J. M. 1993. *The Political Economy of Large Natural Disasters.* Oxford: Clarendon.

Aldrich, John H., and Forrest D. Nelson. 1984. *Linear Probability, Logit and Probit Models.* Sage University Papers series on Quantitative Applications in the Social Sciences, no. 07–045. Beverly Hills, Calif.: Sage.

Alexandratos, Nikos. 1997. *FAO's Cereals Projections to 2010 and Recent Developments: Response to Lester Brown.* Rome: Chief of Global Perspective Studies Unit, Food and Agriculture Organization. Unpublished manuscript, received from John Lupien, director of Food and Nutrition Division, FAO.

Allison, Graham. 1971. *Essence of Decision: Explaining the Cuban Missile Crisis.* Boston, Mass.: Little, Brown.

American Political Network. 1994. 'Lake Victoria: Ecosystem on the Brink, Report Finds', *Greenwire* (lexis-nexis), 29 November.

Amery, Hussein A., and Atif Kubursi. 1992. 'Le Litani, clé de la renaissance economique et de la stabilité politique du Liban' [The Litani, Key to the Economic Renaissance and the Political Stability of Lebanon], *Ecodecision* (September): 55–57.

Anderson, Steven M. 1995. 'Reforming International Institutions to Improve Global Environmental Relations, Agreement and Treaty Enforcement', *Hastings International and Comparative Law Review* 18(4): 771–821.

Anderson, Terry L. 1995. 'Water, Water Everywhere but Not a Drop to Sell', in Simon, ed. (425–433).

Angell, Norman. 1936. *Raw Materials, Population Pressure and War.* New York: World Peace Foundation.

Anon. 1994. 'Development Monitor: Attitudes', *Indicator South Africa* 12(1): 73.

Archer, Dan. 1994. *Twenty-Twenty, A Working Report.* Working Paper 111. Pietermaritzburg: Institute of Natural Resources, University of Natal, August.

Associated Press. 1995. 'China Is Ready to Fight for the Spratlys, Report Says', *International Herald Tribune,* 19 April: 4.

_____. 1997. 'Private Foreign Investment in Poor Nations Hits Peak', *Louisville Courier Journal,* 24 March.

Axelrod, Robert. 1984. *The Evolution of Cooperation.* New York: Basic Books.

Bächler, Günther. 1994. 'Desertification and Conflict. The Marginalization of Poverty and of Environmental Conflicts', paper presented at the Symposium on Desertification and Migration, Almeria, Spain, 9–12 February.

_____. 1998. 'Why Environmental Transformation Causes Violence: A Synthesis', *Environmental Change and Security Project Report* 4: 24–44. Washington, D.C.: Woodrow Wilson International Center for Scholars.

_____. 1999. 'Environmental Degradation in the South as a Cause of Armed Conflict', in Carius and Lietzmann, eds. (107–129).

Bächler, Günther, Volker Böge, Stefan Klötzli, Stephan Libiszewski, and Kurt R. Spillmann. 1996. *Kriegsursache Umweltzerstörung. Ökologische Konflikte in der Dritten Welt und Wege ihrer friedlichen Bearbeitung* [Environmental Destruction as a Cause of War. Ecological Conflicts in the Third World and Peaceful Ways of Resolving Them]. Three vols. Zurich: Rüegger.

Bailey, Jennifer. 1997. 'States, Stocks, and Sovereignty: High Seas Fishing and the Expansion of State Sovereignty', ch. 14 in Gleditsch, ed., 1997b (215–234).

Bailey, Ronald. 1993. *Eco-Scam. The False Prophets of Ecological Apocalypse.* New York: St Martin's.

Ball, Desmond. 1993–1994. 'Arms and Affluence: Military Acquisition in the Asia-Pacific Region', *International Security* 18(3): 78–112.

Ball, George W., and Douglas B. Ball. 1992. *The Passionate Attachment: America's Involvement with Israel. 1947 to the Present.* New York: Norton.

Banks, Arthur S. 1971. *Cross-Polity Time-Series Data.* Cambridge, Mass.: MIT Press.

_____. 1979. *Cross-National Time-Series Data Archive User's Manual.* Binghamton, N.Y.: State University of New York at Binghamton.

Barbier, Edward, and Thomas Homer-Dixon. 1996. *Resource Scarcity, Institutional Adaptation, and Technical Innovation: Can Poor Countries Attain Endogenous Growth?* Toronto, Ontario: University of Toronto and American Association for the Advancement of Science.

Barnard, David. 1994. 'Housing: The Reconstruction Challenge', *Prodder Newsletter: Program for Development Research* 6(4): 1–3.

Battersby, John. 1994. 'Blacks Prepare to Cast Their Ballots', *Christian Science Monitor,* 28 February.

Baumrind, Diana. 1983. 'Specious Causal Attributions in the Social Sciences', *Journal of Personality and Social Psychology* 45(6): 1289–1298.

Beaumont, Peter. 1997. 'Water and Armed Conflict in the Middle East–Fantasy or Reality?', ch. 21 in Gleditsch, ed., 1997b (355–374).

Bendor, Jonathan, and Piotr Swistak. 1997. 'The Evolutionary Stability of Cooperation', *American Political Science Review* 91(2): 290–307.

Benedick, Richard E. 1998. *Ozone Diplomacy: New Directions in Safeguarding the Planet*. Cambridge, Mass.: Harvard University Press.

Bernaur, Thomas. 1995. 'The Effect of International Environmental Institutions: How We Might Learn More', *International Organization* 49(2): 351–377.

Biersteker, Thomas J., and Cynthia Weber, eds. 1996. *State Sovereignty as Social Construct*. Cambridge: Cambridge University Press.

Biswas, Asit, John Kolars, Masahiro Murakami, John Waterbury, and Aaron Wolf. 1997. *Core and Periphery: A Comprehensive Approach to Middle Eastern Water*. Delhi: Oxford University Press.

Blum, Douglas W. 1999. 'Beyond Reciprocity: Governance and Cooperation in the Caspian Sea'. Paper presented at the Workshop on Environmental Cooperation and Regional Peace, Woodrow Wilson International Center for Scholars, Washington, D.C.

Boardman, Joan. 1998. 'An Average Soil Erosion Rate for Europe: Myth or Reality?', *Journal of Soil and Water Conservation* 53(1): 46–50.

Bobrow, Davis. 1984. 'Population, Conflict, and Policy', in *Multidisciplinary Perspectives on Population and Conflict*, pp. 179–194, ed. Nazli Choucri. Syracuse, N.Y.: Syracuse University Press.

Boersema, Nic. 1988. 'Making the Right Move: Migration Decision Making in a Rural Community', in Steyn and Boersema, eds. (99–119).

Bolch, Ben, and Harold Lyons. 1993. *Apocalypse Not: Science, Economics, and Environmentalism*. Washington, D.C.: Cato Institute.

Bollen, Kenneth A. 1993. 'Liberal Democracy: Validity and Method Factors in Cross-National Measures', *American Journal of Political Science* 37(4): 1207–1230.

Botkin, Daniel B., and Edward A. Keller. 1998. *Environmental Science: Earth Is a Living Planet*. New York: Wiley.

Boulding, Kenneth E. 1966. 'Ode, on the General Subject of Water', *Industrial Water Engineering* 3(December): 32–33. Reprinted as part of 'The Feather River Anthology' in Richard B. Beilock, *Beasts, Ballads, and Bouldingisms*, pp. 109–110. New Brunswick, N.J.: Transaction Books.

BP. 1998. *BP Statistical Review of World Energy 1997*, http://www.bp.com/bp-stats/.

Brams, Steven J., and Alan D. Taylor. 1996. *Fair Division: From Cake-Cutting to Dispute Resolution*. Cambridge, England: Cambridge University Press.

_____. 1999. *The Win-Win Solution: Guaranteeing Fair Shares to Everybody*. New York: Norton.

Brams, Steven J., and Jeffrey R. Togman. 1996. 'Camp David: Was the Agreement Fair?', *Conflict Management and Peace Science* 13(3): 99–112.

_____. 1998. 'Camp David: Was the Agreement Fair?', in *Conflict in World Politics: Advances in the Study of Crisis, War and Peace*, pp. 306–323, ed. Frank P. Harvey and Ben D. Mor. London: Macmillan. Revised and expanded version of Brams and Togman, 1996.

Bremer, Stuart. 1992. 'Dangerous Dyads. Conditions Affecting the Likelihood of Interstate War, 1816–1965', *Journal of Conflict Resolution* 36(2): 309–341.

Bremer, Stuart, J. David Singer, and Urs Luterbacher. 1973. 'The Population Density and War Proneness of European Nations, 1816–1965', *Comparative Political Studies* 6(3): 329–348. Reprinted as ch. 8 in J. David Singer et al., 1979, *Explaining War. Selected Papers from the Correlates of War Project*. Beverly Hills, Calif. and London: Sage (189–207).

Brennan, Ellen. 1999. *Population, Urbanization, Environment, and Security: A Summary of the Issues*. Comparative Urban Studies Occasional Paper Series (22). Washington, D.C.: Woodrow Wilson International Center for Scholars.

Broad, Robin, and John Cavanagh. 1999. 'The Death of the Washington Consensus?' *World Policy Journal* 16(3):79–88.

Brock, Lothar. 1991. 'Peace Through Parks: The Environment on the Peace Research Agenda', *Journal of Peace Research* 28(4): 407–423.

Bromberger, Norman, and Francis Antonie. 1993. 'Black Small Farmers in the Homelands', in *State and Market in Post-Apartheid South Africa,* ed. Merle Lipton and Charles Simkins. Johannesburg: Witwatersrand University Press.

Brooks, David. 1995. *Field Study Report: South Africa, Mozambique and East Africa*. Ottawa: International Development Research Centre, Environment and Natural Resources Division, May.

Brown, Lester. 1965. 'Population Growth, Food Needs, and Production Problems', in *World Population and Food Supplies 1980*. ASA special publication 6: Madison, Wisc.: American Society of Agronomy (17–21), at http://www.arec.umd.-edu/arec365/365n1f.htm.

_____. 1998. *Who Will Feed China? Wake-Up Call for a Small Planet*. Washington, D.C.: Worldwatch.

Brown, Neville. 1989. 'Climate, Ecology, and International Security', *Survival* 31 (November/December): 519–532.

Brundtland, Gro Harlem, et al. 1987. *Our Common Future: World Commission on Environment and Development*. Oxford: Oxford University Press.

Bueno de Mesquita, Bruce, and David Lalman. 1988. 'Empirical Support for Systemic and Dyadic Explanations of War', *World Politics* 41(1): 1–20.

Bulloch, John, and Adil Darwish. 1993. *Water Wars: Coming Conflicts in the Middle East*. London: Gollancz.

Bundy, Barbara K, Stephen D. Burns, and Kimberly V. Weichel, eds. 1994. *The Future of the Pacific Rim*. Westport, Conn.: Praeger.

Buol, S. W. 1994. 'Soils', in *Changes in Land Use and Land Cover: A Global Perspective,* pp. 211–229, ed. William B. Meyer and B. L. Turner II. Cambridge: Cambridge University Press.

Butterworth, Robert L. 1976. *Managing Interstate Conflict. 1945–1974*. Pittsburgh, Pa.: University Center for International Studies.

Butts, Kent Hughes. 1999. 'The Case for DOD Involvement in Environmental Security', in Deudney and Matthew, eds. (109–126).

Campbell, Donald T. 1975. 'Degrees of Freedom and the Case Study', *Comparative Political Studies* 8(2): 178–193.

Carius, Alexander, and Kurt M. Lietzmann, 2000. *Environmental Change and Security. A European Perspective*. Berlin: Springer.

Carnegie Commission on Preventing Deadly Conflict. 1997. *Preventing Deadly Conflict: Final Report with Executive Summary.* Washington, D.C.: Carnegie Commission on Preventing Deadly Conflict.

Carson, Rachel. 1962. *Silent Spring.* Boston, Mass.: Houghton Mifflin.

Cartwright, Nancy. 1979. 'Causal Laws and Effective Strategies', *Nous* 13(4): 419–438.

Central Statistical Services. 1992. *South African Statistics 1992.* Pretoria: Central Statistical Services.

Chan, Steve. 1997. 'In Search of Democratic Peace: Problems and Promise', *Mershon International Studies Review* 41(1): 59–91.

Chanda, Nayanda. 1995. 'Long Shadow: Southeast Asians Have China on Their Mind', *Far Eastern Economic Review* 28, December: 17.

Chanda, Nayanda, and Kari Huus. 1995. 'China: The New Nationalism', *Far Eastern Economic Review* 9, November: 22.

Chang, Pao-Min. 1990. 'A New Scramble for the South China Sea Islands', *Contemporary Southeast Asia* 12: 26.

Chang, Teh-Kuang. 1991. 'China's Claim of Sovereignty over Spratly and Paracel Islands: A Historical and Legal Perspective', *Case Western Reserve Journal of International Law* 23(3): 399–420.

Chazan, Naomi. 1994. 'Engaging the State: Associational Life in Sub-Saharan Africa', in *State Power and Social Forces,* pp. 255–292, ed. Joel Migdal, Atul Kohli, and Vivienne Shue. Cambridge: Cambridge University Press.

Chen, Jie. 1994. 'China's Spratlys Policy with Special Reference to the Philippines and Malaysia', *Asian Survey* 34(10): 893–903.

Chen, Qimao. 1993. 'New Approaches in China's Foreign Policy', *Asian Survey* 33(3): 237–251.

Chiras, Daniel D. 1998. *Environmental Science: A Systems Approach to Sustainable Development.* Belmont, Calif.: Wadsworth.

Choucri, Nazli. 1974. *Population Dynamics and International Violence.* Lexington, Mass.: Lexington Books.

———. 1997. 'Environmental Flash Points in the Near East and North Africa', in *Consequences of Environmental Change–Political, Economic, Social (Proceedings of the Environmental Flash Points Workshop, Reston, Virginia, November 12–14. 1997),* pp. 177–196, ed. Robert S. Chen, W. Christopher Lenhardt, and Kara F. Alkire. University Center, Mich.: Consortium for International Earth Science Information Network.

Choucri, Nazli, and Robert C. North. 1975. *Nations in Conflict.* San Francisco, Calif.: Freeman.

———. 1989. 'Lateral Pressure in International Relations: Concept and Theory', in Midlarsky, ed. (289–326).

Choucri, Nazli, Robert North, and Susumu Yamakage. 1992. *The Challenge of Japan Before World War II and After.* London: Routledge.

Choucri, Nazli, ed. 1984. *Multidisciplinary Perspectives on Population and Conflict.* Syracuse, N.Y.: Syracuse University Press.

Chu, Shulong. 1994. 'The PRC Girds for Limited High-Tech War', *Orbis* 38(2): 177–191.

CIA, annual. *World Factbook*. Washington, D.C.: Gale Research, for Central Intelligence Agency.

Clapp, Jennifer. 1994. 'Africa, NGOs, and the International Toxic Waste Trade', *Journal of Environment and Development* 3(2): 17–46.

Coetzee, Henk, and David Cooper. 1991. 'Wasting Water', in *Going Green: People, Politics and the Environment in South Africa*, pp. 129–138, ed. Jacklyn Cock and Eddie Koch. Cape Town: Oxford University Press.

Cohen, J., and J. Rogers. 1992. 'Secondary Associations and Democratic Governance', *Politics and Society* 20(4): 393–472.

Cohen, Joel. 1995. *How Many People Can the Earth Support?* New York: Norton.

COICA. 1998. 'Two Agendas on Amazon Development', in Ken Conca and Geoffrey D. Dabelko, *Green Planet Blues: Environmental Politics from Stockholm to Kyoto*. Boulder, Colo: Westview, for Coordinating Body for the Indigenous Peoples' Organizations of the Amazon Basin (337–342).

Colinvaux, Paul A. 1980. *The Fates of Nations: A Biological Theory of History*. NY: Simon and Schuster. [Paperback edition: Harmondsworth: Penguin. 1983.]

Collier, David. 1993. 'The Comparative Method', in Ada W. Finifter, ed., *Political Science: The State of the Discipline II*. Washington, D.C.: American Political Science Association (105–120).

Collier, David, and Steven Levitsky. 1997. 'Democracy with Adjectives: Conceptual Innovation in Comparative Research', *World Politics* 49(3): 430–451.

Collier, Paul, and Anke Hoeffler. 1998. 'On the Economic Causes of Civil War', *Oxford Economic Papers* 50(4): 563–573.

Conca, Ken. 1993. 'Environmental Change and the Deep Structure of World Politics', in Lipschutz and Conca, eds. (306–326).

_____. 1994. 'In the Name of Sustainability: Peace Studies and Environmental Discourse', *Peace and Change* 19(2): 91–113.

_____. 1995a. 'Environmental Protection, International Norms, and National Sovereignty: The Case of the Brazilian Amazon', in Gene Lyons and Michael Mastanduno, *Beyond Westphalia? State Sovereignty and International Intervention*. Baltimore, MD: Johns Hopkins University Press (147–169).

_____. 1995b. 'Rethinking the Ecology-Sovereignty Debate', *Millennium: Journal of International Studies* 23(3): 701–711.

_____. 1997. *Manufacturing Insecurity: The Rise and Fall of Brazil's Military-Industrial Complex*. Boulder, Colo: Lynne Rienner.

'Concrete Claims'. 1995. *Far Eastern Economic Review* 21 December: 14.

Conway, H. McKinley, and Linda L. Liston. 1972. *The Weather Handbook*. Atlanta, Ga.: Conway Research.

Cooley, John. 1984. 'The War over Water', *Foreign Policy* 54(Spring): 3–26.

Cooper, David. 1991. 'From Soil Erosion to Sustainability', in Jacklyn Cock and Eddie Koch, *Going Green: People, Politics and the Environment in South Africa*. Cape Town: Oxford University Press (176–192).

Cooper, David, and Salim Fakir. 1994. *Commercial Farming and Wood Resources in South Africa: Potential Sources for Poor Communities*. Working Paper, 11. Johannesburg: Land and Agriculture Policy Centre, September.

Cordner, Lee G. 1994. 'The Spratlys Dispute and the Law of the Sea', *Ocean Development and International Law* 25(1): 61–74.

Correia, Francisco Nunes, and Joaquim Evaristo da Silva. 1997. 'Transboundary Issues in Water Resources', in Gleditsch, ed. 1997b (315–334).

Cowan, George, David Pines, and David Meltzer, eds. 1994. *Complexity: Metaphors, Models, and Reality*. Santa Fe Institute Studies in the Sciences of Complexity, Proceedings. 19. Reading, Mass.: Addison-Wesley.

CPI. 1999. *Consumer Price Index 1913–1999*. Washington, D.C.: Bureau of Labor, ftp://ftp.bls.gov/pub/special.requests/cpi/cpiai.txt.

Craig, James R., David J. Vaughan, and Brian J. Skinner. 1996. *Resources of the Earth: Origin, Use and Environmental Impact*. Upper Saddle River, N.J.: Prentice-Hall.

Cross, Catherine, Simon Bekker, and Craig Clark. 1992. 'People on the Move: Migration Streams in the DFR', *Indicator South Africa* 9(3): 43–50.

_____. 1994. 'Migration into DFR Informal Settlements: An Overview of Trends', in Hindson and McCarthy, eds. 1994b (73–82).

Crosson, Pierre. 1995. 'Soil Erosion Estimates and Costs', *Science* 269: 461–464.

_____. 1996. *Resource Degradation*. Federation of American Scientists; Long-term Global Food Project (3), http://www.fas.org/cusp/food/index.html.

_____. 1997a. 'Soil Erosion', *Environment* 39(10): 5.

_____. 1997b. 'Will Erosion Threaten Agricultural Productivity?', *Environment* 39(8): 4–12.

CRS. 1995. *World Oil Production After Year 2000: Business As Usual or Crises?* Joseph P. Riva, Jr., Specialist in Earth Sciences, Science Policy Research Division, 18 August. 1995. Washington, D.C.: Congressional Research Service, Report for Congress, http://www.cnie.org/nle/crs_main.html.

Cunningham, William P., and Barbara Woodworth Saigo. 1997. *Environmental Science: A Global Concern*. Dubuque, Iowa: Wm. C. Brown.

Dabelko, Geoffrey D., and David D. Dabelko. 1995. 'Environmental Security: Issues of Conflict and Redefinition', *Environmental Change and Security Project Report* (1): 3–13. Washington, D.C.: Woodrow Wilson International Center for Scholars.

Dalby, Simon. 1999. 'Threats from the South? Geopolitics, Equity, and Environmental Security', in Deudney and Matthew, eds. (155–186).

Darnton, John. 1993. 'Note of Unity Pervades Peace Prize Ceremony', *New York Times*, 11 December.

Dasgupta, Partha. 1993. *An Inquiry Into Well-Being and Destitution*. Oxford: Clarendon.

_____. 1995. 'Population, Poverty, and the Local Environment', *Scientific American* 272(2): 40–45.

de Blij, Harm J., and Peter O. Muller. 1992. *Geography: Regions and Concepts*. 6th ed. New York: Wiley.

de Haas, Mary, and Paulu Zulu. 1993. 'Ethnic Mobilization: KwaZulu's Politics of Secession', *Indicator South Africa* 10(3): 47–52.

Deininger, Klaus, and Lyn Squire. 1996. 'A New Data Set Measuring Income Inequality', *The World Bank Economic Review* 10(3): 565–591.

de Moor, André P. G. 1998. *Perverse Incentives. Subsidies and Sustainable Development: Key Issues and Reform Strategies*, http://www.ecouncil.ac.cr/rio/focus/report/english/subsidies/.

Denoon, David B. H., and Steven J. Brams. 2001. 'Fair Division in the Spratly Islands Controversy', ch. 10 in this volume. Reprinted with minor changes from *International Negotiation* 2(2): 303–329. 1997.

Denoon, David B. H., and Evelyn Colbert. 1998–99. 'Challenges for the Association of Southeast Asian Nations (ASEAN)', *Pacific Affairs* 71(4): 505–523.

Denoon, David B. H., and Wendy Frieman. 1996. 'China's Security Strategy: The View from Beijing, ASEAN, and Washington', *Asian Survey* 36(4): 422–439.

de Sherbinen, Alex. 1995. 'World Population Growth and U.S. National Security', *Environmental Change and Security Project Report* (1): 24–29. Washington, D.C.: Woodrow Wilson Center for Scholars.

Deshingkar, Priya. 1994. *Integrating Gender Concerns into Natural Resource Management Policies in South Africa*. Johannesburg: Land and Agriculture Policy Centre, April.

de Soysa, Indra. 2000. 'The Resource Curse: Are Civil Wars Driven by Rapacity or Paucity?', in Mats Berdal and David M. Malone, eds, *Greed and Grievance. Economic Agendas in Civil Wars*. Boulder, Colo. and London: Lynne Rienner (113–135).

de Soysa, Indra, and Nils Petter Gleditsch, with Michael Gibson, Margareta Sollenberg, and Arthur Westing. 1999. *To Cultivate Peace. Agriculture in a World of Conflict. PRIO Report* 1/99. Oslo: International Peace Research Institute, Oslo and Washington, D.C.: Future Harvest, available in electronic form at www.futureharvest.org.

Dessler, David. 1991. 'Beyond Correlations: Toward a Causal Theory of War', *International Studies Quarterly* 35(3): 337–355.

_____. 1997. 'Making Research on Environmental Scarcity and Violent Conflict More Useful to Policymakers', paper prepared for the 'Roundtable on the University of Toronto's Project on Environment, Population and Security', presented at the 38th Annual Convention of the International Studies Association, Toronto, 18–22 March.

Deudney, Daniel H. 1990. 'The Case Against Linking Environmental Degradation and National Security', *Millennium* 19(3): 461–476.

_____. 1991. 'Environment and Security: Muddled Thinking', *Bulletin of Atomic Scientists* 47(3): 22–28.

_____. 1993. 'Global Environmental Rescue and the Emergence of World Domestic Politics', in Lipschutz and Conca, eds. (280–305).

_____. 1999a. 'Bringing Nature Back In: Geopolitical Theory from the Greeks to the Global Era', in Deudney and Matthew, eds. (25–57).

_____. 1999b. 'Environmental Security: A Critique', in Deudney and Matthew, eds. (187–219).

Deudney, Daniel H., and Richard A. Matthew, eds. 1999. *Contested Grounds: Security and Conflict in the New Environmental Politics*. Albany, NY: State University of New York Press.

Deutsch, Karl W. 1952. *Nationalism and Social Communication*. Cambridge, Mass.: MIT Press.

_____. 1963. *The Nerves of Government*. New York: Free Press.

Deutsch, Karl W., Sidney A. Burrell, Robert A. Kann, Maurice Lee, Jr., Martin Lichterman, Raymond E. Lindgren, Francis L. Loewenheim, and Richard W. Van

Wagenen. 1957. *Political Community and the North Atlantic Area*. Princeton, N.J.: Princeton University Press.

Development Bank of South Africa. 1994. *South Africa's Nine Provinces: A Human Development Profile*. Pretoria: Development Bank of South Africa.

Dewar, David. 1991. 'Cities Under Stress', in *Restoring the Land*, pp. 91–102, ed. Mamphele Ramphele. London: Panos.

Diebert, Ronald J. 1996. 'From Deep Black to Green? Demystifying the Military Monitoring of the Environment', *Environmental Change and Security Project Report* (2) 28–32. Washington, D.C.: Woodrow Wilson International Center for Scholars.

Diehl, Paul F. 1992. 'What Are They Fighting For? The Importance of Issues in International Conflict Research', *Journal of Peace Research* 29(3): 333–344.

_____. 'Environmental Conflict: An Introduction', *Journal of Peace Research* 35 (3): 275–277.

Dietz, Thomas, and Eugene A. Rosa. 1997. 'Environmental Impacts of Population and Consumption', in *Environmentally Significant Consumption. Research Directions*, pp. 92–99, ed. Paul C. Stern, Thomas Dietz, Vernon W. Ruttan, Robert H. Socolow, and James L. Seeney. Washington, D.C.: National Academy Press.

Dinar, Ariel, Mark W. Rosegrant, and Ruth Meinzen-Dick. 1997. *Water Allocation Mechanisms: Principles and Examples*. Washington, D.C.: World Bank and International Food Policy Research Institute, http://www.worldbank.org/html/-dec/Publications/Workpapers/WPS1700series/wps1779/wps1779.pdf.

Dix, Robert H. 1994. 'History and Democracy Revisited', *Comparative Politics* 27(1): 91–105.

DMU. 1998. *Natur og Miljø 1997: Påvirkninger og tilstand* [Nature and Environment 1997: Influences and Condition]. Roskilde: Danmarks Miljøundersøgelser.

Dobson, Andrew. 1996. 'Representative Democracy and the Environment', in Lafferty and Meadowcroft eds. 1996a (124–139).

DOE. 1997. *Renewable Energy Technology Characterizations*. U.S. Department of Energy and Office of Utility Technologies, http://www.eren.doe.gov/utilities/-techchar.html.

Dolven, Ben, and Lorien Holland. 1999. 'Softly, Softly', *Far Eastern Economic Review* 10 June: 28–30.

Dorplan, Andreas. 1942. *The World of General Haushofer*. New York: Farmer and Rinehart.

Doty, Roxanne Lynn. 1996. *Imperial Encounters: The Politics of Representation in North-South Relations*. Minneapolis, Minn.: University of Minnesota Press.

Downs, George W., David M. Rocke, and Peter N. Barsoom. 1996. 'Is the Good News About Compliance Good News About Cooperation?', *International Organization* 50(3): 379–406.

Doyle, William. 1984. 'The Price of Offices in Pre-Revolutionary France', *Historical Journal* 27(4): 831–860.

Drury, A. Cooper, and Richard Stuart Olson. 1998. 'Disasters and Political Unrest: An Empirical Investigation', *Journal of Contingencies and Crisis Management* 6(3): 153–161.

Durham, William H. 1979. *Scarcity and Survival in Central America: Ecological Origins of the Soccer War*. Stanford, Calif.: Stanford University Press.

Durning, Alan. 1990. *Apartheid's Environmental Toll*. Worldwatch Paper (95). Washington, D.C.: Worldwatch.

Easterbrook, Gregg. 1995. *A Moment on the Earth. The Coming Age of Environmental Optimism*. New York: Viking Penguin. [Paperback edition: New York: Penguin. 1996.]

Eberstadt, Nicholas. 1988. *The Poverty of Communism*. New Brunswick, N.J.: Transaction Books.

———. 1993. *North Korea: Reform, Muddling Through, or Collapse?* NBAR Analysis 4(3). Seattle, Wash.: National Bureau of Asian Research.

———. 1998. 'Demography and International Relations', *Washington Quarterly* 21(2): 33–52.

Eckstein, Harry. 1975. 'Case Study and Theory in Political Science', in *Strategies of Inquiry: Handbook of Political Science, vol. 7*, pp. 79–137, ed. Fred I. Greenstein and Nelson W. Polsby. Reading, Mass.: Addison-Wesley.

Eckstein, Harry, and Ted R. Gurr. 1975. *Patterns of Authority: A Structural Basis for Political Inquiry*. New York: Wiley.

Ehrlich, Anne H., and Paul R. Ehrlich. 1987. *Earth*. London: Methuen.

Ehrlich, Paul R. 1968. *The Population Bomb*. New York: Ballantine.

Ehrlich, Paul R., and Anne H. Ehrlich. 1972. *Population, Resources, Environment. Issues in Human Ecology*, 2d ed. San Francisco, Calif.: Freeman. [Originally published in 1970.]

———. 1991. *The Population Explosion*. New York: Touchstone.

———. 1996. *Betrayal of Science and Reason. How Anti-Environmental Rhetoric Threatens Our Future*. Washington, D.C. and Covelo, Calif.: Island Press.

EIA. 1993. *Renewable Resources in the U.S. Electricity Supply*. Washington, D.C.: Energy Information Agency, U.S. Department of Energy, http://www.eia.-doe.gov/cneaf/electricity/pub_summaries/renew_es.html.

———. 1997a. *Annual Energy Review 1996*. Washington, D.C.: Energy Information Agency, U.S. Department of Energy, http://www.eia.doe.gov/emeu/aer/contents.html.

———. 1997b. *International Energy Outlook 1997*. Energy Information Agency, U.S. Department of Energy, http://www.eia.doe.gov/bookshelf.html.

———. 1998. *International Energy Annual 1996*. Energy Information Agency, U.S. Department of Energy, http://www.eia.doe.gov/emeu/iea/contents.html.

———. 1999. *Annual Energy Outlook 1999*. Energy Information Agency, U.S. Department of Energy, http://www.eia.doe.gov/oiaf/ieo99/pdf/048499.pdf.

El-Ashry, Mohamed T. 1994. 'Commentary, the New GEF', *Environment* 36(6): 37–38.

———. 1995a. 'Water Resources: A Global Environmental Perspective', Stockholm (Sweden) Water Symposium, 16 August. Available at www.worldbank.org/-html/gef/.

———. 1995b. 'Water Resources and Management in the 21st Century', Third Princess Chulabhorn Science Congress, Water and Development: Water Is Life, Bangkok (Thailand). Available at www.worldbank.org/html/gef/.

Ellingsen, Tanja. 2000. 'Colorful Community or Ethnic Witches' Brew? Political Regime and Armed Conflict 1945–92', *Journal of Conflict Resolution* 44(2): 228–249.

Ellingsen, Tanja, and Nils Petter Gleditsch. 1997. 'Democracy and Armed Conflict in the Third World', in Volden and Smith, eds. (69–81).

Engelman, Robert, and Pamela LeRoy. 1993. *Sustaining Water: Population and the Future of Renewable Water Supplies.* Washington, D.C.: Population Action International http://www.cnie.org/pop/pai/h2o-toc.html.

ERS. 1995. *World Population and Projections to 2050.* Database from Economic Research Service, U.S. Department of Agriculture, based on U.S. Census data, http://usda.mannlib.cornell.edu/data-sets/general/95010/.

———. 1997. International Agricultural Baseline Projections to 2005. Economic Research Service, U.S. Department of Agriculture, http://www.econ.ag.gov/-epubs/pdf/aer750/

Escobar, Arturo. 1995. *Encountering Development: The Making and Unmaking of the Third World.* Princeton, N.J.: Princeton University Press.

Esty, Daniel. 1999. 'Pivotal States and the Environment,' in *A New Framework for US Policy in the Developing World,* pp. 290–314, ed. Robert Chase, Emily Hill, and Paul Kennedy. New York: Norton.

Esty, Daniel, Jack A. Goldstone, Ted Robert Gurr, Barbara Harff, Pamela Surko, and Alan N. Unger. 1995. *State Failure Task Force Report.* McLean, Va.: Science Applications International, for State Failure Task Force.

Esty, Daniel, Jack A. Goldstone, Ted Robert Gurr, Barbara Harff, Marc Levy, Geoffrey D. Dabelko, Pamela Surko, and Alan N. Unger. 1998. *State Failure Task Force Report: Phase II Findings.* McLean, Va.: Science Applications International, for State Failure Task Force.

Fairman, David. 1994a. 'Report on Reports, Report of the Independent Evaluation of the Global Environment Facility Pilot Phase', *Environment* 36(6): 25–30.

———. 1994b. 'Commentary, the New GEF', *Environment* 36(6): 39.

Falkenmark, Malin, and Gunnar Lindh. 1993. 'Water and Economic Development', in Gleick, ed., 1993b (80–91).

Falkenmark, Malin, Jan Lundqvist, and Carl G. Widstrand. 1989. 'Macro-Scale Water Scarcity Requires Micro-Scale Approaches', *Natural Resources Forum* 13(4): 258–267.

Falkenmark, Malin, and Carl G. Widstrand. 1992. 'Population and Water Resources: A Delicate Balance', *Population Bulletin* 47(3): 2–36.

FAO, annual. *FAO Production Yearbook.* Rome: Food and Agricultural Organization.

FAO. 1984. *Systematic Index of International Water Resources Treaties, Declarations, Acts, and Cases, by Basin: Volume II.* Legislative Study (34). Rome: Food and Agriculture Organization.

———. 1993. 'Forest Resources Assessment 1990: Tropical Countries', *FAO Forestry Paper* 112. Rome: Food and Agriculture Organization.

———. 1995a. 'Forest Resources Assessment 1990: Global Synthesis', *FAO Forestry Paper* 124. Rome: Food and Agriculture Organization.

———. 1995b. *World Agriculture: Towards 2010. An FAO Study.* Nikos Alexandratos, ed. Rome: Food and Agriculture Organization.

———. 1997. *The State of Food and Agriculture.* Rome: Food and Agriculture Organization. Including electronic database.

———. 1999a. *The State of Food and Agriculture. 1999*. Rome: Food and Agriculture Organization.

———. 1999b. *The State of Food Insecurity in the World. 1999*. Rome: Food and Agriculture Organization.

———. 2000. FAO database, accessible from http:\\www.fao.org.

Feierabend, Ivo K., Rosalind L. Feierabend, and Betty A. Nesvold. 1970. 'Social Change and Political Violence: Cross-National Patterns', in *Violence in America: Historical and Comparative Perspectives*, rev. ed., pp. 632–687, ed. Hugh Davis Graham and Ted Robert Gurr. New York: Praeger. [First published in 1969.]

Fig, David. 1996. 'Environmental Flashpoints in South Africa', *Track Two* 5(4): 4–6.

Finger, Matthias. 1991. 'The Military, the Nation State and the Environment', *Ecologist* 21(5): 220–225.

Finnemore, Martha. 1996. *National Interests in International Society*. Ithaca, N.Y.: Cornell University Press.

Fischer, Hubertus, Martin Wahlen, Jesse Smith, Derek Mastroianni, and Bruce Deck. 1999. 'Ice Core Records of Atmospheric CO_2 Around the Last Three Glacial Terminations', *Science* 283(5408): 1712–1714.

Fisher, Frank. 1994. *The Harvard Middle East Water Project: Brief Summary*. Cambridge, Mass.: Institute for Social and Economic Policy in the Middle East, John F. Kennedy School of Government, Harvard University.

Flanagan, William H., and Ernst Vogelman. 1970. 'Patterns of Political Violence in Comparative Historical Perspective', *Comparative Politics* 3(1): 1–20.

Foran, John, ed. 1997. *Theorizing Revolutions*. London: Routledge.

French, Hilary F. 1994. 'Rebuilding the World Bank', in Lester R. Brown et al., *State of the World 1994*. New York: Norton (156–176).

———. 1995. *Partnership for the Planet: An Environmental Agenda for the United Nations*. Worldwatch Paper (126). Washington, D.C.: Worldwatch.

Gallagher, Michael G. 1994. 'China's Illusory Threat to the South China Sea', *International Security* 19(1): 169–194.

Galtung, Johan. 1969. 'Violence, Peace, and Peace Research', *Journal of Peace Research* 6(3):167–191. Reprinted in Johan Galtung: *Essays in Peace Research*, vol. 1: *Peace: Research–Education–Action*. Copenhagen: Ejlers. 1975 (109–134).

———. 1982. *Environment, Development and Military Activity. Towards Alternative Security Doctrines*. Oslo: Norwegian University Press.

Gandar, Mark. 1991. 'The Imbalance of Power', in *Going Green: People, Politics and the Environment in South Africa*, pp. 94–109, ed. Jacklyn Cock and Eddie Koch. Cape Town: Oxford University Press.

Garavito, R. Michael. 1999. 'Working Knowledge: Aspirin', *Scientific American* 280(5): 96.

Gardner-Outlaw, Tom, and Robert Engelman. 1997. *Sustaining Water, Easing Scarcity: A Second Update*. Revised data for the Population Action International report 1993: *Sustaining Water: Population and the Future of Renewable Water Supplies*. Population Action International, http://www.populationaction.org/-why_pop/water/water-toc.htm.

Garver, John W. 1992. 'China's Push Through the South China Sea', *China Quarterly* (132): 999–1028.

Gastil, Raymond D. 1988. *Freedom in the World: Political Rights and Civil Liberties 1987–1988.* New York: Freedom House.

GEF. 1995. 'Public Involvement in GEF Projects'. Washington, D.C.: Global Environment Facility. Available at www.gefweb.org.

_____. 1996. 'GEF Business Plan for FY98-FY00', prepared for the October 1996 Council Meeting. Washington, D.C.: Global Environment Facility. Available at www.gefweb.org.

_____. 1998a. 'Questions and Answers'. Washington, D.C.: Global Environment Facility. Available at www.gefweb.org.

_____. 1998b. 'Project Performance Report'. Washington, D.C.: Global Environment Facility. Available at www.gefweb.org.

_____. 1999. 'Introduction to the GEF'. Washington, D.C.: Global Environment Facility. Available at www.gefweb.org.

George, Alexander L. 1979. 'Case Studies and Theory Development: The Method of Structured, Focussed Comparison', in *Diplomacy: New Approaches in History, Theory, and Policy,* pp. 43–63, ed. Paul G. Lauren. New York: Free Press.

George, Alexander L., and Andrew Bennett. 2000. *Case Studies and Theory Development.* Cambridge, Mass.: MIT Press.

George, Alexander L., and Timothy McKeown. 1985. 'Case Studies and Theories of Organizational Decision Making', in *Advances in Information Processing in Organizations,* pp. 21–58, ed. Robert Coulam and Richard Smith. London: JAI Press.

George, Susan. 1992. *The Debt Boomerang. How Third World Debt Harms Us All.* Amsterdam: Transnational Institute and Pluto.

Gissinger, Ranveig. 1997. *En kvantitativ analyse av avhengighet, ulikhet og væpnede konflikter.* [A Quantitative Analysis of Dependency, Inequality, and Armed Conflict.] Cand. polit. thesis, Norwegian University of Science and Technology, Trondheim.

Gissinger, Ranveig, and Nils Petter Gleditsch. 1999. 'Globalization and Conflict. Welfare, Distribution, and Political Unrest', *Journal of World-Systems Research* 5(2): 274–300, http://csf.colorado.edu/wsystems/jwsr.html.

Gleditsch, Nils Petter. 1994. 'Conversion and the Environment', ch. 7 in *Green Security or Militarized Environment?* pp. 131–154, ed. Jyrki Käkönen. Aldershot and Brookfield, Vt.: Dartmouth.

_____. 1995. 'Geography, Democracy, and Peace', *International Interactions* 20(4): 297–323.

_____. 1996. 'Det nye sikkerhetsbildet: Mot en demokratisk og fredelig verden?' [The New Security Environment: Towards a Democratic and Peaceful World?], *Internasjonal Politikk* 54(3): 291–310.

_____. 1997a. 'Environmental Conflict and the Democratic Peace', ch. 6 in Gleditsch, ed. 1997b (91–106).

_____. 2000. 'Resource and Environmental Conflict: The State of the Art', in *Responding to Environmental Conflicts: Implications for Theory and Practice,* ed. Alexander Carius. Dordrecht: Kluwer (in press).

_____. 2001. 'Armed Conflict and the Environment', ch. 12 in this volume. Revised version of article published in *Journal of Peace Research* 35(3): 381–400. 1998.

Gleditsch, Nils Petter, and Håvard Hegre. 1997. 'Democracy and Peace: Three Levels of Analysis', *Journal of Conflict Resolution* 41(2): 283–310.

Gleditsch, Nils Petter, and Bjørn Otto Sverdrup. 1996. 'Democracy and the Environment', paper presented to the Fourth National Conference in Political Science, Geilo, Norway, 8–9 January.

Gleditsch, Nils Petter, ed. 1997b. *Conflict and the Environment*. Dordrecht: Kluwer.

Gleick, Peter H. 1989. 'The Implications of Global Climate Changes for International Security', *Climate Change* 15 (October): 303–325.

_____. 1993a. 'An Introduction to Global Freshwater Issues', in Gleick, ed. 1993b (3–12).

_____. 1993c. 'Water and Conflict, Fresh Water Resources and International Security', *International Security* 18(1): 79–112.

_____. 1994. 'Water, War, and Peace in the Middle East', *Environment* 36(3): 6–18.

_____. 1996. 'Basic Water Requirements for Human Activities: Meeting Basic Needs', *Water International* 21(2): 83–92.

_____. 1998a. 'The Human Right to Water', *Water Policy* 1: 487–503.

_____. 1998b. *The World's Water: The Biennial Report on Fresh Water Resources*. Washington, D.C. and Covelo, Calif.: Island Press.

Gleick, Peter H., ed. 1993b. *Water in Crisis. A Guide to the World's Fresh Water Resources*. New York and Oxford: Oxford University Press, for Pacific Institute for Studies in Development, Environment and Security and Stockholm Environment Institute.

Glymour, Clark, Richard Scheines, Peter Spirtes, and Kevin Kelly. 1987. *Discovering Causal Structure: Artificial Intelligence, Philosophy of Science, and Statistical Modelling*. Orlando, Fla.: Academic Press.

Gochman, Charles. 1989. 'Capability-Driven Disputes', in *Prisoners of War? Nation-States in the Modern Era*, pp. 141–160, ed. Charles Gochman and Alan Sabrosky. Lexington, Mass.: Lexington Books.

_____. 1991. 'Interstate Metrics: Conceptualizing, Operationalizing, and Measuring the Geographic Proximity of States Since the Congress of Vienna', *International Interactions* 17(1): 93–112.

Gochman, Charles, and Zeev Maoz. 1984. 'Militarized Interstate Disputes: Procedures, Patterns, and Insights', *Journal of Conflict Resolution* 28(4): 585–615.

Goertz, Gary, and Paul F. Diehl. 1992. *Territorial Changes and International Conflict*. London and New York: Routledge.

Goldstone, Jack A. 1991. *Revolution and Rebellion in the Early Modern World*. Berkeley, Calif.: University of California Press.

_____. 1998a. 'The Soviet Union: Revolution and Transformation', in *Elites, Crises, and the Origins of Regimes*, pp. 95–124, ed. Mattei Dogan and John Higley. Lanham, Md.: Rowman and Littlefield.

_____. 1999a. 'Youth Bulges, Youth Cohorts, and Their Contribution to Periods of Rebellion and Revolution.' Manuscript, University of California, Davis.

_____. 1999b. 'Population and Pivotal States', in *The Pivotal States: A New Framework for US Policy in the Developing World*, pp. 247–269, ed. Robert Chase, Emily Hill, and Paul Kennedy. New York: Norton.

_____, ed. 1994. *Revolutions: Theoretical, Comparative, Historical, and Historical Studies*, 2d ed. Fort Worth, Tex.: Harcourt Brace.

_____, ed. 1998a. *The Encyclopedia of Political Revolutions*. Washington, D.C.: Congressional Quarterly.

Goodwin, Jeff. 1997. 'State-Centered Approaches to Social Revolutions', in *Theorizing Revolutions*, pp. 11–37, ed. John Foran. New York: Routledge.

Gore, Al. 1992. *Earth in the Balance. Ecology and the Human Spirit*. Boston, Mass.: Houghton Mifflin.

Grady, Denise. 1996. 'So, Smoking Causes Cancer: This Is News?', *New York Times*, 27 October, section 4: 3.

Græger, Nina. 1996. 'Environmental Security?', *Journal of Peace Research* 33(1): 109–116.

Grieco, Joseph M. 1990. *Cooperation Among Nations, Europe, America and Non-Tariff Barriers to Trade*. Ithaca, N.Y.: Cornell University Press.

Grunawalt, Richard J. 1993. *Targeting Enemy Merchant Shipping*. Newport, R.I.: Naval War College International Law Studies.

Guha, Ramachandra. 1997. 'The Authoritarian Biologist and the Arrogance of Anti-Humanism: Wildlife Conservation in the Third World', *Ecologist* 27(1): 14–20.

Gupta, Joyeeta. 1995. 'The Global Environment Facility in its North-South Context', *Environmental Politics* 4(1): 19–43.

Gurr, Ted Robert. 1980. *Handbook of Political Conflict*. New York: Free Press.

_____. 1993. *Minorities at Risk: A Global View of Ethnopolitical Conflicts*. Washington, D.C.: U.S. Institute of Peace.

Gurr, Ted Robert, and Barbara Harff. 1994. *Ethnic Conflict in World Politics*. Boulder, Colo.: Westview.

Haas, Ernst B. 1964. *Beyond the Nation-State: A Functional Theory of Politics*. Stanford, Calif.: Stanford University Press.

_____. 1991. *When Knowledge Is Power: Three Models of Change in International Organizations*. Berkeley, Calif.: University of California Press.

Haas, Peter M. 1990. *Saving the Mediterranean: The Politics of International Environmental Cooperation*. New York: Columbia University Press.

_____. 1992. 'Banning Chlorofluorocarbons: Epistemic Community Efforts to Protect Stratospheric Ozone', *International Organization* 46(1): 187–224.

Haas, Peter M., and Ernst B. Haas. 1995. 'Learning to Learn: Improving International Governance', *Global Governance* 1(3): 255–284.

Haas, Peter M., Robert O. Keohane, and Marc A. Levy. 1993. *Institutions for the Earth: Sources of Effective International Environmental Protection*. Cambridge, Mass.: MIT Press.

Haller-Trost, R. 1994. 'International Law and the History of the Claims to the Spratly Islands', preprint. Melbourne: Monash University.

Hammarström, Mats. 1986. *Securing Resources by Force. The Need for Raw Materials and Military Intervention by Major Powers in Less Developed Countries*. Report 27. Uppsala: Department of Peace and Conflict Research, Uppsala University.

————. 1997. 'Mineral Conflict and Mineral Supplies: Results Relevant to Wider Resource Issues', ch. 8 in Gleditsch, ed. 1997b (127–136).

Hardin, Garrett. 1968. 'The Tragedy of the Commons', *Science* 162(3859): 1243–1248. Reprinted in *Managing the Commons*, pp. 16–30, ed. Garrett Hardin and John Baden. New York: Freeman, 1977.

Harre, Rom. 1985. *The Philosophies of Science.* Oxford: Oxford University Press.

Harrison, Philip. 1992. 'The Policies and Politics of Informal Settlement in South Africa: A Historical Perspective', *Africa Insight* 22(1): 14–22.

Hauge, Wenche. 1997. 'Development and Conflict', in Volden and Smith, eds. (33–53).

Hauge, Wenche, and Tanja Ellingsen. 2001. 'Causal Pathways to Conflict', ch. 3 in this volume. Revised version of article published in *Journal of Peace Research* 35(1): 299–317. 1998.

Hauge, Wenche, and Håvard Hegre. 1997. 'Economic Development and Civil Conflict', paper presented to the 38th Annual Convention of the International Studies Association, Toronto, Canada, 18–22 March.

Hayes, Peter, and Lyuba Zarsky. 1994. 'Environmental Issues and Regimes in Northeast Asia', *International Environmental Affairs* 6(4): 283–319.

Haynes, Viktor, and Marko Bojcun. 1990. *The Chernobyl Disaster.* London: Hogarth.

Hegre, Håvard. 2000. 'Development and the Liberal Peace', *Journal of Peace Research* 37(1): 5–30.

Hegre, Håvard, Tanja Ellingsen, Nils Petter Gleditsch, and Scott Gates. 1999. 'Towards a Democratic Civil Peace? Opportunity, Grievance and Civil War 1816–1992', paper presented at the Launch Conference of the World Bank project on the Economics of Civil War, Crime, and Violence, Washington, D.C., 22–23 February, http://www.worldbank.org/research/conflict/ papers.htm.

Heilbroner, Robert L. 1974. *An Inquiry into the Human Prospect.* New York: Norton.

Heisler, Martin. 2000. 'Now and Then, Here and There: Migration and the Transformation of Identities, Borders and Orders', in *Identities, Borders, Orders*, ed. Mathias Albert, David Jacobson, and Yosef Lapid. Minneapolis, Minn.: University of Minnesota Press.

Henderson, Errol A., and J. David Singer. 2000. 'Civil War in the Post-Colonial World. 1945–1992', *Journal of Peace Research* 37(3): 275–299.

Herman, Arthur. 1997. *The Idea of Decline in Western History.* New York: Free Press.

Heske, Henning. 1987. 'Karl Haushofer: His Role in German Geopolitics and Nazi Politics', *Political Geography Quarterly* 6(20): 135–144.

Hill, Richard, Swarupa Ganguli, and Dede Naylor. 1998. 'Environmental Flashpoints in South Asia,' in *Consequences of Environmental Change–Political Economic, Social (Proceedings of the Environmental Flash Points Workshop, Reston, Virginia, 12–14 November 1997)*, pp. 127–176, ed. Robert S. Chen, W. Christopher Lenhardt, and Kara F. Alkire. University Center, Mich.: Consortium for International Earth Science Information Network.

Hille, John. 1995. *Sustainable Norway: Probing the Limits and Equity of Environmental Space.* Oslo: Project for an Alternative Future, http://afux.prosus.nfr.no/-af-pub/sustainable.

Hillel, Daniel. 1994. *Rivers of Eden: The Struggle for Water and the Quest for Peace in the Middle East.* New York: Oxford University Press.

Hindson, Doug, Mark Byerley, and Mike Morris. 1994. 'From Violence to Reconstruction: The Making, Disintegration, and Remaking of an Apartheid City', *Antipode* 26(4): 323–350.

Hindson, Doug, and Jeff McCarthy. 1994a. 'Defining and Gauging the Problem', in Hindson and McCarthy, eds. 1994b (1–28).

Hindson, Doug, and Jeff McCarthy, eds. 1994b. *Here to Stay: Informal Settlements in KwaZulu/Natal.* Dalbridge: Indicator Press.

Hindson, Doug, and Mike Morris. 1994. 'Violence in Natal/KwaZulu: Dynamics, Causes, Trends'. Unpublished paper, March.

Hinman, Helen. 1945. *Population Pressures: War and Poverty.* Newark, N.J.: Arthur W. Cross.

Hirschman, Albert O. 1981. *Essays in Trespassing: Economics to Politics and Beyond.* Cambridge: Cambridge University Press.

Hollick, Ann L. 1995. 'Ocean Law: Senate Approval of the UN Convention', *Strategic Forum* 41: 1–3.

Holst, Johan Jørgen. 1989. 'Security and the Environment: A Preliminary Exploration', *Bulletin of Peace Proposals* 20(2): 123–128.

Holsti, Kalevi J. 1991. *Peace and War. Armed Conflicts and International Order 1648–1989.* Cambridge: Cambridge University Press.

Homer-Dixon, Thomas F. 1991. 'On the Threshold: Environmental Changes as Causes of Acute Conflict', *International Security* 16(2): 76–116. Reprinted in Lynn-Jones and Miller, eds. 1995 (43–83).

_____. 1994. 'Environmental Scarcities and Violent Conflict: Evidence from Cases', *International Security* 19(1): 5–40. Reprinted in Lynn-Jones and Miller, eds. 1995 (144–179).

_____. 1995a. 'Environmental Scarcity and Intergroup Conflict', in Michael Klare and Daniel Thomas, *World Security: Challenges for the New Century*, 2d ed. New York: St. Martin's (290–313).

_____. 1995b. 'The Ingenuity Gap: Can Poor Countries Adapt to Resource Scarcity?', *Population and Development Review* 21(5): 587–612.

_____. 1995c. *Strategies for Studying Causation in Complex Ecological Political Systems.* Toronto: Project on Environment, Population and Security, University College, University of Toronto and Washington, D.C.: American Association for the Advancement of Science.

_____. 1996. 'Strategies for Studying Complex Ecological-Political Systems', *Journal of Environment and Development* 5(2): 132–148.

_____. 1999. *Environment, Scarcity, and Violence.* Princeton, N.J.: Princeton University Press.

Homer-Dixon, Thomas F., Jeffrey H. Boutwell, and George W. Rathjens. 1993. 'Environmental Change and Violent Conflict', *Scientific American* 268(2): 38–45.

Homer-Dixon, Thomas F., and Marc A. Levy. 1995/1996. 'Correspondence: Environment and Security', *International Security* 20(3): 189–198.

Homer-Dixon, Thomas F., and Valerie Percival. 1996. *Environmental Scarcity and Violent Conflict: Briefing Book.* Toronto: Project on Environment, Population, and Security, University of Toronto and Washington, D.C.: American Association for the Advancement of Science.

Homer-Dixon, Thomas F., and Jessica Blitt, eds. 1998. *Ecoviolence: Links Among Environment, Population, and Security*. Lanham, MD and Oxford: Rowman and Littlefield.

Howard, Philip, and Thomas F. Homer-Dixon. 1995. *Environmental Scarcity and Violent Conflict: The Case of Chiapas, Mexico*. Toronto: Project on Environment, Population and Security, University College, University of Toronto and Washington, D.C.: American Association for the Advancement of Science. [Reprinted as ch. 2 of Homer-Dixon and Blitt, eds. 1998.]

Huang, Alexander Chieh-cheng. 1994. 'The Chinese Navy's Offshore Active Defense Strategy: Conceptualizations and Implications', *Naval War College Review* 47(3): 7–31.

Hume, David. 1754. 'Of the Populousness of Ancient Nations'. Reprinted in David Hume. 1985: *Essays: Moral, Political and Literary*. Indianapolis, Ind.: Liberty Classics.

Huntington, Samuel P. 1968. *Political Order in Changing Societies*. New Haven, Conn.: Yale University Press.

_____. 1991. *The Third Wave: Democratization in the Late Twentieth Century*. Norman, Okla., and London: University of Oklahoma Press.

Huth, Paul K. 1996. *Standing Your Ground. Territorial Disputes and International Conflict*. Ann Arbor, Mich.: University of Michigan Press.

IFPRI. 1997. *The World Food Situation: Recent Developments, Emerging Issues, and Long-Term Prospects*. By Per Pinstrup-Andersen, Rajul Pandya-Lorch, and Mark W. Rosegrant. Washington, D.C.: International Food Policy Research Institute, http://www.cgiar.org/ifpri/pubs/2catalog.htm.

Iida, Keisuke. 1993. 'Analytic Uncertainty and International Cooperation: Theory and Application to International Economic Policy Coordination', *International Studies Quarterly* 37(4): 431–457.

IMF. 1999. Data from *International Statistical Yearbook*. Updates available at http://www.imf.org/external/np/res/commod/index.htm.

Inayatullah, Naeem, and David L. Blaney. 1996. 'Knowing Encounters: Beyond Parochialism in International Relations Theory', in *The Return of Culture and Identity in IR Theory*, pp. 65–84, ed. Yosef Lapid and Friedrich Kratochwil. Boulder, Colo.: Lynne Rienner.

Inglehart, Ronald F., Neil Nevitte, and Miguel Basañez. 1996. *The North American Trajectory: Cultural, Economic, and Political Ties Among the United States, Canada, and Mexico*. New York: Aldine de Gruyter.

IPCC. 1995. *IPCC Second Assessment Report: Climate Change*. Geneva: Intergovernmental Panel on Climate Change.

_____. 1997. *The Regional Impacts of Climate Change: An Assessment of Vulnerability*. Geneva: Intergovernmental Panel on Climate Change.

Island Resource Foundation. 1995. 'Global Environment Facility (GEF) Overview and the Role of NGOs in GEF', February. Available at www.microstate.com/pub/micros/gef/gefover.html.

Ivanhoe, L. F. 1995. 'Future World Oil Supplies: There Is a Finite Limit', *World Oil* (October): 77–88.

Jaggers, Keith, and Ted R. Gurr. 1995. 'Tracking Democracy's Third Wave with the Polity III Data', *Journal of Peace Research* 32(4): 469–482.

Jakobsen, Monica S. 1996. 'Peace and Prosperity or Democratic Chaos? A Study of Regime Transitions and Civil War 1945–92', paper presented to the 37th Annual Convention of the International Studies Association, San Diego, Calif., 16–20 April.

Jänicke, Martin. 1996. 'Democracy as a Condition for Environmental Policy Success: The Importance of Non-Institutional Factors', in Lafferty and Meadowcroft eds. 1996a (71–85).

Jerusalem Report. 2000. 'Source of Peace?', 13 March.

Johnson, C. 1995. 'Active Explorations: Wan' An Bei', preprint. Honolulu: East-West Center.

Johnston, Alastair Iain. 1995–1996. 'China's New "Old Thinking": The Concept of Limited Deterrence', *International Security* 20(3): 5–42.

Jones, Daniel, Stuart Bremer, and J. David Singer. 1996. 'Militarized Interstate Disputes, 1816–1992: Rationale, Coding Rules, and Empirical Patterns', *Conflict Management and Peace Science* 15(2): 163–213.

Jordan, Andrew. 1994a. 'Paying the Incremental Costs of Global Environmental Protection: The Evolving Role of GEF', *Environment* 36(6): 12–20, 31–36.

_____. 1994b. 'Commentary, the New GEF', *Environment* 36(6): 38–39.

Kahl, Colin H. 1998. 'Population Growth, Environmental Degradation, and State-Sponsored Violence: The Case of Kenya. 1991–93', *International Security* 23(2): 80–119.

Kaplan, Abraham. 1964. *The Conduct of Inquiry: Methodology for Behavioural Science.* San Francisco, Calif.: Chandler.

Kaplan, Robert. 1994. 'The Coming Anarchy', *Atlantic Monthly* 273(2): 44–76.

Katzenstein, Peter J., ed. 1996. *The Culture of National Security: Norms and Identity in World Politics.* New York: Columbia University Press.

Keck, Margaret, and Kathryn Sikkink. 1998. *Activists Beyond Borders: Advocacy Networks and International Politics.* Ithaca, N.Y.: Cornell University Press.

Kegley, Charles, and Eugene Wittkopf. 1995. 'Population and the Global Habitat', in *The Global Agenda,* 4th ed., pp. 343–357, ed. Charles Kegley and Eugene Wittkopf. New York: McGraw-Hill.

Kelly, Kimberley, and Thomas F. Homer-Dixon. 1995. *Environmental Scarcity and Violent Conflict: The Case of Gaza.* Toronto: Project on Environment, Population and Security, University College, University of Toronto and Washington, D.C.: American Association for the Advancement of Science. [Reprinted as ch. 3 of Homer-Dixon and Blitt, eds. 1998.]

Kelman, Herbert C. 1997. 'Social-Psychological Dimensions of International Conflict,' in *Peacemaking in International Conflict: Methods and Techniques,* pp. 191–237, ed. I. William Zartman and J. Lewis Rasmussen. Washington, D.C.: U.S. Institute of Peace Press.

Kennedy, Donald. 1998. 'Environmental Quality and Regional *Conflict'. Report to the Carnegie Commission on Preventing Deadly Conflict.* Washington, D.C.: Carnegie Corporation.

Keohane, Robert O. 1984. *After Hegemony: Cooperation and Discord in the World Political Economy.* Princeton, N.J.: Princeton University Press.

Keohane, Robert O., and Joseph S. Nye. 1977. *Power and Interdependence: World Politics in Transition*. Boston, Mass.: Little, Brown.

Keohane, Robert O., and Elinor Ostrom, eds. 1995. *Local Commons and Global Interdependence: Heterogeneity and Cooperation in Two Domains*. London: Sage.

Ki, Maha, and Anthony Minnaar. 1994. 'Figuring Out the Problem: Overview of PWV Conflict from 1990–1993', *Indicator South Africa* 11(2): 25–28.

Kim, Hyun-Soo. 1994. 'The 1992 Chinese Territorial Sea Law in the Light of the UN Convention', *International and Comparative Law Quarterly* 43(4): 894–904.

Kincaid, Harold. 1994. 'Defending Laws in the Social Sciences', in *Readings in the Philosophy of Social Science*, pp. 497–514, ed. Michael Martin and Lee C. McIntyre. Cambridge, Mass: MIT Press.

King, Gary, Robert O. Keohane, and Sidney Verba. 1994. *Designing Social Inquiry. Scientific Inference in Qualitative Research*. Princeton, N.J.: Princeton University Press.

Kleinbaum, David G., Lawrence L. Kupper, and Keith E. Muller. 1988. *Applied Regression Analysis and Other Multivariate Methods*, 2d ed. Boston Mass.: PWS–Kent.

Klötzli, Stefan. 1997. 'The "Aral Sea Syndrome" and Regional Cooperation in Central Asia: Opportunity or Obstacle?', ch. 25 in Gleditsch, ed. 1997b (417–434).

Kolars, John, and William Mitchell. 1991. *The Euphrates River and the Southeast Anatolia Development Project*. Carbondale, Ill.: Southern Illinois University Press.

Kolko, Gabriel. 1985. *Anatomy of a War. Vietnam, the United States, and the Modern Historical Experience*. New York: Pantheon.

Krasner, Stephen D. 1985. *Structural Conflict, The Third World Against Global Liberalism*. Berkeley, Calif.: University of California Press.

Kuehls, Thom. 1996. *Beyond Sovereign Territory: The Space of Ecopolitics*. Minneapolis, Minn.: University of Minnesota Press.

Kugler, Jacek, and A.F.K. Organski. 1989. 'The Power Transition: A Retrospective and Prospective Evaluation', in Midlarsky, ed., (171–194).

Kugler, Jacek, and Douglas Lemke, eds. 1996. *Parity and War*. Ann Arbor, Mich.: University of Michigan Press.

LaFeber, Walter. 1980. *America, Russia, and the Cold War 1945–1980*, 4th ed. New York: Wiley. [First edition published in 1967.]

Lafferty, William M., and James Meadowcroft. 1996b. 'Democracy and the Environment: Congruence and Conflict–Preliminary Reflections', in Lafferty and Meadowcroft, eds. 1996a (1–17).

———. 1996c. Democracy and the Environment: Prospects for Greater Congruence', in Lafferty and Meadowcroft, eds. 1996a (256–272).

Lafferty, William M., and James Meadowcroft, eds. 1996a. *Democracy and the Environment: Problems and Prospects*. Cheltenham, England: Edward Elgar.

Lane, David. 1996. 'The Gorbachev Revolution: The Role of the Political Elite in Regime Disintegration', *Political Studies* 44(1): 4–23.

Lawson, Lesley. 1991. 'The Ghetto and the Greenbelt', in *Going Green: People, Politics and the Environment in South Africa*, pp. 46–62, ed. Jacklyn Cock and Eddie Koch. Cape Town: Oxford University Press.

Lee, Kuan Yew. 1995. 'Interview', *The Straits Times,* 13 May: 3.

Lee, Shin-wha. 1996. 'Not a One-Time Event: Environmental Change, Ethnic Rivalry, and Violent Conflict in the Third World', paper presented at the 37th Annual Convention of the International Studies Association, San Diego, Calif., 16–20 April.

Lele, Uma, and Steven Stone. 1989. *Population Pressure, the Environment and Agricultural Intensification: Variations on the Boserup Hypothesis.* MADIA discussion paper 4, Washington, D.C.: World Bank.

Leon, Javier, and Raimundo Soto. 1995. *Structural Breaks and Long-Run Trends in Commodity Prices.* Policy Research Working Paper 1406. Washington, D.C.: World Bank.

Leroy, Marcel. 1978. *Population and World Politics.* Leiden: Nijhoff.

_____. 1986. 'Human Population as a Factor in Strategic Policy and Action', in Westing, ed. (159–182).

Levy, Marc A. 1993. 'European Acid Rain: The Power of Tote-Board Diplomacy', in Haas, Keohane, and Levy, eds. (75–132).

_____. 1995. 'Is the Environment a National Security Issue?', *International Security* 20(2): 35–62.

Lewontin, Richard C. 1976. 'The Analysis of Variance and the Analysis of Causes', in *The IQ Controversy: Critical Readings,* pp. 179–193, ed. Ned J. Block and Gerald Dwarkin. New York: Pantheon.

Libiszewski, Stephan. 1992. 'What Is an Environmental Conflict?', in *Occasional Paper* (1). Bern: Swiss Peace Foundation and Zürich: Center for Security Studies and Conflict Research, Swiss Federal Institute of Technology.

_____. 1997. 'Integrating Political and Technical Approaches: Lessons from the Israeli-Jordanian Water Negotiations', ch. 23 in Gleditsch, ed., 1997b (385–402).

Lichbach, Mark Irving. 1989. 'An Evaluation of Does Economic Inequality Breed Political Conflict', *World Politics* 41(4): 431–470.

Lietzmann, Kurt M., and Gary D. Vest, , 2000. *Environment and Security in an International Context.* Report (232). Brussels: Committee on the Challenges of Modern Society, NATO; Bonn: Federal Ministry for the Environment, Nature Conservation and Nuclear Safety and Washington, D.C.: Department of Defense.

Liggit, Bruce. 1988. *An Investigation into Soil Erosion in the Mflozi Catchment: Final Report to the KwaZulu Bureau of Natural Resources.* Pietermaritzburg: Institute of Natural Resources, University of Natal, Investigational Report I/R.

Lijphart, Arend. 1975. *The Politics of Accommodation: Pluralism and Democracy.* Berkeley, Calif.: University of California Press.

Lipschutz, Ronnie D. 1989. *When Nations Clash: Raw Materials, Ideology, and Foreign Policy.* New York: Harper and Row.

_____. 1992. 'Reconstructing World Politics: The Emergence of Global Civil Society', *Millennium* 21(3): 389–420.

_____. 1997. 'Damming Troubled Waters: Conflict over the Danube. 1950–2000', paper presented at Environment and Security Conference, Institute of War and Peace Studies, Columbia University, New York, 24 October.

Lipschutz, Ronnie D., and John P. Holdren. 1990. 'Crossing Borders: Resource Flows, the Global Environment, and International Security', *Bulletin of Peace Proposals* 21(2): 121–133.

Lipschutz, Ronnie D., with Judith Mayer. 1996. *Global Civil Society and Global Environmental Governance: The Politics of Nature from Place to Planet.* Albany, N.Y.: State University of New York Press.

Lipschutz, Ronnie D., and Ken Conca, eds. 1993. *The State and Social Power in Global Environmental Politics.* New York: Columbia University Press.

Litfin, Karen T. 1994. *Ozone Discourses.* New York: Columbia University Press.

_____. 1995. 'Framing Science: Precautionary Discourse and the Ozone Treaties', *Millennium* 24(2): 251–277.

_____. 1997. 'Sovereignty in World Ecopolitics', *Mershon International Studies Review* 41(2): 167–204.

_____. 1998a. 'Satellites and Sovereign Knowledge: Remote Sensing of the Global Environment', in Litfin, ed. 1998b (193–221).

Litfin, Karen T., ed. 1998b. *The Greening of Sovereignty in World Politics.* Cambridge, Mass.: MIT Press.

Lodgaard, Sverre. 1992. 'Environmental Security, World Order and Environmental Conflict Resolution', in *Conversion and the Environment,* pp. 115–136, ed. Nils Petter Gleditsch. *Proceedings of a Seminar in Perm, Russia, 24–27 November 1991.* PRIO Report (2).

Lomborg, Bjørn. 1998. *Verdens Sande Tilstand* [The True State of the World]. Copenhagen: Centrum. [English language edition forthcoming, Cambridge: Cambridge University Press, 2001.]

_____. 2001. 'Resource Constraints or Abundance?', ch. 7 in this volume.

Lonergan, Steve C. 1994. *Environmental Change and Regional Security in Southeast Asia.* Ottawa: Department of National Defense, Canada, ORAE Report PR 659.

_____. 1997. 'Water Resources and Conflict: Examples from the Middle East', ch. 22 in Gleditsch, ed. 1997b (374–384).

_____. 2001. 'Water Wars: Rhetoric and Reality', ch. 6 in this volume.

Lonergan, Steve C., and David Brooks. 1994. *Watershed: The Role of Freshwater in the Israeli-Palestinian Conflict.* Ottawa: International Development Research Centre Books.

Lonergan, Steve C., Richard DiFrencesco, and Ming-Ko Woo. 1993. 'Climate Change and Transportation in Northern Canada: An Integrated Impact Assessment', *Climatic Change* 24(4): 331–352.

Lonergan, Steve C., ed. 1999. *Environmental Change, Adaptation, and Human Security.* Dordrecht: Kluwer.

Louw, Antoinette. 1992. 'Political Conflict in Natal 1989–92', *Indicator South Africa* 9(3): 57–59.

_____. 1993. 'Wars of Weapons, Wars of Words', *Indicator South Africa* 11(1): 65–70.

_____. 1994a. 'Conflicting Views', *Indicator South Africa* 11(3): 14–18.

_____. 1994b. 'Conflict of Interest', *Indicator South Africa* 11(2): 17–21.

_____. 1994c. 'Post-Election Conflict in KwaZulu-Natal', *Indicator South Africa* 11(4): 14–17.

Lowi, Miriam R. 1993a. 'Bridging the Divide, Transboundary Resource Disputes and the Case of West Bank Water', *International Security* 18(1): 113–138.

_____. 1993b. *Water and Power: The Politics of a Scarce Resource in the Jordan River Basin.* Cambridge: Cambridge University Press.

_____. 1999. 'Water and Conflict in the Middle East and South Asia: Are Environmental Issues and Security Issues Linked?', *Journal of Environment and Development* 8(4): 376–396.

Lund, Michael S. 1996. *Preventing Violent Conflicts, A Strategy for Preventive Diplomacy.* Washington, D.C.: United States Institute of Peace Press.

Lye, Keith, and Shirley Carpenter. 1987. *Encyclopedia of World Geography.* New York: Dorset.

Lynn-Jones, Sean, and Steven E. Miller, eds. 1995. *Global Dangers. Changing Dimensions of International Security.* Cambridge, Mass., and London: MIT Press.

MacKenzie, Craig. 1994. *Degradation of Arable Land Resources: Policy Options and Considerations Within the Context of Rural Restructuring in South Africa.* Working Paper 8. Johannesburg: Land and Agriculture Policy Centre.

Mackie, John L. 1965. 'Causes and Conditions', *American Philosophical Quarterly* 2(4): 245–264.

Maddox, John. 1972. *The Doomsday Syndrome.* New York: McGraw-Hill.

Malthus, Thomas, 1798. *An Essay on the Principle of Population.* Reprinted, Oxford: Oxford University Press. 1993.

Mandel, Robert. 1980. 'Roots of the Modern Interstate Border Dispute', *Journal of Conflict Resolution* 24(3): 427–454.

Markoff, John. 1999. 'Globalization and the Future of Democracy.' *Journal of World-Systems Research* 5(2): 242–262, http://csf.colorado.edu/wsystems/-jwsr.html.

Mathews, Jessica T. 1989. 'Redefining Security', *Foreign Affairs* 68(2): 162–177.

Mbeki, Thabo. 1999. 'Thabo Mbeki's Speech: Full Text', *BBC Online Network News,* 16 June, http://news2.thdo.bbc.co.uk/hi/english/world/africa/newsiid 370000/370679.stm

McGrath, Mike, and Andrew Whiteford. 1994. 'Disparate Circumstances', *Indicator South Africa* 11(3): 47–50.

McHugh, Paul D. 1985. 'Delimitation of Maritime Boundaries', *Natural Resources Journal* 25(4): 1025–1038.

McInnis, Colin, and Mark G. Rolls, eds. 1994. *Post-Cold War Security Issues in the Asia-Pacific Region.* Portland, Oreg.: Frank Cass.

McKeown, Timothy J. 1999. 'Case Studies and the Statistical Worldview', *International Organization* 53(1): 161–190.

McMichael, Anthony J. 1993. *Planetary Overload.* Cambridge: Cambridge University Press. [Paperback edition, Cambridge: Canto. 1995.]

McMillan, Susan M. 1997. 'Interdependence and Conflict', *Mershon International Studies Review* 41(1): 33–58.

Meadows, Donella H., Dennis L. Meadows, and Jørgen Randers. 1992. *Beyond the Limits.* London: Earthscan.

Meadows, Donella H., Dennis Meadows, Jørgen Randers, and William Behrens. 1972. *The Limits to Growth: A Report for the Club of Rome's Project on the Predicament of Mankind.* New York: Universe and London: Potomac Associates.

Merritt, Richard. 1995. 'Population Imbalance and Political Destabilization', *International Political Science Review* 16(4): 405–425.

Meyer, John W., David John Frank, Ann Hironaka, Evan Schofer, and Nancy Brandon Tuma. 1997. 'The Structuring of a World Environmental Regime, 1870–1990', *International Organization* 51(4): 623–651.

Midlarsky, Manus I. 1988. 'Rulers and the Ruled: Patterned Inequality and the On-set of Mass Political Violence', *American Political Science Review* 82(2): 491–509.

_____. 1995. 'Environmental Influences on Democracy: Aridity, Warfare, and a Reversal of the Causal Arrow', *Journal of Conflict Resolution* 39(2): 224–262.

_____. 1998. 'Democracy and Islam: Implications for Civilizational Conflict and the Democratic Peace', *International Studies Quarterly* 42(3): 485–511.

_____. 1999. *The Evolution of Inequality: War, State Survival, and Democracy in Comparative Perspective.* Stanford, Calif.: Stanford University Press.

_____. 2001. 'Democracy and the Environment', ch. 8 in this volume. Revised version of article published in *Journal of Peace Research* 35(3): 341–361. 1998.,

Midlarsky, Manus I., ed. 1989. *Handbook of War Studies.* Boston, Mass.: Unwin Hyman.

Migdal, Joel. 1994. 'The State in Society', in *State Power and Social Forces,* pp. 7–36, ed. Joel Migdal, Atul Kohli, and Vivienne Shue. Cambridge: Cambridge University Press.

Miller, G. Tyler, Jr. 1998. *Living in the Environment: Principles, Connections, and Solutions.* Belmont, Calif.: Wadsworth.

Miller, Richard. 1987. *Fact and Method.* Princeton, N.J.: Princeton University Press.

Minnaar, Anthony. 1992. 'Undisputed Kings: Warlordism in Natal', in *Patterns of Violence: Case Studies of Conflict in Natal,* pp. 61–94, ed. Anthony Minnaar. Pretoria: Human Sciences Research Council.

_____. 1994. *An Overview of Political Violence and Conflict Trends in South Africa with Specific Reference to the Period January-June 1994.* Pretoria: Centre for Socio-Political Analysis, Human Sciences Research Council, July.

Mitchell, Ronald B. 1994. *Intentional Oil Pollution at Sea: Environmental Policy and Treaty Compliance.* Cambridge, Mass.: MIT Press.

Mitrany, David. 1966. *A Working Peace System.* Chicago, Ill.: Quadrangle.

_____. 1976. *The Functionalist Theory of Politics.* New York: St. Martin's.

Mkhondo, Rich. 1993. *Reporting South Africa.* London: Heinemann.

Moller, Valerie. 1994. 'Post-Election Euphoria', *Indicator South Africa* 12(1): 27–32.

Moltzin, Inga. 1991. 'Do-it-Yourself Urban Living', *New Ground* 3(1): 14–17.

Morgenthau, Hans, as revised by Kenneth W. Thompson. 1985. *Politics Among Nations, The Struggle for Power and Peace,* 6th ed. New York: Knopf.

Morris, Mike, and Doug Hindson. 1992. 'The Dis-integration of Apartheid: From Violence to Reconstruction', in *South African Review,* pp. 152–170, ed. Glenn Moss and Ingrid Obery. Braamfontein: Ravan.

_____. 1994. 'Power Relations in Informal Settlements', in Hindson and Mc-Carthy, eds. 1994b (157–166).

Most, Benjamin, and Harvey Starr. 1989. *Inquiry, Logic, and International Politics.* Columbia, S.C.: University of South Carolina Press.

Moulin, Hervé. 1995. *Cooperative Microeconomics: A Game-Theoretic Introduction.* Princeton, N.J.: Princeton University Press.

Moussis, Nicholas. 1995. *Handbook of European Union: Institutions and Policies.* Rixensart: Edit-Eur.

Mueller, John. 1989. *Retreat from Doomsday. The Obsolescence of Major War.* New York: Basic Books. [Paperback edition 1990.]

Muller, Edward N., and Mitchell A. Seligson. 1987. 'Inequality and Insurgency', *American Political Science Review* 81(2): 425–451.

Muller, Edward N., and Erich Weede. 1990. 'Cross National Variation in Political Violence. A Rational Action Approach', *Journal of Conflict Resolution* 34(4): 624–651.

Murdo, P. 1995. 'Evolution of Japan's Fishing Industry: A Cautionary Tale', *Japan Economic Institute Report* 38a: 1–17.

Myers, John G., Stephen Moore, and Julian L. Simon. 1995. 'Trends in Availability of Non-Fuel Minerals' in Simon, ed. 1995a (303–312).

Myers, Norman. 1993. *Ultimate Security: The Environmental Basis of Political Stability.* New York: Norton.

Myers, Norman, and Julian Simon. 1994. *Scarcity and Abundance? A Debate on the Environment.* New York and London: Norton.

Narayan, Deepa. 1995. *The Contribution of People's Participation, Evidence from 121 Rural Water Supply Projects.* Environmentally Sustainable Development Occasional Paper Series no. 1. Washington, D.C.: World Bank.

Nash, Linda. 1993. 'Water Quality and Health', in Gleick, ed. 1993b (25–39).

Nordhaus, William D. 1994. *Managing the Global Commons. The Economics of Climate Change.* Cambridge, Mass.: MIT Press.

North, Robert. 1984. 'Integrating the Perspectives: From Population to Conflict and War', in Choucri, ed. (195–215).

O'Boyle, Lenore. 1970. 'The Problem of an Excess of Educated Men in Western Europe, 1800–1850', *Journal of Modern History* 42(4): 471–495.

Ohlsson, Leif. 1999. *Environment, Scarcity and Conflict: A Study of Malthusian Concerns.* Ph.D. diss. Göteborg: Department of Peace and Development Research, Göteborg University.

Oldeman, L. R. 1992. *Global Extent of Soil Degradation. Bi-Annual Report 1991–1992.* Wageningen: International Soil Reference Center and Nairobi: United Nations Environment Programme.

Oldeman, L. R., R.T.A. Hakkeling, and W. G. Sombroek. 1991. *World Map of the Status of Human-Induced Soil Degradation: An Explanatory Note.* Wageningen: International Soil Reference Center and Nairobi: United Nations Environment Programme, 2d rev. ed.. [First edition published in 1990.]

Olzak, Susan, and Johan Olivier. 1994. 'The Dynamics of Ethnic Collective Action in South Africa and the United States: A Comparative Study'. Unpublished paper, June.

Oneal, John R., and Bruce M. Russett. 1997. 'The Classical Liberals Were Right: Democracy, Interdependence, and Conflict. 1950–1985', *International Studies Quarterly* 41(2): 267–293.

O'Neill, J. O. 1993. *Ecology, Policy and Politics. Human Well-Being and the Natural World.* London: Routledge.

Ong'wen, Oduor. 1995. 'NGOs Want More from the Restructured Global Environment Facility', *Econews Africa*, 20 April. Available at www.web.net/econews/-enav4n8a.html.

Opschoor, Johannes B. 1989. 'North-South Trade, Resource Degradation and Economic Security', *Bulletin of Peace Proposals* 20(2): 135–142.

Organski, A.F.K. 1958. *World Politics*. New York: Knopf.

Organski, A.F.K., Jacek Kugler, J. Timothy Johnson, and Youssef Cohen. 1984. *Births, Deaths, and Taxes*. Chicago, Ill.: University of Chicago Press.

Organski, Katherine, and A.F.K. Organski. 1961. *Population and World Power*. New York: Knopf.

Oye, Kenneth A., ed. 1986. *Cooperation Under Anarchy*. Princeton, N.J.: Princeton University Press.

Paehlke, Robert. 1996. 'Environmental Challenges to Democratic Practice', in Lafferty and Meadowcroft, eds. 1996a (18–38).

Pan, Shiying. 1993. 'The Nansha Islands: A Chinese Point of View', *Window* 13 May: 23–39.

Park, Choon-Ho. 1978. 'The South China Sea Disputes: Who Owns the Islands and the Natural Resources?', *Ocean Development and International Law* 5(1): 27–59.

Park, Jacob. 1995. 'Finding Funds for Asia's Environmental Needs', *Christian Science Monitor*, 18 October.

Parry, Martin, Blantran de Rozari, Chong Ah Look, and Sangsant Panich. 1992. *The Potential Socio-Economic Effects of Climate Change in Southeast Asia*. United Nations Environment Program, Earthwatch Global Environment Monitoring System: Nairobi.

Payne, Rodger A. 1995a. 'Freedom and the Environment', *Journal of Democracy* 6(3): 41–55.

———. 1995b. 'Non-Profit Environmental Organizations in World Politics; Domestic Political Structure and Transnational Relations', *Policy Studies Review* 14(1/2): 171–182.

———. 1996. 'Deliberating Global Environmental Politics', *Journal of Peace Research* 33(2): 129–136.

———. 1997. 'The Democratization of (Sustainable) Development, Recent Innovations at the World Bank and GEF', International Studies Association, Annual Meeting, Toronto, Ontario, March.

Pearce, David W., and R. Kerry Turner. 1990. *Economics of Natural Resources and the Environment*. Baltimore, Md.: Johns Hopkins University Press.

Pearce, E. A., and C. G. Smith. 1984. *The Times Books World Weather Guide*. New York: New York Times Books.

Peden, Morag. 1993. *Tree Utilization in KwaZulu and the Future Provision of Tree Products*. Working paper 88. Pietermaritzburg: Institute of Natural Resources, University of Natal.

Peluso, Nancy. 1993. 'Coercing Conservation,' in Lipschutz and Conca, eds. (46–70).

Percival, Valerie, and Thomas F. Homer-Dixon. 1995. *Environmental Scarcity and Violent Conflict: The Case of Rwanda*. Toronto: Project on Environment, Population and Security, University College, University of Toronto and Washington, D.C.: American Association for the Advancement of Science.

_____. 1998. 'The Case of Rwanda', in Thomas Homer-Dixon and Jessica Blitt, *Ecoviolence: Links Among Environment, Population, and Security.* Lanham, Md.: Rowman and Littlefield (210–222).

_____. 2001. 'The Case of South Africa', ch. 2 in this volume. Revised version of article published in *Journal of Peace Research* 35(3): 279–298. 1998 and as ch. 4 of Homer-Dixon and Blitt, eds. 1998.

Pimentel, David. 1997. 'Soil Erosion', *Environment* 39(10): 4–5.

Pimentel, David, C. Harvey, P. Resosudarmo, K. Sinclair, D. Kurtz, M. McNair, S. Crist, L. Spritz, L. Fitton, R. Saffouri, and R. Blair. 1995a. 'Environmental and Economic Costs of Soil Erosion and Conservation Benefits', *Science* 267(5207): 1117–1123.

_____. 1995b. 'Response', *Science* 269: 465–466.

Pollack, Henry N. 1998. 'Climate Change Record in Subsurface Temperatures: A Global Perspective', *Science* 282(5387): 279– 281.

Potter, David, ed. 1996. *NGOs and Environmental Policies: Asia and Africa.* London: Frank Cass.

Pounds, J. Alan, Michael P. L. Fogden, and John H. Campbell. 1999. 'Biological Response to Climate Change on a Tropical Mountain. (Highland Forests at Monteverde, Costa Rica)', *Nature* 398(6728): 611–614.

Power, Timothy J., and Mark J. Gasiorowski. 1997. 'Institutional Design and Democratic Consolidation in the Third World', *Comparative Political Studies* 30(2): 123–155.

Princen, Thomas, and Matthias Finger, eds. 1994. *Environmental NGOs in World Politics: Linking the Local and the Global.* London: Routledge.

Przeworski, Adam, and Fernando Limongi. 1997. 'Modernization: Theories and Facts', *World Politics* 49(2): 155–183.

Putnam, Robert. 1993. *Making Democracy Work: Civil Traditions in Modern Italy.* Princeton, N.J.: Princeton University Press.

Raknerud, Arvid, and Håvard Hegre. 1997. 'The Hazard of War. Reassessing the Evidence for the Democratic Peace', *Journal of Peace Research* 34(4): 385–404.

Rapkin, David P., and William P. Avery. 1986. 'World Markets and Political Instability Within Less Developed Countries', *Cooperation and Conflict* 21(2): 99–117.

Rasler, Karen, and William Thompson. 1992. 'Assessing the Costs of War', in *Effects of War on Society,* pp. 245–279, ed. G. Ausenda. San Marino: AIEP.

Ray, James L. 1995. *Democracy and International Conflict: An Evaluation of the Democratic Peace Proposition.* Columbia, S.C.: University of South Carolina Press.

Renner, Michael. 1996. *Fighting for Survival. Environmental Decline, Social Conflict, and the New Age of Insecurity.* New York and London: Norton, for Worldwatch.

_____. 1999. *Ending Violent Conflict.* Worldwatch Paper (146). Washington, D.C.: Worldwatch.

Renner, Michael, Mario Pianta, and Cinzia Franchi. 1991. 'International Conflict and Environmental Degradation', ch. 5 in *New Directions in Conflict Theory. Conflict Resolution and Conflict Transformation,* pp. 108–128, ed. Raimo Väyrynen. London: Sage, in association with the International Social Science Council.

Repetto, Robert. 1994. *The 'Second India' Revisited: Population, Poverty, and Environmental Stress over Two Decades.* Washington, D.C.: World Resources Institute.

Rescher, Nicholas. 1998. *Complexity: A Philosophical Overview.* New Brunswick, N.J.: Transaction.

Rich, Bruce. 1994. *Mortgaging the Earth, the World Bank, Environmental Impoverishment and the Crisis of Development.* Boston, Mass.: Beacon.

Richardson, Lewis Fry. 1960. *Statistics of Deadly Quarrels.* Pittsburgh, Pa.: Boxwood/Chicago, Ill.: Quadrangle.

Risse-Kappen, Thomas, ed. 1995. *Bringing Transnational Relations Back in: Non-State Actors, Domestic Structures, and International Institutions.* Cambridge: Cambridge University Press.

Rønnfeldt, Carsten F. 1997. 'Three Generations of Environment and Security Research', *Journal of Peace Research* 34(4): 473–482.

Rosenau, James N. 1990. *Turbulence in World Politics: A Theory of Change and Continuity.* Princeton, N.J.: Princeton University Press.

Rothenberg, Jerome. 1993. 'Economic Perspectives on Time Comparisons: An Evaluation of Time Discounting', in *Global Accord: Environmental Challenges and International Responses,* pp. 307–332, ed. Nazli Choucri. Cambridge, Mass.: MIT Press.

Rothschild, Emma. 1995. 'What Is Security?', *Daedalus* 124(3): 53–91.

Rozanov, Boris G., Viktor Targulian, and D. S. Orlov. 1990. 'Soils', in *The Earth as Transformed by Human Action,* pp. 203–214, B. L. Turner II, William C. Clark, Robert W. Kates, John F. Richards, Jessica T. Mathews, and William B. Meyer. Cambridge: Cambridge University Press.

Ruggie, John G. 1983. 'Continuity and Transformation in the World Polity: Toward a Neorealist Synthesis', *World Politics* 35(2): 261–286.

Rummel, Rudolph J. 1995. 'Democracies ARE Less Warlike than Other Regimes', *European Journal of International Relations* 1(4): 457–479.

Russett, Bruce M. 1993. *Grasping the Democratic Peace: Principles for a Post-Cold War World.* Princeton, N.J.: Princeton University Press.

Russett, Bruce M., and Harvey Starr. 2000. 'From Democratic Peace to Kantian Peace: Democracy and Conflict in the International System', in *Handbook of War Studies II,* pp. 93–128, ed. Manus I. Midlarsky. Ann Arbor, Mich.: University of Michigan Press.

Salameh, Mamdough G. 1995–1996. 'China, Oil and the Risk of Regional Conflict', *Survival* 37(4): 133–146.

Salmon, Wesley C. 1984. *Scientific Explanation and the Causal Structure of the World.* Princeton, N.J.: Princeton University Press.

Saltnes, Turi. 1998. *Forørkning–en konfliktskapende faktor? En kvantitativ analyse av forholdet mellom miljø og borgerkrig* [Desertification and Conflict. A Quantitative Analysis of the Relationship Between the Environment and Civil War]. Thesis for cand. polit. degree, Norwegian University of Science and Technology.

Sayer, Andrew. 1992. *Method in Social Science: A Realist Approach.* New York: Routledge.

Schreurs, Miranda, and Dennis Pirages, eds. 1999. *Ecological Security in Northeast Asia.* Seoul: Yonsei University Press.

Schroll, Henning, et al., eds. 1999. *Fremtidens Pris. Talmagi i Miljøpolitikken* [The Price of the Future. Numbers Magic in Environmental Policy]. Copenhagen: Mellomfolkeligt Samvirke and Det ökologiske råd.

Selin, Shannon. 1994. *Asia-Pacific Arms Buildups–Part Two: Prospects for Control.* Vancouver: University of British Columbia Press.

Shambaugh, David. 1992. 'China's Security Policy in the Post-Cold War Era', *Survival* 34(2): 88–106.

Sharma, Shalendra D. 1996. 'Building Effective International Environmental Regimes: The Case of the Global Environment Facility', *Journal of Environment and Development* 5(1): 73–86.

Shefner, Jon. 1999. 'Pre- and Post- Disaster Political Instability and Contentious Supporters: A Case Study of Political Ferment', *International Journal of Mass Emergencies and Disasters* 17: 137–160.

Shelly, Christine. 1995. Statement by Christine Shelly/acting spokesman, 'Spratlys and the South China Sea', Washington, D.C.: U.S. Department of State, 10 May: 1.

Shephard, Allan. 1994. 'Maritime Tensions in the South China Sea and the Neighborhood: Some Solutions', *Studies in Conflict and Terrorism* 17(2): 181–211.

Shiklomanov, Igor A. 1993. 'World Fresh Water Resources', in Gleick, ed. 1993b (13–24).

Silard, Stephen A. 1995. 'The Global Environment Facility: A New Development in International Law and Organization', *George Washington Journal of International Law and Economics* 28(3): 607–654.

Simkins, Charles. 1991. 'Population Pressures', in Mamphele Ramphele, ed., *Restoring the Land.* London: Panos (21–26).

Simon, Julian L. 1981. *The Ultimate Resource.* Princeton, N.J.: Princeton University Press.

———. 1989. 'Lebensraum: Paradoxically, Population Growth May Eventually End Wars', *Journal of Conflict Resolution* 33(1): 164–180.

———. 1995b: 'Why Do We Hear Prophecies of Doom from Every Side?', *Futurist* 29(1): 19–24.

———. 1996. *The Ultimate Resource 2.* Princeton, N.J.: Princeton University Press.

Simon, Julian L., Guenter Weinrauch, and Stephen Moore. 1994. 'The Reserves of Extracted Resources: Historical Data.' *Non-Renewable Resources* 3 (summer): 325–340, http://www.inform.umd.edu/EdRes/Colleges/BMGT/.Faculty/JSimon/Articles/RESOURCE.txt.

Simon, Julian L., ed. 1995a. *The State of Humanity.* Oxford: Blackwell.

Simon, Julian L., and Herman Kahn, eds. 1984. *The Resourceful Earth.* New York: Blackwell.

Simpson, Dean. 1993. 'The Drowning Pool', in *Rotating the Cube: Environmental Strategies for the 1990s*, pp. 25–30, ed. Rob Preston Whyte and Graham Howe. Dalbridge: Indicator Press.

Singer, J. David, and Melvin Small. 1994. *Correlates of War Project: International and Civil War Data, 1816–1992 (ICPSR 9905).* Ann Arbor, Mich.: Interuniversity Consortium for Political and Social Research.

Singer, Max. 1987. *Passage to a Human World.* Indianapolis, Ind.: Hudson Institute.

Skocpol, Theda. 1979. *States and Social Revolutions: A Comparative Analysis of France, Russia, and China*. Cambridge: Cambridge University Press.

Sloan, Geoffrey R. 1988. *Geopolitics in United States Strategic Policy, 1890–1972*. New York: St. Martin's.

Small, Melvin, and J. David Singer. 1982. *Resort to Arms. International and Civil Wars 1816–1980*. Beverly Hills, Calif.: Sage.

Smil, Vaclav. 1993. *China's Environmental Crisis: An Inquiry into the Limits of National Development*. Armonk, N.Y.: Sharpe.

Smith, Dan, and Willy Østreng, eds. 1997. *Research on Environment, Poverty and Conflict: A Proposal*, PRIO Report (3). Oslo: International Peace Research Institute, Oslo and Fridtjof Nansen Institute.

Snidal, Duncan. 1991. 'Relative Gains and the Pattern of International Cooperation', *American Political Science Review* 85(3): 701–726.

Sober, Elliot. 1988. 'Apportioning Causal Responsibility', *Journal of Philosophy* 85(6): 303–318.

Soroos, Marvin S. 1997a. *The Endangered Atmosphere. Preserving a Global Commons*. Columbia, S.C.: University of South Carolina Press.

_____. 1997b. 'The Turbot War: Resolution of an International Fishery Dispute', ch. 15 in Gleditsch, ed., 1997b (235–252).

South Africa Statistics. 1992. *Republic of South Africa*. Pretoria: Central Statistical Service.

South African Institute of Race Relations. 1994. *Race Relations Survey. 1993–94*. Johannesburg: South African Institute of Race Relations.

Sprinz, Detlef, and Tapani Vaahtoranta. 1994. 'The Interest-Based Explanation of International Environmental Policy', *International Organization* 48(1): 77–105.

Stedman, Stephan John. 1996. 'Negotiation and Mediation in Internal Conflict', in *The International Dimensions of Internal Conflict*, pp. 341–376, ed. Michael Brown. Cambridge, Mass.: MIT Press.

Stern, Eric. 1999. 'The Case for Comprehensive Security', in Deudney and Matthew, eds. (127–154).

Steyn, Hendrik P., and Nic. Boersema. 1988. 'Introduction' and 'Conclusion', in Steyn and Boersema, eds. (1–7, 134–137).

Steyn, Hendrik P., and Nic. Boersema, eds. 1988. *Making a Move: Perspectives on Black Migration Decision Making and Its Context*. Pretoria: Human Sciences Research Council.

Stormont, W. 1994. 'Report: Managing Potential Conflicts in the South China Sea', *Marine Policy* 18: 353–356.

Suliman, Mohamed, ed. 1999. *Ecology, Politics and Violent Conflict*. New York: Zed.

Summers, Robert, and Alan Heston. 1988. 'A New Set of International Comparisons of Real Product and Price Levels Estimates for 130 Countries. 1950–1985', *Review of Income and Wealth* 34(1): 1–25.

_____. 1991. 'The Penn World Table (Mark 5): An Expanded Set of International Comparisons. 1950–1988', *Quarterly Journal of Economics* 106(9): 327–368. Data (Mark 5.6) at http://www.nber.org/pwt56.html.

Susskind, Lawrence E. 1994. *Environmental Diplomacy: Negotiating More Effective Global Agreements*. New York: Oxford University Press.

Suzuki, Motoshi. 1994. 'Economic Interdependence, Relative Gains, and International Cooperation: The Case of Monetary Policy Coordination', *International Studies Quarterly* 38(3): 475–498.

Swain, Ashok. 1996. *The Environmental Trap: The Ganges River Diversion, Bangladeshi, Migration and Conflicts in India*, Report 41. Department of Peace and Conflict Research, Uppsala University.

Swatuk, Larry A. 1997. 'The Environment, Sustainable Development, and Prospects for Southern African Regional Cooperation', in *Bridging the Rift: The New South Africa in Africa*, pp. 127–151, ed. Larry Swatuk and David R. Black. Boulder, Colo.: Westview.

Tamir, Avraham. 1988. *A Soldier in Search of Peace: An Inside Look at Israel's Strategy*. London: Weidenfeld and Nicolson.

Tarrow, Sidney. 1994. *Power in Movement: Social Movements, Collective Action and Politics*. Cambridge: Cambridge University Press.

Tasker, Rodney, and Adam Schwarz. 1994. 'ASEAN Preventive Measures', *Far Eastern Economic Review,* 4 August: 14–15.

Taylor, Charles L., and Michael C. Hudson. 1972. *World Handbook of Political and Social Indicators*, 2d ed. New Haven, Conn., and London: Yale University Press.

Taylor, Charles L., and David A. Jodice. 1983. *World Handbook of Political and Social Indicators*, 3d ed, 2 vols. New Haven, Conn., and London: Yale University Press.

Teitelbaum, Michael S., and Jay Winters. 1998. *A Question of Numbers: High Migration, Low Fertility, and the Politics of National Identity*. New York: Hill and Wang/Farrar, Straus, Giroux.

Terborgh, John. 1999. *Requiem for Nature*. Washington, D.C., and Covelo, Calif.: Island Press.

Thompson, Warren. 1929. *Danger Spots in World Population*. New York: Knopf.

Thompson, Warren, and David Lewis. 1965. *Population Problems*. New York: McGraw-Hill.

Tickner, J. Ann. 1993. *Gender in International Relations: Feminist Perspectives on Achieving Global Security*. New York: Columbia University Press.

Tilly, Charles. 1973. 'Does Modernization Breed Revolution?', *Comparative Politics* 5(3): 425–447.

_____. 1978. *From Mobilization to Revolution*. Reading, Mass.: Addison-Wesley.

Tir, Jaroslav. 1998. 'Demographic Pressure and Interstate Conflict: The Impacts of Population Growth and Technological Development', paper presented at the Annual Meeting of the International Studies Association Midwest, Chicago, Ill., 6–8 November.

Tir, Jaroslav, and Paul F. Diehl. 2001. 'Demographic Pressure and Interstate Conflict', ch. 4 in this volume. Revised version of article published in *Journal of Peace Research* 35(3) 319–340. 1998.

Toset, Hans Petter Wollebæk, Nils Petter Gleditsch, and Håvard Hegre. 2000. 'Shared Rivers and Interstate Conflict', *Political Geography* 20 (in press).

Trittin, Jürgen. 2000. 'Foreword', in Carius and Lietzmann, eds. (vii–ix).

Turner, R. Kerry, David Pearce, and Ian Bateman. 1994. *Environmental Economics: An Elementary Introduction*. New York: Harvester Wheatsheaf.

UN, annual. *Demographic Yearbook.* New York: Department for Economic and Social Information and Policy Analysis, Statistics Division, United Nations.

UN. 1994. *World Population Prospects: The 1994 Revision.* New York: United Nations.

_____. 1996. *Statistical Yearbook.* New York: Department for Economic and Social Information and Policy Analysis, Statistics Division, United Nations.

_____. 1997. Convention on the Law of the Non-Navigational Uses of International Watercourses. UN General Assembly A//51/869, 11 April. New York: United Nations.

_____. 1998. *Strategic Approaches to Freshwater Management.* New York: Report of the Secretary General, for the UN Commission on Sustainable Development.

UNDP. 1996. *Human Development Report 1996.* UN Development Program. New York: Oxford University Press, for United Nations Development Program, http://www.undp.org/undp/news/hdr96pr1.htm

UNEP. 1991. *Status of Desertification and Implementation of the United Nations Plan of Action to Combat Desertification.* Report of the Executive Director, Nairobi: United Nations Environment Program.

_____. 1997. *Global Environment Outlook.* New York: Oxford University Press.

Urban, Michael, Vyacheslav Igrunov, and Sergei Mitrokhin. 1997. *The Rebirth of Politics in Russia.* Cambridge: Cambridge University Press.

U.S. Bureau of the Census. 1999. *World Population Profile 1998.* Report WP/98 Washington, D.C.: U.S. Government Printing Office.

USGS. 1997. *Changing Perceptions of World Oil and Gas Resources as Shown by Recent USGS Petroleum Assessments.* USGS Fact Sheet FS-145-97, http://dr.cr.usgs.gov/fs145-97/intro.htm.

_____. 1998. *Database of 93 minerals.* U.S. Geological Survey, http://minerals.-er.usgs.gov/minerals.

Valencia, Mark J., and Masahiro Miyoshi. 1986. 'Southeast Asian Seas: Joint Development of Hydrocarbons in Overlapping Claim Areas', *Ocean Development and International Law* 16(3): 211–254.

Valencia, Mark J., Jon Van Dyke, and Noel Ludwig. 1995. 'The Solution of the Spratly Islands Ought to Look Like This', *International Herald Tribune,* 10 October.

Van Praag, Nicholas. 1994. 'The Global Environment Facility, Instrument Establishing', *International Legal Materials* 33(5): 1273. Available at www.dc.enews.com/magazines/ ilm/archive.

VanDeveer, Stacy D., and Geoffrey D. Dabelko. 1999. 'Redefining Security Around the Baltic: Environmental Issues in Regional Context'. *Global Governance* 5(2): 221–249.

Vasquez, John A. 1993. *The War Puzzle.* Cambridge: Cambridge University Press.

_____. 1995. 'Why Do Neighbors Fight? Proximity, Interaction, or Territoriality', *Journal of Peace Research* 32(3): 277–293.

Väyrynen, Raimo. 1996. 'The Age of Humanitarian Emergencies', draft paper for the WIDER project on the Political Economy of Humanitarian Emergencies, University of Notre Dame.

Vesilind, Priit J. 1993. 'Middle East Water: Critical Resource', *National Geographic* 183(5): 38–60.

Vicuna, F. 1989. 'Review of Shigeru Oda's *International Control of Sea Resources*', *Ocean Development and International Law* 20: 245–251.

Vine, Jeremy. 1999. 'South Africa Announces Crime Crackdown', *BBC Online Network News*, 28 June, http://news2.thdo.bbc.co.uk/hi/english/world/africa/newsiid380000/380223.stm.

Volden, Ketil, and Dan Smith, eds. 1997. *Causes of Conflict in the Third World*. Oslo: North/South Coalition and International Peace Research Institute, Oslo.

Wallensteen, Peter, and Margareta Sollenberg. 1997. 'Armed Conflicts, Conflict Termination and Peace Agreements. 1989–96, *Journal of Peace Research* 34(3): 339–358.

_____. 1999. 'Armed Conflicts 1989–98', *Journal of Peace Research* 36(5): 593–606.

Waltz, Kenneth N. 1979. *Theory of International Politics*. New York: McGraw-Hill.

Wang, Liyu, and Peter H. Pearse. 1994. 'The New Legal Regime for China's Territorial Sea', *Ocean Development and International Law* 25(4): 431–442.

Wapner, Paul. 1995. 'Politics Beyond the State: Environmental Activism and World Civic Politics', *World Politics* 47(3): 311–340.

_____. 1996. *Environmental Activism and World Civic Politics*. Albany, N.Y.: State University of New York Press.

_____. 1998. 'Reorienting State Sovereignty: Rights and Responsibilities in the Environmental Age', in Litfin, ed., 1998b (193–221).

Weber, Cynthia. 1995. *Simulating Sovereignty: Intervention, the State, and Symbolic Exchange*. Cambridge: Cambridge University Press.

Weiner, Myron. 1971. 'Political Demography: An Inquiry into the Political Consequences of Population Change', in *Rapid Population Growth: Consequences and Policy Implications,* compiled by the National Academy of Sciences. Baltimore, Md.: Johns Hopkins University Press (567–617).

Weiner, Myron, and Sharon Stanton Russell. 2000. *Demography and National Security*. Providence, R.I.: Berghahn.

Weiss, Edith Brown. 1989. *In Fairness to Future Generations: International Law, Common Patrimony, and Intergenerational Equity*. Tokyo: United Nations University.

_____. 1998. 'The Five International Treaties: A Living History', in *Engaging Countries: Strengthening Compliance with International Environmental Accords,* pp. 89–172, ed. Edith Brown Weiss and Harold Jacobson. Cambridge, Mass.: MIT Press.

Wendt, Alexander. 1992. 'Anarchy Is What States Make of It: The Social Construction of Power Politics', *International Organization* 42(2): 391–426.

Westing, Arthur H., ed. 1986. *Global Resources and International Conflict: Environmental Factors in Strategic Policy and Action*. Oxford: Oxford University Press.

_____. 1989. *Comprehensive Security for the Baltic: An Environmental Approach*. London: Sage, for PRIO and UNEP.

_____. 1990. *Environmental Hazards of War. Releasing Dangerous Forces in an Industrialized World*. London: Sage, for PRIO and UNEP.

_____. 1997. *Armed Conflict and Environmental Security*. Special issue of Environment and Security 1(2).

WFS. 1996. *World Food Summit*: Technical Background Documents, vols. 1–15, http://www.fao.org/wfs/final/e/list-e.htm.

Whitmeyer, Joseph, and Rosemary L. Hopcroft. 1996. 'Community, Capitalism, and Rebellion in Chiapas', *Sociological Perspectives* 39(4): 517–539.

WHO. 1992. *Our Planet, Our Health. Report of the WHO Commission on Health and the Environment*. Geneva: World Health Organization.

_____. 1996. *Water Supply and Sanitation Sector Monitoring Report: Sector Status as of 1994*. WHO/EOS/96.15, Geneva: World Health Organization.

Whyte, Anne. 1995. *Building a New South Africa*. Ottawa: International Development Research Centre.

WI, annual since 1984. *State of the World*. New York: Norton, for Worldwatch.

Wigley, T.M.L., R. L. Smith, and B. D. Santer. 1998. 'Anthropogenic Influence on the Autocorrelation Structure of Hemispheric-Mean Temperatures', *Science* 282(5394): 1676.

Wilkins, Nick, and Julian Hofmeyer. 1994. 'Socio-Economic Aspects of Informal Settlements', in Hindson and McCarthy, eds. 1994b (107–122).

Williams, Bruce A., and Albert R. Matheny. 1995. *Democracy, Dialogue, and Environmental Disputes*. New Haven, Conn.: Yale University Press.

Wilmer, Franke. 1993. *The Indigenous Voice in World Politics: Since Time Immemorial*. Newbury Park, Calif.: Sage.

Wilson, Francis. 1991. 'A Land Out of Balance', in *Restoring the Land*, pp. 27–38, ed. Mamphele Ramphele. London: Panos.

Wilson, Francis, and Mamphele Ramphele. 1989. *Uprooting Poverty: The South African Challenge*. New York: Norton.

Wolf, Aaron T. 1999a. 'Water and Human Security', *Aviso: An Information Bulletin on Global Environmental Change and Human Security* (3): 1–7.

_____. 1999b. '"Water Wars" and Water Reality: Conflict and Cooperation Along International Waterways', in Lonergan, ed. (251–265).

Wolf, Aaron T., Jeffrey A. Natharius, Jeffrey J. Danielson, Brian S. Ward, and Jan K. Pender. 1999. 'International River Basins of the World', *International Journal of Water Resources Development* 15(4): 22–35.

Woodrow Wilson Center. 1995–. *Environmental Change and Security Project Report*. Washington, D.C.: Woodrow Wilson International Center for Scholars.

World Almanac and Book of Facts. 1982. New York: Newspaper Enterprise Association.

World Bank, annual. A. *World Debt Tables*. Washington, D.C.: Oxford University Press.

_____. B. *World Development Report*. Washington, D.C.: Oxford University Press.

World Bank. 1992. *World Development Report 1992: Development and the Environment*. Oxford: Oxford University Press.

_____.World Bank. 1993. *Water Resources Management*. World Bank Policy Paper. Washington, D.C.: World Bank.

_____. 1994: *World Development Report: Infrastructure for Development*. Oxford: Oxford University Press.

_____. 1998. *World Development Indicators 1997* (CD-ROM).

WRI, annual. *World Resources*. New York and Oxford: Oxford Unversity Press. Partially available at: www.wri.org/wri/.

Wright, Quincy. 1965. *A Study of War*, 2d ed. Chicago, Ill.: University of Chicago Press. [First published in 1942.]

Wrong, Michela. 1996. 'Uganda Tries to Combat a New Enemy: A Water Weed Threatening Ecological and Political Turmoil', *Financial Times* (Lexis-Nexis). 19 March.

Wu, Kan, and Fereidun Fesharaki. 1994. 'China Energy: Short Memos, Number 4', preprint. Honolulu: East-West Center.

Yee, Albert. 1996. 'The Effects of Ideas on Policies', *International Organization* 50(1): 69–108.

Yi, Xiaoxiong. 1994. 'China's U.S. Policy Conundrum in the 1990s', *Asian Survey* 34(8): 675–691.

Young, H. Peyton, ed. 1991. *Negotiation Analysis*. Ann Arbor, Mich.: University of Michigan Press.

Young, H. Peyton. 1994. *Equity in Theory and Practice*. Princeton, N.J.: Princeton University Press.

Young, Oran R. 1994. *International Governance: Protecting the Environment in a Stateless Society*. Ithaca, N.Y.: Cornell University Press.

_____. 1998. *Creating Regimes: Arctic Accords and International Governance*. Ithaca, N.Y.: Cornell University Press.

Young, Oran R., ed. 1999. *The Effectiveness of International Environmental Regimes: Causal Connections and Behavioral Mechanisms*. Cambridge, Mass.: MIT Press.

Young, Zoe. 1999. 'NGOs and the Global Environmental Facility: Friendly Foes?', *Environmental Politics* 8(1): 243–267.

Zehr, Stephen C. 1994. 'The Centrality of Scientists and the Translation of Interests in the U.S. Acid Rain Controversy,' *Canadian Review of Sociology and Anthropology* 31(3): 325–353.

Zuk, Gary. 1985. 'National Growth and International Conflict: A Reevaluation of Choucri and North's Thesis', *Journal of Politics* 47(1): 269–281.

Index